The
Roosevelt-Litvinov
Agreements

The Roosevelt-Litvinov Agreements

THE AMERICAN VIEW

DONALD G. BISHOP

SYRACUSE UNIVERSITY PRESS

Library of Congress Catalog Card: 65-15852

The author gratefully acknowledges permission to quote passages from:

The Forrestal Diaries, edited by Walter Millis. The Viking Press. Permission granted by the New York *Herald Tribune* and Princeton University.

The Memoirs of Cordell Hull. The Macmillan Company.

Moscow Was My Parish by Georges Bissonnette. Copyright 1956 by the Augustinians of the Assumption. McGraw-Hill Book Company.

Negotiating with the Russians, edited by Raymond Dennett and Joseph E. Johnson. World Peace Foundation.

Postmarked Moscow by Lydia Kirk. Charles Scribner's Sons.

Manufactured in the United States of America

Composition and presswork by The Heffernan Press, Worcester, Mass.
Binding by Vail-Ballou Press, Binghamton, New York

Foreword

Diplomatic relations between the United States and the Soviet Union have been of the greatest significance since 1933 when they began. The importance of the two countries and of their place in world events during this period has guaranteed this.

Diplomatic relations were established in November 1933 when President Roosevelt and Foreign Minister (officially, People's Commissar for Foreign Affairs) Maxim Litvinov exchanged a series of formal notes after several days of negotiations in Washington. In this exchange both governments made promises, but those made by Litvinov, as the "price" of recognition, far exceeded those made by President Roosevelt. Since the American leaders had obtained these promises from a reluctant Soviet leader, the promises themselves were important in setting the pattern for diplomatic relations in the first few years. Since there had previously been much skepticism in the United States on the value of recognition and the willingness of the Soviet leaders to try to live in harmony with other governments, the implementation of these promises took on added importance.

This book studies the implementation of these promises. The first chapter concerns the background of recognition and the negotiations in Washington. Each of the other chapters deals with the implementation of one of the agreements made in November 1933, the problems encountered, and the degree to which the American government believed that the Soviet government was fulfilling the 1933 promise. The popular answer in the United States has been that Soviet promises are always broken; it is the purpose of the present work to discover how much truth there is, in this case, to that assumption.

The research relied primarily on the diplomatic correspondence between the two governments, as filed in the National Archives in Washington, and on State Papers in the Franklin D. Roosevelt Library at Hyde Park, New York. Since comparable Soviet materials are not available, the analysis and conclusions of this book do not show both sides of the diplomatic picture, but only the American. Soviet views and attitudes are revealed only through Soviet response to American proposals as reported by American officials, noted repeatedly throughout this book. The materials used, then, are those available to American officials confronted with specific situations, on which they had to make their policy decisions. Because the Soviet documents have not subsequently been made available, neither the American officials, nor the researcher, nor the reader has access to the Soviet analysis.

Professor Robert Browder, in his *The Origins of Soviet-American Diplomacy*, analyzes the period of nonrecognition (1917-33), the background of the recognition problem, and the conferences in November 1933. Because of his careful presentation of that period, the present book refers only briefly to it, as background, and emphasizes events of the years after 1933.

The documentary materials are open (on a restricted basis) only through 1941, and the reader will discover that most of the examples fall in the period 1933-41, though more recent examples—based on official and nonofficial nondocumentary sources—are cited whenever possible, into 1964.

Although Soviet leadership has changed and diplomatic tactics are somewhat different today than in the 1930's, the conclusions of this study have meaning for analysts of present-day United States–Soviet relations as well as for those interested in studying the early years of our diplomatic relations.

Many people have been helpful in the writing of this book, but two may properly be singled out for specific mention: Dr. E. Taylor Parks of the Historical Office of the Department of State and Mrs. Patricia Dowling of the National Archives. Their assistance has been invaluable.

DONALD G. BISHOP

Syracuse, New York
Autumn 1964

Contents

Foreword   v

I Recognition of the Soviet Government   1

Background, 1.   Moving toward Recognition, 4.
Recognition, 17.   Initial Reactions, 22.

II Noninterference in Internal Affairs   27

The Problem, 27.   Implementation of the Agreement, 41.

III Freedom of Worship   61

Background, 61.   The Agreement, 63.
Implementation, 67.

IV Legal Protection for American Nationals   87

Soviet Policy toward Foreigners in the U.S.S.R., 87.
The Agreement, 90.   The Means of Protecting American
Nationals, 102.   Conclusions, 135.

V Soviet Debts   140

The Debt Situation, 141.   The 1933 Debt "Agreement," 148.
Implementation: Trying To Make an Agreement, 152.
Conclusions, 175.

VI Soviet Claims and Assignments   179

Claims, 179.   Assignments, 181.   Implementation, 196.

VII Economic Espionage   199

The Nature of Economic Espionage, 200.
The Metropolitan-Vickers Trial, 203.   American Experience,
206.

VIII "Normal" Diplomatic Relations   210

The Honeymoon, 211.   Friction and Heat, 213.
Conclusions, 227.

IX Evaluation   233

Broken Promises and Hopes, 233.   Break Diplomatic
Relations?   237.   What Have We Learned?   240.

Appendix: Identification of Officials   247

Notes to Chapters   251

Note on Sources   285

Index   289

TABLES

1. Principal Debts of the Russian Governments   141
2. American Claims against the Soviet Government   142
3. Principal American Corporate Losses   143
4. Russian Property in the United States   184
5. Money Realized from the Litvinov Assignment   195

The
Roosevelt-Litvinov
Agreements

CHAPTER I

Recognition of the Soviet Government

The year 1933 was momentous in the United States. A new administration came to power; a dynamic President called on the people, confused by the enormity of the depression, to join forces and march together; whole batches of "must" legislation were delivered to Congress for enactment; new ideas and reforms of a thousand varieties were tossed in every direction. The New Deal was beginning. In the foreign as well as the domestic field, new suggestions were made and new paths explored. No one was certain where all these rumblings and movements might take the country, but "change" became almost a virtue.

In foreign policy, one of the prospects centered around new relations between the American and Soviet governments. Before 1933 gasped to an exhausted finale, new relations had been established and a new vista lay ahead. The decision of the American leaders to recognize the Soviet government and establish diplomatic relations with it was, without question, one of the more important decisions of that year. For both governments, it was truly a milestone. Yet it would seem now, looking back thirty years, that the change was more significant for the United States than for the Soviet Union. Other important governments had recognized Moscow; the United States was only one more, though the last of the great powers to do so. For the United States, however, this was a change in a policy followed for sixteen years, a change which was to involve the government and people in new relations with a Communist government. Never again would this diplomatic humpty-dumpty be the same. Such a decision is worthy of careful examination.

BACKGROUND

The background of American-Soviet relations is extensive. From the American view, relations with Russia began in 1781 when the Continental Congress sent envoy Francis Dana to Russia. But Catherine the

1

Great refused to receive this representative of what she believed to be a dangerously revolutionary form of government. After two years the American group returned home and it was only in 1809 that Tsar Alexander I agreed to recognize the American government, accepting John Quincy Adams as the first American Minister to St. Petersburg. During the remainder of the nineteenth century, the two governments maintained normal diplomatic relations, relatively unmarred by major difficulties.

On March 22, 1917, the United States became the first country to recognize the Provisional Government of Russia following the abdication of Tsar Nicholas II. Ambassador David R. Francis, who had been accredited to the Tsar's government, remained in Petrograd and worked with the new regime. Georgi Bakhmetyev, Ambassador of the Imperial Russian government in Washington since 1911, resigned on April 20, 1917, and was replaced by Boris Bakhmetyev whom President Wilson received on July 15. The situation was less precise later in 1917 when the Provisional Government was replaced by the Soviet system. Ambassador Francis remained at his post, but he was careful not to accord recognition to the new regime. On February 27, 1918, he removed the Embassy to Vologda, five hundred miles east of Petrograd, and on July 25, 1918, to Archangel. Though he left in November 1918, due to illness, the Embassy remained until September 14, 1919, and certain consular officers stayed until 1923.

Meanwhile the Provisional Workers' and Peasants' Government—later the Soviet government—issued an order on November 28, 1917, dismissing "the Ambassador in the United States of America, Georgi Petrovich Bakhmeteff."[1] On June 5, 1918, the Soviet Foreign Commissar, Chicherin, told Ambassador Francis that "Citizen Litvinov" was nominated as the Soviet representative to the United States; on March 18, 1919, Ludwig C. A. K. Martens was named, though the American government accepted neither.[2] Bakhmetyev retained his status until June 30, 1922. Meanwhile Serge Ughet, the Financial Attaché of the Russian Embassy, was recognized by the American government as custodian of Russian property in the United States, and several consular officers were also permitted to continue to serve.

If this seems confused, Washington was none too sure of its whole policy toward the new Soviet regime. The Wilson administration had replaced the traditional *de facto* recognition policy with a *de jure* policy. If the Soviet system was in fact the government in Russia—and this was far from certain with both the civil war and the Allied intervention continuing—the regime surely failed to meet the test of having come to power through legal methods. Yet there were reasons—

political and military—why the United States wished to do business with the Soviets. Secretary of State Lansing, in a long memorandum dated December 3, 1919, admitted that the Russian situation was of great importance to the American government, especially if it was to reap the fruits of its participation in the First World War, but the Secretary was not specific as to what should be done. He indicated a month later that he thought that an evolutionary process "even if it has now begun has not yet progressed sufficiently to make it possible or desirable to come to an understanding with those who remain in control of affairs at Moscow."[3] On the one hand, the United States government proclaimed itself "[w]ithout any desire to interfere in the internal affairs of the Russian people, or to suggest what kind of government they should have,"[4] yet, on the other, it sent troops into Russia to challenge that regime. The intervention, in turn, was too halfhearted to be effective but strong enough to produce Soviet wrath for years to come.

American policy toward the Soviet government was hardening, however. The leaders of the Soviet government, wrote Secretary of State Colby in 1920, have frequently boasted that they are willing to sign agreements while not having the slightest intention of carrying them out.

> In the view of this Government, there cannot be any common ground upon which it can stand with a Power whose conceptions of international relations are so entirely alien to its own, so utterly repugnant to its moral sense. There can be no mutual confidence or trust, no respect even, if pledges are to be given and agreements made with a cynical repudiation of their obligations already in the mind of one of the parties. We cannot recognize, hold official relations with, or give friendly reception to the agents of a government which is determined and bound to conspire against our institutions; whose diplomats will be the agitators of dangerous revolt; whose spokesmen say that they sign agreements with no intention of keeping them.[5]

Although the American government had decided not to recognize the Soviet government at that time, the question never died down for long. When President Coolidge referred to it in his message to Congress in December, 1923, Foreign Commissar Chicherin immediately followed it up with a query. Secretary of State Hughes stated his views very plainly:

> There would seem to be at this time no reason for negotiations. The American Government . . . is not proposing to barter away its principles. If the Soviet authorities are ready to restore the confiscated property of American citizens or make effective compensation, they

can do so. If the Soviet authorities are ready to repeal their decrees repudiating Russia's obligations to this country and appropriately recognize them, they can do so. It requires no conference or negotiations to accomplish these results which can and should be achieved at Moscow as evidence of good faith. . . . Most serious is the continued propaganda to overthrow the institutions of this country. This Government can enter into no negotiations until these efforts directed from Moscow are abandoned.[6]

Between 1921 and 1933, also, Congress was repeatedly concerned with recognition, which became the subject of several congressional resolutions.[7] Despite these flurries, the question was effectively settled for the decade of the 1920's.

MOVING TOWARD RECOGNITION

With the coming to power of the Roosevelt Administration, there was real opportunity for a policy change. Many forces pushed in this direction.

The Soviet government now showed greater signs of cooperation with the Western governments than previously. She had attended the Geneva Disarmament Conference in 1932 and her contribution had impressed many diplomats. Her need for American credits continued— or increased—as the Five Year Plan sought to industrialize the economy and safeguard the Soviet Union from attack. Relations with Japan, strained since the 1931 invasion of Manchuria, worried Moscow and now, in 1933, the Nazi Fuehrer came to power in Germany, so that Moscow had a "two-front headache." Meanwhile, a depression-ridden American economy needed markets. The Soviet government had already been permitted to establish a trading organization— Amtorg (American Trading Organization)— in New York, and Boris Skvirsky headed a Soviet Information Bureau in Washington. Since the United States had no comparable agencies in the Soviet Union, recognition would be more useful at some points to the American than to the Soviet leaders.

When President Roosevelt sent an appeal for military and economic disarmament to the heads of fifty-four nations on May 16, 1933, he included President Mikhail Kalinin in Moscow. To some it seemed unrealistic to address the head of a government we refused to recognize; indeed, some believed that Roosevelt's action constituted a type of recognition but this was officially denied.[8]

The Soviet government was now courting recognition actively. A year earlier, in April 1932, Peter A. Bogdanov (chairman of the Board of Directors of Amtorg) told W. W. Lancaster of the National City

Bank that if the Soviet government could be sure of not receiving a rebuff—as it had from Secretary Hughes in 1923—it would propose negotiations for settlement of Russian debts and recognition of the Soviet regime. In August 1932 the *New York Times* reported that Soviet leaders, while still not recognizing the obligations of their predecessor regimes, were ready to settle their own financial problems. About the same time, Lancaster—then in Russia—was told that the Soviet government wanted to borrow $100,000,000 and would pay 10 per cent rather than 7 per cent interest. The American government made no reply to any of these overtures; clearly the Hoover administration did not intend to recognize the Soviet Union, and on March 3, 1933, the day before the administration left office, Under Secretary of State William Castle maintained that this had been the best policy.

The question of recognition had been largely absent from the 1932 presidential campaign; neither party referred to it in its platform, and neither candidate devoted any attention to it. The policy of the new administration was not known,[9] although it was widely believed that the new President favored a change.

The Soviet government lost no time in continuing to show its desire for recognition. On March 10, 1933, the Moscow *Daily News* quoted Maxim Litvinov, People's Commissar for Foreign Affairs, to the effect that "states which . . . do not maintain any relations with the Soviet Union . . . are . . . hostile to it."[10] Early in April, Norman H. Davis, an American diplomat, was told that Litvinov would be glad to visit him to discuss the question of recognition; when Davis disclaimed authority to discuss the topic, the matter was dropped. But the next week, Bogdanov (of Amtorg) told Albert M. Creighton, a Boston manufacturer, that the Soviet government was ready to place orders for $25,000,000 worth of goods. With long-term credits, it would buy machinery—$50,000,000 the first year and ten times that by the fifth year. In May, one Soviet journal said that if the United States wished to sell more goods to Russia, it would have to recognize the Soviet government. Despite the nonrecognition policy, the Reconstruction Finance Corporation granted a one-year credit of four million dollars to the Soviet government, to buy American cotton. Thereupon the RFC received a long list of requests for similar loans in other fields. Later that month, Litvinov, in London at the World Economic Conference, stated that the Soviet government would purchase one billion dollars worth of goods abroad if proper credits could be arranged.[11] The American-Russian Chamber of Commerce at once passed a resolution calling for recognition.

It should not be assumed that the Soviet government was motivated solely by considerations of prestige. How much this characterized Soviet thinking is not known, but it was far from the sole concern. Two other important factors were the Far Eastern situation and the possibility of increased foreign trade.

The Soviet leaders were increasingly aware of Japanese power, especially since the invasion of Manchuria in 1931/32. Now Japanese and Soviet troops faced each other across the frontier for hundreds of miles, armed incidents were frequent, and everything seemed to point to a major military explosion in the near future. In early 1933, the Soviet leaders could not foresee the specific nature of the threat that would result from the accession of Hitler to the German chancellorship or from the formation of the German-Japanese Anti-Comintern Pact in 1936, but they did know that their position would be better if they could have at least the goodwill of the United States, as expressed tangibly by recognition.

During the period leading up to American recognition of the Soviet government, it was assumed in Washington that the Japanese threat was a major factor in Moscow's continuing pressure for recognition. Two days after Roosevelt's inauguration, Ambassador Grew in Tokyo reported that "the Japanese are somewhat worried over the possibility that the new administration will bring about the resumption of diplomatic relations between America and Soviet Russia."[12] The Finnish Foreign Minister expressed the view to an American diplomat "that the current year is the ideal time from the Japanese standpoint for further activity, as the military machine of Japan is in efficient working order and the nationalistic spirit of the Japanese people has reached a high pitch."[13]

On March 9, 1933, Grew forwarded information he had received from a reliable source (said to be the head of the Soviet secret police in Japan) to the effect that Japanese officials feared an American-Soviet rapprochement.

> Japan is frantically preparing for war on a large scale . . . with the Soviets, with the United States, or with both. . . . The Soviet Union badly needs the resumption of diplomatic relations with the U.S. . . . In order to obtain American recognition, the Soviets are willing to give economic favors or to grant concessions in return for the cancellation of the old debts.[14]

It was reported that Matsuoka (Japanese diplomat) had predicted that "if Japan embarked on a serious war in the next five years, it would be with the Soviets and in such an eventuality he would not be surprised to see the U.S. on Japan's side."[15] He thought such a war likely.

As the summer of 1933 drew to a close, the Japanese apparently became reconciled to the possibility of American recognition of the Soviet government. Grew reported a "calm acceptance of approaching recognition" so that "it would seem that Japan expects early recognition of Soviet Russia by the U.S."[16]

Similar views were expressed as the time came near when the decision for or against recognition would be made. In September, Secretary Hull wrote to the President that "recognition by the U.S. is greatly desired by the Soviet authorities, since they are apparently convinced that recognition by the U.S. would be a factor in preventing a Japanese attack on the Maritime Provinces."[17] A memorandum prepared by Stanley K. Hornbeck, chief of the Far Eastern division of the Department of State, at the very time when Roosevelt and Litvinov were negotiating, suggests that recognition "now or during the approaching winter would tend to afford to that element in Japan which desires that this war be fought [soon] . . . a reenforcement of that element's conviction and argument that it would be to Japan's advantage to have this war begin soon."[18]

It seems clear, then, that the American leaders believed that the Japanese threat to the Soviet Union bulked large in Moscow's desire to obtain recognition by the United States, especially at that time. If this was true, the Soviet leaders might be willing to make larger concessions than previously; this might be the best time to deal with them. The Japanese threat to the Soviet Union, therefore, was one of the important factors moving toward recognition.

Another such force involved the possibilities of trade following recognition. The United States, in the midst of the greatest depression in its history, was greatly interested in trade and actively looking for markets. In 1930 the Russians were the largest purchasers of American agricultural and industrial equipment. Just as it looked as if the United States could climb out of the depression through trade with the Soviet Union, this hope collapsed, with exports in 1932 being only 10 per cent of 1931 exports. American businessmen were alarmed, on the theory that the Russians, in view of the nonrecognition policy, had taken their business elsewhere. Recognition, it was believed, would put the export trade back on a rosy basis.[19]

As we have seen, Bogdanov and Litvinov had repeatedly held out the prize of huge trade opportunities, if only recognition would be forthcoming. Stalin had remarked in 1929: "It is the development of commercial relations on the basis of mutual advantages that is of importance. . . . The question of diplomatic recognition will solve itself when both parties recognize the advantages of diplomatic relations."[20]

If some voices called hopefully for greater trade possibilities, others cautioned against too much optimism. There will be a strong effort, wrote Secretary Hull to Frank C. Walker of the Treasury Department, on October 29, 1933,

> put forth by the various interests which believe that they can get a large market for American products in Russia, financed by government money, to push the matter of government recognition and a large loan. This whole move appeals to me as exactly the kind of thing which the Harding-Coolidge and Hoover administrations engaged in to our ultimate undoing when we stopped loaning money abroad in 1929.
> . . . There is grave danger that this administration is now preparing to make exactly the same kind of mistake concerning Russia. . . . I fear that a highly centralized administration in the form of the Russians could easily cause us the most serious kind of trouble when the time for repayment comes.[21]

After all, there were realistic difficulties of trading with a country like the Soviet Union. "I think we shall find the Russians . . . very difficult in matters regarding trade relations," wrote Robert P. Skinner, an American diplomat, early in 1933,

> as they will demand everything and yield little. They will propose the usual phrases about reciprocal rights and most-favored-nation privileges, but these . . . mean everything when applied to the United States and nothing when applied to a country organized like Russia which habitually demands, and usually obtains, free admission to the markets of other countries, but gives no equivalent, herself, her foreign trade being carefully guarded as a state monopoly. . . . As to anticipation of important increases in our export business to Russia merely because of the possible resumption of diplomatic relations, they might as well be abandoned at once. Almost every country that has recognized Russia, thus far, has done so in the hope of obtaining trade, and has been disappointed. It is altogether probable that in case we should recognize Russia business will go on very much as at the present time.
> The Russians . . . purchase goods . . . only as they need them, and their requirements will be neither increased or diminished from the fact of recognition.[22]

This was a frank statement, indeed, and most prophetic, as matters turned out. Later in the year, however, the American Legation in Riga indicated that the Soviet leaders might be more desirous of some type of trade accommodation than previously thought. In July, Cole (the Chargé) reported that in its financial dealing with the rest of the world, "the Soviet Government is, and has been for several months, on the verge of extreme financial difficulties. In the beginning of the current year, the German banks came to the rescue with financial credits on the security of Russia's future exports."[23] Following the Nazi revolution, the Soviet government might have to look elsewhere for credit. Cole continued:

> There is no better prospect in Moscow's eyes than the U.S. The extension of cheap credits to Russia by American industry may or may not be advantageous to the enterprises concerned; to Russia it is a matter of the most urgent necessity. With payments to the extent of several millions of dollars to be met in the current year, with a curtailed export trade which is not yielding enough to meet these payments, with a vast unfinished industrial construction program in dire need of foreign assistance and foreign equipment, with former friends and supporters turning their backs—it is not surprising that Russian officials are willing to employ a measure of propaganda and misrepresentation in order to secure financial help from America.
>
> The Russian appeal stresses recognition; actually what is wanted are credits. . . . there has never been a time since the commencement of commercial relations between Soviet Russia and the rest of the world when conditions were worse for the granting of credits to Russia and when the risk involved was greater.

On the file copy of this dispatch, two heavy blue lines have been penciled opposite the last paragraph by a reader in the Department.

From a neighboring Baltic country came similar testimony. Julius Seljamaa, the Estonian Minister to the U.S.S.R., warned an American diplomat that it would be unwise for the United States to expect to receive any tangible results such as foreign trade from recognition. "Under the existing conditions the Soviet authorities were without means to enter into extensive engagements abroad; they had of late even reduced very heavily their imports from Great Britain and from Germany."[24]

The American government had placed no restrictions on trade with the Soviet Union since 1920, nor to ordinary commercial financing so long as no gold was paid and no securities offered for sale to the American people. After 1924 substantial trade had developed between the two countries. It was not, then, that trade was impossible until recognition was accorded. As Under Secretary of State Castle pointed out, "the recognition of the Soviet regime by the Governments of other countries has not resulted in any material change in the attitude of the businessmen of those countries with respect to the risks involved in granting credits to that regime."[25]

Much of this information on the Soviet need for credit was not then known to the American businessmen who were pressing for recognition in hope of increasing their sales. In the middle of the depression, any business opportunity was eagerly sought. President Roosevelt, trying desperately to improve the domestic economic situation, must have been doubly sensitive to this pressure. Even if American officials were not optimistic about the prospects, every possibility had to be explored.

Nothing in the available documents shows just when President Roosevelt decided to approach the Soviet government, although it appears that the decision was made in early autumn of 1933. Bullitt has written that it was in September when the President decided to recognize the Soviet government if the latter "would agree to cease to direct the activities of the American Communist Party and would extend religious freedom to Americans in the Soviet Union."[26]

Soon after his inauguration Roosevelt had asked Henry Morgenthau, Jr., to explore possibilities of reconciliation with the Soviet Union, presumably because the President sensed opposition in the Department of State. "The State Department in 1933, frankly, was unsympathetic if not hostile to the whole idea of opening relations with the Soviet Union."[27] Conversations were held with Amtorg during the summer, but the President became increasingly impatient as little progress resulted.

By this time both the President and Hull were deluged with correspondence and delegations, offering compelling reasons for recognizing or not recognizing the Soviet government. The American Foundations Committee on Russian-American Relations addressed an inquiry to American newspapers, receiving replies from 1,139 daily papers, of which 718 (63 per cent) advocated recognition "now" on the terms of the questionnaire, and only 306 (27 per cent) were in full opposition.[28] A survey of press opinion by the Department of State in September-October 1933 showed that no part of the country was hostile, though several parts lacked enthusiasm. On the other hand, a petition opposing recognition, signed by 673,586 Massachusetts voters, was sent to the President in March 1933, and a month later a mass meeting in Washington—with 160 organizations participating and 6,000 in attendance, listening to Father E. A. Walsh of Georgetown University, President William Green of the American Federation of Labor, and Representative Hamilton Fish, Jr.—was "awakened to the dangers of such a step."[29]

Hull relates[30] that he had talked with diplomats of countries which had already recognized Russia, seeking to learn all possible details of the negotiations and of their experiences in dealing with that government. He spoke about this matter with a number of foreign ministers while at the London Conference in June and July, and also with Litvinov, the Soviet Foreign Commissar. In August Hull discussed recognition in a general way with the President, but they reached no conclusions. Sometime in the fall—he does not give a date—the President asked Hull to give him an opinion "on what we should do." Hull replied:

> I favor recognizing Russia. . . . Russia and we had been traditional friends. . . . The world is moving into a dangerous period both in Europe and in Asia. Russia could be a great help in stabilizing this situation as time goes on and peace becomes more and more threatened.
> The President, without a moment's hesitation, replied, "I agree entirely." He then added: "Two great nations like America and Russia should be on speaking terms. It will be beneficial to both countries to resume diplomatic relations."[31]

Hull thought that the outstanding questions between the two governments should be analyzed in writing and settled by informal conferences, before inviting a Russian governmental representative to the United States, but Roosevelt was ready to use personal diplomacy. "If I could only, myself, talk to some one man representing the Russians," he said to Morgenthau, "I could straighten out the whole question."[32] The President, believing that we should invite the Russian representative to come here and discuss the questions and then agree upon recognition, decided to send a direct letter to President Kalinin in Moscow on October 10.

> Since the beginning of my Administration, I have contemplated the desirability of an effort to end the present abnormal relationship. . . .
> It is most regrettable that these great peoples . . . should now be without a practical method of communicating directly with each other.
> The difficulties that have created this anomalous situation are serious but not, in my opinion, insoluble; and difficulties between great nations can be removed only by frank, friendly conversations. If you are of similar mind, I should be glad to receive any representative you may designate to explore with me personally all questions outstanding between our countries.
> Participation in such a discussion would, of course, not commit either nation to any future course of action, but would indicate a sincere desire to reach a satisfactory solution of the problems involved. It is my hope that such conversations might result in good to the people of both our countries.[33]

A week later, on October 17, Kalinin replied that "difficulties . . . present or arising between the two countries, can be solved only when direct relations exist . . . and that . . . they have no chance for solution in the absence of such relations."[34] In accordance with this view, Kalinin accepted Roosevelt's proposal and designated Maxim Litvinov to come to Washington at a mutually agreeable time. Kalinin's phrase indicated that the problems could be solved only after recognition, which was not Roosevelt's suggestion.

The American government had not come to this decision hastily and carelessly. In March 1917 it had recognized the Provisional Government of Russia almost overnight, with no real awareness of the meaning of the Tsar's abdication or the potentialities of the new regime. This was not the case in 1933. Words of caution had come to the Department from a variety of sources. In February 1933, before Roosevelt was President, the American Minister in Riga listed five available alternatives, one of which was to make recognition "conditional upon previous negotiation of a treaty covering all points."

> Unconditional recognition . . . would leave us without essential guarantees. . . . If the Russians did meet our substantial requirements, there would then be no reason for withholding recognition and those who oppose it would be silenced.
> . . . We must insist upon a contract . . . which covers all our desiderata, as we shall certainly obtain nothing later on.[35]

In his dispatch, Skinner emphasized that "the Russians need us infinitely—(in the original, this word is underlined with pencil and a question mark has been placed in the margin by some reader in the Department)—more than we need them." They would exploit this diplomatic success; "therefore, we must be extremely careful to avoid initiating proposals, even of the most informal character, but should so conduct our affairs that the original tenders come from the Russian side. Russia, today, not only needs us but in all likelihood is prepared —(the last five words are also underlined and questioned, in the original)—to make sacrifices even of principle, to obtain our official friendship."

In April 1933, the Department instructed the Legation in Riga to prepare "a basic documented study of Soviet legal concepts, as embodied in treaties and legislation, with respect to the legal position and rights of foreign nations in Russia."[36] This study, amounting to three hundred pages of typed material, arrived in Washington on December 15, too late to be used in negotiations with Litvinov. The Division of Eastern European Affairs, under the direction of Robert F. Kelley, spent much time in 1933 preparing a series of memoranda dealing with recognition. In May there was a study entitled "Soviet Attitude and Policy with Respect to the Repudiation of Debts and Confiscation of Property," and in July another on "Problems Pertaining to Russian-American Relations which, in the Interest of Friendly Relations between the U.S. and Russia, Should be Settled Prior to Recognition of the Soviet Government," which was handed to President Roosevelt by Under Secretary Phillips on July 27. Kelley himself prepared a series of ten memoranda on "Problems Pertaining to Russian-American Relations," the titles of which indicate the scope of Kelley's examination:

1. Russian Governmental Indebtedness to the Government of the United States
2. Russian Governmental Indebtedness to American Citizens. Dollar Loans Floated in the United States
   a. Recommendations and Considerations in Connection with the Question of Russian Governmental Indebtedness to the Government of the United States
   b. Russian Government Debt to the Government of the United States
3. Private American Claims against Soviet Russia
4. Questions of "Communist Propaganda"
5. Treaty Rights Essential to the Welfare and Protection of American Nationals in Russia
6. Russian Government Property in the United States
7. Dominating Party and Governmental Organizations and Biographies of Prominent Party and Governmental Leaders of the U.S.S.R.
8. Statements by Litvinov on Matters of Foreign Policy that are of Interest to the United States

Since Kelley was not enthusiastic about recognition, it is not surprising that these studies emphasized the difficulties involved in recognition and subsequent diplomatic relations with the Soviet Union.

The departmental inquiry did not stop here, however. On October 24, 1933, Assistant Secretary R. Walton Moore sent a note to Kelley, saying, "Mr. Phillips is now asking our representatives in London to give us a very detailed statement of the problems and difficulties the English have met and are now encountering in dealing with Russia in reference to claims, trade relations, et cet., and the Secretary thinks that we should as far as possible try to obtain the similar experiences of other nations."[37] On the same day, Moore sent a memorandum to Secretary Hull:

My thought is that it may be desirable for you to send some such letter as the following to each of the other Cabinet officers:

"Dear Mr. Secretary:

Without attempting to forcast [*sic*] what may occur but assuming for the moment that there may be conditional recognition of the Russian Government, I am writing to suggest that you indicate to this Department any possible subjects within the jurisdiction of your department or to which your attention has been directed which, in your opinion, should have consideration in determining what conditions should attach to an act of recognition. It is unnecessary to say that we should most carefully guard against overlooking any matters of vital concern to our Government in respect to the situation that is to be dealt with."[38]

Moore's files also contain a thirty-one-page memorandum prepared by Green H. Hackworth, the Department's Legal Adviser, dated October 28, considering on the basis of both international law and American precedent "whether recognition has retroactive effect . . . whether such effect may be limited by an understanding . . . whether Soviet courts are calculated to give fair and speedy trials . . . the effect of Soviet laws on the rights of foreigners . . . and whether counterclaims are likely to be asserted because of Vladivostok and Archangel."[39]

On November 4, when Litvinov was on his way to the United States, Moore sent Hull a document suggesting the conditions to be imposed on the Soviet government if recognition were to be granted. He referred to the domestic as well as the international problem.

In drafting the document we have kept constantly in mind the fact that the treaty making power and the legislative authority of our Government cannot be infringed and thus have made several of the stipulations to be exacted of the Soviet Government unilateral instead of bilateral. The Russian Representative will probably ask for a bilateral stipulation relative to subversive propaganda, but aside from the fact that there is no such propaganda against Russia on foot in this country, the answer is that a bilateral stipulation might well be regarded as invading the authority of the Senate.[40]

Moore, in an undated memorandum, discussed the problem of conditional recognition, referring to the precedents of the recognition of the Dominican Republic in 1903, Haiti in 1911, and Mexico in 1913 and 1923. "The mere statement of conditions would not be very effective. The only way by which the recognizing State may be assured that its demands shall be given effect is to make them *conditions prec-*

edent.[41] But what does this mean? If the "mere statement of conditions" is inadequate assurance, what further guarantee can the recognizing government ask? Can it demand "performance," which might well stretch over a period of years? Once a government is recognized, further, who is to *make* it fulfill its promises? And this, as it turned out, was the crux of the Soviet problem: Soviet leaders were willing to give assurances in 1933 but, in later years, failed—in our view—to do as they promised. Indeed, Moore foresaw this problem, suggesting in his memorandum of October 4 that, "A restricted representation of each country, in the other until otherwise mutually determined, might well be specified and in such manner as to encourage the performance of the conditions accompanying recognition."[42] It is not clear just what Moore had in mind with this unprecedented suggestion. He quoted Oppenheim, the international law authority, to the effect that "conditional recognition, if accepted by the new State, imposed the internationally legal duty upon such State of complying with the condition; failing which a right of intervention is given to the other party for the purpose of making the recognized State comply with the imposed condition."[43] It is not known whether the Soviet leaders wanted recognition so badly in 1933 that they would have paid this kind of price, or whether, if they had, they would have fulfilled their "internationally legal duty" but, in any case, American public opinion in 1933 would surely not have approved intervention to secure the fulfillment of Soviet promises. Philip Marshall Brown, a former American diplomat, wrote to Hull on October 27:

> Please allow me to express my deliberate conviction that no reliance whatever can be placed upon the foreign policy and diplomatic relations of the Soviet Union. These are based on cynical grounds of expediency without the least respect for fundamental principles either of law or of honor. Any assurances they might offer either in treaties or otherwise have but slight value if they believe Marxian principles are endangered.[44]

In the end, Moore himself recognized that, "the only recourse left to the recognizing State, in case the recognized State does not observe the conditions, is the severance of diplomatic relations or reprisals and . . . such action was taken by the British Government as regards Mexico."[45]

The problem in the autumn of 1933, however, was to attempt to state conditions for recognition, in the hope that such procedure would be adequate for the protection of American interests. On the basis of British-Soviet experiences, Moore wrote Hull in October 1933:

Russia is (a) inclined to a more reasonable attitude towards nations that have not accorded the recognition she seeks than towards those that have, and (b) after eagerly seeking and obtaining recognition she becomes more indifferent to her obligations than theretofore.

. . . It may be thought best in advance of actual recognition to take the time necessary to explore the entire situation and endeavor to reach a full agreement between the two governments . . . pertaining to all or most of the very large number of important questions that sooner or later will call for consideration.

. . . Should the President extend recognition without the situation being dealt with in advance as suggested, then for the purpose of eliminating disputable questions as far as possible it might be accompanied by such conditions as may be agreed upon.[46]

The words of caution were not confined to those who were skeptical of the Soviet government. William C. Bullitt, a friend of the President and a Special Assistant to the Secretary of State, was in close touch with Soviet representatives in Washington, and "was particularly friendly towards Russia and was an ardent proponent of recognition."[47] Yet Bullitt was also careful in stating his belief that we should exact a price from the Soviet government prior to recognition.

It seems essential that formal recognition should not be accorded except as the final act of an agreement covering a number of questions in dispute. Before recognition and before loans, we shall find the Soviet Government relatively amenable. After recognition or loans, we should find the Soviet Government adamant. Among the chief agreements which, in my opinion, must be reached before recognition [are] . . . :

1. Prohibition of Communist propaganda in the United States by the Soviet Government and by the Comintern.

2. Protection of the civil and religious rights of Americans in Russia . . .

3. Agreement . . . that the act of recognition . . . shall take effect only from the day on which it may be accorded.

By negotiation before recognition, we should also attempt to obtain an agreement in regard to the repayment of the loans of the Government of the United States to the Kerensky Government, a waiver of Russian counter claims based upon our Vladivostok, Archangel, and Murmansk expeditions; also some sort of provision for the settlement of claims of American nationals and corporations for property, goods and cash seized by the Soviet Government.[48]

The officials of the Department of State, then, had made long and careful preparations for the moment when the question of recognition would be faced directly. Perhaps Moore was being oratorical when he told the country, in a radio address on November 22, after recognition, that

> in performing this task they drew upon the mass of material in the department's Eastern European Division which was so complete as to exclude the risk of any fact or argument being overlooked. The officials who made the survey knew, of course, all that had occurred when some twenty-six other governments . . . including Great Britain, France, Italy and Germany, had granted unconditional recognition. They were well aware that this was not what the President contemplated and that it was their duty to ascertain and enumerate all of the matters as to which the President might require agreements concurrent with and as a basis of recognition.[49]

And yet, something approaching this completeness had been attempted. Hull has related that there were as many as twenty drafts of the proposed agreements, in an effort to make them "ironclad."[50] One final briefing session was held on November 6 at the White House, with Roosevelt, Hull, Phillips, Bullitt, Morgenthau, and Moore present. If a government ever approached a critical negotiation forewarned and—if possible—forearmed, the American government was so prepared as it waited while Litvinov steamed westward across the Atlantic.

RECOGNITION

The Soviet Commissar for Foreign Affairs, Maxim Litvinov, arrived in New York aboard the *S. S. Berengaria* on November 7, the sixteenth anniversary of the Bolshevik revolution. Accompanying him were Ivan Divilkovsky, Secretary to the Commissariat of Foreign Affairs, and Konstantine Umansky, Chief of the Press Bureau of that Commissariat.

Secretary Hull was, at this time, more interested in the upcoming Pan American Conference in Montevideo, which he was planning to attend, than in the recognition of the Soviet government. As we have seen, Kelley, Chief of the Eastern European Division of the Department of State, was not enthusiastic about the prospect of recognition. It is not surprising, then, that at his press conference on October 23, Hull announced that the preparatory work for the negotiations with Litvinov would be organized by Moore and Bullitt.[51] Although Bullitt, as Special Assistant to the Secretary, was a member of the Department, he worked on this matter directly under the President, and the Department was not kept informed of all of his activities, especially during the preliminary stages. When Hull was asked, at his October 21st press conference, if he expected to sit in on the conversations with

Litvinov, he said that "he would not undertake to make any predictions at this time."[52] A week later he was asked again if he had made any plans for talking with Litvinov and he replied that "no plans of any kind had been made so far as he knew."[53] Soon after this, however, in another memorandum—it is handwritten in pencil and undated but must have been written around November 1—Hull noted that "a collection of important problems at the State Department—contrary to plans—cannot be disposed of before November 5th; that in order to pursue them to completion, I have deferred date of sailing to November 11th—that I would not have done this on account of *any one* of these unfinished matters."[54] Later, Hull repeated that he had suggested to the President that he delay his departure for one week, so that he could participate in the conferences with Litvinov. "I told him I especially wanted to be sure that the agreements on no Soviet propaganda and interference in the United States and on religious freedom for Americans in Russia were agreed to before I left. The President consented."[55]

Before his arrival in New York, Litvinov had been quoted as saying that, so far as he was concerned, he "could reach an agreement with President Roosevelt in a half hour."[56] Upon his arrival, he told reporters, "Perhaps less."[57] These statements were presumably made for their diplomatic effect, but, if the recognition had been unconditional as he expected, perhaps this amount of time would have been adequate. On the day of his arrival, Litvinov "indicated that the question of diplomatic relations would be the only one he would discuss with President Roosevelt now and that discussion of other questions would be taken up later if recognition is accorded."[58] Writing while Litvinov was still en route, journalist Walter Duranty, on the basis of his experience in Moscow, analyzed the situation as follows:

> The Soviet feels strongly that a discussion of debts, claims and counterclaims, to say nothing of possible credits and future business or a trade agreement, should not confuse the immediate issue, which the Soviet believes to be the establishment of normal diplomatic relations.
>
> To introduce such discussion now would be only productive of delays and difficulties because the subjects involved belong to a mixed commission of experts.
>
> It is probable that M. Litvinoff will be willing to repeat the pledges given to other nations, that no Soviet citizen will be allowed to engage in propaganda if admitted to the United States. . . . All other subjects will be left to future discussion.[59]

Later, Hull wrote:

> Right off, Litvinov gave us to understand he expected us to agree on recognition, and then we would begin to discuss the moot questions.

He and his Government had drawn this conclusion from the President's letter, although the letter had made no such commitment. . . . I had to disabuse him of this idea before we could get down to real business.[60]

Litvinov first visited the Department of State on November 8. There were at least five such meetings over a period of three days, plus five "vastly more important and pivotal conversations" with the President at the White House. In all, the negotiations were scattered over a period of nine days, coming to an end on November 16. No stenographers were present, and no complete record attempted.[61] Thus information about the meetings must be pieced together. Moore wrote a memorandum on November 9:

> The impression I formed yesterday was confirmed this morning, namely that Mr. Litvinov expects to obtain recognition without making any committal whatever. He is unwilling to go an inch further than to say that the Soviet laws as reasonably interpreted and administered afford American nationals and the institutions of our Government all the protection they can desire, and that so far as concerns our financial demands and the Soviet counter claims their consideration must be postponed until diplomatic relations are established. He is thus not willing to make any of the agreements which we so carefully prepared during the ten days preceding his arrival and he is anxious to place us in the same position occupied by other nations which accorded recognition and then found that they were unable to reach settlements or to save their nations from injustice. . . .
>
> Mr. Litvinov, in answer to a question I asked him this morning, made a categorical reply leaving no doubt that he desires recognition without placing the Soviet Government under any promise or pledges of any character whatever.[62]

Moore should not have been astonished at Litvinov's attitude, since all the other governments had granted unconditional recognition. The American official already saw the possibility that recognition might not be granted and the negotiations broken off. In such a situation, Moore wrote: "It seems to me of prime importance . . . that we should find some proper way of having it understood that this occurred because of the refusal to furnish assurances relative to such questions as those pertaining to propaganda, religion, espionage, et cet., rather than that the financial questions were pivotal."[63] On Wednesday, November 9, there was still no indication as to just how Litvinov would treat specific proposals by the American government. It was decided to make a test on this point, and that afternoon he was handed the proposal touching religious freedom for Americans in the Soviet Union.

He promptly said that the present Russian laws give sufficient assurance against any injuctice [*sic*] and that he is not in position to agree to modify the laws or make any pledge as to their construction and administration. By the notes on the draft handed him he indicated what the laws now are. It may be expected that he will take a similar attitude relative to the proposed agreements on propaganda, the trial of accused persons, economical [*sic*] espionage, et cetera.[64]

Bullitt later declared that Litvinov's persistent refusal prompted the negotiators to hand him a schedule of return steamship sailing dates.[65]

About this time the President entered the negotiations directly.[66] State Department officials had informed him of the fruitless character of the discussions up to that point; the situation called for action by the President, if the stalemate were to be broken. The President agreed.

On the afternoon of the 10th, they met for an hour, with the President turning on his famous charm and Litvinov, it is reported,[67] mellowing considerably, leading to the conclusion that Litvinov, for reasons of prestige, was willing to negotiate agreements only at the highest level. That evening the two men met again, for three hours. On the 11th, Litvinov met Phillips, Moore, Bullitt, and Kelley for an hour at the Department of State. By this time, apparently, the issues of religious freedom and propaganda were settled. On the 12th Litvinov met with Roosevelt for two hours in the evening. On the 13th and 14th there were no conferences; the Soviet leader was presumably waiting for Moscow's approval of the tentative agreements. On the 15th, Litvinov met with the President in the morning and then spent two hours with Bullitt, arguing the subject of debts and claims. Bullitt's memorandum to the President on this meeting concluded, "I think we were a bit too gentle with him this morning."[68] Litvinov and the President met that afternoon and in less than an hour produced a "gentlemen's agreement" on the debt situation. The final session came on the evening of the 16th. Signatures were affixed to a series of statements, most of them parallel notes, in which the two governments entered into the agreements which the American government had considered so essential. These will be discussed below, separately.

The first set of agreements specified recognition. President Roosevelt wrote:

> My Dear Mr. Litvinov: I am very happy to inform you that as a result of our conversations the Government of the United States has decided to establish normal diplomatic relations with the Government of the Union of Soviet Socialist Republics and to exchange ambassadors.
>
> I trust that the relations now established between our peoples may forever remain normal and friendly, and that our nations henceforth

unmistakably show the President's resolute purpose to safeguard the integrity of our Government and the rights of our nationals now or hereafter residing in Soviet territory. That was the primary purpose to which any strictly material question such as the settlement of debts was altogether ancillary.[77]

Moore referred specifically to the agreements on religion and subversion. Apparently hoping to blunt some of the criticism, he quoted Father Edmund A. Walsh of Georgetown University, who had played an important role in protecting Roman Catholic interests in Russia in the early years of the Communist regime:

> Comprehensive and formal guarantees of an unprecedented character in several fields were made by the Soviet Government prior to recognition. This in itself is a significant abandonment of the previous Soviet policy which uniformly demanded recognition first, with detailed discussion and mutual guarantees to follow. All that now remains to achieve normal diplomatic relations is the honest and unequivocal fulfillment of public pledges, publicly given.[78]

There was probably general agreement when he said that "one supreme value attaching to recognition is that henceforth we will have competent and active official representatives in the Soviet Union with full opportunity to do whatever is required to protect those citizens in the full enjoyment" of their rights. The American representatives would have the opportunity; whether they would be able to protect the citizens might be another matter, to be judged only in the future.

Some opposition to recognition was specific rather than general, and thoughtful rather than emotional. On December 16, 1933, for example, Senator J. Hamilton Lewis of Illinois sent Hull a letter from President Walter Dill Scott of Northwestern University, with an attached memorandum: "Some Remarks on the Russian Recognition Agreement," by an unnamed "great scholar" who "knows the Russian situation better than any man in America."[79] This memorandum took issue with the American government's action, both as to what had been done and what had been left undone. It suggested that there should have been only a single paragraph of agreement, granting most-favored-nation treatment to Americans. Undue stress had been placed, the author said, on the religious question; there had been no serious difficulty over religious matters for foreigners in the Soviet Union. The marriage question was not settled since there was no guarantee that a Russian, married to an American, could leave the Soviet Union. The Soviet agreement not to refuse visas on "personal grounds" was dangerous. There was no provision for reentry permits.

The author of the memorandum criticized the agreement on propaganda because it did not even mention the Communist International or the International Organization to Help Revolution in Foreign Countries (MOPR) or the International Workers Relief (Mezhrabpom.) Also, the government should have demanded that American workers not participate in communist propaganda in Russia. Russian trade should be permitted in the United States only on a basis of reciprocity. The agreement covered neither the right for all Americans to trade with Russia nor that of American courts to have jurisdiction over Amtorg. If Americans are to trade with Russia, furthermore, they must be free to disclose the facts and discuss them publicly outside of the Soviet Union; since the statement on economic espionage did not protect this right, it was manifestly unsatisfactory. While the Soviet government was waiving its claims on the Siberian expedition, why did the American government not insist on a similar provision relative to the Archangel and Murmansk actions? The debt question was not settled; concessions by the Soviet government should have been guaranteed.

This authority on the Soviet system thus pinpointed some very specific problems. What is not obvious, with the lack of records, is whether some of these questions were considered during the negotiations but failed to be mentioned in the agreements. What is obvious, three decades later, is that several of his objections later came to be points of controversy between the two governments.

Foreign press comment ranged widely. An editorial in the Vatican newspaper, *Osservatore Romano*, stated that "Official recognition of Russia by the United States may be considered . . . one of the most important historical facts of the post-war epoch."[80] The London *Times* suggested that "possibly some of the hopes . . . will turn out to be exaggerated," but recognized that President Roosevelt

> is too well informed and too astute a politician to be under any illusions as to the real value of M. Litvinov's solemn declaration of the "fixed policy" of the Soviet Government to refrain from interference in the internal affairs of the United States. He probably attaches importance to it only as helping to make his recognition of the Soviet Government more palatable to that large section of American opinion which persists in abominating it and all its works.[81]

The *Nationalzeitung* (Basle) did not think that the pledge on propaganda would be of any real value for two reasons. "Past experience has shown that these pledges were not observed in other countries; also, it is not known what power, if any, the Soviet Government excercizes [*sic*] over the Third International which organizes propaganda of that sort."[82] In his summary, the American diplomat said, "The Swiss press does not appear to attach much importance to the question of debts . . . and suggests that this matter may probably be settled by . . . never mentioning it again."[83] Some of this analysis was prophetic.

The reaction of the Soviet government was first made known in the leading editorial in *Izvestia,* an official government newspaper, on November 20. The editorial was summarized for the Department by Cole (the Chargé in Riga):

> The United States, the greatest capitalist power in the world, has at last been "compelled" to establish normal diplomatic relations. . . . The United States [hoped] "that it could manage to get along without the establishment of normal relations with the U.S.S.R." . . . The ideas of the leaders of American capitalism that they could carry on a policy based on a refusal to maintain normal diplomatic relations with the U.S.S.R. were "purely imaginary."
>
> . . . "The United States could not continue its former policy . . . without causing the greatest injury to itself and to the cause of peace."
>
> . . . Soviet public opinion strove in every manner to come closer to the United States. This arose from the Soviet struggle to maintain peace. The establishment of normal diplomatic relations is "the greatest victory of our peace policy." Soviet public opinion expects business relations between the two countries to increase. . . .
>
> Mutual relations between the two countries will develop on the basis of mutual respect and without interference by either country in the affairs of the other. . . . There is one good side to the fact that the struggle for normal diplomatic relations lasted so long: "It has taught American public opinion to understand that it is not a question of the U.S. 'helping' the U.S.S.R. but of mutual benefit for two equal parties."[84]

Both governments, therefore, were, on the surface, pleased with the results. The American government pointed to the fact that, unlike other governments granting recognition, it had forced the Soviets to negotiate the outstanding problems prior to recognition; the Soviet government emphasized that it had "compelled" the American government to recognize it and deal with it on a basis of equality. Both governments, therefore, could begin the period of "normal diplomatic relations" with feelings of accomplishment and pride.

Recognition, however, was not an end in itself, but only the means by which the governments could settle problems. If the maintenance of diplomatic relations did indeed provide the friendliness and the contribution to the peace of the world to which the President and

Litvinov referred, then recognition was an important key to this new period. If, however, despite recognition, the governments found themselves unable to proceed on such a basis, then recognition produced only frustration and perhaps futility. The remainder of this study will examine relations of these two governments in the post-1933 period, to see how the Roosevelt-Litvinov agreements were implemented, and to what degree they did contribute to friendly, peaceful relations. Each of the agreements will be considered, with a chapter devoted to its implementation and the problems that arose in the process.

CHAPTER II

Noninterference in Internal Affairs

THE PROBLEM

The previous discussion indicates that the American government considered Litvinov's agreement on propaganda and subversion to be the most important of all his promises; it is appropriate, therefore, to begin our analysis of the promises made by him with this one.

There was almost unanimous agreement as to the necessity of some protection for the United States. Here and there a voice opposed this view, but there were not many such. In April 1933 Senator Borah, long a proponent of recognition, stated that never "since Mr. Stalin became dictator of the Russian government" had there been "any attempt . . . to interfere with the governmental affairs of the United States or to seek by propaganda to interfere with the governmental affairs of this country."[1] Just before this, indeed, the American Minister in Riga wrote to the Department that, "As for Russian propaganda in the United States, it is a fair guess that the Russian Government will agree to give it up and perhaps even to undertake to restrain the Communist Party. . . . The Russians will not admit it but the fact is that their propaganda campaign is dying a natural death for the excellent reason that it does not pay."[2] There were not many who took this view; the general belief was that Russian support for the American Communist Party was real, dangerous to the health if not the life of the republic, and that protection was needed. "It is a principle of international law," wrote Robert Kelley, "so universally accepted as to have acquired an almost axiomatic character that the government of one State is obligated not to interfere in the internal affairs of another State with which it is not at war."[3]

The United States government was not willing to rely solely on a principle of international law, even if it was "almost axiomatic." Thus, the Eastern European Affairs Division of the Department of State made a careful study of the problem, analyzing every treaty Soviet

27

Russia had signed. In one memorandum, Kelley devoted forty pages to excerpts from treaties and other agreements on the general topic of interference and propaganda, finding that various governments had requested formal pledges from the Soviet government on such matters as:[4] (1) "Pledges that the Soviet representatives or delegates to the country concerned will not carry on propaganda against the institutions or the government of that country or interfere in the internal affairs"—by Germany, Austria, Norway, Denmark, Japan, Great Britain; (2) "Pledges to the effect that the Soviet Government will not interfere in the internal affairs of the country in question"—France, Poland, Persia, Georgia, Great Britain; (3) "Pledges . . . that the Soviet Government will refrain from any agitation or propaganda against the Government or the institutions of the other country"—Germany, Austria-Hungary, Turkey, Bulgaria, Czechoslovakia, France, China, Great Britain; (4) "Pledges . . . that the Soviet Government will not conduct or assist or encourage outside the borders of the Soviet Union propaganda, direct or indirect, against the institutions of the government in question"—Great Britain, Italy; (5) Pledges that the Soviet Government will not "support with funds or in any other form persons or bodies or agencies or institutions whose aim is to spread discontent or to foment rebellion" in any part of, or in the dominions, colonies, or mandates of the country in question—Great Britain, Japan; and (6) various undertakings "that the Soviet Government will not permit in Soviet territory the formation or the presence of groups or organizations, the object of which is to attack by force of arms the government in question"—practically all countries bordering on the Soviet Union and in the case of Latvia and Estonia this was not limited to armed organizations.

The exacting of promises from the Soviet government had not been adequate, however. Of the thirteen governments that had obtained a pledge of some sort from the Soviet government, eight had found Soviet officials guilty of violating these pledges. Of nine governments that entered into diplomatic relations with the Soviet government but exacted no such pledge, five had also found grounds for complaint. Several governments found that "by repressive police measures they have been able to cope fairly satisfactorily with attacks, directed by Moscow, made upon them within the territories under their control; but have found it much more difficult to meet propaganda and other activities carried on against them by Moscow outside their frontiers."[5] In the spring of 1925 the French government requested the Soviet government to withdraw the 1st Secretary of the Embassy in Paris because he had made a speech promising "the moral and material support of Russia to all neighboring peoples of the great republic who desire to free themselves from exploitation by world capitalism." Again in 1927, the French government demanded the withdrawal of Rakovsky, the Soviet Ambassador, because he had signed a declaration to the effect that "in case of war with the U.S.S.R., the proletarians in capitalistic countries must work for the defeat of their governments and foreign soldiers must join the Red Army."[6]

In practically every case in which a violation of agreements of this type had occurred, the Soviet government took the view "either that the act charged was not of a nature that could be considered a violation of the pledge or has denied in entirety the truth of the charge, branding as untrustworthy or forged the testimony of witnesses or documents adduced in substantiation thereof."[7] As a result, the pledges did little to protect the other governments.

The American officials knew, therefore, that the greatest of caution was needed if they were really to protect American interests against Soviet activity. They prepared an agreement to be presented to Litvinov "by taking a phrase here and a sentence there from twenty-six similar treaties Russia had signed with other countries. . . . When it was finished, there was not a single word in the draft that had not already appeared in some treaty to which Russia had affixed her signature and seal."[8] Hull has already been quoted as saying that Kelley's staff prepared as many as twenty drafts of some of the proposed agreements, and this type of caution surely applied to the agreement under discussion. Hull related that when Litvinov was shown the agreement "he read it and said: 'We can't agree to this.' 'But you have agreed to it,' I replied. 'How?' he exclaimed. I then pointed out how we had prepared it, using entirely the wording of treaties that Russia had already signed. He was greatly impressed and agreed to study it further."[9]

Somehow, Litvinov was brought to the point where he was willing to sign an agreement on this point. The text of the agreement is as follows:

My Dear Mr. President: I have the honor to inform you that coincident with the establishment of diplomatic relations between our two Governments it will be the fixed policy of the Government of the Union of Soviet Socialist Republics:

1. To respect scrupulously the indisputable right of the United States to order its own life within its own jurisdiction in its own way and to refrain from interfering in any manner in the internal affairs of the United States, its territories or possessions.

2. To refrain, and to restrain all persons in government service

and all organizations of the Government or under its direct or indirect control, including the organizations in receipt of any financial assistance from it, from any act overt or covert liable in any way whatsoever to injure the tranquillity, prosperity, order, or security of the whole or any part of the United States, its territories or possessions, and in particular, from any act tending to incite or encourage armed intervention, or any agitation or propaganda having as an aim, the violation of the territorial integrity of the United States, its territories or possessions, or the bringing about by force of a change in the political or social order of the whole or any part of the United States, its territories or possessions.

3. Not to permit the formation or residence on its territory of any organization or group—and to prevent the activity on its territory of any organization or group, or of representatives or officials of any organization or group—which makes claim to be the Government of, or makes attempt upon the territorial integrity of, the United States, its territories or possessions; not to form, subsidize, support or permit on its territory military organizations or groups having the aim of armed struggle against the United States, its territories or possessions, and to prevent any recruiting on behalf of such organizations and groups.

4. Not to permit the formation or residence on its territory of any organization or group—and to prevent the activity on its territory of any organization or group, or of representatives or officials of any organization or group—which has as an aim the overthrow or the preparation for the overthrow of, or the bringing about by force of a change in, the political or social order of the whole or any part of the United States, its territories or possessions.[10]

The President, in his reply, accepted this assurance and then added: "It will be the fixed policy of the Executive of the United States within the limits of the powers conferred by the Constitution and laws of the United States to adhere reciprocally to the engagements above expressed." As we have already seen, Moore believed that the Soviet government would want this agreement to be bilateral, and suggested that we might have to agree to this not because there was such activity in the United States but in order to receive a promise from Litvinov.

From the beginning, the key to the agreement concerned the Communist International. Secretary Hull has reported that he insisted that the agreement "be much broader than the usual agreements the Soviet Government signed, which bound only the Government itself not to conduct propaganda and left all individuals in Russia free to do so, including the Communist International."[11] Morgenthau has written that when Hull pressed Litvinov, during the negotiations, about the Comintern, the latter "disclaimed responsibility, saying that the Comintern had no government standing. 'We have no request to make of any of your organizations in the United States,' he said, 'so why ask us about some of our organizations.' "[12] At the time the agreement was criticized for not having mentioned the Comintern. The London *Times* said:

> Litvinov's letter to Roosevelt, like Sokolnikoff's note to Henderson, contains no explicit mention of the Communist International which . . . is the organization through which the Russian Communist Party conducts its revolutionary propaganda abroad. . . . No undertaking given by the Commissar for Foreign Affairs, however carefully it may be drafted, is likely to have any restraining effect upon the efforts of the Comintern.[13]

The omission of the Comintern was not an oversight. In preparing the text, Kelley believed that if this organization were specifically mentioned by name, the Russians could change the name and claim that it was not covered by the agreement. If *all* such organizations and activity were proscribed, the Comintern would be included.

A present-day reader of these promises inevitably asks how the American officials could have expected the Soviet government to abide by these promises. As early as 1919 Litvinov had said that "If peace were made, Russian Bolshevist propaganda in foreign countries would stop at once,"[14] and again in 1921, "the Soviet republic entirely absorbed in the work of internal reconstruction and of building up its economic life has not the intention of intervening in the internal affairs of America and . . . makes herewith a categorical declaration to this effect."[15] But the problem had continued. On the basis of the Soviet interpretation of similar pledges given to other governments and its insistence that it had no control over the Communist International, the Soviet government would, inevitably, try to evade the intention of the agreement. Did the Americans not know this? If so, then why the insistence on having such an agreement, and why such care in preparing it? The answer to this is not clear. Probably official views represented varying degrees of skepticism. One thing is certain, however, and that is that some agreement on this matter was politically essential, given the climate of American public opinion. It was hard enough for many Americans to accept recognition in any case; without even an attempt to reach an agreement on this topic, the acceptance would have been much less. Dr. Joseph F. Thorning, S.J., wrote in *America*, a Roman Catholic review, immediately after recognition:

The question of subversive propaganda . . . is handled without kid gloves. Although the 3rd International is not mentioned by name, the implication is clear. The American Section of this organization . . . is to be suppressed on Soviet soil as well as throughout the world. Here again, the safeguarding clauses are numerous. An attempt is made to block every avenue of approach for possible agitators who would labor for the incorporation of this republic into the U.S.S.R.

The gap between promises and fulfillment is sometimes more than can be taken in one stride. But, if paper pledges mean anything, President Roosevelt has again obtained the maximum measure of security for his country. . . . Most important of all, knowing President Roosevelt's character and determination as we do, we can feel perfectly sure that, in the event of Soviet nonfulfillment, recognition will be withdrawn ipso facto and relations become as before.[16]

Even after recognition had been secured, the Russians sought to soothe American sensitivity on this matter of propaganda. When Litvinov spoke to the National Press Club in Washington on November 17, he was asked how relations might affect the Third International.

"The Third International is not mentioned in the documents," he said. "You should not read more into the documents than was intended."

One correspondent wanted to know how the Communist Party might be affected.

"What Communist party?" he asked. "The Communist party of Russia doesn't concern America. The Communist Party of America does not concern Russia."

Asked if any Russians were engaged in distributing propaganda in the United States, he said: "I wish you would give me the addresses of any such persons."[17]

The newly appointed Soviet Ambassador, Alexander Troyanovsky, was also reassuring in a press conference in Moscow. " 'Communism cannot be imported from abroad,' he said. . . . 'In any event, I can assure you there will be no Communistic activity on the part of any of our officials in America.' "[18]

The use of a state as a base from which to operate through agencies created by its rulers to achieve the overthrow of other governments was alien to existing conceptions of international law. The Communists openly pointed to the fact that the power and resources of their state were "placed in the service of the world revolution. . . . This is the reason why the imperialist states sever their diplomatic relations with the Soviet Union."[19]

In the early days of the Bolshevik regime, there had been no attempt to conceal the direct connection between the Soviet government and the Communist International. In December 1917 Lenin and Trotsky placed "two million roubles for the needs of the revolutionary international movement at the disposal of the foreign representatives of the Commissariat for Foreign Affairs."[20] In the same month Trotsky, Commissar for Foreign Affairs, stated that "the Soviet power considers diplomatic relations necessary not only with governments but also with revolutionary-socialist parties seeking the overthrow of existing governments."[21] In 1918 and 1919 representatives of the Soviet government were expelled from Germany, Switzerland, Sweden, and England for openly engaging in subversive activity. In 1920 Radek declared that "the Soviet government is fulfilling its duty as a detachment of the International."[22]

Soon, however, the Soviet leaders sought to convince the outside world of the separation of the two agencies. In 1921 Litvinov asserted that there was no "justification for identifying the Third International with the Russian Government";[23] it was incidental that the Comintern headquarters were in Moscow and that some members of the Soviet government held positions in the Executive Committee. In 1924 Rykov stated that the Comintern was "independent of Soviet power"[24] while Zinovyev, then head of the Comintern, declared that the organization was "an absolutely independent organization, entirely independent" of the Soviet government.[25] When the Polish government protested that the discussion by the 6th Comintern Congress of a communist revolution in Poland violated its treaty with the Soviet government, Chicherin "pointed out that the Soviet Government has explained several times that the Communist International was not a governmental organization but was a private organization."[26] The British government insisted that the Soviet government and the Communist International were organizationally connected in such a manner as to form, to all intents and purposes, a single organization; that therefore obligations assumed by the Soviet government rest also upon the Communist International and that the activities of the Communist International, directed against themselves constitute, therefore, violation of the pledges made by the Soviet government. Although there were heated exchanges between the British and Soviet representatives in 1921, 1923, 1924, 1927, and 1929, the Soviet government refused to accept responsibility for the Comintern. In 1931, certain British Conservatives favored breaking diplomatic relations with Moscow unless that government were willing to assume this responsibility, but the Prime Minister restrained them. "If we broke, should we be in a better position to handle the situation today? We say 'No.' "[27]

Moscow maintained this story of the separation of the two agencies at the time of the American recognition in 1933, with no concern that the facts seemed to be otherwise and that its version was not accepted in authoritative places. As Kelley wrote, "the foreign policy of the Bolshevist regime as a whole is determined, fully and definitively, by the All-Union Communist Party, which assigns to the Communist International the parts of that policy falling within 'the sphere of the international revolutionary movement,' and to the Soviet government the parts of that policy falling within 'the sphere of the foreign policy of the Soviet Union.' "[28] He pointed out that "it is not without significance" that Trotsky, Chicherin, and Litvinov—the only three persons who had held the post of Foreign Commissar—had all participated in the work of the Comintern, even if in 1928 Litvinov had emphasized that no principal member of the Soviet government had worked actively at the 6th Congress the previous year.[29]

Indeed, Moscow's own story did not fit together. The editor of *Izvestia*, the official government newspaper, declared that "the close organic and spiritual bond between the Soviet Republic . . . and the Communist International cannot be doubted. And even if the connection had not been admitted many times by both sides, it would, nevertheless, be clear to all."[30] In 1929, the official organ of the Comintern declared that "the two are, therefore, inseparably associated not only by reason of the fact that they both, by their very existence deny the whole capitalist world . . . ; they are also the representatives of a uniform process of world revolution."[31] Even Stalin admitted the hollowness of the Soviet claim. Speaking to the Central Committee of the Soviet party in April 1929 about a situation which had developed the previous year at the 6th Congress of the Comintern, he said:

> Ordinarily the theses are submitted to a preliminary examination by the delegation of the All-Union Communist Party. However, in this case, this condition was not observed. The result was that the theses signed by Comrade Bukharin, sent to the delegation of the All-Union Communist Party, were at the same time sent to the foreign delegations of the 6th Congress. But these theses proved . . . to be unsatisfactory. . . . The delegation of the All-Union Communist Party had to make about twenty corrections in the theses . . . Why did Comrade Bukharin send the theses to the foreign delegations before they were examined by the delegation of the All-Union Communist Party? . . . This embarrassment would not have occurred had Comrade Bukharin not been in a hurry.[32]

The relation of the Soviet government and the Communist International was never settled. Moscow maintained that the two were completely separate, and the other governments maintained but never proved completely that this was nonsense.

It was easier to establish the relation between the Communist International in Moscow and the American Communist Party in the United States. The Constitution of the party at the time of recognition began, "The name of this organization shall be the COMMUNIST PARTY OF U.S. OF AMERICA, section of the Communist International." A member of the party adhered to the "program and statutes of the Communist International."[33] Article IV of the Constitution stated:

> The Communist Party, like all sections of the Comintern, is built upon the principle of democratic centralization. These principles are: . . . immediate and exact application of the decisions of the Executive Committee of the Communist International. . . . After a decision has been adopted at the congress of the Comintern, . . . it must be carried out unconditionally, even if some members or some of the local organizations are not in agreement with the decision.[34]

Other similar controls were included in the constitution of the Comintern, adopted at the 6th Congress in 1928. There was no question, then, that the American Communist Party was under the control of the Comintern in Moscow.

An analysis of Communist activities by the Department of State listed seven methods used by the Comintern to control the American party *directly*.

1. *Visits to the United States* by representatives of the Comintern, as in the case of John Pepper (the alias of Joseph Pogany), A. Lozovsky, Dengel, and Pollitt, who attended the 6th National Convention in March 1929. These "C. I. representatives" could see that the party did what Moscow wanted.

2. *Financial contributions.* It was reported that Lozovsky brought $35,000 to the United States in 1922, that Foster brought $10,000 after his visit to Moscow in 1921, and that in April 1923 $90,000 was received from Moscow for trade union work.

3. *Visits of representatives* of the American party to Moscow for conversations, meetings of organizations, and as liaison. Thus William Z. Foster was in Moscow for six weeks in 1924, 1925, and 1926 in his capacity as a member of the Executive Committee of the Comintern and the Executive Bureau of the Profintern; in 1928 at the 6th Congress of the Comintern and the 4th Congress of the Profintern; in May 1929, December 1929, in 1931, and in 1933 he went on business of an "unknown nature." Earl Browder visited Moscow in 1921, 1924, 1926, 1928, 1930, and 1932.

4. *Assignment of American Communists* to Moscow for training in agitation and propaganda to be carried on in the United States. In 1931 the American Embassy in London forwarded a list of Communists, some of them American citizens, who arrived in Helsinki on November 3, 1930, and left for the U.S.S.R. the next day. "They were proceeding to the Agitation and Propaganda School in Moscow and were not reticent in the expression of their extremist views."[35] This group "according to the Director of the Detective Central Police have expressed their intention of later returning to the U.S. to instruct their fellow countrymen in Marxist principles."[36] A year later, an official of the Department talked with a Dutch diplomat who said "that many Americans destined for Russia were now passing through Holland. . . . He understood that American communists were being signed up [by Amtorg] ostensibly for technical work in Russia but in reality were going to communist schools there."[37] In this connection, "Amtorg recently announced in New York City that it was making arrangements to send some 6,000 American workmen to Soviet Russia."[38]

5. *Discussions of and decisions* with respect to questions concerning communism in the United States.

6. *Written orders on tactics* and organization, and orders to expel certain members, as in the case of Jay Lovestone, Alexander Bittelman, and Benjamin Gitlow, all one-time high party officials.

7. *Published material* of a theoretical nature, as found in the *Communist International, International Press Correspondence, Pravda,* and authoritative books. Let us now discuss these last three methods.

The theoretical material would be, normally, the same for American and other Communists. Articles appearing in the *Communist International* "have nearly the same force as direct instructions from the Communist International to the Communist Party under discussion."[39] Thus in 1931 the Executive Committee of the Communist International (ECCI) decided that "Communists should increase their agitation towards explaining to the masses the achievements of the U.S.S.R.";[40] in 1933 this same body recommended that "communist parties . . . make pertinent proposals to the respective central committees of the social-democratic parties affiliated with the Socialist International . . . concerning joint action against fascism and the advance of capitalism."[41]

Beyond the general area of ideology, Moscow was specifically interested in the activities of the American party. On November 8, 1933 —the first day of the conversations with Litvinov in Washington— the American Legation in Riga telegraphed that the current issue of the *Communist International* contained "more material concerning revolutionary movement of the Communist Party in the U.S. than any other issue known to me . . . devoted to the best methods . . . to take advantage of the increased labor unrest in the U.S. and to struggle against the President's recovery program."[42]

Moscow repeatedly make known its displeasure with the American party: "In the United States, the efforts of the communists to base their work on the plants and factories, to put the work on the 'enterprise principle,' have met with very little success. . . . The work at the enterprises and the trade union work of the Party is especially poor."[43] On another occasion, the party was criticized for its "incorrect understanding of the situation in the U. S. . . . [and of] the mutual relations between the American Communist Party and the Communist International."[44]

It is not surprising, then, that Moscow should give specific instructions to the American comrades: "The *Daily Worker* must be more firmly controlled by the Central Committee. . . . At the same time, the Party must establish firmer control over the language press and must see to it that its agitation is in line with that of the *Daily Worker*."[45] "It is the task of the American Communist Party to seize upon and organize all demonstrations, disturbances and strikes that may appear, and to exploit them to the advantage of the cause which the Communists advocate. . . . They are to be turned into strikes having a political character."[46] Some of these instructions brought immediate response. The ECCI in September 1932 instructed the American party "to mobilize the masses, putting foremost the struggle . . . for social insurance, against the reduction of wages, and for the immediate relief of the unemployed."[47] The Central Committee of the American party agreeably decided that "The immediate, central task of the Party is . . . in the extension and intensification of the struggle of the unemployed for immediate relief, and for unemployment and social insurance."[48] When the American government imposed an embargo on imports of timber from the Soviet Union, on the grounds that it was produced with forced labor, the Soviet Foreign Affairs Commissariat

> instructed the Amtorg, and the representatives of the institutions concerned in the U.S. to ascertain urgently the circumstances leading to the decision of the Department . . . in order that we may dispute its legality. As we have already denied that forced convict labor is utilized in the U.S.S.R., we . . . instruct all the camps of the Ogpu to obtain from all prisoners on special work a signed document testifying that their work is voluntary.[49]

Concern of Soviet leaders with the success of the American Communist Party is obvious.

In addition to the seven types of direct control just discussed, there was an indirect method by which Moscow could accomplish its hopes in the United States. This involved the use of subsidiary organizations —front organizations—whose decisions were made in Moscow and whose representatives came to the United States, bringing instructions and money and exercising control over the American portion of the international organization, with interlocking directorates into the party and Comintern in both Moscow and the United States. The American Legation in Riga prepared a 260-page summary of "Moscow Agencies for Propaganda in Countries Outside of Russia," analyzing the organization, the tasks and activities of the groups, their relation to the Communist International, and their connections in the United States. The organizations discussed were:

Communist International
Red International of Labor Unions (RILU, Profintern)
Peasant International
Red Sport International
International of Proletarian Freethinkers
International of War Veterans and War Victims
Anti-War Committees
Anti-Imperialist League
International Red Aid (MOPR)
Workers International Relief (Mezhrabpom)
International Association of Revolutionary Writers
Union of Proletarian Esperantists
International of Apartment Tenants
International of Revolutionary Painters
Friends of the Soviet Union
International of Seamen and Harbor Workers
International Union of the Revolutionary Theater (MORT)
International of Educational Workers
International Conference of Negro Workers
International Music Bureau
Society for Cultural Relations with Foreign Countries (VOKS)
Intourist
All-Union Society for the Land Settlement of Toiling Jews
Section for the Advancement of Scientific and Technical Collaboration with U.S.A.

There is room to consider only a few of these, to illustrate the manner in which they served Moscow's purpose. According to its statutes, the Red International of Labor Unions was "an International which, together with the Communist International, organizes the labor class for the overthrow of the bourgeoisie, for the destruction of the bourgeois state, for the establishment of a dictatorship of the proletariat, for the seizure of the weapons and arms of production, and for the installation of communism."[50] Its tasks included "broad propaganda and agitation for the ideas of revolutionary and class struggle, of social revolution and of the dictatorship of the proletariat" and "mass revolutionary action in the aim of overthrowing the capitalist system and bourgeois government." As Kuusinen said in 1930, "The organizations of the revolutionary labor union movement should . . . embrace not only communists but also those revolutionary workmen who are not yet members of the Party. . . . They must be schools of communism. . . . But they also have certain functions in common with Communist parties. First of all they have a common aim. . . . This common aim results in unity of action."[51] The North American section of the RILU was the Trade Union Unity League (TUUL) created in 1920 under the leadership of the Communist Party. It was never very successful; the organ of the RILU declared in April 1932 that the "organization work of the American Trade Union Unity League . . . makes it evident that the instructions of the Red International of Labor Unions . . . are not always put into effect."[52] It did, however, claim credit for important participation in a number of strikes during the depression.

The Workers International Relief, organized in 1921 to aid the starving people of Soviet Russia, later emphasized industrial assistance to the Soviet Union and subversion elsewhere. As its head, Willi Muenzenberg, said, "the fight of the Workers International Relief is determined by the recognition that . . . the abolition of the capitalist system is more important than relief activity."[53] It claimed the collection and distribution of about seventeen million dollars between 1921 and 1931, much of it contributed by Russian labor unions, and was called "one of the most successful mouthpieces"[54] of the U.S.S.R. It maintained nine district headquarters in the United States, aided in the textile strikes in Pennsylvania and North Carolina, and collected funds for tractors for the Soviet Union.

The Communist International was important in coordinating the work of all these organizations. Lozovsky pointed out that the instructions which the RILU issued "were always coordinated with the Communist International" and "the political and tactical line of policy in the world labor union movement . . . is the line of the Communist International and of our party."[55] Lozovsky was, himself, an example of the coordination, being at various times Secretary General of the RILU, member of ECCI, and Assistant Commissar for Foreign Affairs of the Soviet government. "Comrade Herman" in 1924 declared that "the Mezhrabpom . . . must note that there is only one single vanguard which directs the proletariat in all these battles, and that is the Communist International."[56]

To aid this large task of integration, the *International Press Correspondence (Inprecorr)* was founded in 1921 when the ECCI decided to start the publication of a Correspondence Leaflet two or three times a week, to appear in German, English, and French.

> The Bulletin of the Communist International publishes resolutions and circulars of the Executive Committee. . . . Its field included . . . instructions of an official nature. The "International Press Correspondence" . . . takes upon itself the remaining part of political information and acts, furthermore, as an intermediary between the Communist Parties in matters of their mutual orientation in international affairs.[57]

Shortly after the establishment of this new medium, ECCI, deciding that the problems of the international trade union movement had been receiving practically no attention, resolved "that henceforth not less than one quarter of the 'International Press Correspondence' is devoted to questions of the trade union movement."[58]

Here, then, was another method by which Moscow could keep in close touch with Communist parties in various parts of the world, including the United States, so that every member, in "his adherence to the program and statutes of the Communist International" would have authentic knowledge of what was expected of him at all times.

On July 18, 1931, Acting Secretary of State Castle called the attention of all American diplomatic and consular officers to the provisions of the Immigration Acts of 1917 and 1918 which prohibited the entry of certain people into the country. The Secretary listed more than a dozen organizations—including the Communist International, Communist International of Youth, Red International of Labor Unions, and Workers International Relief—stating that people "who have participated or are participating in any capacity in the work of these organizations" were ineligible to come into the United States. "The list of organizations . . . while believed to contain the names of the principal organizations membership in or affiliation with which renders an alien inadmissible to the United States is not to be taken, however, as an inclusive list of such organizations and may be added to from time to time."[59]

Most Americans were not aware, at the time of recognition, of this web of Communist organizations and activities. They may have understood vaguely that Communism sought to undermine the American system of government, but they failed to see that the American Communist Party was only a small part, carefully created and controlled, in an effort to replace the whole of the American system. Kelley made this point very specific:

> [The system] consists, in general, of forming, subsidizing and actively directing and controlling from Moscow a small, disciplined group of communists in each country . . . and the resultant establishment of a communist government. It, thus, resolves itself into active interference in the domestic affairs of each state concerned,—directed and controlled by an alien power and inimical to the continuance of the existing order in, and existing government of, each such state.[60]

Such intention was no secret. The last paragraph of the *Program* adopted by the 6th Comintern World Congress (1928) stated that Communists "openly proclaim that their aims can be achieved only by means of a forcible overthrow of the entire present social order."[61]

It was to defeat such activity that the American leaders made Litvinov promise that there would be no interference in the domestic affairs of the United States, and that the Soviet government would not permit on its soil any organization or activities intended to aid in the overthrow of the American system of government. It was this purpose which led some Americans to believe that the promise to end Communist propaganda and subversion in the United States might mean the end of the Comintern: "The American section of this organization . . . is to be suppressed on Soviet soil as well as throughout the world." "Great Britain, France, Germany and Italy have only to follow President Roosevelt's lead, and the Third International, now 'in residence' in Russia, is ended forever."[62] The governmental leaders may not have expected such complete success.

IMPLEMENTATION OF THE AGREEMENT

The ink was hardly dry on the Litvinov promise before it was involved in contention. Benjamin Gitlow, once head of the American Communist Party but later expelled by the Comintern, has told that Litvinov met privately with the leaders of the American Party in New York and assured them that the commitment did not affect their party or its relations with the Comintern. "After all, comrades," he is quoted as saying, "you should by this time know how to handle the fiction of the tie-up between the Comintern and the Soviet government. . . . The letter is a scrap of paper which will soon be forgotten."[63] He is also quoted as having said to newsmen, "The Third International is not mentioned in the document. You must not read into it more than was mentioned," while the New York *Daily Worker* proclaimed on

November 21, "The capitalist press . . . Roosevelt . . . and the capitalist class . . . know that every attempt to claim that Article 4 of the Litvinov pact applies to the Communist International will meet with defeat. Just as every attempt of the British government, for example, to do that failed."[64] This was only the first scene in a long, bitter controversy in which Litvinov claimed that the agreement did not cover the Comintern and the American leaders maintained that it did.

Within six weeks of the signing of the pledge, evidence showed that the American Communist Party was not free from Moscow's influence, when the American Legation in Riga informed the Department that an article in *Bolshevik*, the official organ of the All-Union Communist Party, declared that "America . . . may be confronted with serious political strikes. The American Communist Party should now guide the incitement of the masses in this direction."[65] In May 1934 Moore sent a memorandum to Bullitt: "This was written in our Legal Division. It may assist you in your investigation of the alleged activities of the Third Internationale [*sic*] in Moscow in contravention of the pledge given the President by Litvinov."[66] Such evidence continued to pile up, and Matthew Woll (Vice President of the American Federation of Labor) presented a "mass of evidence to the Department tending to show that propagandist activities are carried on in Moscow in disregard of the pledge made by Mr. Litvinov to the President"; the State Department concluded that "in at least two instances . . . there [had] been a violation of the pledge."[67] Moore requested Woll "not to agitate the subject in any way, pending our effort to conclude an agreement as to debts," yet later, in June 1934, Moore wrote to Bullitt that he had had an opportunity to tell Troyanovsky that "we have evidence that Litvinoff's propaganda pledge has been disregarded."[68]

Secretary Hull, in August 1934, instructed Ambassador Bullitt to bring to Litvinov's attention—in view of the forthcoming Comintern Congress—a list of five occasions, "evidence of which seems indisputable,"[69] which constituted violations of Litvinov's note. The violations concerned: (1) discussion of the policies and activities of the American Communist Party at a Comintern meeting in December 1933, with the adoption of a program to apply to the United States; (2) a message from the Comintern in January 1934 urging the *Daily Worker* to become a "real collective agitator and organizer of the workers' struggle"; (3) the consideration by the Red International of Labor Unions in December 1933 of a report on the organization of revolutionary elements within the American Federation of Labor; (4)

the participation of two representatives of the American Communist Party in the ECCI; and (5) the participation of an American Communist Party representative in the proceedings of the Executive Bureau of the RILU. Within the first few months, an impressive list of violations was already building up.

Well might Woll and other labor leaders be concerned about the violation of the pledge given by Litvinov, for a new tactic had been devised in an effort to take over the American labor unions. The *Communist International* of October 1, 1934, "stressed the need"— in other words, gave the order—of "creating strong revolutionary [Communist] opposition groups within the American Federation of Labor unions," and stated that "the Communist Party of the U.S. should concentrate its efforts on work in the American Federation of Labor unions and attempt to acquire the leadership in some of the local unions. . . . The communist unions are not to be entirely abandoned, but they are, for the time being at least, to play only a secondary role."[70]

Early in 1935 the American Consul in Moscow reported a conversation with an American citizen who was working as an advisor to the Azerbaijan Petroleum Trust, stating that a Shop Committee had asked him in May 1934 to write an open letter telling how well the workers in Soviet plants were being treated. "He was told that should he write such a letter, it would find its way into every penal institution in the U.S."[71] Later in 1935 the Department of State received two letters, one from an individual in Washington and the other from a bank in Cincinnati, protesting against circulars received from the International Book Company in Moscow, advertising the Workers' and Peasants' Red Army Album. While not important matters, these were further indications of the various ways in which Moscow continued to involve itself in American domestic affairs.

The agreement, it will be recalled, was reciprocal in nature. Earlier, Litvinov had been concerned by the "hundreds of thousands of press organs in almost all countries [which] have . . . been daily libelling the Soviet Union, attacking the Soviet system and insulting the Soviet Government."[72] It is not surprising, then, that the Soviet Ambassador should, at some point, have used the Roosevelt-Litvinov agreement to defend his government's interests, as he did in 1935, referring to articles printed in the "White Russian" press—such as *Novoye Russkoye Slovo* in New York City—and the activities of Russian organizations that attacked the Soviet government. The American official to whom Troyanovsky protested disclaimed responsibility for such actions:

> I pointed out that the undertakings of Mr. Litvinov and the President
> . . . were not entirely reciprocal, that the President undertook only to
> do what was in the power of the Executive here to do . . . that there
> is not in this country, as there is in the Soviet Union, any law giving
> the Federal Government control over the press. He said he realized
> this, but thought that the President's undertaking must have some
> meaning. . . . He asked whether there is not some Federal law which
> forbids the publication of articles urging the overthrow of foreign
> governments. I told him I did not know of such a law and felt quite
> sure there was none.[73]

Neither the American nor the Soviet government, then, was happy
with the interpretations of the agreement.

The biggest single problem in the implementation of this agreement, however, involved the 7th World Congress of the Communist
International, held in Moscow in 1935. The Congress was originally
scheduled for the latter part of 1934 but was quietly rescheduled
until the "first half of 1935." At the time of this change, the Lithuanian
Minister in Moscow, "whose knowledge of the activities of the Third
International Party is intimate, has expressed the opinion to me that
the Comintern Congress will be postponed indefinitely as the Soviet
Government is unwilling to have the friendly relations it is now culti-
vating with many countries jeopardized by wild speeches in Moscow."[74] By the middle of 1935, however, the Soviet government was in
a better position to hold such a meeting. The debt negotiations with
the United States were essentially and unsuccessfully ended, while a
new treaty with France strengthened the Soviet hand in Europe. In
May the Department of State informed Ambassador Bullitt of the
farewell banquet to be given on June 8 for the American delegates to
the Congress. Bullitt reported:

> It is extraordinarily difficult to obtain any exact information here as to
> the meeting of the Third International which is scheduled to take
> place soon in Moscow.
> Borodin a few days ago went so far as to say "it will take place on"
> then caught himself and said, "I really do not know the date. It is
> you know to be an absolutely secret conference."[75]

In June Bullitt wired that the delegates were being hidden in the
country near Moscow and that the Congress would be confined to
private meetings of the ECCI. Within a week, however, he reported
that Louis Fischer, a journalist, had called on him, "obviously under
the instructions of some agency of the Soviet Government" to inform
him that, as an unexpected result of these secret meetings, "It had

been decided that a full Congress . . . should be held in Moscow at the end of July or the beginning of August."[76] Fischer asked whether the United States would protest if an American Communist attacked the United States during the Congress, saying that "he felt personally that such a speech at such a Congress would constitute a violation of Litvinov's pledge . . . and that he was most disturbed because of the possible effect on Soviet-American relations." The Ambassador refused to answer such a hypothetical question but was told the next day that the Department believed that discussion of the activities in the United States, and participation of representatives of the American Communist Party in such meetings did constitute violations of Litvinov's pledges and that, if asked, he should say that "the American Government expects that the Soviet Government will take appropriate means to prevent acts in disregard of the solemn pledges given by Mr. Litvinoff on behalf of the Soviet Government."[77]

Even well into July, however, the Soviet leaders professed to know nothing of such a Congress. On July 8 Bullitt understood that it would begin on or about July 20 and close on or about August 5. That afternoon, he referred to the meeting while talking with Litvinov, who replied:

> "What? Is there to be one?" I answered: "Yes, on the 20th of this month." Litvinov replied with a broad grin: "You know more about the Third International than I do. The other day when I was talking with Stalin I said that I had heard there was to be a meeting of the Third International on the tenth of this month. Stalin replied: "Is there?" He knew no more about it than I do. . . ."
>
> It seems to me clear from Litvinov's demeanor today that he intends to take the attitude that the Soviet Government has no connection with the Third International and knows nothing whatsoever about its activities.[78]

Five days later the Ambassador, talking with Litvinov again, expressed the hope that the Congress would not take place:

> He replied "What Congress? I know nothing about it."
>
> I said . . . that the Government of the United States . . . was recalling vividly at this moment the promises . . . of his note to the President . . . [and] expected the promises of the Soviet Government to be respected.
>
> He mumbled with distinct signs of annoyance and rising temper: "I remember I said I could not promise anything about the Third International." I answered that I feared most serious consequences if the pledge of his Government should not be respected.[79]

Bullitt understood, however, that Litvinov, Voroshilov, and Molotov had protested to Stalin against holding the meeting, and expressed the view that the decision to do so might be reversed.

The Congress did meet, however, convening on July 25 and continuing until August 20. At the opening session, two Americans—Earl Browder and William Z. Foster—were elected to the Presidium. The keynote speech contained no reference to the United States except for one slight mention of the Washington "bonus marchers." On July 29, however, Browder spoke to the Congress, reporting on the elimination of factionalism from the American party (as directed by the 6th Congress in 1928), the growth of the party, the influence of the party in labor union and youth organizations, and other matters then under discussion in the United States. The Congress was no longer ignoring the United States. On August 2, Georgy Dimitrov—one of the most important leaders in the 7th Congress—discussed the problem of the United States, in view of the new "united front" tactic. He complimented the American party for having shown initiative in the creation of a Farmer-Labor Party, adding: "But they must still take active measures in order that the creation of such a party should become the affair of the masses themselves."[80] In concluding his speech, Dimitrov hailed

> Tom Mooney who has been languishing in prison for eighteen years and the thousands of other prisoners of capitalism and fascism (stormy applause) and we say to them, "brothers . . . you are not forgotten. We are with you. Every hour of our lives, every drop of our blood we will give for your liberation and the emancipation of all toilers from the disgraceful fascist regime." (Stormy applause, all in the hall rise.)

In the resolutions adopted by the Congress, there was no important reference to the United States. The resolutions were binding on all Communist Parties, including the American—as, for example, when Communists were ordered "to strive . . . to bring about a united front both on a national and international scale" and to concentrate attention on the "further consolidation of their ranks and the winning over of the majority of the working class to the side of communism"[81] —but no mention was made of the American situation.

On August 21 Bullitt summarized the participation of the American delegates. The following Americans had been elected to office or given committee assignments: Browder, Foster, Green, Sherman, Darcy, and Ford; speeches had been made by Browder, Foster, Green, Caruthers, Darcy, Ford, Hudson, and Stone. The Ambassador also listed the following participants who were connected with the Soviet government apparatus: Stalin, Andreev, Zhdanov, Ezhov, Krupskaya,

Hohov, Pyatnitski, Manuilski, Lozovsky, and Knorin. It will be noted that Litvinov is not listed.

The day after the Congress had closed, the American Ambassador sent a series of telegrams to Washington, evaluating the meetings:

> The Congress of the Communist International . . . was a flagrant violation of Litvinov's pledge to the President.
>
> The mere holding of the Congress in Moscow under control of the Soviet Government would have constituted a technical breach of Litvinov's pledge. The violation, however, was far more serious.
>
> The participation of American delegates in the Congress, the inclusion of Browder and Foster in the Presidium . . . the inclusion of Americans in other committees . . . , the numerous references to the United States in other addresses and the election . . . of the Americans Browder, Green and Foster to the Executive Committee of the Communist International, place beyond the question of fact that the Government of the United States would be juridically and morally justified in severing diplomatic relations with the Soviet Government.
>
> In mitigation the Soviet Government can plead only that attacks on the Government of the United States were less severe than attacks on other governments and that no direct attacks were made personally by members of the Soviet Government.[82]

Having justified a rupture in diplomatic relations as satisfying "the indignation we all feel," the Ambassador admitted that the decision should rest on some other basis. He expressed the view that relations, if broken, would be most difficult to reestablish during the next decade and he foresaw, during this period, either an attack on the Soviet Union or unprecedented development by the Soviet system. In either case, it was desirable for the United States to have an official observation post in Moscow. If relations were broken, further, the United States would be without representation in the Soviet Union while the Soviet government would still have representation in the United States unless all Soviet citizens—including the officials of such organizations as Amtorg and Intourist—were expelled along with the diplomats. Bullitt concluded, therefore, that we should not break relations with the Soviet government. "At a moment when the peace . . . is threatened . . . a government like ours which deeply cares for peace must hesitate to shake the unstable structure of international peace by withhold action (withholding?) diplomatic relations with any other government."[83]

Bullitt made several other suggestions: we should not make a written protest to the Soviet government, for it would be fruitless; we should use the occasion to clarify to the American people the

Soviet government's aims as embodied in the new "united front" tactic; we should revoke the exequaturs of Soviet consuls in New York and San Francisco, and reduce to a minimum the number of visas granted to Soviet citizens by refusing visas "unless they present entirely satisfactory evidence proving that they are not and have never been members of the Communist Party or Communist International and . . . Profintern." He admitted that he had weighed the advisability of withdrawing our Military Attaché from Moscow[84] and having the Soviet service attachés dismissed from Washington, but he thought this should be held in reserve. Bullitt suggested that the President call attention to Litvinov's pledge and the facts of the Comintern and the 7th Congress. It must be made clear to the people, he said, that Dimitrov had laid a new policy line:

> Communists in all democratic countries have been ordered . . . to worm their way into the labor unions, farmers organizations, the women's peace organizations, all organizations of youth, all liberal, political, social and religious organizations and into the ranks of the intellectuals, there to work as bosom friends of their fellow members . . . until the day comes when they hope to be able to establish Soviet tyrrany [sic] in the United States and destroy their fellow workers who have trusted them.[85]

Despite Bullitt's advice, Roosevelt and Hull believed that a formal written protest was necessary. The note was sent on August 23 and presented two days later to Krestinsky, Litvinov's assistant, who said, "If your note is a protest with regard to the Congress of the Communist International, I can tell you before reading it that it will be rejected."[86] Although the Soviet policy had been established in advance, he did agree to read it. The note firmly and clearly expressed the attitude of the American government on this "flagrant violation" of Litvinov's promise. It called attention to the activities, "involving interference in the internal affairs of the United States," in connection with the Comintern Congress and lodged

> a most emphatic protest against this flagrant violation of the pledge given by the Government of the Union of Soviet Socialist Republics on November 16, 1933, with respect to non-interference in the internal affairs of the United States.
>
> .   .   .   .   .
>
> . . . The American people resent most strongly interference by foreign countries in their internal affairs . . . and the Government of the United States considers the strict fulfillment of the pledge of non-interference an essential prerequisite to the maintenance of normal and friendly relations. . . .

The Government of the United States would be lacking in candor if it failed to state frankly that it anticipates the most serious consequences if the Government of the Union of Soviet Socialist Republics is unwilling, or unable, to take appropriate measures to prevent further acts in disregard of the solemn pledge given by it to the Government of the United States.

. . . The development of friendly relations between the Russian and American peoples will inevitably be precluded by the continuance on territory of the Union of Soviet Socialist Republics, in violation of the promise of the Government of the Union of Soviet Socialist Republics, of activities involving interference in the internal affairs of the American people.[87]

Other protests were made by the governments of Great Britain, Latvia, and Italy.

Two days later, on the 27th, Krestinsky handed to Bullitt his government's reply which read, in part:

The Government of the Union of Soviet Socialist Republics has always regarded and still regards with the greatest respect all obligations which it has taken upon itself including naturally the mutual obligation concerning non-interference in internal affairs provided for in the exchange of notes of November 16, 1933. . . . There are contained no facts of any kind in your note of August 25 which could be considered as a violation on the part of the Soviet Government of its obligations.

. . . It is certainly not new to the Government of the United States that the Government of the Union of Soviet Socialist Republics cannot take upon itself and has not taken upon itself obligations of any kind with regard to the Communist International.

Hence the assertion concerning the violation by the Government of the Union of Soviet Socialist Republics of the obligations contained in the note of November 16, 1933, does not emanate from obligations accepted by both sides in consequence of which I cannot accept your protest and am obliged to decline it.[88]

The note closed with the Soviet government's declaration that it shared the opinion of the American government "that strict mutual non-interference in internal affairs is an essential prerequisite for the maintenance of friendly relations." There it was again, the same assertion of the separateness of the Soviet government and Comintern, with the former having no responsibility for the acts of the latter. Both governments believed completely in noninterference; they just couldn't agree on what constituted it. And yet, it did appear that the Soviet government felt guilty, for it took the offensive, charging that the fault was really in the United States. On August 26, the Soviet Ambassador in Washington referred publicly to a campaign then being conducted in the United States "against our government and against our form of government." In an allusion which was particularly interesting since it came from the representative of an atheistic government, he recalled the biblical injunction: "And why beholdest thou the mote which is in thy brother's eye but perceivest not the beam that is in thine own eye?" adding that anything said in Moscow by American citizens about the United States was "very insignificant" compared to the continuous anti-Soviet propaganda in the United States. "I have even seen suggestions that our government should somehow stop the activity of American organizations and American citizens in the United States. It is obvious that my government will not interfere in the internal affairs of the United States in this or any other way."[89] It was a weak answer to a strong protest. Or, was the American protest so strong, after all?

Bullitt's advice had been disregarded, but he was not silenced. He wired Hull:

> I consider that a statement by you is infinitely to be preferred to another note. . . . I feel profoundly that your statement must be accompanied by action. . . .
>
> If . . . not . . . the Government of the U.S. would be placed in the position of having issued a most stern admonition and then weakened it to an empty gesture. Thereby our position in all future dealings with the Soviet Government would be gravely prejudiced. . . .
>
> I therefore recommend as strongly as possible that in your statement you should announce that you have cancelled the exequaturs of Soviet Consuls in the United States; that the President has ordered the withdrawal of our Military Attaché in Moscow and requested the withdrawal of the Soviet Military, Naval and Air Attachés in Washington; that the granting of American visas to Soviet citizens will be restricted to a minimum and that other measures of protection are under consideration.[90]

Having made his recommendations, Bullitt emphasized again the desirability of the recommended action. "The Soviet Foreign Office," he said, "does not understand the meaning of honor or fair dealing but it does understand the meaning of acts. Unless we are now ready to back by acts the words we have used the Soviet government will feel free to behave as it pleases in its relations with us." He ended with one last warning: "We shall never find a better moment to act against the direction of the Communist movement in the United States by the Dictator in the Kremlin."

But Washington was not ready to take such action. "I discussed with the President again this afternoon," Hull telegraphed Bullitt, "action to be taken with respect to Soviet note. We went over your suggestions very carefully. . . . He asked me to convey the following message to you. 'I think suggestion to return Russian Consuls and Attachés at this time is a premature step, and instead we should only at this moment put out a formal statement of great dignity.' "[91] And this is what was done.[92] On August 31 Hull released an answer to Krestinsky's claim. He reviewed the background of the non-interference pledge and quoted from it, especially paragraph 4. The language of that paragraph, said Hull,

> irrefutably covers activities of the Communist International, which was then, and still is, the outstanding world communist organization, with headquarters in Moscow.
> . . . The Soviet Government denies having made any promise "not to permit . . . and to prevent" such activities of that organization on Soviet territory, asserting that it "has not taken upon itself obligations of any kind with regard to the Communist International." That the language of the pledge . . . is absolutely clear and in no way ambiguous and that there has been a clean-cut disregard and disavowal of the pledge by the Soviet Government is obvious.
> . . . When in its reply the Soviet Government indicated an intention entirely to disregard its promise "to prevent" such activities as those complained of it struck a severe blow at the fabric of friendly relations between the two countries.
> . . . It is not possible for the Soviet Government to disclaim its obligation to prevent activities on its territory directed toward overthrowing the political or social order in the United States. And that Government does not and cannot disclaim responsibility on the ground of inability to carry out its pledge, for its authority within its territorial limits is supreme and its power to control the acts and utterances of organizations and individuals within those limits is absolute.[93]

Whether the relations between the two countries would be impaired, the Secretary concluded, "will depend upon the attitude and action of the Soviet Government." The Soviet press said only that Hull had made a statement; the Soviet government made no comment. Bullitt was informed "that the Soviet Government is anxious now not to envenom further its relations with the United States" and that it was unlikely that hostile comments would appear in the government-controlled press.

One aspect of this problem has never been clarified. Immediately after the Comintern Congress, Umansky (then Censor of the Foreign Office and later Ambassador to Washington) defended the Soviet position by asserting to correspondents in Moscow that "it had been clearly understood in Washington by both sides that the Comintern was not included in Litvinov's assurance," which is the same, wrote Bullitt, as a charge "that the President of the United States had entered into a secret agreement with Mr. Litvinov whereby the latter's pledges had been entirely negatived and had been published to the American people as mere 'eye-wash.' "[94] Bullitt, worried by this suggestion of a secret agreement in 1933, telegraphed the Secretary: "This implication has been made specific now by the Foreign Office. It is, of course, a flat lie but the lie is being propagated not only to foreign press correspondents by Umanski but also to ambassadors and ministers by Krestinski."[95]

Litvinov testified in his own behalf a few months later when, lunching with Bullitt and Kelley, he asserted

> that he had an entirely clear conscience: that I must know that he had said to the President that he could not be responsible for the Third International; and that the President had replied that he would hold the Soviet Union to its pledge only in case of important injury to the interests of the United States.
>
> I replied that my memory was entirely different. That I recalled that he had said he could make no promises about the Third International but that the President had told him that he would hold him to strict accountability with regard to the Third International and that he, Litvinov, had subsequently signed the pledge. He replied that he had made his statement to the President after signing the pledge.
>
> . . . Litvinov then made it clear that the Soviet Government would not in any way restrain the activities of the Communist International in the United States or the Soviet Union, or of American Communists connected with the Communist International in the Soviet Union.[96]

In 1938, however, Walter Duranty informed a member of the State Department that he had asked Litvinov if one of the 1933 communications covered the activities of the Communist International. "Litvinov's reply was evasive. A similar inquiry made of President Roosevelt at the time the texts . . . were released had evoked an affirmative answer."[97]

There the matter rests, on the reputation of the two men, with no official record to provide final verification. It would seem, especially on the basis of the latter part of the Litvinov statement, just quoted, that the Soviet government never had any intention of restraining the Comintern. The Soviet leaders, especially Litvinov, either refused to honor a pledge made or had been able to "trick" the American government into believing that the Comintern was included, and then later they relied on interpretation to make as good a case as they could for themselves, knowing that there was no verbatim record by which they could be challenged.

Whatever the facts really were, whatever the intentions of the participants, whatever the interpretation made of the words used in the promise, one thing was clear: the American government was no more successful in actually protecting itself against Soviet Communist interference in its internal affairs than had been the other governments that had recognized the Soviet government. American officials, with their precise preparation, may have hoped to protect their society, but—despite all their knowledge of the experiences of the other governments—they failed to do better than the others. Eventually, it all boiled down to the fact that neither government would accept the view of the other. The Soviet government could protect itself against interference by the nature of its system; we could not protect ourselves by appealing to Moscow but only by careful attention to our own internal problems. "Unfortunately," the *Warsaw Courier* pointed out on August 28, 1935, "bourgeois countries do not carry their actions to their logical conclusions, as do the Soviets. . . . Nothing will happen."[98]

This was essentially true, in the immediate and direct sense. In the longer view, however, something did happen. Probably never again were relations between the two governments as friendly. None could escape the fact that the honeymoon was now over and that rivalry and suspicion had replaced the friendly and hopeful climate that had previously existed. If Kelley had never been very optimistic about Soviet actions, he must now have been very cynical about the situation, though he remained with the Department until 1937. For Bullitt, however, this was understandably a personal matter. He had followed the Soviet problem since 1919; he had played an important role in the 1933 negotiations; and he had enthusiastically hoped that he could conduct the diplomatic relations in a notable and successful fashion. This hope was now dust and ashes. His usefulness as spokesman for his government was greatly reduced, both by the Soviet opposition and the unwillingness of his own government to follow the strong policy he had recommended; he became hostile and bitter in his dealings with the Russians, though he continued in the Moscow post until mid-1936. The contention over the Comintern Congress, in other words, would appear to have been a major turning point in American-Soviet relations.

What developed subsequently? The issue over the Comintern Congress did not end the struggle over implementation of the noninterference agreement. Nor did it terminate the interference. The first meeting of the Central Committee of the American Communist Party following the 7th World Congress, occurred in New York on November 16-18, 1935. One of the more significant actions taken was approval of a resolution on the formation of a Farmer-Labor Party in the United States. Speaking on the resolution, Browder stated that "the Farmer-Labor Party will not be born spontaneously. It must be led and organized by a united front coalition of the most advanced workers and toilers,"[99] which is just what he had heard Dimitrov order at the meeting in Moscow.

In October 1935 the Embassy in Moscow notified the Department that the Cooperative Publishing Society of Foreign Workers in the Soviet Union[100] had invoiced five thousand copies of Stalin's "Marxism and the National and Colonial Question," to be shipped to the International Publishers in New York. About the same time it was announced that "half a million copies of the historic speech" of Georgy Dimitrov at the recent Congress "are being rushed off the press for mass distribution throughout the country," with a special popular edition to sell for a nickel.[101] The American Embassy in Moscow raised the question, in view of the recent conflict over the Comintern Congress, whether the Department wished to do anything about this large shipment of Communist propaganda.

> If we were to refuse to certify the consular invoice for these pamphlets we might merely give the Communist Party of the United States an excellent opportunity to make propaganda in favor of the Soviet Union. Seizure . . . might produce a similar result. On the other hand the printing of the pamphlet in Moscow and its shipment to the United States constitutes an act in violation of Litvinov's pledge to the President.[102]

The American government decided not to interfere with the shipment.

Another highly publicized issue arose during the presidential election campaign of 1936. It began on August 8 with publication in the Chicago *Tribune* of a dispatch from Donald Day in Riga, stating that the Communist International had issued "instructions to the American Communist Party to support the candidacy of President Roosevelt." Since these instructions would constitute a clear intervention in American internal affairs, the American government was very interested. On August 20, a departmental memorandum stated:

> The most important charge in the *Tribune* item, namely that "instructions have been sent to the American Communist Party to support the candidacy of President Roosevelt" is not in accordance with the facts. No such "instructions" appear in the issue of *Communist International*

referred to (#13, July 1936), and, in so far as is known, no such instructions have been issued. In fact, as disclosed by material appearing in the Communist press in this country, American Communists do not support, but oppose, Roosevelt in the present campaign.[103]

Browder was quoted as saying, "we do not support Roosevelt," although on August 17 the N.Y. *Daily Worker* said, "The Communist Party declares without qualification that the Landon–Hearst–Wall Street ticket is the chief enemy of the liberty, peace, and prosperity of the American people."[104] The only possible justification for the newspaper story, the memorandum stated, was that Browder's statements "might be assumed to have been determined by the Communist International and therefore to represent the essence of instructions from the Communist International and the fact that the Browder article appears in the *Communist International* which, as the official organ . . . might be assumed to contain only material which is approved." The memorandum concluded by saying that, "while it is, of course, probable that that position has been fully approved by the Executive Committee of the Communist International it is inaccurate to state that the statement constitutes 'instructions' to the American Communist Party."

This refutation of the *Tribune* story did not end the rumors. On August 27 Secretary Hull sent identical telegrams to Moscow and Riga, saying:

> It is rumored that the Communist International is preparing a document or instructions for circulation in this country advising people how they should vote in the Presidential election. Obviously any such move would be a covert move to injure and defeat the Administration. Please endeavor to ascertain whether this is true and, if so, furnish all information available as quickly as possible.[105]

The next day, Lane cabled from Riga: "I have no direct evidence that the Communist International is preparing material of the nature indicated for circulation in the United States." He reported, however, that a year earlier Cole had reported from Riga a remark made to him by the Soviet Minister that in the forthcoming elections "the American Communist Party will not only not oppose President Roosevelt but on the contrary will render him every support."[106] On September 9, Henderson cabled from Moscow that he had talked with a Soviet official who often acted in an informal liaison capacity between the Embassy and the Kremlin, who had discussed this question of the election with officials of the Communist International and affiliated organizations—"who were of sufficient importance to know whether or not any kind of instruction . . . had been issued or was being planned" —and they had stated that "the matter of interfering in the American elections had not been discussed or even thought of by them and expressed considerable surprise that the question had been raised. . . . He was personally convinced . . . that no such interference was being planned."[107] "I have thus far," the Chargé said, "been unable to find any evidence that the Communist International is preparing instructions for circulation in the United States with regard to the elections." Later, Lane wired from Riga, "I have found no (repeat no) direct evidence (either here or in Estonia) that the Communist International intends to instruct voters in the United States to vote for the President";[108] still later, "I was informed in Kovno by Soviet sources there that there is no truth in the report that Moscow is endeavoring to influence voters in the United States."[109]

So concerned was the American government about this matter that two Foreign Service officers talked with Donald Day, who admitted that he had not originally noticed that the article in *Communist International* was signed by Browder but had decided to let his dispatch go through anyway. He insisted that he was not basically in error, since "it is well known that the Comintern maintains iron discipline, and anything written by Browder must have been done on orders from Moscow."[110] Day had, the Department was informed, "cleverly based certain statements on inference which on the whole are justifiable," even though his references were "overemphasized and misleading."[111]

The fact that American officials would devote so much time and effort to a newspaper story which, so far as they could ascertain, was never fully justified would seem to indicate that they were extremely sensitive on the question of Soviet interference in internal affairs. They may even have regretted that no stronger action was taken following the Comintern Congress. It is not that Moscow was unable, or unwilling, to instruct American Communists on how to vote; the incident demonstrates that she was now almost automatically suspect.

In any case, Soviet interference involved a different theory after the 7th Congress. The emphasis on direct revolution was now played down by Moscow, and the party line was that of the "united front tactic." This does not mean that the Soviet government had surrendered its mission of interference, but that its new devices, being less objectionable, might evoke less direct opposition from other governments. In 1939 when the Soviet Union was celebrating the twentieth anniversary of the founding of the Comintern, it did not escape the notice of the American Embassy in Moscow, that *Pravda* made no reference whatever to the United States except to state the number of members in the American Communist Party.

Other changes were in the wind. In 1935 the Soviet leaders demonstrated that they preferred to offend certain governments, including some whose help they badly needed, rather than surrender the organizational links which were their connections with the discontented elements in those countries. The leaders of other governments, however, could also deal with this matter. On October 17, 1940, the Anti-Subversive Activities Act—the Voorhis Act—was approved by the American government, requiring registration of every organization subject to foreign control which engages in political activity in the United States. The constitution of the American Communist Party at that time stated that the party was "affiliated to the Communist International." Since this might bring the party under the Voorhis Act, a special convention of the party on November 16-17, 1940, adopted a new constitution which omitted all reference to the Comintern.[112] Article VI stated that "decisions of the National Convention are final," which attempted to end all doubt about the international activities of the party except as (Article V) all members were to pay money into an International Solidarity Fund to aid the "workers and toilers of other lands." All organizational ties with the Comintern were to be severed as of January 1, 1941, according to Earl Browder. Ambassador Steinhardt in Moscow was not impressed:

> In view of the fact that the control exercised by the Comintern over its member parties in other countries is not effected through public channels, this ostensible severance of organizational ties is meaningless, especially in view of the resolution of the special congress that despite this act the American Communist Party would continue to serve the cause of Lenin and Stalin.[113]

The Department of State said officially that the Communist action was taken "solely" to avoid the Voorhis Act. "Actually, no change has taken place in the Party's program, policies, or activities. It is still regarded as a tool of the Communist International, serving the interests of the Soviet Union."[114]

With the German attack on the Soviet Union in 1941, the Soviet leaders needed all the American aid they could get. This, to some degree, depended upon American confidence in the Soviet Union, and on May 23, 1943, Moscow announced that the Communist International was being dissolved since, it was said, it had fulfilled its original purpose. This led, in turn, to a convention of the Communist Party, U.S.A., in May 1944 which replaced the Party with the Communist Political Association, "a nonparty association" with no ostensible international connections. The April 1945 issue of *Cahiers du Communisme*, theoretical journal of the French Communist Party, however, contained an article by Jacques Duclos, a leader of the French party, entitled "On the Dissolution of the Communist Party of the United States." After reviewing Browder's explanation of the reasons for this action, Duclos returned to the tactics of the 7th World Congress:

> American Communists were right in supporting the candidacy of President Roosevelt in the last election but it was not at all necessary . . . to dissolve the Communist Party. . . . On the contrary, the formation of the Communist Political Association could not but trouble the minds and obscure the perspectives in the eyes of the working masses. . . . And it is clear that if Comrade Earl Browder had seen, as a Marxist-Leninist, this important aspect of the problems . . . he would have arrived at a conclusion quite other than the dissolution of the Communist Party of the United States.[115]

Browder's answer was instantaneous, appearing in the same issue of the New York *Daily Worker* as the Duclos article. He admitted:

> Unquestionably, while this is the personal article . . . it reflects the general trend of opinion of European Marxists . . . and this demands our most respectful consideration.
>
> It has been clear . . . that the end of the war in Europe would require a fundamental review of all problems by American Marxists. . . . We must make the most careful inventory. . . . The article of Duclos may conveniently provide a starting point for this fundamental review.[116]

Sixty days later, a convention in New York unanimously rejected the "revisionist" Browder and reconstituted the Communist Party of the United States of America under the leadership of William Z. Foster. It appeared that the international influence—"direction"—over the party would continue, even if not directly from Moscow.[117]

Subsequent developments cannot be followed carefully, since the records are not open to the researcher, but it is apparent that the story did not end with the Second World War. In November 1951, for example, the Soviet government demanded that the General Assembly of the United Nations open a full debate on Moscow's charges that the United States government was violating the noninterference agreement of 1933. The charge arose out of the provisions of the Mutual Security Act of 1951, which authorized "the use of up to $100,000,000 for assistance to persons residing in or fleeing from Russia or other

Communist-controlled areas." Moscow claimed that, by encouraging the anti-Communist underground inside the Iron Curtain, the American government was interfering in its internal affairs. The *New York Times* reported that, while the State Department

> would have preferred that the Mutual Security Act did not state that any of the $100,000,000 would be used for political purposes within the Soviet Union, well-informed observers said that it was clearly the intent of Congress that some part of the fund be used for that purpose. They also expressed the view that the United States public would also support such activities. . . .
>
> At the present time, however, the propaganda policy of the State Department is not directed to the purpose of helping the people of the Soviet Union to overthrow their Government although the effort is constantly made to encourage the people of the Soviet satellites to express their national interest and break away from their masters in Moscow.[118]

The article stated that the State Department "is ready to send a note to Moscow accusing the Kremlin of having tried to subvert and overthrow the United States Government ever since the agreement was signed. Officials here regard the Soviet protest as a model of propaganda and audacity, but both legally and factually baseless."

On December 19, 1951, the American Embassy in Moscow gave to the Soviet Foreign Ministry a note which

> categorically rejects the Soviet Government's allegations that the Act constitutes interference in the internal affairs of the U.S.S.R. or a violation of the undertakings in the Roosevelt-Litvinov correspondence of November 16, 1933.
>
> . . . . .
>
> . . . The United States Government denies the implication of the reference note that rendering assistance to refugees from oppression and refusal to return them to the oppressor governments constitutes subversion or interference in the internal affairs of those governments.
>
> . . . . .
>
> The United States Government states in conclusion that false charges of interference in Soviet internal affairs come with singular ill-grace from a regime which has for many years consistently supported subversive activities directed against the United States and other nations of the Free World.[119]

Again, the following year, Stalin declared at the closing session of the 19th Party Congress in Moscow that "Soviet Russia will support Communist parties in other lands 'in their struggle for liberation and . . . the preservation of peace.' "

When Stalin mentions "capitalist countries" he of course has the United States in mind. . . . Therefore, when Stalin publicly promised Communist parties in capitalist countries that Soviet Russia would support them "in their struggle for liberation," he was in effect saying that Soviet Russia would support the Communist Party of the United States in an effort to overthrow the United States Government.

Obviously, this Stalin pledge shatters the agreement that was made when the United States accorded recognition to Soviet Russia.[120]

Or, perhaps, the agreement had been shattered long before 1952.

Such sporadic outbreaks are not likely to be of lasting significance. They are important largely for their immediate propaganda effect. The basic issues were settled in the 1930's. Faith in paper pledges was shown to be futile. There is no evidence that the Soviet government ever intended to fulfill the 1933 agreement as the Americans understood it. The failure then of the United States government to convince the Soviet government that the agreement did apply to all organizations and activities on its soil and within its control essentially meant that no subsequent attempts were likely to be more successful. Given the American interpretation of the agreement, the Soviet government violated this agreement more directly and more completely than in the case of any of the other 1933 agreements. It was apparently never within the realm of possibility that the two governments could reach a common understanding. This story, then, is really one of expectation rather than interpretation.

CHAPTER III

Freedom of Worship

BACKGROUND

It was not surprising that President Roosevelt and his advisors should have included the religious aspect of American-Soviet relations in the negotiations with Litvinov. If religion had not bulked large in discussion between the two governments, the same could not be said of American public opinion. The Soviet policy toward religion was a thing which the "man on the street" could understand. He may have been confused by the talk of political, economic, and social theory, but he could react to a policy that sought to do away with religion. Many Americans had religious and ethnic interest in those in the Soviet Union who were being denied the chance to worship or were even punished for doing so.

The files of the Department of State for 1930 contain numerous queries and protests from American citizens relative to the Soviet government's antireligious policy, following issuance of a decree regarding Religious Associations on April 8, 1929. This law (the translation of which covers twenty-four pages) was very comprehensive. It sought to keep the practice of religion under the control of local authorities as far as possible through a "licensing" system. It was clear that the Soviet government was not relaxing its antireligious campaign, that religious groups might not hold funds or property, hire premises, nor enter into agreements and transactions. They might, however, obtain from the local political authorities the right to use—free of charge— special houses of worship and other objects intended solely for worship. They might collect contributions, but only from their members. The restrictions on religious instruction were vague but ominous.

It was not long, accordingly, before news stories from the Soviet Union spoke of the arrest of clergymen, heavy taxes levied on them and their churches, confiscation of church property including bells and other metal adornments and fees collected by confessors, anti-Sunday laws, abolition of religious holidays, petitions signed under duress by both laity and clergy requesting the closing of certain churches, and the dissolution of the whole Ukrainian Autocephalous (Orthodox) Church. Such matters inevitably came to official attention, as on January 7, 1931, when Frederick Coleman, the American Minister in Riga, wrote the Department of State that "sometime ago there were indications that prosecutions for having possession of small coin were being directed particularly against clergymen, in spite of their right under the law to make collections."[1] The first official denial of any persecution was given by A. I. Rykov in February 1930:

> Cases of repression are unknown to me. . . . Does this . . . mean that none of the servants of religious cults has ever been arrested, tried and convicted? There have been, and there are, such arrests; but these arrests and these sentences are in no way connected with the religious beliefs of the persons sentenced, nor with religious cults in general. In these cases, servants of religious cults were punished for crimes punishable under our criminal law. And, for such offenses, servants of religious cults are held liable on terms of absolute equality with all other citizens. . . . No doubt, some of the churches are being closed down. This is being done consequent upon resolutions adopted by mass meetings in cases where the population itself . . . prefers to utilize the surplus churches for cultural purposes.[2]

Rykov's statement gives a clear tip-off to Soviet policy. The government would not relax its antireligious campaign, but cloak it under the garb of absolute legality, using innocent-sounding explanations. In May 1931 a new law established a complete administrative system for supervising religious matters.

These things disturbed many Americans, some of whom protested to their officials. One of these protests, indeed, came from Secretary of the Interior Ray Lyman Wilbur who asked if something could be done. The answer of Joseph P. Cotton, Acting Secretary of State, was direct: "The religious situation in Russia sounds outrageous but it seems to me that this government as a government must keep its hands off. The President must make that answer to any delegation if he sees them."[3] This was not an American but a Soviet problem and any interest shown by the American government, whatever the personal beliefs or sympathies of individual officials, would almost inevitably be branded by the Soviet leaders as an unwarranted intervention in the internal affairs of their country.[4] It was reported, in fact, that the Soviet Minister in Kovno had complained to the Lithuanian Foreign Office because of agitation in that country against religious persecutions in the U.S.S.R.

It was this background which focused American interest on the religious situation in Russia. If the American people and their government were unable to alter the policy of the Soviet government toward its people, the same thing need not be true for American citizens resident in the Soviet Union. This was one aspect over which control might be exerted.

THE AGREEMENT

This problem was not of major importance, so far as official policy was concerned. It did not officially possess anything like the same weight as the questions of revolutionary aims or repudiated debts. In fact, the question of religion was not even mentioned in the memorandum prepared by the Chief of the Division of Eastern European Affairs or the letter from the Secretary of State to the President on September 21, 1933. The Secretary, however, had requested Moore and Bullitt to prepare memoranda "on the more important conditions and understandings that might be considered significant in connection with the development of plans for the recognition of the Russian government" and both of these memoranda mention—in a single word only—the question of religious rights. The President insisted on inclusion of this matter in the negotiations, as a prerequisite to recognition, and was said to be very proud of this fact.[5]

When Litvinov was handed the draft agreement on freedom of worship, he objected that this was impossible. It developed that he had understood the provisions to apply to Russians as well as Americans in the Soviet Union. He then maintained that the Russian laws were "sufficient for the purpose indicated and that he had no authority to say that they would be changed"; he could not tell how a particular court might interpret the law or how it might be administered, but "he was certain that they would be interpreted and administered fairly."[6] When Hull asked him to consider the draft and present his comments in writing, he said: "I prefer to do it right away. I'll write my comments on it here,"[7] and did so. Where it was proposed that Americans should be permitted to have full liberty of conscience and the free exercise of religious worship, he wrote "Yes." On their exemption from all disability or persecution because of religious faith or worship, he wrote, "No disability or persecution." At the end of the sentence giving them permission to conduct religious services, he wrote "Yes" but eliminated the part that gave them the right to own and lease buildings for these purposes. When it came to religious instruction for children singly or in groups, he struck out "or in groups" and the sentence ended "only privately." As to burial of the dead, he wrote "Yes." He materially changed the sentence which protected clergy from discrimination or persecution, giving them "right of entry" but removing the guarantee that they should be treated as well as nonecclesiastical Americans with respect to the rental of living quarters and the purchase of food; he did agree that they were not to be subject to any special attacks. In the sentence on the use of funds for religious, educational, and philanthropic work, he wrote "No" for religious work and added "subject to laws governing charity" in their application to philanthropic work.[8]

Among the official notes exchanged on November 16, those on religious freedoms are the longest, covering more than three pages of the published report. The President began by referring to his expectation that, after the establishment of normal relations, "many Americans will wish to reside temporarily or permanently within the territory" of the Soviet Union; "I am deeply concerned that they should enjoy in all respects the same freedom of conscience and religious liberty which they enjoy at home."[9] He then pointed out that the United States government had always striven to protect its people, at home and abroad, "in the free exercise of liberty of conscience and religious worship, and from all disability or persecution on account of their religious faith or worship." Then the President became specific in the enumeration of the rights involved. His government would expect that nationals of the United States when within the territory of the Soviet Union "will be allowed to conduct without annoyance or molestation of any kind religious services and rites of a ceremonial nature, including baptismal, confirmation, communion, marriage, and burial rites, in the English language, or in any other language which is customarily used in the practice of the religious faith to which they belong, in churches, houses, or other buildings appropriate for such service, which they will be given the right and opportunity to lease, erect or maintain in convenient situations." It was expected that American nationals "will have the right to collect from their co-religionists and to receive from abroad voluntary offerings for religious purposes; that they will be entitled without restriction to impart religious instruction to their children, either singly or in groups, or to have such instruction imparted by persons whom they may employ for such purpose; that they will be given and protected in the right to bury their dead according to their religious customs in suitable and convenient places . . . and given the right and opportunity to lease, lay out, occupy and maintain such burial grounds subject to reasonable sanitary laws and regulations." Finally, it was expected that religious groups "will be given the right to have their spiritual needs ministered to by clergymen, priests, rabbis or other ecclesiastical functionaries who are nationals of the United States, and that such clergymen, priests, rabbis or other ecclesiastical functionaries will be protected from all disability or persecution and will not be denied entry into the territory of the Soviet Union because of their ecclesiastical status."

Litvinov replied by stating that his Government "as a fixed policy accords the nationals of the United States within the territory of the Union of Soviet Socialist Republics the following rights" and then quotes Roosevelt's statements, often in identical language. He supported his assertion by references to relevant Soviet laws and to the German-Soviet Treaty of October 12, 1925. Moore understood that the laws were not to be set forth in the agreement, but that the language contained in the laws should be used where possible. Somehow the laws themselves were quoted by Litvinov. "This has been found extremely difficult," wrote Moore, "for the reason that the laws do not touch several important points."[10] Litvinov agreed, moreover, to grant these rights "immediately upon the establishment of relations" between the two governments, so that they were not dependent upon any other action or agreement, although a consular convention to provide most-favored-nation treatment for American nationals was foreseen. He made only one qualification: the Soviet government reserved the right to refuse visas to Americans wishing to enter the Soviet Union "on personal grounds," but "does not intend to base such refusals on the fact of such persons having an ecclesiastical status."

An analysis of these two letters reveals a number of noteworthy features:

1. There was surely an attempt by President Roosevelt to head off possible Soviet opposition or interpretation by making the agreements as specific and as inclusive as possible. The right to receive funds from abroad as well as collections from members of the group, the right to use English or whatever other language was customary in religious services, and the right to lay out burial grounds illustrate this. Whatever might happen in the implementation of this agreement, it would be difficult to claim that more careful phrasing should have been produced by the American negotiators, as was true in certain of the other agreements.

2. It will be noted that this agreement was not reciprocal. The Soviet government made certain promises; the American government promised nothing, and thus no rights for the Soviet people were secured, although the Soviet government claimed reciprocal rights in 1955, as we shall see.

3. The agreement applies only to "American nationals" in the Soviet Union and has, therefore, nothing to do with the attitude of the Soviet government toward its own people or other foreigners. The agreement even specifies that the clergymen shall be "nationals of the United States of America." The Soviet government agreed to give religious rights to Americans and no one else. The question as to whether a person was an American national will be examined in Chapter IV.

4. Litvinov's citation of various laws relative to the status of religion in the Soviet Union was intended, no doubt, both to convince readers that the Soviet policy was less evil than had been charged and also to reassure the President and the American people that these rights would actually be forthcoming. Whether this was an intentional camouflage is not ascertainable; it later served an important propaganda function. Kelley's memoranda had clearly shown that the Soviet leaders were adroit at appearing to do what they did not actually do, and that the administration of law in the Soviet Union was often more significant than the statement of the law itself.[11] Soviet interpretation was known to be skillfully used to the advantage of the Soviet regime; "reading between the lines" was essential in dealing with it. There is more suspicion of Soviet motives and techniques today than in 1933, but it is impossible to read Litvinov's reference to the Decree of January 23, 1918—"A free performance of religious rites is guaranteed as long as it does not interfere with public order and is not accompanied by interference with the rights of citizens of the Soviet Union"—without understanding that this decree really grants nothing at all until we know what "interfere with public order" and "interference with the rights of citizens" means. These are the telling phrases in what purports to be a grant of freedom. Litvinov was frank in referring to religious instruction in quoting the law: "The school is separated from the Church. Instruction in religious doctrines is not permitted in any governmental and common schools. . . . Persons may give or receive religious instruction in a private manner." This would seem to indicate that whatever parents taught their children at home was sanctioned, just so long as the schools did not become the vehicles of religious instruction. But earlier, Emelyan Yaroslavsky, President of the Society of Militant Atheists, wrote in *Bezbozhnik*, the official publication of that agency:

> The law does not restrain religious parents from educating their children at home in a religious spirit. But, since the school in the U.S.S.R. is separated from the Church, and instruction at the school is based on the firm foundation of science, religious instruction contrary to science is considered harmful by our Constitution.[12]

If, therefore, parents in the privacy of their homes were to teach what the Soviet authorities might consider "contrary to science,"—a term sufficiently vague to be fairly inclusive—the right of "religious instruction in a private manner" becomes meaningless. It might be said, accordingly, that Litvinov's inclusion of Soviet legal statements undermined rather than strengthened the grant of freedom. Although the Soviet government conceded nothing that was not already granted, President Roosevelt was apparently satisfied with the Litvinov promise.

5. Along this same line was Litvinov's willingness to provide most-favored-nation treatment to American nationals. Kelley had already demonstrated that the differences between the Soviet and other systems were so great as to make this usually helpful statement of rights practically meaningless when applied by the Soviet leaders. Litvinov quoted Article 9 of the German-Soviet treaty of 1925, the only relevant treaty, giving Germans the right to hold religious services in the Soviet Union "according to the laws of the country." He did not, however, include another part of the same article of that treaty which included the phrase "so long as their doctrines and practices are not contrary to the laws of the country,"[13] which even more clearly emphasized the supremacy of Soviet law. It is likely that the insertion of this phrase was intended to enable the Soviet government to deny the right to establish religious schools.

6. Most of these facts are now judged by the wisdom of hindsight. Lacking this, in 1933, there was a fairly high degree of confidence that the exchange of letters on religious freedoms had pretty well eliminated this as a handicap to friendly future relations between the two governments. A noted Catholic clergyman expressed great hope:

> A principle of human right . . . is vindicated in the most thrilling diplomatic duel of modern times. To be sure, the rights of conscience are claimed for and conceded only to American citizens who may be resident in Russia. . . . But the principle is as clearly established for Russians as for American nationals. . . . It may yet prove the opening wedge in the godless ring of steel.[14]

Moore said, in his radio speech of November 22, 1933, "assuming as we must that the agreement will be observed, it is not perceived how our nationals of any denomination or their spiritual leaders will be under any disadvantage or subject to any discrimination whatever."

IMPLEMENTATION

Let us, then, see how the agreement worked out in practice. Only three religious groups, under normal circumstances, were likely to be represented among the American nationals resident in the Soviet

Union: Catholic, Jewish, and Protestant. Let us consider each, in turn.

The second of these groups may be eliminated at once. No attempt has been made, so far as is known, to establish a separate Jewish congregation or to obtain an American rabbi to minister to the needs of these Americans. Two synagogues have been available in Moscow where Jewish members of the foreign diplomatic staffs and business representatives can practice their faith. If, as must have been assumed in 1933, a large number of American businessmen had become residents of the Soviet Union, this might not have been an adequate disposition of the problem. The Roosevelt-Litvinov agreement on religion has really not been applicable to Jews.

The problem has hardly been more real for Protestants. On November 13, 1933, while Litvinov was in this country, the Rev. George L. Parker (of Keene, New Hampshire) addressed a letter to the President relative to the British-American Church which had been open in St. Petersburg prior to the Soviet regime. Mr. Parker, as former pastor in this church, stated that it had been known as the "official Embassy chapel." "The Church's work was solely among and for English-speaking residents. No attempt was desired, or allowed or made, to go beyond this limit or propagandize Russian people in the slightest degree."[15] When he and others had left under "convoy" of Sir George Buchanan (the British Ambassador) in 1918, a claim was filed with the Soviet Government regarding the church. Could this, Mr. Parker inquired, be resecured for those British-American residents of Leningrad who would be interested, now that the American government proposed to recognize the Soviet government? In April 1934 Parker offered further information and asked, now that the agreement was official, about the status of this church. Department of State files show nothing further and the church was apparently never reopened.

Other Protestant clergymen were interested in the possibility of such a church in Moscow. On January 28, 1935, Dr. Henry Smith Leiper (Executive Secretary of the Universal Christian Council in New York City) wrote to Secretary Hull, inquiring about "a question which has been repeatedly referred to us, namely, the possibility of the establishment of an American church in Moscow. . . . We would like to know . . . how many Americans there are actually in Moscow at the present time."[16] In his reply of February 4, the Secretary said that the Department had no pertinent data covering Moscow alone. Specific information was made available a month later when the Embassy informed the Secretary that "at the present time there are 453 Americans residing in Moscow. . . . Over two-thirds of them are of native Russian or Jewish origin and therefore could not be counted on as prospective Protestant communicants. . . . The Embassy has received no inquiries concerning the possible establishment of an American church here nor have there been other indications of active interest on the part of the native American citizens in having their spiritual needs administered."[17]

About the same time Bishop Wade of the Methodist church inquired about this possibility, having read that "Russia is permitting the erection of the first Christian Church in Moscow since the Revolution. It is to be used exclusively by American residents and visitors." "May I inquire," said Bishop Wade, "whether this is correct?"[18] The American Chargé replied, "So far as I am aware, no project for the erection of a Christian Church . . . is under contemplation."

The Embassy in Moscow was also advised that the American Federation of Churches had written to the Archbishop of Canterbury asking whether the Church of England would be interested in a joint project, with a building being used by the Anglican congregation on Sunday mornings and by an American Protestant clergyman on Sunday afternoons, the cost to be divided. The Embassy informed Washington that there were so few Americans in Moscow and the financial and administrative problems of opening a church so great that it could not recommend such action.

> An American Protestant Church in Moscow . . . could hardly be self-supporting and would probably be compelled to convert a considerable portion of such contributions as it might receive from abroad into Soviet currency at the prohibitive official rate of exchange. . . . A clergyman, regardless of his nationality, is compelled to pay taxes in the Soviet Union which are relatively high and he would probably be compelled to assume responsibility for the payment of church rentals and the cost of church upkeep. Moreover, it is understood that churches in the Soviet Union encounter considerable difficulty in obtaining from the Soviet government fuel and other supplies necessary for their maintenance. . . .
>
> Through strictly confidential sources, the Embassy has learned that the position of the three foreign clergymen—Roman Catholic priests—now in the Soviet Union would be intolerable were it not . . . that they are residing in foreign Embassies. It is understood . . . that persons who dare to call upon them are frequently placed under arrest, examined, and at times even sent into exile.[19]

This description hardly sounded like freedom of religious worship, which was the President's goal. The Embassy in Moscow did not think that the Soviet authorities would "overtly object" to an American clergyman ministering to the needs of American citizens but emphasized that Soviet citizens would certainly not be permitted to maintain relations with or receive guidance from such a clergyman. "The amount of religious work which an American clergyman would be able to perform in Moscow would therefore be extremely limited."

Under these circumstances, it did not seem practicable to try to establish an American Protestant church in Moscow, and thus the Roosevelt-Litvinov agreement on religion did not benefit the Protestants.[20] In 1962, however, the National Council of Churches secured the agreement of the Soviet government to the stationing of a Protestant clergyman in Moscow, and the Rev. Donald V. Roberts, a thirty-five-year old Presbyterian minister, was designated. The newspapers gave no indication that the Soviet government had raised any objection to his being sent to Moscow, thirty years after the agreement had been signed. He held his first religious service on November 4, 1962, in the British Embassy with about sixty diplomats and their wives—American, British, Canadian, and Western European—in attendance. It was reported on January 26, 1964, that the first Protestant church in Moscow had been dedicated that day, in the apartment of Mr. Roberts. No information is available as to relations between this clergyman and the Soviet government during the still brief period of his service.

The real effectiveness of the agreement, then, relates to the presence of American Roman Catholics in the Soviet Union, and here the agreement has received some testing. It should be stated at the outset that the agreement was generally fulfilled. Over the years, religious services were held Sunday after Sunday, in the language normally used, with collections being taken, and so on. As is frequently the case, it was not the general unobtrusive fulfillment of the agreement but the few cases where problems arose that came to the attention of the American Embassy in Moscow and the Department of State in Washington. Most of the time no question arose in implementing the agreement.

The Assumptionist Fathers had been active in Russia for many years; after the 1917 revolution most of them were forced to leave. One who remained was Father Pie Neveu, a French citizen, who in 1926 was consecrated as Bishop and Apostolic Administrator of Moscow; he was the only foreign Catholic priest in Moscow. With the conclusion of the Roosevelt-Litvinov agreement, it was decided to send an American priest of the same order, and Father Leopold Braun joined Bishop Neveu late in 1933.[21] All American priests since that time have been Assumptionists. These priests, and their period of service, are as follows: Father Leopold Braun (1933-45), Father

George A. Laberge (1945-49), Father John A. Brassard (1950-53), Father Georges Bissonnette (1953-55), Father Louis F. Dion (1959-61), and Father Joseph Richard (1961——). It is apparent that the Soviet government has been willing to permit Roman Catholic priests to enter the Soviet Union and minister to the spiritual needs of American Catholics in Moscow.[22] Only one such priest at a time has been granted entry except in 1947 when an assistant to Father Laberge was also present. The question of an assistant was first raised in 1938, and repeatedly thereafter, as we shall see. Let us examine the record, to see how the Roosevelt-Litvinov agreement on religious freedom has been applied to this Catholic group.

Knowing that the presence of foreigners was dependent upon the willingness of the Soviet government to grant entrance visas, President Roosevelt was careful to include a provision which said that the American government would "expect" that "clergymen, priests, rabbis or other ecclesiastical functionaries . . . will not be denied entry into the territory of the Soviet Union because of their ecclesiastical status." Litvinov, in reply, promised that the government of the U.S.S.R., while reserving the right to refuse visas to Americans "on personal grounds, does not intend to base such refusals on the fact of such persons having an ecclesiastical status." How was this promise fulfilled?

Father Braun apparently had no difficulty in obtaining a visa to enter the Soviet Union in 1933. He remained for a dozen years, partly because of the fear that if he should leave, he might not be able to return. In 1938 Bullitt wired the Department that he

> had heard authoritatively that Fr. Braun . . . is seriously overworked. . . . I . . . asked if the French government would have any objection to the presence of another American priest in Moscow, pointing out . . . that the Catholic Church in Moscow had always been under the protection of the French Embassy and registered as French Embassy property. Bonnet replied that the French government would have no objection whatsoever. . . .
>
> I should be obliged if the Department would inform me if it would be prepared to insist that the Soviet government should accord a visa to an assistant for Fr. Braun.[23]

In reply the Secretary wired, "Should an American priest be appointed to collaborate with Fr. Braun and should he encounter difficulty in obtaining a Soviet visa, we should be glad to assist him. In view, however, of the spirit of the President's letter . . . we doubt whether it will be possible for us 'to insist' that the Soviet authorities grant a visa."[24] No action was taken at that time.

In September 1943 the question came up again, but it was not thought to be a propitious moment. In February 1944, the Assumptionist Order announced that it wished to send Fr. Laberge in this capacity, and the Embassy raised this question with the Soviet Foreign Office. "The Foreign Office asked whom Fr. Braun served and was told that he served the American community and a number of parishioners and that he was very busy. . . . The Foreign Office also asked whether this was a request of the American government and was told that the Embassy had been instructed by the Department to take the matter up with the Foreign Office."[25] Repeatedly during 1944, the American Embassy in Moscow raised the question of this visa with the Soviet Foreign Office. Vyshinsky said that the question of Fr. Laberge's coming to the Soviet Union should be considered only "from the practical point of view of whether his presence in Moscow as assistant to Fr. Braun was needed. He indicated he would look into the matter."[26] Near the end of November, the Embassy cabled the Department:

> If it could be made clear to the Soviet authorities that the arrival of Fr. Laberge or of some other ecclesiastical official . . . would be immediately followed by Fr. Braun's departure . . . the question of a visa might receive more prompt treatment here. I suspect . . . that the reason for the hesitation in granting a visa . . . is a desire on the part of the Soviet authorities that there should not be more than one such official in Moscow.

Apparently this was done, for in 1945 Laberge arrived in Moscow as a replacement for Braun.[27]

In 1949 Laberge received a Soviet exit visa to consult his religious superiors in London and visit the United States, and a reentry permit was granted in advance. He had hardly reached the United States, however, when his reentry permit was declared invalid by the Soviet government and thus he was barred from the Soviet Union. Here for the first time, is a question of possible violation of the Litvinov agreement. From the Soviet view, of course, there was no violation; Laberge was not denied reentry on the grounds of his "ecclesiastical status," to use Litvinov's phrase, or any other specific grounds. He was just refused the necessary document; no explanation was given. In the strict sense, the Soviet government was completely within its rights. Here again was a matter of interpretation. But the result was the same as if there had been a violation of this part of the agreement. The Soviet intention seemed to be clear; it had, by an administrative device, cut off relations between the American Catholics in Moscow and an American priest, since a period of eleven months was to elapse before a visa was granted to Fr. Brassard, Laberge's replacement.

This, too, in a queer way, was no violation of the 1933 agreement which nowhere specifically called for the presence of American clergy in Moscow. Roosevelt stated that the American government "will expect that religious groups . . . will be given the right to have their spiritual needs ministered to by . . . priests," but Litvinov's reply did not repeat this part of the statement. His promise did specify that "as a fixed policy" the Soviet government gave American nationals the right "to conduct . . . religious services and rites of a ceremonial nature,"—which clearly implied the presence of clergymen, but did not say so. This was a "gray" area where the American government— and certainly the Roman Catholic Church—assumed an air-tight agreement and later believed that the Russian leaders were improper in their interpretation and action.

Father Bissonnette, Brassard's replacement, had to wait only four months for his entrance visa when he took up his duties in the Soviet Union, but this fact was more than balanced by developments beginning in 1955. At this time Ambassador Bohlen informed Bissonnette that the Soviet Foreign Office had said that the latter's presence in Moscow was no longer desirable and that he would have to leave within a few days. On March 2, writes Bissonnette, "the Moscow office of the MVD called and asked me to present myself, without fail, before 5:30 that afternoon. . . . 'Mr. Bissonnette,' the colonel said, 'I must inform you that you must leave the Soviet Union by March 4. Would there be any special way you would like to leave or any border point you would like to cross?' "[28] This was the first time in which an American priest had been expelled by the Soviet government although, as we have seen, it was not the first time that the American Catholics in Moscow had been deprived of a clergyman to minister to them.

Neither Bohlen nor Bissonnette was given any explanation of this Soviet action. "The officer . . . gave me no reason at all," the priest related. "He just said that my exit visa was ready and I could leave the country on March 2, 3 or 4."[29] For a time, the Soviet government would make no statement at all, but on March 8 "a Soviet note explained . . . that the Rev. Georges Bissonnette . . . had been expelled from Moscow in reprisal for the United States' refusal to extend the visa of a Russian clergyman."[30] This was Archbishop Boris, who had come to the United States in December 1954 on a sixty-day visa; his application for an extension had been denied by the State Department. It was in retaliation for this action that Bissonnette was told to leave

Moscow the day after Boris had sailed from New York. The Soviet note contended that in the agreement of November 16, 1933, "both countries had bound themselves to 'extend on the territory of their countries to citizens of the other party the right to satisfaction of their spiritual needs by priests, pastors, rabbis or other ecclesiastical functionaries who are citizens of the other party.' "[31] As we have seen, there was nothing in the agreement to make it reciprocal, and this was a surprising claim by the Soviet government.

The Department of State immediately protested that this was a direct violation of the Litvinov agreement, and that the cases of the two clergymen were not comparable at all. "Father Bissonnette's presence in Moscow was under the terms of the Litvinov Agreement and was in no way related to cases of temporary visits to the United States and the Union of Soviet Socialist Republics by ecclesiastical figures of the respective countries which have occurred from time to time."[32] The Department also emphasized that there was nothing reciprocal in the promise made by Litvinov in 1933.

> There is no condition of reciprocity contained in the Soviet note of November 16, 1933 and the proposal of the United States note of that date was confined to rights for American clergymen. . . . The Soviet government gave no indication at that time of being concerned with the problem of sending Soviet clergymen abroad. Furthermore, the fact that the notes contained no provision for reciprocity cannot be regarded as accidental since another exchange of notes . . . on the same day . . . contains a provision for reciprocal adherence to the engagements undertaken.
>
> It is therefore the view of the United States government that there is no basis for the claim of the Soviet government that the United States is bound by the terms of the November 16, 1933 agreement to admit clergymen from the Soviet Union.[33]

The agreement gave Americans in the Soviet Union the right to conduct their religious services in the normal way. This was now denied them by the Soviet government's action in expelling their clergyman. The Department analyzed the paragraph on entry into the Soviet Union. The meaning of the phrase that the Soviet government reserved the right to refuse a visa on "personal grounds"

> would appear to be that a visa would be refused if an individual applicant were objectionable on some ground other than his being a clergyman. The reservation . . . is not applicable in the present instance, since Fr. Bissonnette was not expelled because of objection to him personally but simply in retaliation for action taken by the United States government in connection with Archbishop Boris. . . . The

United States government regards the action of the Soviet government in expelling Fr. Bissonnette as a violation of the terms of the 1933 agreement.[34]

Whether the Soviet position was proper or not, the diplomatic jockeying which followed turned largely on this matter of reciprocity. Immediately after the expulsion of Bissonnette, Father Louis F. Dion —scheduled to replace him—applied to the Soviet Embassy in Washington for a visa to enter the Soviet Union. On March 23, 1955, he was assured that his application had been sent to Moscow and that speedy action would follow. On June 27 the State Department, in an effort to end the six-month stalemate, stated that "if the Soviet government now considers it desirable that Soviet clergymen be admitted to the United States in order to minister to the religious needs of Soviet nationals, the United States government is prepared in the interest of reciprocity to extend to a Soviet clergyman the same possibilities of entry and religious activities as those accorded to American clergymen in the Soviet Union under the terms of the November 16, 1933 agreement."[35] The American government agreed to accept a Soviet clergyman in the United States on a permanent basis if the Soviet government would issue a permanent visa to an American clergyman. Since previous visas for Moscow had been temporary, requiring periodic renewals, this would be advantageous from our standpoint. The Soviet Foreign Office made no direct reply to this American proposal until September when it notified Father Dion that he could come to the Soviet Embassy in Washington and obtain his visa. The visa was for no fixed period. On November 2 Dion received his visa and two days later visas were issued by the American Embassy in Moscow to the Archbishop and his secretary. If it seemed that the impasse was broken, this was a delusion.

The American government had proposed not only a reciprocal exchange of clergymen but a reciprocity in the conditions under which they would serve. The American priests in Moscow had confined themselves to relations with the American and other foreign Catholics there; they had no contact with Catholics who were Soviet citizens or with Soviet churches, either Roman or Orthodox. The American government now insisted that Archbishop Boris function similarly in this country: "Archbishop Boris will enjoy in the United States the right to minister to the religious needs of Soviet nationals."[36] Since most Soviet nationals in the United States belonged to the diplomatic group, most of them were Communists and, thus, officially atheists, and the American "concession" was not very large. The American note of June 27, 1955, maintained that the status of the two clergymen had not been equivalent:

> Archbishop Boris was admitted into the United States on a temporary visa to deal with matters pertaining to that faction of the Russian Orthodox Church in the United States which is administratively subordinate to the Moscow Patriarchate. In this capacity, Archbishop Boris was in contact with American citizens who are members of the Russian Orthodox Church and had the possibility of holding religious services in many different churches in a number of American cities which he visited. . . . In contrast . . . Fr. Bissonnette resided in Moscow. . . . He served the spiritual needs of Americans in Moscow and had no contact with Soviet citizens of the Roman Catholic faith. Due to action of the Soviet government, Fr. Bissonnette was unable to hold services in the Roman Catholic church in Moscow and was forced to use his small apartment for this purpose.[37]

This kind of reciprocity was not what Moscow had in mind and on November 10, 1955, it sent a note to the State Department emphasizing the Archbishop's intention to fulfill his full churchly obligations and authority while in the United States. "It is apparent to everyone that . . . the religious functions of an Exarch could not be placed on the same footing with the functions of an American priest."[38] Moscow did not desire reciprocity so much as an appearance of reciprocity, being willing neither to enlarge the status of the American priest in Moscow nor to agree to a reduced role for its clergyman in the United States. The State Department reacted accordingly on November 12, cancelling the visa granted to the Archbishop.

> From the . . . Soviet response of November 10, 1955, it is apparent that the Soviet government continues to insist that the admission of Fr. Dion to tend the spiritual needs of a few American Catholics in Moscow requires the admission of Archbishop Boris into the United States for an indefinite period to head an American church organization.[39]

This jeopardized the Soviet visa granted to Fr. Dion. The Department understood that "a member of the Assumptionist Order has been advised orally by the Soviet Embassy in Washington that Fr. Dion should not attempt to utilize his Soviet visa until such time as the question of the entry of Archbishop Boris into the United States is resolved."[40] Everything was just where it had been nine months previously.

At this point the problem was put "in the freezer." Occasionally during the next three years inquiry was made but the stalemate was acknowledged by both sides. It was resolved, finally, on November

21, 1958, when the State Department announced that it had reached an understanding with the Soviet Foreign Minister that the arrival of Archbishop Boris in the United States and the application of Fr. Dion to go to Moscow were two separate matters. The Soviet government indicated that it was prepared to permit Fr. Dion to enter the Soviet Union and that it would accept his visa application, while the American government announced that the Archbishop was on his way to the United States, a three-months' visitor's visa having been granted. Father Dion arrived in Moscow in January 1959.

The entry of American priests into the Soviet Union has thus involved a number of problems, some of them only indirectly. This has also been closely tied with the fact that only one priest has been present in Moscow at a time. In view of the much larger number of Americans there in recent years, many of them tourists but others for longer periods, the pressure of work on the priest must be very heavy, but there is no evidence that requests for additional priests have been submitted to the Soviet government.

The agreement on religion included more than just the matter of entrance into the Soviet Union, however, and we now turn to some of these other problems. It should be emphasized initially that the priests that have served in Moscow have done so in a private capacity. They owe their presence to an agreement concluded by the American government, but they are not a part of the official Mission, are not included on the Diplomatic List, have no diplomatic immunity, and, under the principle of separation of church and state, properly receive no different treatment or better protection than other American citizens in residence. In 1944, the question of Braun's ecclesiastical status in Moscow involved this very relationship. Father Braun considered that he was by rights apostolic administrator in Moscow and that he should be recognized in this capacity by the American Embassy.

> I explained to Fr. Braun that the Embassy could not be concerned in this question which would have to remain a matter for himself and the Soviet authorities. Fr. Braun said that he realized this but that he would wish at least to be known to the Embassy in the capacity which he considers himself to enjoy here. I suggested to him that he might wish to ask his ecclesiastical superiors to consider informing our Government, for its information, of their conception of his status. . . .
>
> Fr. Braun understands clearly, I think, that the United States government and this Embassy cannot take any step to influence his status in the Soviet Union.[41]

While this priest has no official diplomatic status in Moscow, it is also true that he has not been treated as just another American but has been given special status from time to time. It was not surprising, in view of this, that when Fr. Braun struck a servant of the French Embassy during an altercation in 1944 the French asked whether the American Ambassador wanted to take steps to stop the resulting court action. Braun was not viewed as just another American citizen in Moscow by the French, or perhaps by anyone else.

Another problem, resulting from the presence of American priests in Moscow, has already been alluded to: with whom would they have contact while there? Laberge, beginning in 1945, took frequent long trips, bringing baptism, confirmation, Communion, marriage, and burial to Catholics far from Moscow. Bissonnette has reported that, in so doing, he was ministering to Catholics of Soviet nationality "as he was entitled to do under the Roosevelt-Litvinov Agreement." This interpretation of the agreement, however—giving the foreign Catholic priest the right to minister not only to Catholics of foreign countries but to Soviet nationals—was not accepted by the Communist government, and Father Laberge "had to manage to keep out of the clutches of the Soviet police while doing his duty as he saw it."[42] This is a surprising statement, moreover, inasmuch as the Litvinov agreement refers in three places to "American nationals" and nowhere grants rights to anyone else. It would seem in this case that the Soviet interpretation was correct, and that Laberge and Bissonnette, however their attitudes may have been justified on other grounds, were not within the proper interpretation of the agreement.

This conclusion is strengthened by the fact that Laberge's successor believed he must not give the Soviet authorities any right to claim that he was ministering to Soviet citizens, so that he, and those who have followed him, have dealt only with foreigners in Moscow. Since his chapel was in a building rented only to foreigners, a police guard prevented all Soviet citizens from entering. For more than three years, moreover, he never left the city; only as his stay there was ending did he, with police permission, travel outside Moscow to visit the Monastery of St. Sergius in Zagorsk.

Bissonnette was also very cautious about this, writing about a trip to Kiev:

> It may come as a surprise to some that I did not intend to celebrate Mass. I had a portable altar which could have served very well, but the Embassy authorities had decided that by celebrating Mass I might open myself to charges of not confining myself to the spiritual needs of Americans at the Embassy in Moscow and thereby violate the Roosevelt-Litvinov Agreement. The Church had never gone along with

that interpretation, which seemed to contradict the plain meaning of the agreement, but since my orders from my religious superiors were to refrain from everything that might have an adverse effect on the Moscow Mission, I did not celebrate Mass when I was away from Moscow.[43]

This cautious attitude aided the American government, at the time of Bissonnette's expulsion from the Soviet Union, when the Soviet government claimed the reciprocal right of Boris to reside in the United States and minister to members of the Russian Orthodox Church here. As we have seen, the American government was able to state that Bissonnette "served the spiritual needs of Americans in Moscow and had no contact with Soviet citizens of the Roman Catholic faith."

The United States government was fearful that the priests' activities might give the Soviet authorities an excuse for interference. Thus, in 1939 the Embassy was concerned lest Fr. Braun's position be rendered untenable in Soviet eyes by conversations between the Polish and Soviet governments relative to the reopening of the Polish Catholic church in Moscow. If the church were to be reopened, the Polish Embassy proposed that Fr. Braun be appointed to officiate temporarily, pending the appointment and arrival of a regular priest. "Father Braun has told me," wrote Henderson,

> that he does not desire to take over this church since he fears that if he does so he may come in conflict with the Soviet authorities and be ordered to leave this country. . . .
> I believe that Braun is right. . . . A rather difficult situation might arise if such an order should be issued while Fr. Braun is acting as the priest of the Polish Catholic Church since the American Embassy . . . might find itself involved in one of the acrimonious disputes which are usually taking place between the Polish Embassy and the Soviet authorities. From the point of view of the American government it would be much better if Fr. Braun would not extend his activities into fields which are almost certain to increase the probability of conflicts between himself and the Soviet government.[44]

The Department's position was set forth in a reply from the Secretary, emphasizing again the thin line which the Department tried to draw in defining Braun's status in Moscow:

> If Fr. Braun broaches the matter . . . you may state in your discretion that decisions with regard to the scope of his work in the Soviet Union must rest entirely with himself; that it is difficult for the Embassy to advise him with respect to such decisions; but . . . the more he engages in activities unrelated to the spiritual needs of the American

colony, the more handicapped the Embassy will be in its endeavors to assist him on the basis of the . . . notes of November 16, 1933, in case the Soviet government should endeavor to expel him from the country.[45]

A comparable situation arose in 1941 when Braun wrote a long letter to Myron C. Taylor, the President's personal representative at the Vatican, describing the unfortunate state of the Roman Catholic church in the Soviet Union. Under Secretary Welles wrote to Taylor saying that "in view of the peculiar position of Fr. Braun in the Soviet Union it would appear that his presence is tolerated primarily because he administers spiritual aid to certain members of our Embassy staff —it would be inadvisable to reply to him or to undertake to convey messages of a political nature from him to the Holy See,"[46] and suggesting that only an informal method be used to tell Braun that his views were considered with interest.

There was, further, uncertainty over the definition of "religious worship" as used in the Litvinov agreement. In 1936, for example, a prominent American clergyman reported to the Embassy in Moscow that while visiting the Soviet Union he had been a member of a group that interviewed Emelyan Yaroslavsky, President of the Society of Militant Atheists. The clergyman said to this leader of Soviet policy on religion: "Under Article 124 of the proposed Constitution the right of freedom of worship and the right of anti-religious propaganda are granted. When does a religious rite cease to be a rite and become propaganda?" To this, Yaroslavsky replied: "According to the constitution there is no freedom granted for religious propaganda. But at the same time we do not forbid it. Any priest can preach religion. That is propaganda. He can make sermons. That is propaganda. If he adds to them, however, any anti-governmental elements, that is not allowed. . . . He can say all that he likes that is not propaganda against the State."[47]

While this was ostensibly an interpretation of the new Soviet Constitution as it applied to Soviet clergy in their relations with Soviet citizens, there was no attempt to exclude such foreign clergy as Braun, then in Moscow. This may have been doubly significant in view of the fact that Yaroslavsky was speaking to an all-American group. There was no definition of "anti-governmental elements" or "propaganda against the State," leaving the Soviet administrative officials free to interpret as they wished. Although there is no known occasion when the American priest was told what he could or could not say, or when the Soviet government objected to something that had been said, he must, whenever he prepared to meet his congregation, have been conscious of the wide marginal area between what was and what was not safe to say.

In the 1933 agreement, Litvinov said that it would be the fixed policy of the Soviet government to permit American nationals "to conduct without annoyance or molestation of any kind religious services and rites of a ceremonial nature." There have been repeated occasions of various types of annoyances, though there is, again, the matter of interpretation whether or not these acts constitute "annoyances" within the meaning of the agreement.

It is impossible to conduct religious services unless there is a place to hold the services. President Roosevelt specifically mentioned that the Americans in the Soviet Union should have the "opportunity to lease, erect or maintain in convenient situations" "churches, houses, or other buildings appropriate for such services," and Litvinov repeated the words in setting forth his government's policy. While the Soviet government has closed thousands of places of worship, it has never denied a place to worship to the American Catholics in Moscow. Whether there has been annoyance is another matter.

The church of St. Louis des Français had long been used by foreign Catholics resident in Moscow. The ownership of this property was vested in the French Embassy, and the Soviet government never nationalized this property. It was in this church that Braun and Laberge served, and it was here that the foreign Catholics enjoyed the religious freedom the Litvinov Agreement had obtained for them. After Laberge's departure, however, this was altered. Two Russian women and a representative of the Council for Religious Affairs called upon Fr. Thomas (a French Assumptionist who had been sent to help Bishop Neveu) to say that the congregation wanted a priest who could speak their language. (Laberge had preached in Russian, French, and English; Thomas, only in French.) The government official supported their demand, declaring that failure to turn over the keys of the church would result in "unpleasant consequences." Fr. Thomas, he said, would be permitted to officiate at one service each day for foreigners, but henceforth Soviet citizens could attend only services at which a Russian-speaking priest officiated.[48]

When, after waiting eleven months for his entrance visa, Fr. Brassard reached Moscow, he found St. Louis des Français in the hands of the Rev. Josef Butorovich Adamovich who was under the jurisdiction of Archbishop Antony Springovics of Riga, now a part of the U.S.S.R. Although the ecclesiastical authority of the Archbishop of Riga did not extend to Moscow and although the priest had no credentials—they had, he asserted, been deposited with the Council for Religious Affairs and he had a Soviet government certificate of authority—Brassard decided not to compromise the Latvian priest's position, which might only lead to the closing of the church, since this was at a very serious period of the "cold war." Brassard and his successors did not serve in this church.[49]

This made it necessary to find some other place. The French government came to the rescue again; it rented—with the approval of Burobin, the agency of the Soviet government that provides all housing space to foreigners—a small three-room flat which has since served both as a chapel and as a residence for the American priest. In this process, the Soviet government had managed not only to separate the American Catholics and their priest from the St. Louis church, but also to keep Soviet Catholics from coming into contact with the foreign priest.

An unusual event occurred in July 1959 when an American couple —the bridegroom was a graduate student at Moscow University—was married in the church of St. Louis, the first time in memory that Americans had been married there. The vows were recited in Russian, after the pastor, the Rev. Vitold Bronitsky. Then a nuptial mass was conducted by Fr. Dion in his little chapel, and finally a reception was held at Spaso House, the home of the American Ambassador. The Soviet government offered no objection,[50] and this part of the Litvinov agreement was fully satisfied. In June 1963 Fr. Richard was permitted to say Mass in St. Louis des Français, at a special ceremony honoring Pope John XXIII. Soviet officials also permitted Fr. Richard to hold a memorial service for President Kennedy in this church in November 1963.

A more serious type of "annoyance and molestation" occurred in 1940/41, while the American priest was still officiating at the church of St. Louis, when there was a series of robberies. On February 17, 1941, Ambassador Steinhardt notified Foreign Commissar Molotov that this church had been forcibly entered on December 6, 1939, and robbed of chalices, altar lace, trays and liturgical objects; again on April 9, 1940, when church appurtenances and currency were stolen; on December 25, 1940; on December 29, 1940, when the church was not only entered and robbed but "outrageously desecrated";[51] and finally on February 13, 1941, when the church was entered and damaged, and the gold and silver implements stolen. In every case, the robbery was immediately reported to the police. In one case the police admitted they had heard people in the church but had not investigated. After the fourth occurrence, the Ambassador had notified the Soviet government; "as is almost invariably the practice, however, I have not re-

ceived the courtesy of a reply to this note." The Ambassador concluded
that "it may reasonably be assumed, therefore, that the robberies
which I have brought to the attention of the Commissariat for Foreign
Affairs may be regarded as part of a deliberate plan to induce Fr.
Braun to close his church, which is now the only foreign church
functioning in Moscow." The conclusion was logical, indeed, for the
church is located in front of the building of the People's Commissariat
for Internal Affairs—the secret police—which was guarded day and
night by police who could scarcely have failed to know that the
church was being broken into and robbed.

On February 28, the Ambassador notified the Department that
he had now received a reply from the Foreign Office. Instead of admitting its own carelessness or guilt, the Soviet government placed
the blame upon the church, emphasizing that the treatment of religious establishments in the Soviet Union is regulated by special agreements between local authorities and "believers," that the church and
all its appurtenances were obtained from the Moscow Soviet "for use
free of charge," and that, under the terms of this agreement, the congregation is obligated "to safeguard the church and its property and
to bear financial responsibility in the event of loss or damage."[52] This
statement was apparently included, the Ambassador said, to explain
the bill which had been presented to Fr. Braun for the articles stolen
from the church. The repeated robberies, the Soviet note continued,
"are evidence that the council of the church has been derelict in safeguarding the premises." "This conclusion is confirmed by the 'careful
investigation of the facts of the robbery,' which the Embassy communi-
cated to the People's Commissariat." "After having invited my attention to the generosity of the Moscow Soviet in returning to the
church the premises and contents previously seized by the Soviets," the
Soviet government admitted that two minors had been arrested on
February 10, 1941, and a considerable portion of the articles stolen by
them were found and returned to an employee of the church. An
investigation of the robbery of February 13, it was said, indicated that
it "could have been committed by any of the visitors of the church remaining there especially for this purpose, and that the entry of the
criminals into the church could have occurred with the cooperation
of a confederate who was within the church." This evidenced a "failure
of proper measures on the part of the church" and "the inattentive
and careless attitude of the administration of the church toward the
fulfillment of its obligations is also characterized by the fact that the
administration of the church could not even indicate precisely the
location within the church of the articles that were stolen or the time

of their theft." The Soviet note did conclude, however, by saying that measures were being taken for the apprehension of the criminals, and the Embassy would be informed of the results.

This was done; on March 19, 1941, the Ambassador reported to the Department of State that, according to information received from the competent authorities,

> the thefts which occurred . . . on the night of December 6, 1939, and April 9, 1940, were committed by three professional thieves whose names are set forth . . . and that the thefts on December 25 and December 29, 1940, and on February 14, 1941, were committed by a professional thief whose name is given. The note continues that all of the persons named, who have long criminal records, as well as a professional receiver of stolen goods who is also named, were arrested on March 14, 1941, and are being prosecuted under the penal laws. The note concludes that a "considerable part" of the articles stolen from the Church have been located, that the search for the balance of the stolen articles is being continued, and that those already recovered will be returned within a few days to the "church attendant."[53]

The Ambassador was also able to inform the Department that "during the past two weeks the police have been affording the church adequate protection."[54]

What conclusions can be drawn from these incidents? It is easy to assert that the pugnacious attitude by which the Soviet government attempted to put all the blame on the negligence of the church was, in truth, only a smokescreen behind which the Soviet government was innocently trying to hide, thus proving its own guilt. It can be pointed out that the Ambassador would never have implied the existence of a deliberate plan to force the closing of the church had he not believed that he was on firm ground. His were strong words, the very type which Soviet officials were most likely to resent. It can be asserted also that, in the midst of the war, the Soviet police would be doubly protective of foreign property. It can be suggested that the comparative ease with which the Soviet government found the criminals and the stolen property indicates that it could, just as easily, have prevented the robberies in the first place if it had really wished to do so, and that the mere occurrence of the robberies shows a type of official connivance. These things can all be said, but they cannot be proved. Perhaps all of this is true; but does it establish that this was a Soviet attempt to molest and annoy Fr. Braun and his congregation, and that it thus constituted a violation of the 1933 agreement? Or is this, again, not another instance where the Soviet government has kept just within the line of legality and thus—whatever an individual may think—within the terms of the Litvinov agreement?

The idea of "religious freedom" was subjected to other types of annoyances and obstructions. Admiral Standley, American Ambassador in Moscow in the mid-1940's, states that Fr. Braun's food ration had been cut so low by Soviet officials that, even with the help of his parishioners, he "was hard put to keep up strength enough to carry on his heavy duties," and the Chargé, Thurston, had written a number of letters to Burobin without any helpful action. Since Braun had no diplomatic status, he could not buy at the Embassy commissary; since he had little money, he could not afford to buy food in the open market. "On numerous occasions," wrote Standley, "I gave him food from my own mess and also furnished him with firewood."[55]

In 1941 Steinhardt reported that he had been informed by Braun that "in addition to the repeated violations of his church he had been subjected to other vexations through the imposition of what he regards as excessively high income taxes, electric light and property tax assessments, and the coercion of his altar boys to the point where they now fear to officiate in his church."[56]

On another occasion, the Embassy sent word to Washington that the Soviet annoyance was then taking the form of refusing to grant Braun a residence permit for more than three months at a time, though he was charged the full year's fee of five rubles every three months. This meant filling out new forms every three months and reporting to the authorities with hours of waiting until the renewal was approved. It also meant the uncertainty of never knowing if there would be a renewal, one of the reasons why the American government was pleased to have the Russians agree to the issuance of a permanent visa in 1955.

Later, Fr. Bissonnette planned to take a trip by car to the Caucasus-Crimean area. Since it was necessary to obtain permission from various Soviet government agencies, the proper inquiries were made.

> The answers from the Ministry of Defense and Foreign Affairs (for two other Americans going on the trip) were favorable; the towns were all open, the roads were clear. . . . Finally I went down to OVIR (the registration and visa office). . . . The officer in charge informed me that the roads mentioned in my letter were impassable. Landslides, he said; it might take weeks. . . . Mr. Bohlen was furious. He called Protocol and asked them to inform OVIR that the American Ambassador could not understand how the same roads could be impassable for Fr. Bissonnette and in a splendid state of repair for Miss Wojnar and Mrs. Demo. A few hours later, when I returned to OVIR to have the necessary notations made in my residency permit, the same officer I had seen earlier told me without a smile that OVIR had been informed that the roads had just been repaired. "The landslides, too?" I said, and he said yes.[57]

There was, therefore, a rather constant stream of things—some major and some very small—by which the Soviet authorities made life uncertain and unpleasant for the American priest in Moscow and, to a lesser degree, for the American Ambassador who was responsible for the fulfillment of the 1933 agreements where this was possible. It should be remembered that Litvinov agreed to the right to "conduct without annoyance . . . religious services"; there was no promise to avoid annoyances in the daily life of the American clergymen, and it is not certain how anyone could have hoped to prevent or avoid such annoyances in a totalitarian society. It would have stretched the intentions of the negotiators to have maintained that these problems constituted a persecution of the clergy, against which the agreement protected them. The Soviet government never came right out and flatly violated the agreement, perhaps, except in the cases of Fr. Laberge's reentry visa and the expulsion of Fr. Bissonnette; it resorted, instead, to a series of staged pin pricks which made it clear that the American priest was not welcome in Moscow and could never be certain how much longer he might be able to stay or how effectively he could serve while there. This was the way the Soviet leaders had treated their own churches and religious leaders: some churches had been closed in one great fell swoop, but most had been eliminated by a "nibbling" process of annoyances, resort to subterfuge against the clergy or members, or taxation[58] until almost nothing was left in the whole Soviet Union.[59]

The American representatives who conferred with Litvinov in November 1933 had surely not envisaged that the agreement on religious freedom was going to produce the harassed treatment described above. They were unable to foresee the continuing opposition of the Soviet leaders toward religion and, even if this could have been predicted, they must have hoped for better treatment than the Americans received. They may have thought that a careful drawing of the specifications would produce the type of religious freedom practiced in the United States, but they were inexperienced in the deviousness of Soviet administrative techniques. This chapter has demonstrated how different were the goal and the achievement. It is unlikely, however, that Americans—and perhaps other foreigners—in Moscow would have received even this minimal type of acceptance had it not been for the inclusion of this among the promises made by Litvinov.

CHAPTER IV

Legal Protection for American Nationals

In contemplating recognition of the Soviet government, the American government was particularly conscious of the need to provide legal protection for American nationals in the Soviet Union. This is an obligation of every government, and the American government would find itself vulnerable, indeed, if it did not appear to be seriously concerned with this matter. The Department of State was aware that other governments had encountered problems in trying to protect their citizens in the Soviet Union, and had tried to find some formula to safeguard the rights of their people. It is not surprising, therefore, that the President and his advisors should have concentrated on this topic at one stage of the discussions with the Soviet representative.

SOVIET POLICY TOWARD FOREIGNERS IN THE U.S.S.R.

Although the United States government had had no diplomatic representatives in the Soviet Union, it was not ignorant about developments there. Riga, Latvia, was used as an "observation post" where people going in or coming out of the Soviet Union could be interviewed and where Soviet newspaper, periodical, and other materials could be assembled and analyzed. In 1933 the American Legation in Riga prepared an analysis, *Foreigners in Russia*, which covered three hundred pages. Kelley's fifth memorandum, entitled *Treaty Rights Essential to the Welfare and Protection of American Nationals in Russia*, also dealt with this topic. The American government accordingly knew a great deal about this problem, although the memorandum prepared in Riga did not arrive in time to be considered during the Roosevelt-Litvinov negotiations.

It was understood that legal protection for nationals in the Soviet Union was very different than in other countries, and that the Soviet system did not fit in with the usual principles of international law. "Up to the present time," wrote Kelley, "no treaty principles have been devised which seriously limit the power of the Soviet authorities to deal just about as they please with the foreigners residing in or traveling on their territory. . . . It is doubtful whether any such principle can be found which would be conceivably acceptable to the Russian authorities."[1] The memorandum prepared in Riga underlined this: "There is in the Soviet Union today no fixed system of familiar and *internationally-accepted legal concepts*, principles, and established practices. In fact, the whole Soviet system is, and intends to be, a negation of the legal systems known as Roman and Anglo-Saxon law."[2]

A person living in another country experiences an almost infinite variety of situations; no treaty can hope to cover them adequately. Certain principles have been developed, therefore, to provide a standard for the treatment of foreigners in specific cases. In many cases, the principle of the most-favored nation has been applied; elsewhere, reciprocity has been widely accepted. Neither of these principles, however, was adequate in the case of the Soviet Union.

Both the Kelley and Riga memoranda emphasized that most-favored-nation treatment was inapplicable in the Soviet Union where discrimination rests upon the rights of a class and not of a national group. Thus the first paragraph of the Civil Code of the Russian Socialist Federated Soviet Republic (R.S.F.S.R.) provided that civil rights shall not receive the protection of the law when "they are exercised in contradiction to their social and economic purpose," a concept open to wide interpretation, and Article 411 of the same code provided that "in fixing the measure of compensation for injury, the court in all cases must take into consideration the property position of the person suffering and the person giving the injury."[3] In Soviet law, both citizens and foreigners are divided into "toilers" and "non-toilers"; distinctions based on the nationality of a person do not normally occur in Soviet Russia.

Similarly, reciprocity is hardly suitable, since few states are so organized that they resort to the same variety of measures as the Soviet state. Neither the United States nor the Soviet Union is philosophically or administratively equipped to treat foreigners as they are treated in the other country. The existence of a foreign trade monopoly and the administrative power of the central authorities in Moscow, for example, give the Soviet government a wide range of free action that few other governments enjoy. Surely the American government had no right to expect that its nationals would receive the same treatment in Moscow as they did at home, and yet, in a sense, this is what it did expect.

One trouble was that, if the old principles for international legal protection were unsuitable in the Soviet Union, no new principles had been developed. "None of the existing commercial treaties with the Soviet Union have shown any serious attempt to meet the new conditions presented . . . by the peculiar character of the Soviet State. Without exception, they regulate commercial relations in a way much more favorable to the Union than to the other contracting parties."[4]

One basic difference between the American and Soviet legal systems is that in the latter every agency is the servant of the executive branch. Courts are not independent but exist to administer the policies of the Kremlin. Thus, matters—such as searches and seizures, confiscation of property, entrance into or exit out of the country, residence and travel, and taxation—which would be subject to certain legal principles in the United States, lie within the discretion of the executive in the Soviet Union. The central executive authority, moreover, controls all local authorities and many other presumably independent agencies such as labor unions, local courts, and patriotic organizations. "No general treaty provisions can be very effective in protecting . . . foreigners in Russia under these conditions—barring the establishment of a system of extraterritoriality, to which the Soviet government would never consent. . . . Russia's administrative system is sufficiently pliable, its legislation sufficiently ambiguous . . . that formal justification can always be found for the violation of any mere treaty restriction . . . if the ruling group so desires."[5]

Foreigners actually had only such rights as could be obtained through diplomatic pressure. "The position of foreigners in the Soviet Union who were unprotected by treaty provisions has been in no way worse, and in some instances even better, than those whose status was supposedly regulated by treaty."[6] If it appears that foreigners in the Soviet Union had no assurance of legal protection, the facts show that they received, generally speaking, exceptionally good treatment— because, in the early years of the Soviet system, it was to the political advantage of the Soviet government to provide this. Unless foreigners had received this type of treatment, they would not have remained and this would have both embarrassed and handicapped the Soviet government. The impelling force was political rather than legal, and the policy was as temporary or permanent as the needs of the Soviet leaders. A state was likely to obtain rights for its citizens in the Soviet Union in direct proportion to its ability and willingness to bring pressure on the Soviet government. Reciprocity in the form of retaliation was effective. When, indeed, foreign governments were not bound by treaty provisions, they sometimes found they were better able to help their citizens.

To do this, a foreign government needed information about violations of the rights of its citizens, as quickly and completely as possible. When a group of British engineers was arrested early in 1933—the Metropolitan-Vickers case—it was several days before the British Embassy in Moscow could obtain information concerning the whereabouts of the prisoners, the charges against them, the judicial authorities who were to handle the case, and whether or not a trial was to be held. The Soviet Foreign Office repeatedly denied knowledge of these matters. When British officials, including the Ambassador himself, were finally permitted to visit the prisoners, there were difficulties in conducting the conversation in a non-Russian language, four Soviet officials were present at the interview, and the British engineers were "all obviously terrified of speaking and confined themselves to a minimum of replies."[7] Since this incident occurred only a short time before the Roosevelt-Litvinov negotiations, it cast a particularly long shadow over the thinking of the American negotiators when dealing with the question of protection for American citizens in the Soviet Union.

THE AGREEMENT

The agreement on this topic consists of a letter from Litvinov to the President, followed by an acknowledgment from the President, thus reversing the order of presentations that was used in regard to religious freedom. Litvinov said that the Soviet government was prepared to negotiate a consular convention immediately after establishment of diplomatic relations, giving to American nationals "rights with reference to legal protection which shall not be less favorable than those enjoyed in the Union of Soviet Socialist Republics by nationals of the nation most favored in this respect." Indeed, such rights would be granted to American nationals immediately after establishment of relations. He concluded by quoting from the 1925 German-Soviet Agreement Concerning Conditions of Residence and Legal Protection in General which was, by general consent, the basis for the most-favored-nation treatment. Litvinov specifically cited Article 11 of that agreement, in which the two signatories undertook to adopt the measures necessary to inform the consul of the other government "as soon as possible" whenever a national of his country was arrested. The consul might be notified either by the authorities themselves or by the prisoner, and such communications "shall be made within a period not exceeding seven times twenty-four hours, and in large towns, including capitals of districts, within a period not exceeding three times twenty-four hours." Provision was also made for the prisoners to be visited "in places of detention of all kinds" by the consuls or their representatives. Requests for such visits were to be granted "without delay." The foreign consul, however, could not require officials of the government making the arrest to withdraw during the interview with the prisoner.[8]

In his reply, President Roosevelt noted the provisions of this agreement, said that he was glad that these rights would become effective immediately upon establishment of relations between the two countries, and expressed readiness to negotiate a consular convention as soon as practicable. Then, in an obvious effort to emphasize the importance of this agreement and in an attempt to sharpen it, the President stated: "Let me add that American diplomatic and consular officers in the Soviet Union will be zealous in guarding the rights of American nationals, particularly the right to a fair, public and speedy trial, and the right to be represented by counsel of their choice. We shall expect that the nearest American diplomatic or consular officer shall be notified immediately of any arrest or detention of an American national, and that he shall promptly be afforded the opportunity to communicate and converse with such national."

In analyzing this agreement, we need to remember certain facts. (1) Again, as we saw with the agreement on religious freedom, there was an obvious attempt to make the statement as specific as possible. The President was much more precise than Litvinov whose statement referred generally to "rights with reference to legal protection," except as he used the German-Soviet agreement as an example. Whether the President hoped and expected that American nationals would really obtain these rights when in the Soviet Union as if they were still in the United States is not clear. At any rate, Litvinov raised no objection and expressed his government's agreement to such an effort. (2) It is important to note that these rights became available automatically upon establishment of relations between the governments and did not depend upon the negotiation and approval of the consular convention. This was fortunate from our view, for no consular convention was agreed upon. (3) This agreement was unilateral rather than reciprocal. Nowhere does it grant rights to the Soviet government or to Soviet citizens; all rights granted accrued to Americans.[9] It was possible that a consular convention might embody the principle of reciprocity, but there was no assurance of this. The agreement, as made, was not reciprocal. The benefactors of the agreement, accordingly, were "American nationals" only. (4) The agreement relied upon the most-favored-nation principle, despite warnings as to the valuelessness of such a principle when dealing with the Soviet government. Whether this action ignored the warning, or whether it was adopted as the "least bad" of the available alternatives, is not apparent since there are no detailed notes of the negotiations. Whatever their motivation, the American negotiators, in using this principle, hoped to secure for American nationals the sum total of all the legal protection which had been secured up to that time by other governments on behalf of their citizens.

The detailed provisions on this topic were contained in the German-Soviet agreement of October 12, 1925, and a number of other governments relied on this as a basis for treatment of their nationals. These provisions had not been deemed adequate, and in 1928 negotiations between the German and Soviet governments led to further agreement. The right of consular officers to visit prisoners was clarified, for example, with the Russians agreeing not to hinder such visits on the grounds of the Russian law which forbade visits to prisoners before completion of the preliminary examination. They also agreed not to prevent such visits on the pretext that the citizenship of the arrested person had not been fully established. A fixed and uniform schedule of fees for issuance and extension of entrance, exit, and transit visas, and residence permits was also created. Norway, Sweden, Turkey, Germany, and Italy had also contracted with the Soviet government not to impress their nationals into military service while in the Soviet Union.

Under the most-favored-nation principle, all of these rights were to be available to American nationals while in the Soviet Union. Whether or not this was to be very significant remained to be seen. Litvinov's reference to the agreement with Germany was an attempt to show that there was nothing really new about this problem, and that it had already been handled satisfactorily with other governments. The American government, then, concluded an agreement by which it hoped to provide adequate protection to its nationals in the Soviet Union, protection at least as good as that secured by any other government up to that time. The degree to which these hopes were realized, and the problems involved, are the subject of the remainder of the present chapter.

Who are "American nationals"? The term "American national" was used repeatedly in the agreements between President Roosevelt and Litvinov. There was no attempt to define the term, although the participants must have realized that puzzling problems had arisen over the exact nature of the term. In the general sense, "national" and "citizen" mean about the same and are often used interchangeably. More specifically, the former term is broader than the latter. According to Green Hackworth (Legal Adviser in the Department of State in 1933) the term *citizen* "is applicable only to a person who is endowed with full political and civil rights in the body politic of the state; the term *national* includes a *citizen* as well as a person who, though not a citizen, owes permanent allegiance to the state and is entitled to its protection as, for example, natives of certain of the outlying possessions of the United States."[10] Further ramifications of the term need not concern us here; the important thing is that "American nationals" owe allegiance to the United States and are entitled to protection from the American government. It was these persons who were covered by this agreement. This might appear fairly simple: the American government would know who were its nationals and would give them protection when in the Soviet Union, under the most-favored-nation treatment.

American citizens are those who were born in this country and have American citizenship by *jus soli*, those who were born abroad of American parents and have citizenship according to *jus sanguinis*, or those who have surrendered their former citizenship and acquired American citizenship through naturalization. The American government recognizes the right of expatriation, *i.e.*, the right to surrender citizenship and acquire that of another country; some other governments do not, which leads to the possibility of dual citizenship, with two governments both claiming the individual as one of their nationals. Such an individual normally has no difficulty as long as he remains in the country where he has acquired citizenship, but if he returns to his former country, the government of that country may claim that he stills owes it allegiance. Since he is then under its jurisdiction, he may find that his acquired citizenship has no real meaning, and the government of his new country may find itself unable to help him.

Section 4 of a Soviet decree of April 22, 1931, provided that "Foreign citizens who have acquired the citizenship of the U.S.S.R. do not enjoy the rights and do not have to fulfill the duties connected with the citizenship of another country."[11] It seems clear, Secretary of State Stimson told the Consul General in Berlin (who dealt with this problem before 1933),

> that naturalization in Soviet Russia . . . results in expatriation of any American citizen who is naturalized in Soviet Russia. . . . Consequently, whenever it comes to your attention that an American citizen has been naturalized in conformity with a decree of Soviet Russia, you will consider him to have expatriated himself and as not being entitled to protection as a citizen of the United States.[12]

Prior to American recognition of the Soviet government, accordingly, the American government was willing to accept the word of the Soviet government that an individual had been naturalized into Soviet citizenship. The existence of this Departmental instruction may well have accounted for the fact that, after recognition, some Embassy personnel in Moscow were not more zealous in attempting to press for the rights of some who by American law were entitled to the protection of this government.

The attitude of the American government changed, however, and in 1935 the Embassy in Moscow was informed that "the right of the Soviet authorities to consider the American born child of a Soviet father a Soviet citizen is recognized, but they may be informed that since he now desires to assert his American citizenship also acquired at birth and return to the United States for permanent residence, he should be granted a Soviet exit visa or permitted to renounce his Soviet citizenship unless there is pending against him some charge justifying his detention in Soviet territory."[13]

This problem of dual nationality was an important part of our problem with the Soviet government. Many people born in Russia emigrated to the United States. If they, or even their children, returned to Russia they might well find that the Soviet government claimed them as its nationals, refusing to recognize that they had—in their view and in that of the American government—become "American nationals." Thus, in 1926 the Norwegian Minister in Moscow called at the Soviet Foreign Office on behalf of three Americans—this was prior to American recognition—imprisoned in Russia, two of whom were of Russian birth. Litvinov explained the situation of such dual nationals in the Soviet Union as follows:

> Even if they had later become naturalized American citizens, they would be regarded and treated as Russian citizens as soon as they returned to Russia. When a person in their position sought a visa to enter Russia, he was obliged, if he intended to return for good, to sign a declaration to the effect that he should be regarded as a Russian citizen from the moment he set foot on Russian territory. If he sought a visa for a shorter sojourn in Russia he was advised that as long as he remained in Russia he would be regarded as a Russian citizen.[14]

There were many of these people, especially after the Soviet Technical Aid Society in the United States organized groups to go to the Soviet Union to help build up the new society. The Society gave certificates to these people, which became the basis for entrance visas into the Soviet Union and, often, for assuming Soviet citizenship. The problem of dual nationality was further complicated by the boundary changes in

Eastern Europe after two world wars. Even at best, difficulties were inevitable. In addition, the American government became increasingly convinced that the Soviet government was not even trying to eliminate problems when possible.

Take, for example, the case of Mieczyslaw Roszkowski who was born in Fall River, Massachusetts, in October 1920. His parents took him to Poland as an infant. He never set foot in the Soviet Union of his own volition but was seized in eastern Poland by the Soviet authorities at the time of the September 1939 invasion.[15] Having been born in the United States, he was an American citizen; he had, in fact, applied on January 8, 1940, at the American Consulate General in Warsaw for an American passport and was ready to depart for the United States whenever there was an opportunity. He was arrested by the Soviet authorities and sentenced to "three years of reformatory labor camp for unlawful keeping of arms" in view of the fact that he was found to possess an old gun in his home, a gun which—by his statement—the police had declared to be unusable. Was he an American national, entitled to protection by the American government?

During a conversation between Under Secretary Sumner Welles and Soviet Ambassador Umansky, on December 16, 1940, the latter "said that Roskowski [*sic*] had never been in the United States and that his only claim to American citizenship arose from the fact that he had apparently applied for certain American documents in 1939."[16] To this Welles replied that there must be a mistake, since no one could take out first papers without having been in the United States.[17] Informed of this, the American Embassy in Moscow wrote to the Department, "In view of the fact that Roszkowski is a native born American citizen, Umanski's statement that he had never been in the United States . . . is not in conformity with the facts. . . . The present status of the case is that the Soviet authorities continue to refuse . . . to recognize his American citizenship."[18] The Soviet authorities refused to allow the American Ambassador in Moscow to visit Roszkowski or even to know the charges against him. "They have also failed to reply to urgent notes from the Embassy dated August 17, November 28, and December 10, 1940."[19]

On January 15, 1941, however, the Soviet government agreed to reopen the question and on January 21 "Oumansky stated that his government now agreed that Mr. Roszkowski was an American citizen, born in the United States, and that the reason for the original denial of the Soviet Union . . . was due to the fact that he possessed the same name as another individual in the same locality who had been born in Russia."[20] But, as if he foresaw this attempted justification,

Steinhardt had already written to the Department that "the Embassy has made representations in behalf of no other person with a like or similar name, nor is there any other case pending in which American citizenship is in doubt."[21]

In the Roszkowski case, therefore, it developed that there was really no question of dual nationality. At best, it was an error on the part of the Soviet government in the confusion of taking control of the eastern half of Poland. Unless the American government had insisted that Roszkowski was an American national, he would not have been freed from a "reformatory labor camp" and allowed to return to the United States, as he was.

A number of cases which did involve dual citizenship arose during the 1930's. In January 1930, for example, the Department of State received a letter from Mrs. Sarah Barr, asking "who protects American citizens in the Soviet Union" and seeking information about her son Edward. The Department could only reply that, having no diplomatic relations with the Soviet Union at the time, it could do nothing. In October 1934 Mrs. Barr wrote again, asking the Department to help get her son back home now that diplomatic relations did exist. On January 4, 1935, the Embassy in Moscow notified the Department that it had established contact with Edward Barr, who had written that "as soon as I feel stronger I am going to take a trip to Moscow and see the Consul."[22] More than two years later, Mrs. Barr wrote again, and in November 1937 the Embassy stated that it had written both to the Soviet Foreign Office and to Edward Barr, with no reply from either. On February 7, 1938, the Embassy reported a reply from the Soviet Foreign Office: "Unfortunately the whereabouts of Citizen E. L. Barr cannot be established."[23] The Embassy noted that the Foreign Office seldom could provide information regarding dual nationals, that "no information is available" was a standard reply in such cases, and that Barr was "undoubtedly a Soviet citizen at the present time." The facts indicate that Edward Barr was interested neither in returning home to his mother nor in maintaining allegiance to his native country. In such a case, he may well have forfeited—morally though not legally— any claim to protection by the American government.

The case of John Arola was different. He was born in New York City in 1917 and in 1932 arrived in the Soviet Union, being included on the passport of his parents who were Finnish citizens. Soon after this, the parents applied for and were granted Soviet citizenship and, as a minor, John was included. When on May 8, 1937, the American Embassy in Moscow inquired about the circumstances surrounding his acquisition of Soviet citizenship, the Soviet Foreign Office asked "in what connection the Embassy is interested in the citizen status of John Arola who arrived in the U.S.S.R. as a citizen of Finland." During an exchange of inquiries, an official of the People's Commissariat for Foreign Affairs advised the Embassy: "The People's Commissariat finds it inconvenient to give the details of the acquisition of Soviet citizenship by minor children in each particular case. . . . In such case it *should* be considered that the naturalization took place in accordance with the existing law."[24] On December 5, 1938, John Arola's wife notified the American Embassy that her husband had been arrested on June 21, 1938, just a month before the Commissariat's phone call.

What was the American government to do now? If Edward Barr had accepted Soviet citizenship by his own decision, there was no such evidence in this case. Arola was fifteen or sixteen years old when, by his parents' decision, he was made a Soviet citizen. Under American law and international law, he still had a legitimate right to claim American citizenship if he wished to; under American law and international law, the American government had a legal right to offer protection to him, at least until it became apparent that he refused it. The Soviet government, however, took the view in such cases that the person is a Soviet citizen—only a Soviet citizen—and that no information might properly be asked by another government. Since the individual was in their possession, the American government could do little but protest. It might have a proper *legal* interest in knowing why John Arola was arrested, where he was, how he was, and so on, but it was not likely to obtain answers to its questions. In the light of the instruction given by Secretary Stimson on April 12, 1932, referred to above, the American representatives should not proceed to interest themselves in the case but should acquiesce—as they did—and accept the Soviet government's statement.

Elmer John Nousiainen (also spelled Nausiainen in the records) was by American law an American citizen with dual nationality. On July 18, 1938, he visited the American Embassy in Moscow, stating that numerous arrests had been made among his neighbors at Petrozavodsk[25] and that he was afraid he, too, might be arrested. On August 1, the Embassy received a letter from his mother stating that he had never returned home after his visit to the Embassy. It was suspected that he was being detained by the Soviet police. Inquiries by the Embassy met a stone wall of silence. In November, Henderson wrote:

> The Soviet government apparently does not recognize that a person can have the status of dual citizenship. It refused to recognize that another government can have an interest in any person whom it re-

gards as a Soviet citizen. . . . There is little which the American government can do in this matter. No protest or action, in my opinion, can change these Soviet practices which are almost an integral part of the whole Soviet system.[26]

The strongest statement about this Soviet practice, however, came in connection with the case of George Sviridoff who came to the United States as a boy of fifteen, became an American citizen a month after his arrival when his father (who had preceded him to this country) was naturalized, and later got the wanderlust and returned to Russia. Apparently as a youthful prank, he decided to stow away on a ship bound from the Soviet Union to the United States and was caught and returned to the Soviet Union where he disappeared, presumably in a labor camp for punishment. Inquiries by the Embassy elicited nothing. Finally, Henderson was told that "it would appear that Mr. Sviridoff is also a Soviet citizen and that so long as he is in the Soviet Union, the Soviet authorities must consider him as being a Soviet citizen only."[27] At this point, George Kennan, then a member of the Mission in Moscow, tried to state the exact position of the Soviet and American governments on persons of dual citizenship:

> The Soviet government has the administrative power to arrest and hold incommunicado indefinitely any American citizen in the Soviet Union. In case the person in question has Soviet citizenship under Soviet law, the Soviet authorities consider him as having Soviet citizenship *only* and hold themselves under no obligation to give us any information. . . . Should this person have at the time of his arrest only American nationality, the Soviet authorities apparently have only to notify us that he has been admitted to Soviet citizenship in order to create a situation in which . . . we would not press further representations in his behalf. Indeed, there are indications that once an American citizen in Russia is classified by the Soviet authorities as a Soviet citizen he is not normally allowed to visit the American Embassy even for purposes of discussing his citizenship status.
> . . . In reality no American citizen *resident* in the Soviet Union has any assurance that we will be able to help him. . . . These people are virtually at the mercy of the Soviet authorities. We ourselves are practically powerless to influence their decisions.
> I do not believe that there is anything that we can do to alter the attitude or the practices of the Soviet authorities in this respect or to obtain a greater degree of power to protect our own citizens.[28]

The situation was serious enough that it was proposed in 1935 to advise "American citizens of Russian origin or of dual nationality who contemplate travel to U.S.S.R. . . . of likelihood of their being considered Soviet citizens and consequent difficulty of leaving the Soviet Union."[29] The Department, however, did not consider it politic to make such an announcement.

Another factor made the problem even worse. Since 1868 the American government has recognized the right of a person to divest himself of his original citizenship and assume a new allegiance. If an American citizen wished to become a Soviet citizen, his right to do so was recognized, and the *New York Times* reported on November 17, 1939, that more than a thousand Americans had acquired Soviet nationality in recent years. The principle of expatriation was built, however, on the foundation of the right of an individual to make such a decision for himself and it was thus a matter of his own choice. On April 12, 1932, the Secretary of State stated that "naturalization in Soviet Russia is granted only upon the request of or voluntary acceptance by the person naturalized."[30] Later, however, there were indications that the choice in the Soviet Union was not always voluntary but that people were pressured into accepting Soviet citizenship, with little opportunity to refuse. This put the Soviet refusal to recognize dual nationality in an even worse light, for, if the United States accepted this claim, it might be refusing protection to some who were entitled to it and desired it, even if they were not at the moment free to say so.

Ambassador Bullitt had hardly established the Mission in Moscow when he cabled the Department that "since opening of office nineteen persons claiming American citizenship have reported their passports were taken up by the Soviet authorities and they were either forced to accept or were granted Soviet citizenship without their knowledge."[31]

As an example, Michael Devenis was born in Lithuania, migrated to the United States, and became a naturalized citizen. His wife was not an American citizen, but their three children were. In 1929 Dr. Devenis returned to Lithuania to practice medicine. In June 1940 he began arrangements for a return to the United States but was arrested on July 22. Mrs. Devenis and the children were permitted to leave in September; he was moved from one jail to another. In December 1940 the Department wired that it considered "Michael Devenis to have continued in status of American citizen. . . . Issuance of passport to . . . enable him return United States permanent residence was authorized July 22, 1940. On that date he was arrested and thus prevented from departing from Lithuania. Advise appropriate Soviet authorities . . . and request his prompt release on basis . . . acquisition Soviet nationality . . . involuntary."[32] The American government, in other words, considered him still an American citizen; the Soviet government considered him a Soviet citizen on the basis of the Soviet law which gave citizenship to all those of Lithuanian citizenship. Dr. Devenis had nothing to say about whether he was a Soviet citizen; he just happened to belong to a group which was affected, en masse. The American government was finally able to secure his release.

Sol Drypool was born in Brooklyn; he left the United States at the age of seven when his parents returned to Russia. After the First World War he attempted to establish his American citizenship through the American consulate in Riga; in 1924 the Department of State authorized a passport for him, but he claimed that he was never allowed to leave the Soviet Union to apply for it. He called at the American Embassy in Moscow in 1937. The following month he returned to the Embassy, having been told by Soviet authorities that he was in the Soviet Union illegally, that he must get a petition for Soviet citizenship within three days, or present evidence of trying to get an American passport. He chose the latter alternative and was given a general statement by the Embassy; this was submitted to the Soviet Foreign Office. Two months later—March 1938—he called at the Embassy to see if a reply had been received; at 11:30 that night his mother telephoned to inquire about her son who had not returned. The following day his wife called; it was feared that he had been arrested leaving the Embassy. An inquiry by the Embassy from the Foreign Office brought no reply. The implication seems clear: when he refused the offer of Soviet citizenship, he jeopardized his situation and brought swift action against himself.

Peter Krassnoff was born in Hawaii of Russian parents; in 1931— aged seventeen—he went to the Soviet Union on an American passport. This was taken from him by the Soviet officials, who considered him a Soviet citizen because of his parents' nationality. On March 27, 1937, his brother advised the American Embassy in Moscow that Peter Krassnoff had been arrested two days earlier for ripping up the Soviet passport offered him, in front of the Chief of the Soviet at Krivoi Rog. On April 9 the Embassy inquired about his citizenship status; on August 4 it asked the Commissariat for Foreign Affairs about the charges against him and when he might be released; another inquiry was made on November 10; on November 22 the American consul called at the Foreign Office; on December 13 another note was sent. On December 25, 1937, the People's Commissariat stated that "it had no facilities for conducting investigations with regard to Soviet citizens."[33] This was, again, a situation where the refusal of a person to accept the Soviet interpretation of his citizenship—the acceptance of the Soviet passport would have been such an acknowledgment—led the Soviet officials to arrest him rather than admit the possibility of his having American citizenship.

Hjalmar S. Nordeen was born in Sweden but emigrated to the United States where he was naturalized. In 1933 he went to the Soviet Union. Eighteen months later, he applied for an American passport to return to the United States, alleging that he had meanwhile been forced into applying for and accepting Soviet citizenship. On February 4, 1935, the Department of State held that Nordeen had not voluntarily acquired Soviet citizenship and authorized the Embassy in Moscow to issue a passport. On April 24, 1935, he applied to renounce his Soviet citizenship; the following January the Foreign Office said that this request had been denied. Nordeen appealed this decision; the American Embassy interested itself in the case, which dragged on for two years. On November 23, 1937, the Embassy was informed that Nordeen had been arrested two days before. Later the Department was told that nothing much had been done by the Embassy, following his arrest, "since Mr. Nordeen is considered by the Soviet government to have acquired Soviet citizenship in conformity with its citizenship laws."[34] Here was another man who, forced to accept Soviet citizenship, tried to fight the Soviet policy, only to find himself in trouble with the Soviet law; the American Embassy, despite its legal rights in the matter, was unable to do anything that would effectively offer this citizen the protection to which he was entitled.

There were occasions, however, when the Soviet attempt to force its citizenship did not succeed. One such case was that of John Schweiger, an American citizen who sought work in the Soviet Union during the depression. He changed his mind and wanted to return to the United States, with the following results, as attested in an affidavit filed with the American Embassy in Moscow on July 24, 1934. He had frequently been asked for his American passport for the purpose of registration with the police and for extensions of his residence permit; the passport was always returned promptly until December 1931 when it was not. Becoming anxious about this—his passport was his best tangible evidence of American citizenship—he inquired and was told it was not yet ready. Six months later he inquired again, whereupon he was told by the Soviet officials "that he would never get his passport back again and that it had been sent to Moscow; that . . . the Foreign Department . . . had made an application for him to become a Soviet citizen."[35] When he protested against this, stating that he did not want to become a Soviet citizen, he was merely told that he would have to wait and see what action was taken by the Soviet government on the application. In January 1933 he asked again for his American passport, saying that he wished to return to the United States immediately. He was informed that it would be necessary for him to travel to Moscow, to make application to renounce his Soviet citizenship (now an established fact), and that if his application were approved he would have to pay 500 gold rubles for the privilege. On November 11, 1933—now in Moscow—he urgently requested permission to leave the country and appealed for return of his American passport. He was permitted to fill out an application to leave the Soviet Union, for which he had to pay 154 rubles. On December 27, 1933, his request was refused. In January 1934, however, his son approached Kalinin's office[36] and, as a result of his representations, was given permission to leave the Soviet Union, taking his father and mother with him. In July 1934 Schweiger was issued a new passport by the American Embassy, enabling him to use his exit visa and leave the Soviet Union. In his affidavit, he swore that he had "never signed any application or papers which to his knowledge were applications for Soviet citizenship; that he only signed one paper and that was for his Soviet [internal] passport for travel to Moscow."[37] If the Schweiger case appears to be the most brazen, callous disregard of what Americans consider the rights of an individual, it may be only because facts were made available about this situation. The Embassy staff in Moscow realized that there was nothing they could do to prevent this Soviet pressure or help those victimized by it.

If the American negotiators in November 1933 inserted the phrase "American nationals" into the agreement with Litvinov just because it was the normal, accepted term in such a situation, they had little idea of some of the complications which were to arise from this usage. The Soviet government, through its refusal to accept the idea of dual nationality and by forcing certain people to accept its citizenship even against their wishes, made this little phrase in the agreement a major stumbling block to good relations between the two countries. This was only the first of the problems, however, which arose from the implementation of this agreement; we next turn to an explanation of the remainder of that statement.

THE MEANS OF PROTECTING AMERICAN NATIONALS

The problem of determining who was entitled to the protection of the American government was relatively simple, compared with that of deciding how such protection could best be provided. Of the different ways in which the American government normally offers protection to its nationals abroad, several were applicable to the Soviet situation. Most of these were specified or implied in the November 16, 1933, agreement. They may be listed as: (1) a consular convention; (2) the exercise of consular functions; (3) the right of Americans to visit the Embassy in Moscow; (4) investigations made by the Embassy upon request; (5) the Soviet promise to notify the American government when American nationals were arrested; (6) the Soviet promise to allow representatives of the American government to visit and interview arrested American nationals; (7) the expectation of a fair and speedy public trial; and (8) the right to leave the country unless serving a sentence imposed by a court. Each of these will now be considered.

Both Roosevelt and Litvinov, in their statements of November 16, 1933, looked foward to negotiation of a consular convention between the two governments, following establishment of normal relations, and discussions began on November 20. "We discussed at some length a consular convention and I asked Mr. Carr to join us at this point. Mr. Carr handed Mr. Litvinov several sample conventions in [sic] which the United States had been a party."[38] As matters turned out, no such agreement was concluded. If it had been, it would presumably have made specific provision for many of the legal rights to which American nationals were entitled, and the means of affording these rights. Such a convention might not have been very significant, actually, in protecting the rights of citizens in view of the Soviet administrative system but it would have constituted a formal statement—another and a more specific statement than that made by Roosevelt and Litvinov—of the rights of American citizens.

Late in 1963, after years of inactivity, hopes were revived for a Soviet-American consular convention and discussions initiated. It was predicted that there was a very good chance of establishing consulates in Leningrad and either New York or Chicago. A major American objective was a "clause that would promise prompt notification of the arrest of United States citizens in the Soviet Union and access to them by United States officials."[39] It was not clear why such a promise made in 1963 would have much greater validity than the same promise made by Litvinov in 1933—specific violations will be discussed later in this chapter—but, in any case, the hopes were rudely jarred by the Soviet arrest of Professor Frederick Barghoorn of Yale University on October 31 and the Soviet refusal to do either of those things in his case. Nothing more was heard of the proposed consular convention in the months that followed. On March 22, 1964, announcing the Soviet agreement to release three U.S. Air Force officers shot down over

East Germany, Secretary of State Dean Rusk suggested that the way was again open toward new agreements with the Soviet Union, notably on the establishment of consulates in the two countries. A consular agreement between the two governments was signed in Moscow on June 1, 1964, and is now awaiting approval by the United States Senate.

Fortunately from the American point of view, however, no such consular convention was required as a basis for the second method, consular protection of the rights of Americans. Roosevelt and Litvinov had agreed that this protection was to follow "immediately upon the establishment of relations between our two countries," so that this provision took effect automatically. All that was necessary, it appeared, was that normal relations be established, and American consular officials arrive in the Soviet Union with full power to offer protection there as in other countries. In 1932 Kelley had to tell one petitioner that "inasmuch as there are no American diplomatic and consular officers stationed in Russia at the present time, this government is not in a position to render to Americans who may be in Russia the assistance which it ordinarily is able to render to Americans in countries in which such officers are located."[40] Following recognition, however, this would presumably not be true. Almost from the beginning, however, there were difficulties. In April 1934 Acting Secretary Moore wired Bullitt that "for the moment it would seem that only the Consulate at Leningrad should be seriously considered."[41] Three months later, Moore wrote to Assistant Secretary Sayre: "If we are to have any real activity in Russia, there should of course be Consulates established at Leningrad, Odessa, and other points, but this we have discouraged until we have some performance on the promises relative to debts made by Litvinov to the President."[42] It had been decided, apparently, to tie the question of establishment of our consulates to the political question of the continuing unwillingness of the Soviet government to reach an understanding on the debt question. If the Soviet government was, as thought, chiefly interested in American trade, we would not encourage this thinking by trying to establish a number of consulates prior to further settlement of claims.

Nor was the problem of a consulate in Leningrad cleared up. In April 1934 Bullitt wired: "If the Department should desire to open a consular office in Leningrad there are available a 50-room palace in excellent repair, owned by the Leningrad Soviet, and the second floor of the former Italian Embassy, the first floor of which is now used by the Italian Consulate. As yet I have been unable to obtain definite figures for the rental of either of these properties."[43] Later, it was stated that

> at the time of Mr. Hanson's preliminary survey everything was very agreeable with the Soviets. When we got down to definite arrangements they put everything in our way to hold up the proposal. The only building we were able to obtain needed a lot of repair and was offered at an exhorbitant rent. Negotiations over Leningrad and Vladivostok covered a long period of time and we had the same trouble of finding appropriate quarters in Vladivostok. We were only able to open Vladivostok by intimating that we would make the Soviets close down the Soviet Consulate at San Francisco if we could not open in Vlad.[44]

It was thirteen years later, in 1947, before the Department could announce that "the Soviet government has now agreed to the opening of an American Consular office in Leningrad."[45] Before the office was actually opened, however, the Kasenkina incident led to abandonment of the whole proposal. The result was that Moscow and Vladivostok were the only cities in the Soviet Union where American consular offices were ever established.[46]

A more important problem, from the standpoint of protecting American rights, however, came in the regulations that the Soviet government imposed upon the operation of American consular officials. The establishment of consular districts is normally left to the discretion of the government being represented. Early in 1934, however, Bullitt wired the Department that "it will be impossible to organize consular districts in the Soviet Union in accordance with the customary practice of our government. Soviet government refused to allow a Consulate General in Moscow to exercise jurisdiction over the entire Union, and permits Consulates to have jurisdiction only over the place in which they are authorized established and adjacent oblasts."[47] The Soviet government's claim that the general American practice was incompatible with its own usage was interpreted by the American government as a Soviet refusal to allow it to determine the districts of its consular officers in the Soviet Union. The American government thereupon closed its Consulate-General in Moscow on February 6, 1935. As an alternative, the American government established a Consular Section in the Embassy at Moscow which, with Soviet approval, had as its jurisdiction the whole territory of the Soviet Union.

There would probably have been serious difficulties in trying to protect American nationals in the Soviet Union no matter how many consulates we might have been permitted to establish. This problem involves the basic differences of opinion between the two governments as to the rights of individual citizens and the relations between those citizens and their respective governments. The mere presence of consular officials was inadequate for this task, given Soviet regulations on their performance.

In the third place, there was need of access to the American Embassy. Normally an American traveling abroad and faced with deprivation of his rights is likely to turn first to the nearest American Embassy for help. He needs to know just what his rights are under the law of the country where he is, and how these can best be protected. Even when there is no specific problem of arrest or trial, the American citizen is well advised to keep in close contact with his Embassy, especially in countries where the principles of democratic government are not well established. This has particular relevance to the Soviet Union where the Embassy needs to know of the citizen's presence so that he does not just disappear. He, in turn, needs to see that he has in order his passport and such other documents as the local government requires him to possess. Thus the citizen needs to have access to his Embassy in case of trouble. In a totalitarian country where the government controls all forms of communication, the citizen may wish to visit the Embassy in person rather than rely on the mail, telephone, or telegraph services. The important thing, however, is that he have right of access.

We have already seen the case of Sol Drypool who, while in Russia before American recognition, attempted to establish his American citizenship through the American Consulate in Riga. In 1924 the Department of State authorized a passport for him, but he later claimed that he was never allowed to leave the Soviet Union to apply in person for it, as American regulations required. This case involved travel out of the Soviet Union to a nearby American consulate, but even within the Soviet Union access to the Embassy was not always possible.

Thus, at the end of 1939—a critical period in view of the Second World War—the Chief of the Division of Controls in the State Department wrote a memorandum about the case of two American oil companies, some of whose employees were then in the Soviet Union installing equipment. The president of the Lummus Company, for example, had just "received another telegram from the company's engineers at Ufa stating that the Soviet authorities had refused to permit them to leave that city."[48] At the same time Max B. Miller and Co. informed the Department that six of its engineers and their families, then in Grozny, had been refused permission to travel to Moscow to have their passports validated at the Embassy, whereupon the Secretary of State instructed the Embassy in Moscow to

inform the Soviet authorities that this government is requiring all
bearers of American passports in Europe to appear in person at the
appropriate American diplomatic Missions and Consulates . . . to
have their passports validated and that your government is astonished
to learn that the local Soviet authorities are not permitting American
citizens . . . to comply with this government's requirements. You may
add that this government cannot encourage its citizens to continue to
reside in any country the officials of which will not permit them to have
ready access to American diplomatic and consular offices.[49]

The following day, Ambassador Steinhardt reported that, as a result
of continued pressure, the engineers had been granted permission to
go to Moscow but that, after having been promised transportation, they
were now told that none was available. He also declared that statements by Soviet officials were "a deliberate evasion" and a "misrepre-
sentation,"[50] apparently convinced that the Soviet government was
intentionally denying these Americans access to the Embassy. On that
same day, however, he was able to inform the Department that a Foreign Office official "has acquiesced in the principle that the movements
of American citizens within the Soviet Union are not subject to restriction and . . . has assured me that instructions will be issued immediately that all American citizens within the Soviet Union be permitted
to proceed to Moscow at once for the purpose of validating their
passports."[51]

The following month, however, the issue was opened again when
the Ambassador informed Washington that the Soviet government was
now requiring all Americans in the Soviet Union—with the exception
of the Embassy staff, engineers under contract to the Soviet government, and newspaper correspondents—to pay their rail transportation
within the country in American currency. "As many American citizens
do not possess and cannot obtain the substantial amount of American
currency that is necessary this requirement is tantamount to a denial
of freedom of movement."[52]

It is not surprising that the Soviet government, which controls the
movements of its own citizens through a system of internal passports,
should not wish to have foreigners traveling freely through the country, but the tight controls exercised over transportation would seem to
prevent this. The Soviet government claimed in this case that it feared
that these trips to Moscow were just preliminaries to the complete
withdrawal of American engineers from the Soviet Union, leaving a
number of strategically important industrial plants half completed
just when, in view of the European war, they would be needed most.
The Soviet policy almost led to this.

A special aspect of this problem of access to the Embassy arose from Soviet aggression in Poland in September 1939. In 1940 it was believed that there were more than six hundred persons in Soviet-occupied Poland who had claims on American citizenship. But the Soviet authorities refused to permit these people to proceed to Moscow to apply for passport services. Thus, American citizens without passports or whose passports had expired were being deprived of any opportunity to appear at the Embassy and obtain the proper papers at the same time that regulations provided that only American citizens bearing valid passports could be evacuated from this area. "The Embassy is of the opinion that the Soviet authorities are now forcing those American citizens . . . to accept Soviet passports and Soviet citizenship."[53] Some were harassed by Soviet officials who told them that "if they were in fact American citizens, they would be receiving protection from the American government and its representatives."[54] Indeed, prior to August 2, 1940, the Soviet Foreign Office informed the American Embassy that, under regulations issued by the People's Commissariat for Internal Affairs, no non-Soviet nationals in "Western White Russia" and "Western Ukraine" might travel to Moscow to apply for non-Soviet passports, and that no person in these areas, whether Soviet or non-Soviet, might travel to Moscow to apply for an exit visa.[55] On August 2 this statement was modified and the official said he "would endeavor" to obtain permission for travel to Moscow of Americans bearing expired passports who also possess the necessary funds and transportation for their repatriation to the United States.

> When it was brought to his attention on August 10 that the Embassy continued to receive telegrams from the three persons mentioned in my 953 . . . stating that they are unable to receive permission to travel to Moscow he stated that the Commissariat Internal Affairs had thus far not modified in favor of Americans bearing expired passports its basic regulation restricting all travel from these areas to Moscow.[56]

Two months later, a Foreign Office official indicated that these cases were "being examined" and that "those who are not vested with Soviet citizenship will probably be permitted to visit the Embassy."[57] By January 1941, the American government estimated that five hundred of these people had not been allowed to go to Moscow to prove their claims to American citizenship. More than eighty notes on the matter had been delivered to the Soviet government. Ambassador Umansky stated that "unquestionably a great many individuals were claiming American citizenship in order to get to Moscow and that unless there was some reasonable proof that the individuals claiming American citizenship were in fact entitled to a recognition of such claim, the Soviet authorities did not wish great masses of people coming to Moscow without some valid reason."[58] To this, Under Secretary Welles replied that surely the Ambassador must realize that "many of these individuals might have had their papers destroyed by bombardment or in their hurried flight have lost their papers and the mere fact that an individual did not, in view of these circumstances, possess full documentation was by no means an indication that he was not entitled to American citizenship."[59] At one stage in these discussions, in fact, the Under Secretary used this Soviet refusal as an argument against allowing American engineers to return to the U.S.S.R. to erect high-octane gasoline plants: it was not safe there, he said; they were not free to travel.

This was unquestionably an extraordinary wartime situation. The Soviet government's caution might have been understandable except that, in times when no such excuses existed, it had still been unwilling to permit American nationals free access to their Embassy in Moscow. This was not just a "wartime policy."

Right of access to the Embassy implies the use of this right without punishment. For a citizen to be punished for visiting his Embassy, or for him to fear punishment if he does, is essentially to deny the right. Yet this seemed to be the Soviet policy. On July 18, 1938, as we have seen, Elmer Nousiainen, an American citizen possessing dual nationality, visited the American Embassy in Moscow but failed to return to his home afterwards. "It is not known definitely what happened to Mr. Nousiainen and Mr. Ranta but it is suspected that they were detained by the Soviet authorities while in Moscow. Several similar disappearances have recently occurred and it is reliably reported that some of these individuals were arrested and detained by the Soviet authorities after their visit to this mission."[60] Others who were reported to have been arrested, or who disappeared, after visiting the Embassy in 1938 are Ivan Dubin, Michael Aisenstein, Tamara A. Aisenstein, Sam Bess, and Sol Drypool. Eleven others were listed as having been stopped and questioned, though not arrested, on leaving the Embassy. "The number of callers at the Consular Section of the American Embassy in Moscow has declined considerably."[61]

Associated with this denial of access to the Embassy was the Soviet policy of forcing Americans to surrender their passports to the Soviet authorities. One American citizen, working on a Soviet state farm, had an expired residence permit; his hotel director sent his passport to the Grain Trust for a renewal. It was not returned, the Grain Trust denying that it had ever received the document, although it was later safely returned. "Since it is an open secret that the personnel of the Moscow hotels . . . is strictly accountable to the secret police . . . the statement that the passport was lost in the manner described seems somewhat dubious. It is not improbable that the Soviet authorities wanted the use of this passport . . . and simply took this means of obtaining it."[62] One group of American workmen in the U.S.S.R. complained that they had been forced to surrender their passports, which were then withheld; the Soviet answer was that the delay—more than three months— was due to difficulty in obtaining the necessary photographs.

If there was any justification for denying access to the Embassy to those of dual nationality, there was none in the case of those on whom the Soviet government had no claim at all. Again, we see that one of the devices by which American citizens might have their rights protected was undercut by the administration of the Soviet law.

A fourth way to protect the rights of American citizens abroad is through investigations conducted by the Embassy or Consular staff upon request, usually of relatives. This is a particularly useful device in a country such as the Soviet Union where people "disappear," because the Embassy might not otherwise be aware of the presence of the individual being sought. Many of these cases are purely routine, as was Harry Alpert's inquiry in 1937 about his sister, Bessie, last known to be living at a Moscow address which he provided. More than three months later, the Department was told that Bessie Alpert had called at the Embassy the previous September, wanting to return to the United States. She stated that she had applied for Soviet citizenship a year earlier. Two months later the Embassy forwarded a note from the People's Commissariat for Foreign Affairs saying that Bessie Alpert was accepted into Soviet citizenship "in acordance with her own petition."[63] This information was passed on to the inquirer.

A letter from James Henderson inquired about his nephew, William H. Brady, "who supposedly went to Russia or Siberia about 1930 planning to sign up with the Soviet government for three years." Three months later, the Department was informed that the People's Commissariat for Foreign Affairs "has been unable to obtain any information regarding the present whereabouts or fate of Mr. William H. Brady."[64] This news was sent to Henderson, together with the suggestion that Amtorg, which had recruited workers in the United States, might have some information.

Sometimes the Department can be specific and helpful, as in the case of Mrs. Harry C. Cronk who inquired of the whereabouts of her husband, giving his last known address in Leningrad. The Embassy replied: "The Central Address Bureau in Leningrad . . . advised this office that Mr. Harry Cronk is now residing at . . ."[65]

Other cases have a more foreboding aspect, as in the case of Nicholas Comisaroff whose sister in the United States was trying to locate him, on the theory that he was imprisoned in the Soviet Union. The Department was notified that communications addressed by the Embassy to Comisaroff had been returned by the Stalingrad postal authorities with a notation to the effect that the addressee had departed and his whereabouts were not known. Since Comisaroff had replied to past communications from the Embassy and since all persons are required to register a change of address with the Soviet housing authorities, "it is usually assumed that a postal notation . . . similar to that placed on the envelope addressed to Mr. Comisaroff is an indication that the addressee has been arrested by the Soviet authorities . . . it would seem probable that he is in a Soviet prison."[66]

Embassy investigations can do nothing for persons who have adopted Soviet citizenship and little for those about whom no information can be secured. It can be argued that it is necessary for the American government to inform the Soviet government of the former's constant awareness and interest in these cases, but this is of little practical value. It would appear that this procedure is more helpful in providing information to those inquiring than it is in safeguarding the rights of those inquired about.

A fifth protective device resulted from the promise of the Soviet government to notify the American consul "as soon as possible" whenever an American national was arrested. The consul, as we have seen, was to be notified either by a "communication from the person arrested or by the authorities themselves direct." "As soon as possible" was defined in the 1925 German-Soviet agreement as "within a period not exceeding seven times twenty-four hours, and in large towns, including capitals of districts, within a period not exceeding three times twenty-four hours." This seems to be specific and clear, and adequate to prevent American nationals from being swallowed up in Soviet prisons without anyone knowing it. It was surely thought to afford real protection to Americans in danger of losing their rights.

As in the case of the other devices, this hope was to be dashed. It was not, as in the case of access to the Embassy or investigations upon request, a matter of general international law which the Soviet government had never specifically accepted. This was Litvinov's own promise, a promise which he had offered, so far as is known, freely and voluntarily, as an evidence of the good faith of the Soviet government and of its interest in the maintenance of "normal diplomatic relations" with the American government. How did the performance of the Soviet government accord with its promise?

Obviously those of dual nationality will complicate this problem, with the American government maintaining that it has a right to be informed about them and the Soviet government refusing to recognize any obligation to inform the American government about them. We have already mentioned John Arola as belonging to this group. A letter to the American Embassy in Moscow from Arola's wife on December 5, 1938, stated that he had been arrested, reason unknown, the previous June 21. This was the first knowledge of his detention which the Embassy had received. The case of Hjalmar Nordeen has also been mentioned. While the Embassy was pressing its inquiry about him, it was "unofficially but reliably informed" that he had been arrested on November 21, 1937. The Embassy claimed not to be in a position to take action, lest it compromise its informer who was already having trouble with the Soviet government. Eight months later, the Embassy received a letter from a German citizen, stating he had met Nordeen in a Moscow prison and had been asked to advise the American Embassy when possible. Meanwhile, no information of Nordeen's detention came from the Soviet government. The only information on this case which was ever provided by the Soviet government came when a member of the Soviet Foreign Office orally informed a member of the Embassy staff on October 27, 1939, that Hjalmar S. Nordeen had died on October 25, 1938—a year earlier—in one of the northern regions of the Soviet Union.

The case of George Sviridoff is also relevant. On November 24, 1936, Mr. Kliment Sviridoff wrote to the Department with reference to the alleged imprisonment of his son, who wished to return to the United States. On February 12, 1937, the Department requested the Embassy to try to get in touch with George Sviridoff, and inform him that he was presumably entitled to an American passport. The Embassy thereupon sent a registered letter to Sviridoff at Mine 1, Pechorski Camp, Vorkuta. It was known that the letter was received at the mine, but there was no assurance that Sviridoff himself had received it. In June 1937 the Embassy sent an inquiry to the Soviet Foreign Commissariat; no reply was received. In August a second note was sent; in reply the Commissariat stated that it was impossible to establish Sviridoff's whereabouts. Several months later, on April 29, 1938, the Soviet government claimed that Sviridoff was a Soviet citizen, although it offered no evidence to substantiate this bare statement.[67]

It would seem that those who negotiated the agreements in November 1933 should have realized that, again and again, this matter of dual nationality might plague them and embitter relations between the two governments. Lacking this, it would seem that, once this problem had arisen, some supplementary agreement should have been made, so that the thorn would not further infect the sore spot. Since this was not done, we may well conclude that neither government wanted to put itself in the position of admitting an error of judgment or overlapping interpretation, preferring to allow the problem to go unsolved. So far as the American government was concerned, this meant that the rights of some of those claimed as American citizens went unprotected, and the Soviet government won round after round by default. It was a one-sided business, since there were virtually no Soviet citizens—apart from diplomats—in the United States.

But the Soviet government could not always hide behind the question of dual nationality in justifying failure to notify the American government of the arrest and detention of citizens, for there were cases in which no claim of dual nationality was made. The case of Mieczyslaw Roszkowski has been cited in another connection (pp. 95–96). He was not of dual nationality. He was arrested on June 29, 1940, for alleged illegal possession of firearms; the first the Embassy knew of the arrest was August 16, scarcely within the time limit set by the Litvinov promise. In the case of Ivan Hatalowich, the Soviet Foreign Office stated that he had not applied for Soviet citizenship and, upon presentation of an American passport, would be granted a visa to leave the U.S.S.R. When the passport was issued and sent to him, it was returned since he was no longer at that address. On December 7, 1937, the Embassy received a letter from him stating that he had been arrested on November 29. No notification had been made by the Soviet government; this exceeded the Litvinov time limit. More than a year later, the Embassy had still learned nothing of Hatalowich's whereabouts or welfare.

On December 18, 1935, Bruno H. Wuori and four others were arrested for beating a Russian in an argument. On December 31, the Embassy received a letter from Wuori saying that he had been sentenced to one and a half years of imprisonment. No information regarding the arrest of Mr. Wuori was received from the People's Commissariat for Foreign Affairs until April 27, 1936.[68]

The case of Irene Teodozja Pyk was unusual largely because she was already under sentence of death before the American Embassy heard about the case. She later told Ambassador Steinhardt—when the American government tried to ascertain the charges against her—that she had been arrested and sentenced for membership in a student society that favored Ukrainian independence. Thirty-nine other students—not American—had been arrested and, so far as she knew, executed. But no word came from the Soviet government.

Frank Hrinkevich was born in Russia, went to the United States in 1913, and resided there until 1931. He returned to Russia, married a Soviet citizen and later applied unsuccessfully for Soviet citizenship. At the beginning of 1937 he got in touch with the American Embassy to renew his passport. He was supposed to return but failed to. On March 15, 1937, the Foreign Office sent his old passport—it is not clear when they secured it or for what purpose—to the Embassy, asking that it be renewed so that Hrinkevich could be deported. He had been found guilty, it was explained, of having "committed systematic violations of the regulations . . . for residence of foreigners." The Foreign Office was told that Hrinkevich would have to appear in person to renew his passport; no reply. Six months later the Embassy inquired again; no answer. On October 16 the Foreign Office informed the Embassy that Hrinkevich had been arrested on July 19—eighty-seven days earlier. This action produced an explosion within the Department. "This is, in my opinion, a serious matter," wrote George Kennan, "and the handling of it may involve questions of policy. The Soviet government has now violated in two important points the engagements which it at one time appears to have undertaken. . . . It has failed to notify our authorities of the arrest of an American citizen within the time prescribed. It has also orally refused permission for a representative of our Embassy there to visit the arrested citizen."[69]

The case of Arthur Kujala is also relevant. On June 27, 1938, his sister sent a letter to the "Minister of Foreign Affairs" in Washington, saying that her brother had been missing in Russia for a year and that the family would send tickets to bring him home if they could only find out where he was. A month later—more quickly than in most of these cases—the Embassy in Moscow notified the Department that Kujala had written the Embassy on July 21, 1937, inquiring whether money had been received for his assistance and requesting assistance in returning to the United States. The Embassy received no reply to two letters sent to him; in 1938 it addressed a "double registered letter" to his address, but no signature card was ever received by the Soviet postal authorities. On July 22, 1938, the Embassy informed the Soviet Foreign Office of the report of his arrest and asked for information; none was forthcoming until November 13, 1938, when the Foreign Office notified the Embassy that Kujala had been "arrested in 1938 'for reprehensible actions . . . .' Kujala was sentenced to five years in a reformatory labor camp and is now serving his term of detention."[70]

The statement that he had been arrested in 1938 is in error, for the arrest took place on September 23, 1937, but it was only in November 1938—almost fourteen months later—that the Soviet government notified the American Embassy of this fact. Since the maximum allotted under the Litvinov agreement, no matter how remote the place of the arrest, was seven days, the conclusion is inescapable. It also appears that Kujala's offense was not very heinous—not that this would justify the Soviet action in any case; after his deportation from the Soviet Union in 1939, Kujala declared that the only reason for his arrest was that he "didn't have a passport," and it seems that the real trouble was that he did not have sufficient American currency to get his passport renewed.

One cannot read cases such as this without wondering whether the interest of the American government was not almost a "kiss of death." In several cases, about the time the Embassy in Moscow was visited by the person or opened correspondence with him, the Soviet government was alerted and arrest followed soon afterwards. It should be remembered that, at the time of the Great Purge in 1936-38, the Soviet authorities were using any available device to separate foreigners from the native population, and the interest of the American Embassy would focus attention on some who might otherwise be unnoticed. If there is any significance here, the desire of the American government to protect its nationals, far from protecting them, only endangered them.

The last case to be cited on this point involves Mrs. Donald L. (Ruth) Robinson who, it turned out, was not Mrs. Robinson but Mrs. Rubens under false papers. The Embassy was notified on December 8, 1937, by American journalists that they had heard that an American citizen who had been living at the National Hotel in Moscow had been arrested several days earlier. A visit found "Mrs. Robinson" who said that her husband had taken ill and removed to a hospital on December 2. She did not know where he was, and had been told by the hotel manager that he was too ill to be visited. By the next day, "Mrs. Robinson" also disappeared. Inquiry at the Foreign Office elicited nothing; on December 10 a Soviet official hoped to have information "that day." The next day the Secretary of State told Troyanovsky in Washington, "My government and its officials at Moscow do not think it possible for Americans to go into Russia without . . . their movements being known to the Soviet government; and, therefore, the present whereabouts of this Robinson couple is unquestionably known to the officials of the Soviet government."[71] In the next few days the Soviet Foreign Office said half a dozen times that it had no information. By December

16 it was apparent that these Americans had been arrested, but by this time their identity was in question and the case became complicated in several ways. Early in January Mrs. Rubens' identity had been established and the Embassy was instructed to "request information with regard to the present whereabouts of Mrs. Rubens . . . [and to tell the Soviet Government that] this Government desires to be informed of the specific charges under which she is being held."[72] Daily inquiries by the Embassy produced no information, except that a Soviet official said that he could not understand why the American government was attaching so much importance to a woman who had come to the Soviet Union with a fraudulent passport. Loy Henderson of the American Embassy wrote:

> I replied that the case was important not merely because it involved the fate of a person believed to be an American citizen but because it provided an opportunity to the Soviet authorities to demonstrate whether or not they were prepared to accord that degree of cooperation to the American institutions charged with the protection of American citizens abroad as those institutions are accustomed to receive from authorities of other countries. . . . Mr. Weinberg said that this case appeared to be unusually complicated and that the American government should not become impatient merely because it did not receive a prompt reply to its inquiry.[73]

Despite American pressure, it was not until January 17 that the Soviet government admitted that Mrs. Rubens was under arrest. She had been arrested on either December 8 or 9; this was January 17. Litvinov had agreed that when Americans were arrested, the American consul would be notified "within a period not exceeding three times twenty-four hours" in "large towns," and Moscow came within that category. Further, the fact that all of these inquiries and denials were made in Moscow, where Mrs. Rubens had been arrested and where, presumably, she was being detained, only makes Soviet failure to comply with Litvinov's promise more apparent. Whatever the problem over false identity and fraudulent passports, when Mrs. Rubens was arrested she was living at the National Hotel whose director had her passport which clearly indicated that she was an American citizen. Had the Soviet government promptly notified the American government of her arrest and complications developed later, the Soviet government could have emphasized that it had kept its promise. As it was, the Soviet government did not do this, and then tried to take refuge behind the irrelevant complexities of the case.

The Americans arrested in the Soviet Union were a heterogeneous lot, some just on the verge of legality. But, Litvinov had not promised notification just in the case of decent, respectable American nationals who offered no problems either to their own or to the Soviet government; he had made a blanket promise to cover all American nationals, and it should have been presumed in 1933 that those who were likely to be arrested were the very people who were problematical and marginal. It was mainly to protect this type of person that the agreement had been made,[74] and Soviet failure to do this constituted a clear violation of this part of the agreement.

Because the Soviet government did not fulfill its promise, the story of what happened to Americans in the Soviet Union will probably never be fully known. In 1938, Johannes Pfister, a Swiss citizen, reported to the American Legation in Latvia that there were thirty-six American, or former American, prisoners at Ivanov, all sentenced to ten years' imprisonment and sent to Tomsk. The American government had no record of these people and obtained no information from the Soviet government. The people just disappeared, without trace.

There would appear to be one defense for the Soviet government, which was that the "right hand" did not know what the "left hand" was doing. The Litvinov agreement had said that the "Soviet government" would notify American consular officials, but the Soviet government was a complex assortment of many agencies that did not always act in perfect coordination. The American Embassy in Moscow was, by Soviet regulations, restricted to dealings with the Soviet Foreign Office. In saying that the "Soviet government" would notify American officials, Litvinov was really saying that the Foreign Office would provide the notification, which presumed that the Foreign Office would have the facts on which such notification was based. An early Circular Instruction of the People's Commissariat for Foreign Affairs, undated but "apparently issued 1918" stated that "ordinary judicial organs . . . are required immediately to report each case of the arrest of a foreigner and the reason therefore to the People's Commissariat for Foreign Affairs which, in turn, notifies the representative of the country of which the said persons are citizens. Locally, except in Moscow, where there are consuls of a country of which the arrested is a citizen, the consul is immediately and directly informed of the arrest."[75] Article 160 of the Code of Criminal Procedure of the R.S.F.S.R. provided that "if the accused is a citizen of a foreign state, then the copy of the accusatory conclusion shall also be forwarded to the People's Commissariat for Foreign Affairs," though this statement was partly undercut by a proposal of the People's Commissariat for Justice that the

Commissariat for Foreign Affairs be informed "only with respect to those persons detained . . . whose foreign citizenship has been established by appropriate documents."[76]

Apparently, however, this was not always done; a Soviet journal pointed out in 1928 that "in practice, there have been cases where the People's Commissariat for Foreign Affairs was not informed of the arrest of foreign citizens who were even brought to accountability under Articles of the Criminal Code."[77]

The continuing power and growth of the People's Commissariat for Internal Affairs (the secret police) over the lives of Soviet citizens —including all whom the Soviet government chose to classify as its citizens—made extra complications for the People's Commissariat for Foreign Affairs in this connection. In 1935 the Moscow Embassy notified the Department that control of residence and travel of foreigners was being shifted from local executive committees to the local militia (the secret police). Time after time, in response to American inquiries, "the People's Commissariat [for Foreign Affairs] informed the Embassy . . . that it was impracticable to transmit the information concerning . . . citizenship status . . . as the appropriate organs of the Union of Soviet Socialist Republics do not have the information which is of interest to the Embassy."[78] In this statement, "appropriate organs" means the Foreign Office, and it was increasingly apparent that such a sentence really meant that the People's Commissariat for Internal Affairs had custody of the arrested person and information concerning him, but that the Foreign Office could not obtain it. From our standpoint the difficulty was international; for the Soviets, it was internal. In the Sviridoff case cited above, Henderson's memorandum of his conversation with Khaim Weinberg of the Foreign Office notes that: "The People's Commissariat for Foreign Affairs . . . is as a rule unable to obtain information from the People's Commissariat for Internal Affairs regarding the fate or whereabouts of Soviet citizens who have been arrested." In commenting upon this, the Embassy in Moscow pointed out:

> Mr. Weinberg's statement confirms previous statements of other members of the Commissariat to members of the staff of the Embassy to the effect that the Commissariat for Foreign Affairs' failure to furnish information on the whereabouts of arrested Soviet nationals (even though these persons may also be American citizens through dual nationality) is not because it does not desire to cooperate with the Embassy, but because the Commissariat itself is unable to elicit the desired informa-
> Affairs. This factor is of great interest in that it gives an indication
> tion on such persons from the People's Commissariat for Internal

of the impotence of the Commissariat for Foreign Affairs in some phases of foreign relations, as well as an indication of the extent to which the Commissariat for Internal Affairs may effectively control some phases of foreign relations.[79]

Having promised to notify the American government of the arrest of its nationals, the Soviet government was legally obligated to conduct its internal affairs so that it could fulfill its international promise. Had the Soviet government failed to provide notification in one or two cases because of lack of internal coordination, moreover, this would have been understandable; its failure to do so in case after case makes this a very different matter.

This leads to the sixth phase of this problem. The concern of the American government in being notified of arrest and detention, great as it was, was important largely in connection with the ability of representatives of the government to visit and interview those who were being detained. Embassy officials could not hope to visit prisoners when unaware that an arrest had been made, but the chief protection to the citizen came from the visit rather than the notification of arrest. Thus, in his draft for the President to submit to Litvinov, Moore proposed that the "American Ambassador or Consul or anyone designated by either of them shall have the right to interview the accused at any time and in private."[80] Litvinov refused to accept the last three words.

The right to visit a prisoner involves the knowledge of the prisoner's whereabouts. Sometimes in the Soviet Union this is very difficult to ascertain. Dr. Michael Devenis was arrested in Kovno on July 22, 1940. In turn, he was moved to Ukmerge, Vilna, Ust Kozhva, Naryan Mar, and finally to a state cattle farm. Solomon Lozovsky suggested that Devenis was probably no longer under control of Soviet authorities, because of the German military advance in 1941. A month later, on August 15, Ambassador Laurence Steinhardt wrote, "The Commissariat has advised me . . . that it has been unable to obtain any information as to the present whereabouts of . . . Devenis."[81] Two months later, Mrs. Devenis (who had been allowed to return to the United States) informed the Department of State that she had received word that her husband had been removed from Vilna and sent to the Archangel region. Two months more passed, and on December 11, 1941, the Soviet Foreign Office "promised to investigate the question of Devenis' alleged whereabouts and report its findings . . . as soon as possible."[82] On March 27, 1942, it advised the Embassy that Dr. Devenis "had been located in the Ural area and that negotiations for his release were in progress." He was released on May 6 and arrived safely in the United States in September 1942. Thus, these negotiations continued over a period of nearly two years. Even after the Soviet government agreed to release him, almost a year elapsed before he was located and freed. During all of this time, the American government was effectively prevented from having any contact whatever with a man it considered its citizen. Obviously, American officials could not visit or interview him during this period.

If Devenis possessed dual nationality, the same could not be said for Frank Hrinkevich, inasmuch as his application for Soviet citizenship had been refused. As we have seen, eighty-seven days elapsed between his arrest on July 19, 1937, and the announcement of this fact by the Soviet government on October 16. The American request for an interview was refused by the Soviet authorities: "Foreign Office stated orally today . . . that Durbrow, who . . . will arrive this evening in Minsk, may not interview Hrinkevich."[83] In reply, the Secretary of State cabled Ambassador Davies:

> The Department desires that you address to Mr. Litvinov at the earliest possible moment a note stating that you are instructed by your Government to request that permission be granted for a representative of this Government to interview Hrinkevich and asking for an early reply. . . . You may call their attention to the provisions of Art. 11 and the Protocol to Art. 11 of the German-Soviet agreement of October 12, 1925, and to the statement made in Litvinov's letter of November 16, 1933 to the President. . . . You should make it plain, if necessary, that this Government would expect the granting of such permission even in the absence of all written guarantees.[84]

A week later the Department was told that Litvinov had "stated . . . that in his opinion there would be no doubt but what we would have an opportunity to confer with the accused."[85] In 1933 Litvinov promised such an interview unreservedly; in 1937 he thought it would be possible. A formal note sent to the Soviet government on October 25 was acknowledged on November 1, but nothing more. On October 29 the American Ambassador discussed the matter with Litvinov and Stomonyakov; on November 10 the Ambassador again discussed the matter with Stomonyakov (now acting People's Commissar for Foreign Affairs); the next day the Embassy was orally informed that a member of the Embassy might visit Hrinkevich and interview him at once. "Durbrow will proceed to Minsk tomorrow."[86]

On November 16, the Embassy in Moscow informed the Department that two members of the staff had interviewed Hrinkevich at Minsk. This was 24 days after the Embassy had first requested permission to visit him and 12 days after the American Ambassador had first talked with Litvinov about the matter. This means that Hrinkevich was first visited by a representative of his government 114 days— nearly four months—after he was arrested. Litvinov had said that "requests made by consular representatives to visit nationals of their country under arrest . . . shall be granted without delay." "Without delay"—114 days in prison, 65 of them in solitary confinement!!

The interview itself was none too satisfactory. "The circumstances in which officers of our Embassy in Moscow were permitted to interview the prisoner were such as to render the visit largely useless."[87] The representatives of the Embassy were cautioned beforehand by the Soviet authorities that "the interview could be in the Russian language only and that it could not touch upon his arrest, incarceration, and examination."[88] They were not allowed to examine the dossier in the case.

> When asked if he had requested permission to communicate with an American Consular officer, he stated that he did not realize he had that right and the police authorities had not suggested it. . . . The officer of the militia was asked why the Embassy had not been informed within three days after Hrinkevich's arrest. . . . The official stated that he was unable to explain the delay and added that this matter should be taken up with the People's Commissariat for Foreign Affairs in Moscow. . . . The prisoner succeeded in communicating [to the Embassy staff members] that he had been held incommunicado for the first 65 days of his incarceration. He also stated that he had been unaware for the first 60 days . . . of the reasons for his arrest. The Soviet official present at the interview stated to him, "You know now that you are under arrest for having made remarks against the Soviet regime."

The interview lasted for one and a half hours, following which the Embassy officials returned to the local headquarters of the Soviet Foreign Office. They "asked again why the United States government had not been informed of Hrinkevich's arrest within three days. . . . The official was unable to explain this delay and stated that this matter should be taken up with the People's Commissariat for Foreign Affairs in Moscow."[89] The Soviet insistence on holding the interview in Russian was standard practice and did not violate the Litvinov agreement; the presence of a Soviet representative at the interview was specifically reserved in the agreement. Whether such factors prevent an interview with a prisoner from being useful is debatable. A departmental memorandum concluded that an interview such as this "renders largely valueless the assurances given by Mr. Litvinov to President Roosevelt."[90]

The interview between Mrs. Rubens and two representatives of the Embassy demonstrates some of the same features. It lasted an hour and was conducted in the presence of a Soviet investigating magistrate, a brigadier commander of the military tribunal, an officer of the same tribunal who acted as interpreter, and a representative of the Soviet Foreign Office.

> Prior to the interview, the commander informed us that the prisoner was to answer no question until after it had been translated to him and he had given his permission to reply. He also requested that we show him the list of questions which we intended to ask. . . . He stated that the interview was to be limited strictly to questions and answers. I informed him that I could not present him with a full list of questions since we could not ascertain in advance precisely what we may desire to ask. We did furnish him, however, a list of subjects which we intended to discuss.
>
> We were handicapped during the interview by the fact that the commander refused to permit us to ask a number of questions regarding her movements abroad, including those in the Soviet Union; regarding the passports employed by her; and regarding her husband. . . . She failed to answer several questions on the ground that she preferred not to, that her memory failed her or that she did not know the answers.[91]

When asked if there were anything the Embassy could do to make her more comfortable or assist her, she replied, "I am grateful for your offer of assistance but I request you not to try to help me. I intend to stick to my husband." When the Embassy representatives tried to ascertain the nature of the charges against her, the commander intervened, saying that the investigations were not complete.[92] "In general she showed a desire . . . to say nothing to which the commander could take exception and at the same time, apparently did not wish to offend us by failing to cooperate.

> Mr. Ward and I obtained the distinct impression . . . that Mrs. Rubens was under the complete domination of Major Yamnitsky. . . . There was no doubt that she felt it to be in her interest to cooperate with him rather than with us. . . .
>
> We also obtained the impression that Mrs. Rubens thought she was assisting her husband by withholding information from us, by requesting that the American government make no effort to aid her, and by stating that the treatment . . . received from the Soviet authorities was justified.[93]

This contrasts strangely, and impressively, with the practice followed by the American government in December 1938 when M. N.

Gorin, a Soviet citizen, was arrested in Los Angeles. The Soviet Ambassador made his first contact with the American government the day after the arrest. Meanwhile, the Soviet Embassy had been notified and Gorin had already been in touch with the Soviet Embassy in Washington, even before the arrest had been formally made. Charges against Gorin were presented within twenty-four hours. The American government arranged with the authorities in charge of the case for Gorin to have an interview with the Soviet consul at once, specifying that an American official be present and the interview be conducted in English. There is no evidence that such an example had any effect upon subsequent Soviet practice.

In the case of Arthur Kujala the Soviet government attempted to redefine the promise given by Litvinov in 1933. This American citizen was arrested on September 23, 1937, but the Soviet Foreign Office did not notify the American Embassy until November 13, 1938, after he had been given a five-year sentence in a reformatory labor camp. The Embassy immediately began an inquiry into the charges against him, his whereabouts, and when he might be visited by a member of the staff. On November 17 the Foreign Office informed the Embassy that "the People's Commissariat has not failed to request appropriate information from the competent authorities and upon the receipt of a reply the Embassy will be informed without delay."[94] Four "follow-up" notes were sent to the Commissariat on December 13, December 29, January 17, and February 17, without result. On February 8, 1939, during a call on Litvinov, "I brought to his attention the Commissariat's failure to furnish the information desired . . . and he made the same reply as he had made in regard to similar protection cases, namely that the Commissariat was taking every possible step to obtain the desired information but that the actual matters involved were within the jurisdiction of other authorities of the Soviet government."[95] No information was received until April 11 when a Foreign Office official stated orally that Mr. Kujala was in perfect health and that it was probable his case would be reviewed with the idea of suspending the unfinished portion of his prison sentence. "When Mr. Vinogradov was questioned as to Mr. Kujala's whereabouts and the date on which a representative of the Embassy might visit him, he stated, 'I have no information on those points.'"[96] In June 1939 the Department was informed that "notwithstanding two written and several oral representations the Embassy has received neither information regarding Kujula's whereabouts nor permission for a member of the staff to visit him."[97] Later that month, however, following an interview with Potemkin (Assistant People's Commissar), a communication was received which stated that "Kujala was subject to being expelled from the Soviet Union and requesting the issuance to him of a travel document to enable him to depart. . . . The Embassy is requesting an opportunity for an official to take Kujala's application for the renewal of his passport."[98] There was no opportunity to visit Kujala until August 17. Steinhardt wrote: "I interviewed Kujala in the reception room of the People's Commissariat for Internal Affairs. . . . Kujala appears to be in reasonably good health and makes no complaint of the treatment accorded him other than the loss of his liberty."[99]

In 1933 Litvinov had promised that requests to visit detained nationals should be granted without delay; Kujala was first visited by a representative of his government nine months after the Soviet government had notified the Embassy of his arrest, and twenty-three months after his arrest.

This delay was exceeded in the case of Isaiah Oggins who was arrested in February 1939; it was September 1942—forty-three months later and thirty-one months after he had been sentenced—before the Embassy was notified that "no objections perceived to his being visited by a representative of the Embassy."[100] But it was still three more months before the visit was held. And yet—during the same hectic war period—the Soviet government was able to arrange a visit by the Embassy staff to an interned U.S. Air Force bomber crew within two weeks of its arrival in the Soviet Union, and the time would have been even less had the crew not been transferred from one place to another;[101] the Soviet government could move rapidly when it wished.

These flagrant violations of the Litvinov agreement did not go unchallenged. Late in 1939, when Kujala was safely out of the Soviet Union, the Secretary of State instructed the Ambassador in Moscow, at his discretion, "to address a note to the Foreign Office pointing out the apparent violations of the Litvinov pledge . . . and requesting on behalf of your government an explanation therefor. If no explanation is received, or if such is unsatisfactory, the advisability of lodging a strong protest at a later date will be considered."[102] Two days later such a note was delivered to the Soviet government, and on December 22 Molotov made what the American government considered a completely evasive reply. In an earlier note, Molotov said, the People's Commissariat for Foreign Affairs had informed the Embassy that Kujala

> had lived in the Union of Soviet Socialist Republics since 1936 without any documents whatsoever. Therefore, I do not perceive in the actions of the Soviet authorities . . . any departure whatsoever from the

agreement reached in 1933 between the President of the United States, Mr. Roosevelt, and the People's Commissar for Foreign Affairs of the Union of Soviet Socialist Republics, Litvinov. It is entirely obvious that the above-mentioned agreement cannot be extended to persons who are not in possession of proof of their American citizenship. . . . As soon as it had been established that Mr. Kujala was really a citizen of the United States of America the appropriate authorities of the Union of Soviet Socialist Republics not only carried out the above-mentioned agreement but also afforded Mr. Kujala the possibility of leaving for the United States before the expiration of the sentence given him.[103]

It may have been "entirely obvious" to Molotov that the agreement could not be extended to persons not in possession of proof of their citizenship, but Litvinov had made no such specification in 1933; he had spoken of "American nationals" without any mention of whether or not they possessed proof of citizenship. International usage, moreover,—though this may not have impressed the Soviet authorities at all—was on the side of the American government. On December 27, 1939, therefore, Ambassador Steinhardt sent another note to Molotov in which he stated that "the explanation offered in regard to the failure of the Soviet government to notify this mission of the arrest of this American citizen and the failure to permit a member of this Embassy, in accordance with the above-mentioned agreement, to visit Mr. Kujala within a reasonable period of time cannot be regarded as satisfactory."[104] He specifically denied that Molotov had stated the facts of the case correctly, pointing out that the Soviet government had recognized Mr. Kujala's American citizenship in its note of November 11, 1938, but that not until August 1939 was an American representative permitted to interview him, "despite the clear and unequivocal obligation contained in the above-mentioned agreement to grant to this Embassy the right of visit to an arrested American citizen without delay."

In answer to Molotov's argument that the agreement could not cover those not in possession of proof of their citizenship, the Ambassador invited Molotov's attention to the protocol signed on December 21, 1928, at Moscow, between Germany and the Soviet Union, supplementing Article 11 as quoted in the Roosevelt-Litvinov agreement, which provided that "insufficient proof of the citizenship of the person arrested shall not revoke the obligation in respect of notification and right of visit provided thereunder" and calling attention to the fact that American nationals were to be accorded rights no less favorable than those enjoyed by nationals of the most-favored nation. "In the light of the foregoing," Ambassador Steinhardt concluded, ". . . I consider that the actions of the Soviet authorities in the case of Mr. Kujala were not in conformity with either the letter or the spirit of the agreement between the President of the United States and the then Commissar for Foreign Affairs of the Union of Soviet Socialist Republics."[105]

Steinhardt was no more satisfied with Molotov's reply of February 11, 1940, writing that "Molotov reiterates the contentions of the Soviet government . . . and studiously avoids taking cognizance of the specific points emphasized by me."[106] Molotov did, however, shift ground at this point, trying once again to interpret the 1933 agreement to justify the Soviet actions. The Government of the Soviet Union, he maintained, "had never taken upon itself the obligation to grant to the representatives of foreign missions permission to interview their citizens who are serving sentences in conformity with a court decision."[107] The American Ambassador found this new interpretation of some interest. "Under this restricted interpretation of the Litvinov agreement, it would only be necessary for the Soviet authorities, in order to deprive the Embassy of the right of access to American nationals while under detention, to hold a hasty 'trial' and render a court 'decision' before permitting knowledge of the detention to reach the Embassy."[108]

In making this new interpretation, Molotov was only carrying one step further a restriction of the agreement already claimed by the Soviet government. On January 21, 1938, in connection with the Rubens case, the Embassy had been orally informed that the Litvinov promise was worded precisely like the protocol to the German agreement "which had always been interpreted to mean that a representative could visit a prisoner only *after* the investigations had been concluded, that internal authorities permitted the foreign representatives of no country to visit their nationals in prison during the course of investigations and could make no exception with respect to the United States."[109] Two weeks later the Soviet Foreign Office, referring to the protocol to Article 11 of the German-Soviet agreement, stated that "it is clear that the article . . . could not have in view the granting of an interview to the prejudice of the interests of the investigation. The practice prevailing in the Soviet Union provides for granting of interviews only *upon the termination* of such an investigation."[110]

What the Soviet government said in 1938 was that there could be no interviewing of American nationals following their arrest, until the police investigation had been terminated. Since, however, it was Soviet practice to hold the trial immediately after the conclusion of this investigation, no visits by representatives of the American government would be permitted until after the trial was concluded and the sentence passed. In his statement of February 11, 1940, Molotov was trying to establish that the Soviet government had no obligation to permit interviews with persons "serving sentences in conformity with a court decision." Putting these two interpretations together, therefore, we find that the Soviet position was that no visit or interview would be possible until after the sentence had been carried out. Litvinov in 1933 had promised to grant requests "without delay"; by 1940 the Soviet interpretation would make this entirely impossible until after a sentence had been served and the prisoner released. It was to prevent just this possibility that the principle had been established in international law that foreigners are entitled to the protection of their government.

The American government obviously would not agree to this new interpretation of the Litvinov pledge, and on April 19, 1940, the Secretary of State cabled the American Ambassador in Moscow as follows:

Please address a formal note to Molotov in which . . . you should state as follows:

(a) Your government has instructed you to reiterate its refusal, as expressed in the Embassy's note of January 25, 1938, to accept any interpretation of the obligations undertaken by Mr. Litvinov on behalf of the Soviet government, November 16, 1933, which would operate to restrict in any way whatsoever the granting without delay of requests to visit American nationals under arrest. . . .

(b) The failure of the Soviet authorities to notify the Embassy of the arrest of Mr. Kujala, thus rendering it impossible for a member of the Embassy staff to visit him before his trial, and the subsequent failure to permit representatives of the Embassy to visit him after the trial, are regarded by your government as incompatible with the commitments entered into by Mr. Litvinov on November 16, 1933.

(c) Your government will continue to expect that, in accordance with the agreement . . . the Embassy will be notified promptly of the arrest of American citizens in the Soviet Union, and that representatives of this government, upon the request of the Embassy, will be permitted without delay to visit American nationals under arrest in places of detention of all kinds.[111]

The American government experienced these same problems in 1960 in the case of Francis Gary Powers, the U-2 pilot arrested by the Soviet government. On May 10 the Embassy requested "that an officer of the Embassy be permitted to interview Mr. Powers." On July 30 the United States government stated that "the Embassy has made frequent and repeated requests that the Soviet government . . . permit an Embassy officer to interview Mr. Powers" and, on August 9, that

"Powers has been in the exclusive control of the Soviet authorities for 101 days; despite all efforts of this government no one other than his jailers and captors has had access to him." In a press conference on May 12, Khrushchev said that he could not answer the question of access to Powers because "the investigation is proceeding"; no formal answer to the American request was made until August 13 when a Soviet note stated that "the competent Soviet organs consider it possible to solve the question of a meeting of an official of the United States Embassy with F. Powers at the end of F. Powers' trial," thus reiterating the general Soviet position of twenty years earlier, though without insisting on the 1940 Molotov interpretation.[112]

Attention was dramatically focused on this problem in 1963—the thirtieth anniversary of the Litvinov pledge—when Professor Frederick C. Barghoorn of Yale University was arrested on the evening of October 31 in Moscow, taken to Lubyanka prison, and accused of espionage. The American Embassy in Moscow was not notified of his arrest until November 12; by past Soviet standards, this two-week delay was fairly short. The American Embassy made six protests to the Soviet government to no avail. Ambassador Kohler personally visited the Soviet Foreign Ministry, demanding Barghoorn's release and permission for Embassy officials to visit him. On November 15 President Kennedy took a firm—even sharp—attitude toward the situation at his press conference, and next day the Soviet government announced that "in view of the personal concern expressed by President Kennedy," Barghoorn was being released. He was flown to London that afternoon without any U.S. government official having seen or talked with him. The *New York Times* reported that American Embassy officials in Moscow were told that such an opportunity would be afforded, but because of "a misunderstanding over schedules"[113] the meeting did not occur. When Deputy Foreign Minister Zorin—emerging from the Moscow celebration of thirty years of Soviet-American relations—was asked whether there were a Soviet law that prevented an American official from visiting an American citizen in a Soviet jail, he replied, "I do not know. That is a matter for administrative decision."[114] It appears that the Soviet government was pressured into freeing Barghoorn by the tremendous wave of indignation that followed revelation of its action. In most of the other cases, where there was no such outcry and pressure, the results were quite different.

Whatever the expectations of the American government, the Soviet government—having the American citizen in its custody—could do as it pleased and, whatever the legal rights involved, there was very little the American government could do to help itself. In other words, there was very little success in getting the Soviet government to fulfill this part of the Litvinov pledge.

The seventh protective device, the right to a fair, public, and speedy trial, was not specifically mentioned by Litvinov although his statement on the "rights with reference to legal protection" might be interpreted to include this. President Roosevelt, however, was more specific, stating that "American diplomatic and consular officers in the Soviet Union will be zealous in guarding the rights of American nationals particularly the right to a fair, public and speedy trial and the right to be represented by counsel of their choice." Loy Henderson wrote, in connection with the Rubens case, that "the request . . . that Mrs. Rubens be given a trial or be released is based upon our own policy of insisting that American citizens in foreign countries be not punished without trial rather than upon a Soviet treaty obligation."[115]

What constitutes a "fair" trial is a matter of interpretation, and the American government hardly expected that the same legal standards would be applied in a Soviet courtroom as in the United States.[116] The speed of the trial was no particular obstacle, once the Soviet government had concluded its investigations. The American government criticized the length of the investigations, but once these were finished a trial was likely to be held immediately, and ended quickly. The trials were normally public when cases were tried in regular Soviet courts; those handled by the secret police were not.

Certain problems did arise. There was the language problem, for example. Section 22 of the Code of Criminal Procedure of the R.S.F.S.R. provided that "in case the defendant does not have a command of the language in which the trial is conducted, the court must call in an interpreter and keep the defendant informed through the medium of the interpreter of every action taken by the court."[117] Albert Hovi was arrested in November 1936 for having broken a man's arm in an automobile accident. He was brought to trial in May 1937, found responsible for the accident, and sentenced to reformative labor for one year and a deduction of 25 per cent of his wages during that period. When the American Embassy later discovered that he had been arrested and tried, it conducted an investigation. When Hovi was asked, "Did you understand the court proceedings?" he replied, "I understood the proceedings of the court not very perfect for it was translated in Finnish, which I do not understand perfectly."[118] It is possible that the Soviet officials were trying to be helpful, in holding the trial in Finnish since it occurred in the Karelian A.S.S.R. where this language was generally understood. Such an assumption, however, would afford poor comfort to the prisoner.

President Roosevelt specified that American nationals brought to trial would have the right to be represented by counsel of their choice. Soviet law provided that only Soviet lawyers were available. The English engineers, said *Izvestia* at the time of the Metropolitan-Vickers case (see Chapter VII, pp. 203–05), "are entitled to engage as counsel any member of the body of legal defenders whom they may choose or any other specified in the law. According to our laws, foreign lawyers cannot appear as counsel for the defense."[119] During the antiforeign campaign of the Great Purge period, a Soviet lawyer was not likely to be very zealous in his defense of a foreigner accused by the Soviet government. Actually, even this provision was not always honored. When Albert Hovi was questioned about his trial, he was asked "Were you represented in court by an attorney?" and he answered, "I was not represented by an attorney in court, because it was difficult to get an attorney to my trial which was held a distance from the city of 'Petrosavodsk.' Also I did not have a chance to afford an attorney."[120]

Bruno H. Wuori and four others were arrested on December 18, 1935, for beating up a Russian in an argument. On December 31 he wrote the Embassy that he had been sentenced—there was no lack of speed here—to one and a half years of imprisonment. In his statement to the Embassy, Wuori said, "I didn't have anyone to represent me, not even a reliable interpreter."[121]

In 1960 in the Powers trial, the Soviet government assigned a member of the Moscow City Lawyers' Collegium to defend Powers and refused to allow American attorneys to participate in the trial, although it did agree to let members of Powers' family meet with Griniv, the Soviet lawyer.

The worst example of a trial, apparently, came in the Kujala case. The trial lasted less than five minutes; the accused was asked to give his name, nationality, and occupation, whereupon he was given a five-year sentence. This did not even meet the standards of Soviet law.

Despite certain aspects of the Rubens case that weakened the position of the American government, the latter pressed for a trial of the prisoner.

> I feel that we should no longer postpone making at least an informal request that she either be brought to trial or be released. It would seem that after a period of more than one year the investigation of her case should be almost completed. . . . It would be a bad precedent for the American government to permit, at least without a strong display of interest, an American citizen who has not been tried or against whom no formal charges have been made, indefinitely to remain in the prison of a dictatorial country.[122]

She was brought to trial four months after Embassy officials were permitted to interview her. The trial lasted about forty-five minutes; she was asked in what language she would plead and chose English; when the judge asked whether she acknowledged her guilt, Mrs. Rubens inquired "her guilt of what," to which the judge replied her guilt of the charge that she had entered the Soviet Union illegally. After a fifteen-minute hearing, the judges retired, returning half an hour later to announce that since she admitted her guilt, Mrs. Rubens was sentenced to eighteen months' deprivation of liberty. The commencement of this sentence was set at the time of her arrest, so the sentence would be completed the day after the trial. "The trial which was attended in addition to Ward and myself by all the American as well as several of the French and British correspondents in Moscow was conducted throughout in a businesslike manner."[123] The right to trial, then, offered some problems but much less difficulty than several of the other devices used to protect the rights of Americans in the Soviet Union.

Nothing was said in the Roosevelt-Litvinov exchange about the Soviet government's practice of refusing to permit people to leave the country, listed as an eighth means of protecting the rights of American nationals. If Arthur Kujala were arrested and sentenced for not possessing the proper documents, he faced a lifetime of prospective arrests unless he were willing to accept Soviet citizenship or unless, as happened in this case, the American government were able to persuade the Soviet government to permit him to leave the country. By its system of exit visas, the Soviet government is able to prevent anyone— foreign or otherwise—from leaving the country until it is willing for them to do so. The Instructions of the People's Commissariat for Internal Affairs of the R.S.F.S.R. in 1923 provided that visas for departure might be refused:

> (a) in case of non-fulfillment of various kinds of compulsory duties and of non-payment of taxes, until their fulfillment or payment;
> (b) in case the applicant for visa for departure is under trial or if an investigation takes place against him;
> (c) in case of non-compliance with the rules established by the regulations.[124]

This looked quite simple—except for the third part of the statement which, like so many Soviet regulations, meant everything or nothing— but it has not seemed to be so. At any rate, a great many Americans have been refused permission to leave the Soviet Union at one time or other, and their detention within that area has been as complete as if they were detained in a cell-block. What protection of the legal rights of Americans is there really when a man is interviewed by his consul or given a speedy, fair trial only to be refused the right to leave the country where these problems continue to exist?

Just after the Second World War opened, for example, Under Secretary Sumner Welles said that the Department would give sympathetic consideration to passport applications by American engineers desiring to go to the Soviet Union, when the Department was convinced that their work there would be advantageous to the United States or helpful to American-Soviet relations. "This decision was based on the understanding that American citizens in the Soviet Union would be free to visit the American Embassy at any time or to leave the Soviet Union when they desired to do so."[125] Experience had shown, in other words, that Americans were not free to leave the Soviet Union when they chose, even though their presence there had been to the economic advantage of the Soviet government. At about this time, the American Ambassador in Moscow considered this a sufficiently important problem to

> venture to suggest that the Department consider the desirability of advising American citizens who may hereafter contemplate entering into contracts which require their presence or that of any current employees in the Soviet Union to include a clause providing that the individual may depart from the Soviet Union at any time that the Embassy, acting on instructions from the Department, advises all Americans to depart from the Soviet Union, any provision containing a fixed period of time to the contrary notwithstanding.[126]

The Ambassador later suggested that passports good for travel in the Soviet Union should not be issued to American citizens other than Foreign Service officers and newspaper correspondents. Among the reasons given for so drastic a curtailment were "the difficulties encountered by the Embassy in maintaining contact with American citizens within the Soviet Union; the failure of the Soviet authorities to reply with reasonable promptness to communications and inquiries concerning the welfare or whereabouts of American citizens, and the present extreme difficulty of obtaining exit visas and the possibility of a refusal to issue the same or of delay tantamount to refusal."[127]

Reference has already been made to the large number of Americans caught up in eastern Poland in September 1939 with the entry of Soviet armed forces. If most of these people were prevented from having access to the American Embassy in Moscow, they were also prevented from leaving the Soviet Union and returning home. Ambassador Steinhardt reported to the Department that after he had taken up a dozen questions, including this one, with Lozovsky and had "told him bluntly that I would oppose any further concessions in Washington until the Soviet government had given tangible evidence of its appreciation of those already granted by removing the grievances,"[128] the Soviet attitude changed. On November 29, 1940, accordingly, Steinhardt informed the Department that thirty-eight Americans in the Lwow area had been permitted to depart for the United States. There were another five hundred cases, however, on which no action had yet been taken.

This inability of Americans to leave the Soviet Union became worse rather than better after the Second World War. In 1947 the United States government called

> to the attention of the [Soviet] Embassy . . . [the case] of persons in the Soviet Union who, notwithstanding all their personal efforts and the repeated representations of the American Embassy in Moscow, have not been permitted to leave the Soviet Union for the United States. The first category consists of persons with claims to American citizenship who have been forcibly removed to the Soviet Union from various countries of eastern Europe. All efforts of the American Embassy to obtain permission to interview these people with a view to establishing their American citizenship and arranging for their return to the United States have been fruitless.[129]

In December 1949 the Department of State estimated that there were two thousand American citizens in the Soviet Union.

> Of the thirteen American citizens documented by the Soviet government as stateless persons, only one had been granted permission to depart. Of the 20 American citizens who are considered to have been erroneously declared to be Soviet citizens by the Soviet government, only 3 have been permitted to depart. Of the approximately 2,000 persons having claim to American citizenship, including minor children unable to join surviving parents now residing in the United States and women who are being kept apart from husbands or children now living in the United States, only one woman has been granted departure permission. Of the 32 U.S. citizens detained at forced labor, 23 have been allowed to depart for Eastern European countries but there is no indication that they will be permitted to proceed to the United States.[130]

It was not that the Soviet government was occupied with other matters and did not find time to issue exit visas to these people. The Embassy noted that "repressive measures of a serious nature, including administrative fines, arrests, and discrimination with respect to employment, have been taken recently against American citizens attempting to obtain Soviet exit permits for return to the United States."[131] The Soviet government refused permission for American diplomats to travel to many parts of the country as well as for these people to travel to Moscow to visit the Embassy; many were afraid to communicate with the Embassy by mail or telephone, and even those who lived in Moscow were often dissuaded from visiting the Embassy. Many of these people, refused permission to leave the Soviet Union, were certainly forced to accept Soviet citizenship; had they continued to live there without opportunity to renew their American passports, they would be violating the Soviet laws and subject to imprisonment; they had little option.

In one way, the American government may have been fortunate in being unable to obtain exit visas for all of these persons, for there was mounting evidence that many of those allowed to leave the Soviet Union did so because of potential usefulness to the Soviet government. We have cited the case of Albert Hovi who was imprisoned in 1937/38. Not long after termination of his sentence, he was arrested in Helsinki on a charge of espionage for the Soviet government. When interviewed by the American Vice Consul, Hovi reported that the agents of the G.P.U. had told him that his mother would be exiled and that his step-father was already in prison; he consented to help them. "It is believed," stated a departmental memorandum on this case, "that that part of the testimony relative to espionage on behalf of the Soviet Union is, in general, true. The Embassy in Moscow has on various occasions reported incidents in which American citizens, arrested or detained by the Soviet authorities for some minor offense, have been asked to act as Soviet agents abroad."[132] Later, Hermann R. Habicht, a newsman who stayed on in Moscow in an effort to obtain exit visas for Mrs. Habicht and two children, disclosed to the Embassy that "he has been approached on three separate occasions during the past six years by the GPU to return to the United States and act as one of their agents there, and it was intimated to him three years ago that if he would acquiesce in this proposal an exit visa would be granted to his wife. He expressed the opinion that his wife's arrest had resulted from his rejection of the GPU's proposal."[133]

This Soviet policy was apparently not applied only in isolated cases. The Embassy in Moscow notified the Department in 1940 that one of the more intelligent applicants for a visa had experienced trouble in obtaining a Soviet exit visa.

> The applicant stated that he was in considerable disfavor with the local authorities . . . in Soviet occupied Poland because he had refused to accept repeated offers from them to issue to him the desired

exit visa and to facilitate his departure from the Soviet Union . . . and even to pay him substantial and regular compensation in the United States provided he would sign an agreement to undertake espionage work in the United States. He said the Soviet authorities had told him they were not granting permission to anyone to leave the Soviet Union unless the individual gave an undertaking to the foregoing effect and that he was foolish to refuse if he really wished or hoped to leave the Soviet Union.[134]

"This is the first information which the Department has received," wrote the Under Secretary of State to President Roosevelt, "that places under suspicion all persons emigrating from the Soviet Union to this country."[135]

In 1941, during the discussion on getting Lithuanian refugees into the United States, the American Ambassador in Moscow reported that one of the refugees "stated categorically that from 10 to 20 per cent of all these individuals have been and are being solicited by the . . . [GPU] to act as its agents after their arrival in the United States. Hafftka attributed the delays . . . in the issuance of Soviet transit and exit visas . . . to the slow process of selection by the GPU of the individuals it desired to solicit and to the necessity in many cases of 'working on' the individuals before they could be induced to accede to the GPU proposals."[136] Ambassador Steinhardt further pointed out that "the fact that relatives of applicants are already in exile or prison creates a reasonable assumption that many of the applicants have obtained their Soviet visas after agreeing to cooperate with the GPU on their arrival in the United States or, in any event, that they are particularly vulnerable to future pressure."[137] The American government viewed this situation so seriously that the Secretary issued a Circular Telegram in June 1941 stating that "the Department considers that both immigration and nonimmigration visas should be withheld for all aliens having close relatives still residing in territories controlled by . . . [Germany, Italy, Russia] if it is believed that such applicants may be induced through such threats to act as agents."[138] This same problem must have continued in recent years.

It was a complex situation: at the very time that we were trying to free many American citizens from the areas controlled by the Soviet government, we were forced to be wary of the presence of security risks among those who did obtain permission to leave.

CONCLUSIONS

The Soviet government was more directly violative of this part of the Roosevelt-Litvinov agreements than the parts already discussed.

Not only were the instances more numerous, but the violations were more flagrant. The Soviet government did not even attempt to justify its action in certain situations but just kept silent. Its attempts to reinterpret the agreement on two occasions would also seem to demonstrate Soviet awareness of the need for strengthening its position.

The American government should perhaps be held somewhat responsible for the fact that its citizens were not given better protection. When six British engineers were arrested in 1933, the British government made such strong representations that it was generally admitted that the Soviet government had not only been surprised by the British reaction but had been forced to retreat in the face of it.[139] Rarely was the American policy so aggressive. The Barghoorn case was an exception, and perhaps the satisfactory results were in direct proportion to the pressure applied. Inquiries were certainly made, at times repeatedly and forcefully. At other times, however, the Department needed to be prodded into action. Devenis was arrested on July 22, but it was not until December 14 that the Department established that he was entitled to the protection of the government. The following year, on August 15 the Commissariat for Foreign Affairs stated that it had no information of Devenis' whereabouts; nothing was done until October when Mrs. Devenis, in the United States, forwarded word about her husband's location; in December the Foreign Office was still promising to investigate the whereabouts; and it was March 1942 before he was located. In the case of Edward Barr, his mother wrote the Department in October 1934; the Embassy wrote to Barr and nothing happened; the mother wrote again in May 1937, still trying to locate her son. On November 22, 1941, the Soviet authorities announced the arrest of Edward H. Speier in Vladivostok; it was November 19, 1942, before the Department had verified the fact that Speier was an American citizen and was entitled to protection. This was nine months after his trial and sentencing. In the Speier case, one Department instruction was sent by pouch not telegram and took two months to reach Vladivostok by which time Speier, now serving his sentence, had been transferred.[140] Admitting that the United States government was mainly concerned with the war effort in 1942, it is not clear that this is sufficient justification for such inaction.

Most of the trouble, obviously, was not the fault of the American but the Soviet government. There is no better example than the case of Robert Petty, who had been employed by the Soviet government as a petroleum expert. When several of his associates were arrested, Petty decided to return to the United States. On October 2 he called at Burovitz (the Moscow office that handled visas), was given a receipt for his American passport, and told to return on October 7. On October 7 he returned, was told to come back on the 10th; on the 10th he returned, was told to come back on the 20th; on the 20th he was told to come back on the 25th; on the 25th, come back on the 29th; on the 29th, come on November 3. Meanwhile he had called twice at the American Embassy which had sent a note to the Foreign Office and was now making daily telephone inquiries. On November 3 the Chief of the Consular Section of the U.S. Embassy went to Burovitz—the passport would be ready on the 10th. When the American official asked for an interview with the head of Burovitz, he was told that Burovitz would know the following day, November 4, when the passport would be ready; on the 4th, an American Embassy clerk was told that the 5th might be impossible but the 9th, "without fail." On the 9th it was not ready "due to the holidays," but it was actually delivered in the late afternoon of November 10th, following a call on the Acting Commissar of the Foreign Office by the American Ambassador. It is not strange that Petty, meanwhile, had taken to drinking large quantities of vodka; when the Soviet government refused to continue to pay his hotel bills during this long wait and after the secret police had told him that he was being held to testify against a former fellow-employee in an espionage case, Petty struck the Soviet official. This makes it surprising that he was allowed to leave the Soviet Union at all. This long, exasperating delay was caused by failure of the Soviet government to affix a stamp on an American passport.

It is not certain just what the American government could have done in these cases. Written communications, personal calls, and protests were of no avail. On one occasion the Embassy failed to act lest it compromise its informer who was already having difficulty with Soviet authorities. On two occasions it feared to issue a strong protest lest it anger the Soviet officials who would only resort to further delay or other charges against the citizen involved who might, then, never receive permission to leave the Soviet Union.

The frustrated anger of the American Embassy officials who had to deal with the Soviet officials under such trying conditions was often apparent. Perhaps there is no better way to end this chapter than to quote the statement prepared by Ambassador Steinhardt, reviewing the Kujala case after this man was safely out of the Soviet Union. This case, wrote the Ambassador,

> represents so flagrant a violation of the agreement between the United States and the Soviet Union . . . and of generally accepted principles of international law . . . that the Department may wish to give consideration to the advisability of making formal representations to the

Soviet government . . . with the object of endeavoring to extract an explanation and perhaps an apology for the course pursued by the Soviet authorities.

. . . The Soviet authorities might exercise greater care in the future before arresting American citizens and holding them incommunicado for months or even years by reason of a strongly worded protest. . . .

It is doubtful that a more brazen case could be found on which to base a formal protest. There are several elements in the Kujala case which are most unlikely to be found in combination in any single case. . . .

1. Kujala is a native-born American citizen; there can be no quibbling arising out of naturalization, loss of citizenship, or dual citizenship.

2. The Soviet authorities were well aware . . . that Kujala was an American citizen at the time of his arrest for his American passport had been previously repeatedly exhibited to the officials who caused his arrest. . . . The monthly residence permits issued to Kujala by these same authorities were . . . issued to him on the grounds of his possession of an American passport.

3. The failure to deliver or at least transmit through the mails Kujala's three letters to the Embassy was deliberate, for otherwise at least one of the three letters would have reached the Embassy. The suppression of these letters is indicative of the knowledge of the Soviet authorities that they held an American citizen . . . and had not only failed to notify the Embassy within the requisite period of time but went further and refused to permit Kujala to advise the Embassy that he was under detention.

4. Neither Kujala nor the Embassy has at any time been advised either formally or even informally of the charge on which Kujala is said to have been arrested, convicted and sentenced. . . .

5. The so-called trial . . . was travesty of justice and did not conform to Soviet statutory requirements. . . .

6. The People's Commissariat, as recently as two weeks ago, informed the Embassy that it had no knowledge of Kujala's whereabouts. As Kujala stated that he was brought to Moscow and confined about two months ago, it must be assumed that either the Soviet internal authorities kept the Commissariat for Foreign Affairs in ignorance of Kujala's whereabouts or the Commissariat deliberately misinformed the Embassy. . . . In the light of the unsatisfactory results obtained by the Embassy in connection with inquiries regarding other American citizens who have been under arrest in the Soviet Union, it would appear that little credence can be attached to statements from the Commissariat with regard to the whereabouts of arrested Americans. . . .

It is my opinion that if the Department desires to avoid further [such] cases . . . we should not allow the opportunity afforded by the Kujala case to pass without a vigorous protest implying that any like occurrence will have serious consequences, including a demand for indemnification, and that the United States government will not be satisfied with the mere release of one of its citizens after he has served a term of imprisonment apparently with no reason whatsoever in flagrant violation of the agreement between the two countries.[141]

American diplomats repeatedly stated that Americans were not treated worse than others by the Soviet leaders. If the Litvinov promise was repeatedly violated, our people were still better off than some others.[142] The continuing, varied violations, however, and not the fact that other governments' citizens were treated worse than ours, were paramount in shaping American-Soviet relations during this period. Having recognized the Soviet government late, we had hoped to safeguard ourselves against this sort of thing. We did not. "We can . . . bear this in mind," wrote Loy Henderson in Moscow, "when evaluating the statements sometimes made that the Soviet government desires to have genuinely friendly relations with the great democratic countries, including the United States."[143]

CHAPTER V

Soviet Debts

One of the most acute problems between the two governments was that of the Soviet government's debts. This held widespread interest in the United States because it involved the government itself, a number of American corporations and their stockholders, and a considerable number of private American citizens, all of whom had suffered losses through the conduct of the Soviet government. The problem was basically legal, but in a larger sense it was political and psychological, since it involved the American belief in the sanctity of private property. Few Americans knew much in 1933 about the history of the Soviet system, but its violation of private property was known to more people than any of its other activities.

The Tsar's government (as we have seen in Chapter I) was replaced in March 1917 with the Provisional government which, in turn, gave way to Bolshevist control on November 7. On January 28, 1918, the new Soviet government repudiated the debts owed by its predecessors:

> (1) All State loans concluded by the governments of the Russian landowners and the Russian bourgeoisie enumerated in a list which is being especially published are annulled (annihilated) as from December 1, 1917.
>
> (2) In the same manner are annulled all guarantees given by the said governments of the loans of various enterprises and institutions.
>
> (3) All foreign loans are annulled unconditionally without any exception.[1]

In so doing, it sloughed off an indebtedness of approximately twelve billion rubles, of which seven billion were war loans and the remainder were bonds issued or guaranteed by the Imperial Russian government. There was some initial uncertainty about the repudiation. On January 26, 1918, Ambassador Francis telegraphed: "Apparently repudiation national debt not absolutely decreed. . . . Assistant Commissaire Foreign Affairs now says repudiation is a law 'but its enforcement in hands of Council of Commissary' this evidently means that commissaries authorized to withhold enforcement of law if creditors recognize Soviet government and extend further assistance."[2]

The repudiation was followed by a series of decrees nationalizing private property in the Russian Socialist Federated Soviet Republic which included the area in which most foreign interests were located, which led to the statement that the Soviet leaders inherited all of the assets of their predecessors but none of the liabilities. It was apparent that this revolutionary regime was unwilling to honor the generally accepted principles governing the conduct of nations: "Among these principles is the duty of . . . a Government to honor the financial obligations contracted by a State under preceding Governments."[3] This confiscation constituted one of the chief bases for refusal of the United States to recognize the Soviet government before 1933. When the question of recognition was faced, this problem of repudiated debts and confiscated property was vital.

THE DEBT SITUATION

Direct commercial relations between the United States and Russia had not been very important before the First World War. Hence, American claims were small compared with those of other governments, especially the French and British. The debts were divided among the major creditors, as follows:

TABLE 1[4]
PRINCIPAL DEBTS OF THE RUSSIAN GOVERNMENTS

	Prewar Government	Industrial	War Debts
Great Britain	14%	25%	70%
France	80	32	19
United States	—*	6	7
Belgium	—	15	—
Germany	—	16	—

*Approximately $2,600,000 of "4% Rentes of 1894" had been purchased by Americans.

So far as the United States was concerned, there were three kinds of debts: to the United States government which held obligations of Russian governments; to American nationals who held Russian government securities; and to American corporations and nationals who had owned property in Russia. The Department of State in 1933 estimated that American losses from repudiation and confiscation were as follows:

TABLE 2[5]

AMERICAN CLAIMS AGAINST THE SOVIET GOVERNMENT

I. Russian Government obligations held by government of United States	
A. Obligations of Provisional Government, representing cash advanced under Liberty Loan Acts	$187,729,750.00
B. Other Obligations	
1. Obligations received on account of sales, surplus war material	406,082.30
2. Obligations received on account of relief supplies furnished	4,465,465.07
TOTAL	$192,601,297.37

II. Russian Government obligations held by American nationals	
A. Loans floated in the United States	
1. Imperial Russian Government external loan (5 year) issued . . . on November 18, 1916; . . . 5½%	25,000,000.00
2. Imperial Russian Government 3-year credit . . . ; offered June 18, 1916; 6½%	50,000,000.00
3. Russian Treasury notes purchased by National City Bank, April 1916, 5% (later 6%)	11,000,000.00
TOTAL	$86,000,000.00
B. Loans floated elsewhere—chiefly domestic War Loans sold by Russian Government in United States	
1. Bonds of 5½% war loan of 1915-16	12,802,598.24
2. Bonds of Liberty Loan of 1917	5,138,016.31
3. Bonds of Loan of 1894	2,614,025.70
4. Miscellaneous issues of Russian bonds	329,517.50
TOTAL	$20,884,157.75

III. Confiscated property rights and interests of American nationals	
A. Properties and assets of American concerns and real and personal property of individuals confiscated by Soviet authorities	115,141,931.03
B. Bank deposits confiscated	209,825,348.82
C. Debts of Russian Government to private concerns	2,667,281.14
D. Miscellaneous claims	9,057,210.04
TOTAL	$336,691,771.03

This totalled $636,177,226.15 but the State Department estimated that on March 1, 1933, the total, including interest, was $771,159,000.15. Some of these totals were only estimates on the basis of claims known to the Department. Thus in the case of confiscated property (Item III) 750 cases of alleged claims had been reported by October 1933. Of these, the National City Bank had eleven claims for losses resulting from the operation of its branches in Russia totalling $180,000,000. In 1933 it was judged that the recoverable value was about $36,000,000 and in 1927 the President of the Bank had offered to accept $24,000,-000, payable in installments, to settle the whole claim. It was hard to know the worth of the claims.

More than half of the total loss—$336,691,771.03—had been suffered by American firms and nationals whose property, including bank deposits, was nationalized. The largest losses reported to the Department by October 1933 included:[6]

TABLE 3
PRINCIPAL AMERICAN CORPORATE LOSSES

Singer Mfg. Co., and Its Russian subsidiary	claim:	$38,556,000
International Harvester Co., a Russian subsidiary	loss:	40,940,815
National City Bank	claim:	180,108,025
New York Life Insurance Co., Russian-chartered subsidiary	claim:	67,347,479
Equitable Life Assurance Society	claim:	9,968,000
Guaranty Trust Co.	loss:	1,669,673
Vacuum Oil Co. (owned 95% of Russian subsidiary)	claim:	1,650,000

Other American corporations did not report their losses.

Two corporations—International Harvester and International General Electric—offered interesting exceptions to the general rule. The International Harvester Company was allowed to retain possession of its plant. At the time of nationalization in June 1918, Colonel Robins was negotiating with Lenin about American economic aid to the new regime; Lenin exempted American property from the decree. George Romney, Vice President and Treasurer of the International Harvester Company, said in June 1923, "The Soviet authorities did not nationalize our factory, but they did take over the Narodny Bank which, in effect, nationalized our customer. . . . Of late, they have been crowding us to put more money into the business which we have declined to do."[7] This Soviet attitude seems based on a desire to facilitate the operation of a factory that produced essential agricultural implements. In 1924 the company withdrew its managing personnel because of unsatisfactory conditions.

> The works at Lubertsy were taken over and a receipt given the Company's representatives before their departure. The decision to take over the works followed the refusal of the Company to consider any negotiations about the works unless its property rights were first conceded. The Soviets wanted the Company to take a lease of its own property and furnish the capital needed to keep the works. . . . The words *"nationalization," "requisition," "confiscation"* were avoided. The verbal explanation was that such important works could not be allowed to lie idle.[8]

The International General Electric Company owned forty thousand shares of Russian General Electric. Nationalization of this company led to a claim of approximately $1,850,000, but on October 9, 1928, in a special arrangement, Amtorg—the Soviet agency in New York—agreed to buy $5,000,000 to $10,000,000 worth of goods from International General Electric within the next two years, with a cash payment before shipment of 25 per cent and the balance covered by trade acceptances falling due within five years. On the satisfactory completion of the first two years of the contract, Amtorg agreed to purchase at least $4,000,000 worth of goods a year for four more years, so that General Electric's total sales would surpass $25,000,000. Interest at $9\frac{1}{4}$ per cent would compensate for the claim against the Soviet government. As Clark Minor, President of the Company, said, "Provision is made upon the completion of this contract for the settlement of all claims of our Company against the Soviet government arising from decrees and actions of that government with regard to the nationalization or annulment of property rights relating to our interests in Russia."[9]

The largest single item in Table 2 is $209,825,348.82 of confiscated bank deposits. The value of these deposits was uncertain. Several American concerns had more than 30,000,000 rubles of deposits because of foreign exchange restrictions in force before November 1917. Many of these rubles had been purchased at two to a dollar; with the declining value of the ruble, their value in 1933 was not clear. Some settlements were made at the rate of seven to a dollar.

Whatever the uncertainties, the amount owed to the American government and its nationals was large, especially in a depression period. Thousands of citizens were directly concerned with the possibilities of payment of the private claims, and all taxpayers were interested in the payment of amounts owed to their government. But the Soviet government had an important share in this controversy, too.

Soviet statements on the debt situation were varied and confusing, designed to upset the creditors, with gloom and hope alternating, and thus obtain maximum benefit for the Soviet government. On January 22, 1919, President Wilson invited all political and military groups in Russia to send representatives to Prinkipo, in an effort to solve the intervention problem; on February 4 Chicherin, the Soviet Foreign Affairs Commissar, accepted by radio, noting that the Soviet government "did not refuse to recognize its financial obligations to its creditors who were subjects of the Entente powers."[10] Early in 1919 Litvinov and Vorovsky (the Soviet representative in Stockholm) stated that "in order to work out its economic order, Russia needs the . . . material assistance that other countries can offer. For this reason, in case there is agreement with the Allies, the Soviet government would be ready to revise its decrees as concern the foreign obligations of Russia toward other countries without . . . in any way violating the fundamental principles."[11] Whether such a sentence meant anything was not certain. A similar statement was given Bullitt who, after the failure of the Prinkipo Conference, went to Moscow to confer with Lenin and returned to the Paris Peace Conference with a proposal that the Soviet government guaranteed to accept. By April 10, 1919, the Allied and Associated governments suggested a conference with the Soviet government: "The Soviet governments . . . shall recognize their respect for the financial obligations of the former Russian Empire, to foreign parties to this agreement and to the nationals of such States." But again there was a qualification: "detailed arrangements for the payment of these debts to be agreed upon at the Conference, regard being had to the present financial position of Russia," and the United States government was to "take over all Russia's obligations to European powers and cancel a corresponding volume of Allied debts to the United States."[12] Since the rapid advance of the White armies at that time made the fall of the Soviet government appear inevitable, the Paris Conference ignored this proposal.

Chicherin's letter to Lloyd George when the Genoa Conference opened on April 10, 1922, stands out as the "high spot of Soviet concessions" on the debt situation; the Soviet delegation waived Russian counterclaims, refused to pay war debts, and agreed to pay the Russian government loans to foreign nationals. However, the waiving of the counterclaims and the payment of the prewar debts were contingent upon the granting to the Soviet regime of large credits, and formal de jure recognition. The Soviet offers were usually accompanied by enormous bills of counterclaims because of the Allied intervention and blockade—that presented at the Genoa Conference was for twenty-five billion dollars.

The experience with Germany was enlightening. The victorious Germans inserted a provision in the Brest-Litovsk Treaty that "each contracting party . . . will immediately upon the ratification of the Peace Treaty, resume payment of its obligations, especially payment of public obligations to the nationals of the other party." On August 27, 1918, this was replaced with a Supplementary Financial Agreement whereby the Soviets would pay an indemnity of six billion marks. On November 13, two days after the armistice, a Soviet decree repudiated Brest-Litovsk. In the Rapallo Treaty, the Soviet leaders secured one of their first important diplomatic victories: "Germany waives all claims against Russia . . . on condition that the Government of the R.S.F.S.R. does not satisfy claims for compensation of a similar nature made by a third Party."[13] This was balanced by abandonment of all Soviet claims for damages resulting from German action. On the tenth anniversary of the Rapallo Treaty, *Pravda* pointed to its importance:

> How sensible this was may be concluded from the fact that similar claims held by other states for ten years against the Soviet Union have not been recognized. Moreover, these states have not profited in any way from the formal maintenance of these claims but have only had to forego the privileges and advantages which would have accrued to them if their relations with the Soviet Union had been placed on a normal basis from the start.[14]

Neither the British nor the French had been more successful. The British claim was much larger than the American one: government and railway bonds—$330,000,000; commercial investments—$261,000,000; war debt—$2,766,000,000; total—$3,357,000,000. The following declaration was attached to the Anglo-Soviet trade agreement of 1921: "The Russian Soviet government . . . recognizes in principle that it is liable to pay compensation to private persons who have supplied goods or services to Russia for which they have not been paid. The detailed mode of discharging this liability shall be regulated by the treaty referred to in the preamble."[15] This treaty became the General Treaty of August 8, 1924, in which the Soviet government agreed to satisfy the British bondholders' claims, as reduced because of Russian financial conditions; if the British government produced an agreement on the amount of these claims with half the bondholders, the settlement would bind them all. The war loans were left in "cold storage." It was of this that Lloyd George said, "What a remarkable document to be called a Treaty when there is not a single point settled."[16] With the fall of the MacDonald government, the treaty was not ratified. When diplomatic relations were resumed in 1929 the Soviet leaders, at the first session, demanded full resumption of relations with a discussion of outstanding questions to follow, but, with Stalin demanding either a loan or credits as the price for any debt settlement, no further progress was made.

During French-Soviet debt negotiations in 1925, Krassin (Soviet Ambassador in Paris) said that his government "was disposed to do something for the small French bondholders," but stated categorically that "any claim for the credits extended Russia by the French Treasury would be followed by counter-claims for intervention of a much higher figure."[17] A French-Soviet debt conference met in 1926/27 but adjourned without a settlement. The Soviet leaders were not willing to recognize in principle the obligations contracted by previous governments though they were willing to make some small financial settlement in the form of extra interest on future loans.

The Soviet attitude toward the American government was similar. The latter had not joined with the other powers protesting Soviet repudiation of the loans in 1918. Secretary of State Lansing wired Ambassador Francis, "Department regards any protests relative to repudiation of loans as grave error. . . . Protest would not influence Soviet and would only aid German propaganda."[18] This policy must have seemed justified a year later, when Bullitt wired the Commission to Negotiate Peace, "Tchicherin and Litvinov state positively that in principle the Soviet Government is willing to pay its foreign debt; the only question being how to meet immediate payments because of the present difficult financial position of the Government. . . . I am certain . . . that the Soviet Government is disposed to be reasonable."[19] Bullitt's view was even more hopeful a few days later: "Lenine [*sic*], Tchitcherin, Litvinov and all other leaders of the Soviet Government with whom I talked expressed in the most straightforward, unequivocal manner the determination of the Soviet Government to pay its foreign debts, and I am convinced that there will be no dispute on this point."[20] After all, this seemed logical. "The members of the Soviet government realize fully that as a preliminary step to the obtaining of credit the payment of foreign debts must be resumed and, therefore, are ready to pay such debts."[21]

It did not take long for this optimistic view to be dissipated. In August 1920 Litvinov inquired "what bearing it would have if he brought . . . a written statement from Lenin. . . . I replied that . . . our Government had repeatedly expressed its opinion that no credence is to be given to any statement of the Soviet government which has so often violated the most solemn agreements."[22] In January 1922, Krassin (head of the Soviet delegation in London) told the American Consul-General that "American claims must be in connection with Russian counter claims."[23] The Soviet leaders were apparently irked by American insistence on debt payment. In 1925, Litvinov was quoted as saying:

> America up to this time does not wish to recognize us, demanding that we first should recognize our debts to it. It does not even wish to carry on negotiations with respect to the recognition of the payment of debts. England, France first recognized us and afterwards talked of debts, but America does not even wish to talk with us before the recognition of the debts.[24]

Some Americans later must have wished that this policy had been retained. But Litvinov's statements were now widely suspect. As Kelley wrote, "the statements . . . made by Litvinov concerning the Soviet government's policy with respect to property claims made against it by non-communist governments have varied so considerably in both tone and substance, that it must be concluded that he has been activated largely by considerations of expediency in each case."[25] If Soviet policy was now firm, the justification was novel.

> The Soviets will not, in principle, recognize the $75,000,000 prewar loans of U.S. bankers to the Czarist government because the money was used for police oppression of the Russian masses.
>
> The Soviets also will not recognize the $86,000,000 war loans from America to the Czar, because war is inimical to the people's interests.
>
> The Soviets will pay the Kerensky loan of $187,000,000 without argument about the principle, but, following allied precedents, they wish the payments to be spread over a period of years.
>
> However, the Soviet is ready to discuss the debts on a practical basis.[26]

THE 1933 DEBT "AGREEMENT"

The Department of State should, therefore, have been duly warned when in 1933 it prepared to ask the Soviet government to pay its debts. As noted earlier, the Eastern European Affairs division of the Department prepared a memorandum, "Soviet Attitude and Policy with Respect to the Repudiation of Debts and Confiscation of Property," a 147-page analysis of the Bolshevist theory of property, action by the Soviet government, history of the debt wrangle, and the experiences of the British, French, and Americans in dealing with the Soviet government on this subject. Five of Kelley's memoranda also dealt with aspects of the debt question. The Moore papers at Hyde Park contain three more memoranda: 13 pages of charts and statistical tables on Soviet-American trade, 23 pages of statistics on imports and estimated imports from the Soviet Union, and 13 pages on "How could the Soviet Union pay for increased purchases in the United States?"

Kelley recommended that the items of $406,082.30 and $4,465,465.07 of the indebtedness not be presented to Litvinov, since these items represented obligations for sales of relief supplies and surplus war materials to the Kolchak "government," which was never recognized by the United States as the government of Russia. Except for this, however, the full obligation should be presented and the Soviet government expected to arrange for payment:

> The Soviet government should be required to acknowledge liability on

the debt . . . incurred by the Russian Provisional Government to the Government of the United States.

No principle is more firmly established in international law than the principle that a change in the internal constitution of a State does not affect the public debt of the State, and that a new Government succeeds to the financial obligations contracted by previous Governments.

. . . The United States as a great creditor nation and as a country whose citizens are engaged in world-wide financial activities has a profound interest in the maintenance and strengthening of the principle. . . .

Inasmuch as the Russian debt represents money advanced to Russia by the Government of the United States to aid in the prosecution of the war against Germany, the Russian debt should be treated on the same basis as the debts incurred by other countries under the same circumstances. . . .

The money loaned by the Government of the United States to the Russian Government was advanced to the Provisional Government of Russia. . . . Almost all, if not all, other indebtedness of the Russian Government to foreign Governments was incurred by the Imperial Russian Government. It has been suggested that the Soviet Government could undertake to honor the indebtedness of the Russian Provisional Government without modifying any position it may have taken towards the indebtedness contracted by the Russian Imperial Government.[27]

It was also emphasized that it was important that Litvinov accept the disposition of the Russian property in the United States—comprising bank deposits and valid claims to the value of at least ten million dollars—as made since 1917.

Litvinov and Roosevelt did not reach formal agreement on the debt problem. A memorandum from Bullitt to the President spoke of a two-hour argument with Litvinov on November 15:

I finally managed to shake him a bit by telling him that the Johnson Bill, forbidding loans to countries in default on their indebtedness to the Government of the United States, was certain to be passed in January and that if the Soviet Government should make any absurd offer of settlement such an offer would surely be turned down by Congress and the Soviet Government would be unable to obtain one penny of credit from either the Government or any private corporation or individual in the United States, or their agencies abroad.[28]

Bullitt and Litvinov disagreed on the facts, the latter claiming that most of the money loaned to the Kerensky Government had been spent on supplies for the Kolchak army while the former was sure that two-thirds of the money was used in fighting Germany. Litvinov asserted, further, that the private claims—listed at $336,000,000—were by now so padded that $50,000,000 would be a fair settlement figure; Bullitt urged the President to get at least twice that. Bullitt had stated in 1919 that there would be no dispute on the debt problem and that the Soviet government would be reasonable; he may not have thought this in November 1933.

On the afternoon of November 15, Litvinov, meeting with the President; Henry Morgenthau, Jr., just appointed Acting Secretary of the Treasury and hardly yet familiar with his duties; and Bullitt entered into a "gentleman's agreement" which, not being released at the time, became a center of controversy later. It provided

> that over and above all claims of the Soviet Government and its nationals against the Government of the United States and its nationals, the Soviet Government will pay to the Government of the United States on account of the Kerensky debt or otherwise a sum to be not less than $75,000,000 in the form of a percentage above the ordinary rate of interest on a loan to be granted to it by the Government of the United States or its nationals, all other claims of the Government of the United States or its nationals and of the Government of the Union of Soviet Socialist Republics or its nationals to be regarded as eliminated.
>
> The President said that he believed confidently that he could persuade Congress to accept a sum of $150,000,000, but that he feared that Congress would not accept any smaller sum. Mr. Litvinov then said he could not on his own authority accept any such minimum, as his Government had already stated that it considered this sum excessive.
>
> Mr. Litvinov said that he had entire confidence in the fairmindedness of the President and felt sure that when the President had looked into the facts he would not feel that a sum greater than $75,000,000 was justified. So far as he personally was concerned, and without making any commitment, he would be inclined to advise his Government to accept $100,000,000 if the President should still consider such a sum fair.
>
> Mr. Litvinov agreed to remain in Washington after resumption of relations and to discuss with Mr. Morgenthau and Mr. Bullitt the exact sum between the limits of $75,000,000 and $150,000,000 to be paid by the Soviet Government.[29]

The only reference to the debt problem in the November 16 agreements came when the Soviet government released and assigned certain claims to the United States government (see chapter VI) "preparatory to a final settlement of the claims and counter claims" between the governments and their nationals. It was mentioned, also, in a Joint Statement, dated November 16 but issued the next day as a White House press release, in which the two men said:

> In addition to the agreements which we have signed today, there has taken place an exchange of views with regard to methods of settling all

outstanding questions of indebtedness and claims that permits us to hope for a speedy and satisfactory solution of these questions which both our governments desire to have out of the way as soon as possible.

Mr. Litvinov will remain in Washington for several days for further discussion.[30]

It is almost impossible to understand, looking back after thirty years, how high-level public officials could have hoped that such statements would be adequate to the situation. Given the experiences of other governments with the Soviet government, the hundreds of assertions of policy on both sides, the warning memoranda so carefully prepared—the history of the previous sixteen years—how could this have been done? Such faith would seem to run counter to everything known about the Soviet government. Why should the press release state that there was reason "to hope for a speedy and satisfactory solution to these questions" when no agreement had been possible? Why should it be expected that a "gentleman's agreement" would be useful when a formal agreement was impossible? Why enter into a gentleman's agreement until the two disputants were able to agree on the facts?

The main "villain" as it turned out, was the November 15 memorandum by Roosevelt and Litvinov. Purporting to be an agreement, it was no agreement at all. Only two things were agreed to: that the Soviet government would pay a sum of at least $75,000,000 to the United States government, and that Litvinov would remain in Washington to discuss the amount to be paid. Everything else was assumption, and this was the worst place for that, as the history of Soviet debt negotiations had clearly shown. There were several specific problems that needed to be faced and settled, if a settlement were to be made: (1) how much did the Soviet government owe? (2) how was this payment to be made? (3) was the payment to cover the money loaned or was it also to include an amount for interest? (4) if the latter were included, what would the rate of interest be? and (5) just what was expected from the American government and was this dependent upon the Soviet government's fulfilling its part of the agreement? These matters needed the most precise statement during the negotiations, and the most specific agreement if misunderstanding were to be avoided later. Not one of these questions had been answered in the "gentleman's agreement"; not one of them ever was.

It is easy to look back now and spot the ineptness of the diplomacy. It was not possible on November 15 or 16 to foresee what problems would develop, though there was no reason to believe that those that had arisen in the case of other governments would be absent from

American-Soviet relations. The November 15th agreement seems a carelessly drawn statement. Bullitt refers to a 2:00 meeting; the memorandum is dated 2:45, which sounds as if, following a difficult two-hour wrangle in the morning, a forty-five-minute session seemed to indicate some agreement and, with everyone busy with other matters (in chapter I we spoke of another negotiating session that afternoon) the President dictated a quick, off-the-cuff statement. After signing it both men went off to other duties. Such action at this level of government would seem indefensible; if the action is defensible, the statement is less so.

And yet, is this important? Since when have words been so powerful that a tightly knit phrase could ensnare a wily, unwilling opponent? Have we not seen carefully prepared, specifically worded phrases in the agreements on subversion and propaganda, religious freedom, and the protection of American nationals? Did we not, also, find that none of these agreements, however expertly turned out, was adequate to the wishes of the American government? Without excusing hasty action and careless phrasing, if this does represent the action of the afternoon of November 15, we cannot necessarily conclude that caution would have produced the opposite results. One view held in the Department of State was that "in spite . . . of the fundamental difference between the American and Soviet economic systems, the Bolsheviks have show relative favor to Americans from the beginning of this regime. It is an open secret that they are anxious for American recognition."[31] Suppose that, in view of this opinion, President Roosevelt had decided that there would be no recognition until there was a full and final settlement of the debt question, and that Litvinov had accepted the proffered document and agreed to a specific payment. This would have provided a momentary triumph for American diplomacy, but would the payments have been greater than they actually were?

The error made by American negotiators may well lie not in the statement itself but in their willingness to present it, giving Soviet leaders a chance to escape payment. The fact that they did present it made their position appear weak and indefensible. Having disregarded their own warnings against granting recognition before all problems were settled, they made themselves look bad later on, and thus violated a cardinal rule of politics.

IMPLEMENTATION: TRYING TO MAKE AN AGREEMENT

Having gotten off to such a start, it is not surprising that American diplomats never succeeded in getting what they desired. As the debt negotiations were long and complicated, no detailed description will be attempted here. What is proposed, rather, is (1) a general account of the negotiations followed by (2) an analysis of the problems that prevented agreement. It is believed that the Soviet attitude will be better demonstrated in this fashion than by a stage-by-stage discussion.

The November 16 press release said that Mr. Litvinov would remain in Washington for further discussions. These did not prove to be fruitful, and on November 22 Acting Secretary of State Phillips wired Hull of his plans to publish a statement that, "owing to intricacy of questions it has been impossible to reach definite conclusions before Litvinov's departure,"[32] but that responsible officers of both governments would continue the discussions, and a speedy solution was hoped for.

After this, there was no obvious action, although Kelley, Hackworth, Wiley, and Moore met almost daily. Moore reported that they were in touch with the Treasury, the Federal Trade Commission, and certain bankers. "The situation is being carefully explored."[33] On February 10, 1934, Bullitt and Troyanovsky talked, the latter asking if the United States government was ready to begin the discussions. These started within ten days; after some tentative approaches, the main conversations were transferred to Moscow where both Bullitt and Litvinov were. Early in March the United States presented a proposal, based on the November 1933 conversations, which became the basis for negotiations during the next few months.

Meanwhile, in Washington, Congress passed the Johnson Act, "an act to prohibit financial transactions with any foreign government in default on its obligations to the United States." (48 Statutes, 574) The bill, which became law on April 13, stated that

> hereafter it shall be unlawful within the United States . . . for any person to purchase or sell bonds, securities or other obligations of any foreign government or political subdivision thereof or any organization or association acting for or on behalf of a foreign government . . . or to make any loan to such foreign government, political subdivision, organization or association . . . while such government [etc.] . . . is in default in the payment of its obligations or any part thereof, to the Government of the United States.[34]

The Attorney General issued an official opinion that "the Soviet Government is in default, within the contemplation of the statute."[35] Litvinov had been warned of the application of this law to his government during the November discussions; yet on June 16, 1934, he angrily declared that "there would be no purchases until the Johnson bill had been withdrawn or amended. I replied that there was not the faintest possibility of the Johnson bill being withdrawn or amended."[36]

Another development in Washington was the establishment of the Export-Import Bank on February 2, 1934, intended largely though not solely to develop trade with the Soviet Union. Early in the Bank's history, however, the Board of Trustees adopted a resolution that, as it turned out, prevented that trade development:

> It is the sense of the board of trustees . . . that no actual credit transactions with the Soviet Government shall be undertaken unless and until that government shall submit to the President of the United States an acceptable agreement respecting the payment of the Russian indebtedness to the Government of the United States and its nationals.[37]

Trade with the Soviet Union could have been financed under the Johnson Act, but the Bank's resolution prevented that, and thus was really responsible for blocking the Soviet government which naturally resented this action. Moore attempted to justify the resolution:

> When I was with Mr. Rubinin the other day, I explained to him how reasonable it was for the bank to take that action, in view of the fact that it was always understood that the two subjects of a debt agreement and the support by the bank of Russian purchases in this country were so linked together that it would be perfectly illogical for us to extend any credit in advance of a satisfactory debt agreement.[38]

The effect of these two developments was to put pressure on the debt negotiators, and during May and June 1934 almost daily messages passed between Moscow and Washington. The cordial spirit of November 1933 had been rapidly replaced by a new atmosphere. As early as April 8 Litvinov told Bullitt that "he had said his last word and made his maximum offer . . . ; so far as he was concerned the matter was closed."[39] In June, Litvinov asserted that "his Government would make no further concession but would prefer to let the entire matter drop."[40] In early July he said that "so far as the Soviet Government was concerned the matter was now at rest."[41] By July there was a "complete breakdown" in Moscow and the negotiations were, at Bullitt's suggestion, transferred back to Washington. On August 24, Troyanovsky handed the Secretary of State what he termed a compromise proposal; this proved to be so disappointing to the United States that, that same day, the Department of State published the first intimation of the possibility that no agreement could be reached.[42] With no appreciable progress in Washington, Troyanovsky returned to Moscow for consultation. Hull wired Bullitt that "our information is . . . that Troyanovsky believes" that the American proposal "should be accepted and that his trip to Moscow is on his own initiative to endeavor to persuade his government to accept it."[43]

This appears to be the only time when a settlement might really have been reached. Washington was ready to make a concession on the interest question, and Moscow to allow the Export-Import Bank to approve its purchases in the United States, and to pay 10 per cent interest. But nothing developed when Troyanovsky got to Moscow. He stayed longer than anticipated and returned to the United States by way of the Orient, so that the debt negotiations could not be renewed until the end of January 1935.

On January 30, while lunching with Bullitt, then in Washington, Troyanovsky admitted "that he was afraid to discuss the question with the Secretary of State, that he feared their conversation might result disastrously. . . . He then said, 'Could I not, instead of going to the Department of State, just have private conversations with you here?' "[44] The answer was negative. On the following day, the conversation concluded as Troyanovsky feared it might. When the Secretary of State inquired about the position of the Soviet government, the Ambassador stated that "his Government, while desiring to have friendly relations with the United States, could not go beyond the proposal which he had presented to the Department prior to his departure." The Secretary said that "he was profoundly disappointed. The United States had gone to the limit to which it could go and had made considerable concessions. In view of the position taken by the Soviet Government the negotiations would seem to have come to an end. The Ambassador agreed and said he had no proposals to make."[45] It was reported later that the whole conversation lasted four and a half minutes.

Later that day, the Department took action designed to impress the Soviet government with the seriousness of the situation. It was anticipated, Hull cabled to Moscow,

> that the Export-Import Bank will be abolished immediately, that the Naval and Air Attachés will be withdrawn, the Consulate General abolished, and the personnel of the Embassy reduced. . . .
> In discussing these actions with members of the Soviet Government and others in Moscow you should endeavor to convey clearly the fact . . . that Litvinov has shown so little disposition to permit the development of friendly relations with the United States that the Government of the United States is convinced that no real friendship can be developed so long as he adheres to his present attitude.
> Ambassador thinks it desirable that both Nimmer and White in their farewell conversations with Voroshilov should refer to the numerous

unnecessary obstacles to the development of Soviet-American friendship, which have been created by Litvinov.[46]

This brought the debt negotiations to an end after fifteen months of fairly active and often quite bellicose diplomacy.

Let us now turn to some of the specific issues involved in the negotiations and the differences between the two governments. The major questions at stake were these: (1) how much payment would the Soviet government make? (2) was the United States government, in return, to make a loan or offer credits to the Soviet government? (3) how much, if any, interest was to be paid? and (4) what effect would Soviet payment to the United States have on its relations with other creditor governments? Let us discuss these, in turn.

How much would the Soviet government pay? As indicated in the "gentleman's agreement," Litvinov was willing to promise payment of $75,000,000 while the President did not think that Congress would accept anything less than $150,000,000.[47] Bullitt told Troyanovsky in February 1934 that he considered $150,000,000 an "absolute minimum," pointing out that the dollar had been devalued so that this was now equal to $90,000,000 at the old rate of exchange. The effect of devaluation was also emphasized by Hull and the President. Since the United States government later disclaimed responsibility for Soviet internal pressures, this emphasis on devaluation of the dollar appears a weak argument, though apparently Litvinov never told the American negotiators that he was not impressed by it. When Bullitt reminded Litvinov in April of his promise to Roosevelt to recommend a payment of $100,000,000, the Soviet diplomat said that he was "still ready to do so" but that documents turned over to the Soviet Embassy in Washington showed that the Kerensky government had received "almost none" of the funds placed at its disposal, Bakhmetyev and Ughet having spent the money for their own support and for attacks on the Soviet government. Troyanovsky told the President in April that Litvinov still thought the total amount should not be more than $75,000,000 but that "if this seemed to the President too small an amount, Mr. Litvinoff would consider increasing it,"[48] which was an odd offer from one supposed to be as astute a bargainer as Litvinov. But the "ante" was being raised. In May a Soviet representative told Bullitt that he assumed that "our government would accept $100,000,000 in payment of indebtedness. I replied that I had specific orders not to accept a sum as low as $100,000,000."[49] But American officials were already admitting, within their own walls, that the payment of $150,000,000 was unlikely. "In no event," wrote one Assistant Secretary to another, "can we expect the Soviet to promise to pay more than $100,000,000," adding that the amount of the "debt agreement . . . is not in itself very important"[50] since the claims totalled more than $600,000,000. Troyanovsky, interviewed by a *New York Herald Tribune* correspondent in August 1934 did not limit the debt payment to $100,000,000 but talked about $150,000,000. Both sides were somewhat flexible, therefore, on the total amount to be paid. Apparently this was never a serious stumbling block to the success of the negotiations.

Was the United States government to make a loan? Far more serious, and thus of more importance during the negotiations, was the question of whether the United States government would make a loan to the Soviet government, or whether it would only provide credits of some type. Here the careless phrasing of the November 1933 negotiations rose to haunt the participants. From the first, the American representatives maintained that no loan had ever been intended. In his first conversation about debts with Litvinov, on March 15, 1934, Bullitt, who had been present and taken a most important role during the November conferences, and who should have known if anyone did, emphasized

> that the President had never had any idea of a direct loan to the Soviet Government but only of a loan in the form of credits. I pointed out that no loan could possibly be made by the United States to any foreign country at the present time and that we had assumed that he was fully aware that a loan in the form of credits was the only possibility. He agreed that he had known that it would be extraordinarily difficult for the Government of the United States to make any loan to the Soviet Union but insisted that he had thought the President would find a way to do so. I feel sure that the President never envisaged a loan in any other form than that of a commercial credit to be expended in the United States.[51]

When the Ambassador asked for Presidential support, Hull sent the assurance: "You may inform Litvinoff that the President expressly states that he has never had any thought of a direct loan to the Soviet Government and that there is not the slightest possibility of such a loan being made."[52] Bullitt informed the Department that Litvinov at first "categorically refused to consider anything but a cash loan. However, after long argument he agreed to refer the entire matter to Stalin."[53] Three days later, however, Litvinov's view was unchanged: " 'We shall never accept credits in place of a loan. We might agree to spend the entire proceeds of a loan in the United States but what we insist upon is a straight loan like the one the Swedish Government has just granted us so that we can pay for all our American purchases in cash.' I replied that the message I had received from the President was decisive, that no loan could or would be granted."[54] Within a few days, Litvinov seemed more conciliatory. "Litvinov today informed me that the Council of People's Commissars had decided that it would arrange the matter of indebtedness . . . by way of a long-term credit operation and that the Soviet Government would not insist upon a loan."[55] What Litvinov proposed was a twenty-year credit to be extended by the Export-Import Bank for twice the sum agreed on as the total of the Soviet debt obligation. This would enable the Soviet government to make all its purchases in the United States for cash. Bullitt regarded the proposal as "wholly unacceptable. It substitutes for a loan . . . a credit which is the equivalent of a loan,"[56] pointing out that if the credit were extended as proposed, the Soviet indebtedness would be twice as large at the end of the twenty years as at the beginning. This was so "unreasonable not to say fantastic" that he did not even comment on other aspects of the proposal.

Thus the negotiations now turned to the possibility of an extension of credit, despite the Export-Import Bank resolution, and the telegrams were filled with detailed proposals about the total amount of the credits, the discount arrangements, length of time for payment, and so on. On one thing the Soviet leaders were clear: the total amount of the credit had to be twice the amount which they paid to the United States government, and the figures of $200,000,000 and $100,000,000, respectively, were generally mentioned. Bullitt refused to accept this, and was supported by the Department:

> Of course approve your refusal to accept proposition, which practically means an unconditional loan of $200,000,000. Since all credit transactions would be placed under the control of Amtorg with power to decide terms, class of goods purchased, and what preference given producers, it would to a large extent place our business at the will of Amtorg.[57]

Discussions about credit aroused American fears that the Soviet government might spend much of the money on munitions or weapons, or place manufacturers of the same products in bitter competition with each other; this we wanted to be able to control. On the other hand, the Soviet leaders were wary of any arrangement which would give the Export-Import Bank the right to approve or disapprove of Soviet transactions in the United States, fearing that this would permit the United States government to control Soviet trade.

The argument on credit had essentially reached a stalemate in the summer of 1934. Troyanovsky was told that "Amtorg would be free to select the exporters with whom it wanted to deal and to purchase whatever goods it desired. The Bank, however, must reserve the right to disapprove a particular transaction."[58] "Such a right was reserved by all governments which guarantee credits extended to the Soviet government. This phraseology did not mean that the Bank would participate in the determination of the terms of sale between the exporter and Amtorg. . . . It was thought that there would be no difficulty in clarifying the phraseology so as to dispel Moscow's worries."[59] But Troyanovsky's "compromise proposal" of August 24 contained the same arrangement.

> The twenty-year credit . . . was in actuality a loan, and . . . terms of that length of time were unheard of in commercial transactions. . . . The proposal amounted in its essence to the United States granting the Soviet Government a loan equal to the amount of its indebtedness to the United States and in addition a revolving credit of an equivalent amount. Congress would certainly never approve of such a transaction, and it would be severely criticized by public opinion.[60]

Moore told the Soviet Ambassador that it was "out of the question" for the American government to extend a loan to the Soviet government as proposed by either Litvinov or Troyanovsky. "If the Soviet Government insisted on this requirement, there was no possibility of reaching a settlement on the matter." Troyanovsky said that he would be very glad to have another meeting if any suggestions occurred to us, but he did not hold out the "slightest possibility of his Government yielding on the question of a loan."[61] Moore cabled Bullitt, "We can only for the present let the matter ride."[62] And there, indeed, the matter rested. When Bullitt talked with Litvinov a month later, the latter said that his government "had no desire even for a loan except at a very low interest rate; that it desired to let the entire matter drop."[63] And on January 31, 1935, when the negotiations broke down, Troyanovsky still maintained that "his Government could not but insist on the extension to it of a $100,000,000 loan."[64]

Thus the United States government refused to consider a loan of any type, maintaining that this had never even been considered during the talks in Washington. When the Soviet government agreed to accept a credit transaction, the American government found itself unable to agree on the terms proposed. The American government refused to pledge its credit unless it had some control over the use made of it; it refused to accept uncontrolled credit, whereas the Soviet government refused to accept controlled credit.

The year-long argument about whether the United States would make a loan to the Soviet government sounds less than statesmanlike after this passage of time, however politically popular it may have been. The fact is that the United States government was very vulnerable, and Litvinov knew it and took as much advantage of his position as he could. When the matter deadlocked in midsummer of 1934, Bullitt, who had been present at all the conferences in Washington, was asked to summarize his understanding of the situation. He wrote:

> It was clearly impossible that the Government of the United States should give either a loan or an uncontrolled credit and Litvinov never indicated that he expected either a loan or uncontrolled credit. I was as you know astounded when he took that position after my arrival in Moscow. The President and I talked over the matter repeatedly and there was in our minds never the faintest idea of a straight loan or uncontrolled credit.[65]

But the American position had not been stated so clearly in November 1933. When Bullitt asked Litvinov how he could have imagined that he was going to get a loan, in view of public opposition in the United States to further loans, Litvinov replied that "the President had used the word 'loan', that . . . he thought the President could find a way to get it."[66] In the very next sentence of his telegram, Bullitt agreed to the correctness of Litvinov's position, admitting that "from time to time in speaking of credits the word 'loan' was used synonymously therewith by the President. It is my impression that the word 'loan' was even used in the conversation of which a memorandum was made." The documents verify this. In Bullitt's memorandum for the President on November 15, 1933, he reported that he had threatened Litvinov with the Johnson Act, then pending, which forbade loans. In the "gentleman's agreement" signed later that same day, Litvinov offered to have his Government pay a certain sum as extra interest "on a loan to be granted to it by the Government of the United States or its nationals."[67] So the term "loan" was used both orally and in writing during the Washington talks.

The American position was even weaker than this. The archives contain a memorandum signed by Assistant Secretary Moore on April 28, 1934, dealing with the debt negotiations. Attached to this is a proposal drafted before Bullitt left, "to be suggested to the Soviet as expressing the general understanding reached while Mr. Litvinov was here." Three phrases from this paper are relevant here: "On all credits or loans to be extended . . ."; "A credit or loan is deemed to be extended . . . upon either the opening of an irrevocable credit or the granting of a loan"; and "My Government will submit . . . from time to time . . . a schedule of all credits or loans extended to it by nationals of your Government."[68] If the third statement mentions loans by American nationals, the other two do not, and the difference is implicit. It is not surprising, then, that Litvinov exhibited to Wiley (the American Chargé) on October 20, 1934, "the undated memorandum of his conversation with the President in which the term 'loan' was employed." Wiley pointed out that " 'loan' without any modifying adjective was not sufficient to substantiate his thesis," to which Litvinov replied that "had anything but a straight loan been considered in Washington he would have left without recognition rather than subscribe to a proposal so disadvantageous to Soviet relations with both France and England."[69] It was easier for Litvinov to make this assertion than for Bullitt or Wiley to maintain that the United States government had never even thought of a loan.

In February 1935, after the negotiations had broken down and Moscow was seeking to avoid blame for the failure, Litvinov showed Walter Duranty, the *New York Times* correspondent in Moscow, the undated memorandum initialed by the President, and later he was authorized to state on the "most competent authority and most categorically"

> that the word credit was not even mentioned in the negotiations, only the word loan was employed. Though there was no mention of any limitation of the right of the Soviet Government to dispose of the 'loan' as it pleased, the Soviet Government . . . [later] offered to stipulate that the loan be used exclusively to finance Soviet purchases in the United States. The Soviet Government never requested that the loan be paid over. It had merely expected that the 'loan' would be placed at the disposal of the Soviet Government in order to cover purchases.[70]

This whole question developed, then, to the embarrassment of the American government, which tried to make the best case it could. One cannot surely ascertain now what was in the minds of the participants at the time, but if there was no intention of a loan, the word should not have been used. If it was used unintentionally in the give-and-take of oral discussion, it should never have been used in writing. However clear the understanding reached in Washington—Bullitt reported that he and the President discussed the question of whether recognition should be held up until the debt agreement had been worked out in detail, but the President "felt that this was not necessary as he thought his understanding with Litvinov was clear"[71]—at least there was no necessity for affording Litvinov so large and tempting an opening in which to operate. This was not American diplomacy at its best.

How much interest was to be paid? Another annoying aspect of the debt negotiations concerned interest payments on the debt. As we have seen, Litvinov in November 1933 promised that the Soviet government would pay its debt "in the form of a percentage above the ordinary rate of interest" so that the question was complicated by having two kinds of interest, normal and extra, a device previously used by Moscow in the 1924 debt agreement treaty with Britain and in 1927 with France. Litvinov insisted that his government would pay the debt only by extra interest.

This topic came into the discussions at Bullitt's first talk with Troyanovsky on February 10, 1934, with the former pointing out that the Soviet government had been paying 15 per cent and 14 per cent, respectively, on normal credits from Britain and Germany and that no foreign government could expect to borrow at less than 7 per cent in the United States at that time. Bullitt emphasized that the larger the rate for the additional interest and the smaller the rate for the normal, the better it was for the Soviet government. To this, Litvinov sent a quick reply that the gentleman's agreement did not provide for the payment of interest on the amount to be paid in settling claims against the Soviet government. When Bullitt talked with Litvinov, the latter "was vehement in his objection to interest,"[72] maintaining that he had not agreed to pay any extra interest on any credits whatever but only on loans to be given to his government to be used for purchases anywhere." While he was making his case, Litvinov also objected to fixing the additional interest at 10 per cent. To all of this, Bullitt replied that "when the existence of a debt was admitted interest accrued on it until payment unless there was something said or understood to the contrary, and that this would mean interest at a reasonable rate in all the circumstances."[73] Both Roosevelt and Bullitt were convinced "that Litvinov had agreed to pay extra interest on all loans or credits of whatsoever nature obtained from any American individual or corporation" and, as we have seen, the President believed the understanding so clear that it was unnecessary to hold up recognition until the details could be worked out. While in Washington, Litvinov had said that he was ready to offer a total rate of 7 per cent. "Morgenthau greeted this with laughter and indicated that the total rate would have to be at least 10 per cent."[74]

From here on, the discussions emphasized details rather than principles. The amounts of interest, of both types, varied from time to time, sometimes also whether the interest applied to the whole amount or only to part, sometimes as to the period in which payment would be made. Once, asked what additional interest his government proposed to pay, Troyanovsky said that "although his Government did not think that it should pay any interest, he proposed the payment of one per cent."[75] When Litvinov reported that his government had been offered credits by Germany at 7 per cent, Bullitt told him that, so far as he knew, the Soviet Union had never gotten credits below 11 per cent. Later Litvinov maintained that the Soviet government was not paying and would not pay more than 6 per cent. "I asked him where he got these figures. He replied, from the Soviet Credit Department. I suggested ingenuously that he have them checked, as personally, I did not believe them. He replied somewhat weakly that of course there might be some indirect extra payments."[76] On another occasion, Litvinov read to Bullitt the rates for credit then being paid by the Soviet government, including 5 per cent from various British banks. "I replied that I had no knowledge of such interest rates, that Rosengoltz [Commissar of Foreign Trade] had admitted to me yesterday that the Soviet Government had not yet been able to obtain credits in England at less than 11 per cent. This Litvinov denied vehemently and stated that the memorandum in his hand had been prepared by Rosengoltz."[77] The rates most frequently suggested by Litvinov were 4 per cent plus 3 per cent, though once he "inadvertently began to discuss this figure as 5 plus 5 percent confirming my guess that he is ready to accept a 10 percent total interest rate."[78]

In dealing with this question as with previous ones, American representatives were careless in their negotiations, proceeding on assumptions rather than clear statements and facts, when they knew the wily nature of their adversary. It might have made no difference, so far as money payments went, but the position could have been easily and proudly defended.

What effect would Soviet payment to the United States have on relations with other governments? This question occupied a major position in the Soviet argument. Since little was heard about it in the earlier stages of the negotiations, it may well have been a rationalization, in which case the Soviet leaders discovered the strength of the argument and used it as they could. Their position was that a payment to the United States government of a debt based upon loans to pre-Soviet Russian governments, would immediately open the floodgates to demands by the British, French, Germans, and others for similar payments to them. It will be recalled that the waiving of German claims against Russian in the Treaty of Rapallo rested specifically on the fact that similar claims by third parties were not honored by the Soviet government. Since the claims of these other governments were much larger than those of the American government—exclusive of nationalized property, these other claims totalled about $9 billion—the

Soviet government was properly reticent about putting itself in a position where it had to meet them. "The only solution in such a case would be to sell the whole of the Soviet Union or parcel it out in settlement."[79] Litvinov stated the case very plainly:

> We sincerely desire the best possible relations with the United States but we cannot jeopardize our relations with the rest of the world. The claims against the Soviet Union of England, France, Germany and various other nations are far larger than the claims of (America?). Those claims have now been shelved and forgotten but the moment we make any settlement with the United States all other nations will demand immediate settlements. We must therefore make a settlement with the United States which will be on a basis that no other nation will be able to accept.[80]

Litvinov concluded that "it is physically impossible for either the British, French, or Germans to lend us double the amount of their claims, the sum is too large. Therefore, we can settle with the United States on that basis." He was undoubtedly correct that if his government paid by means of extra interest on commercial credits, other governments would ask the same treatment.

On this question, however, the Soviet government was on the defensive. Hull told Troyanovsky that Litvinov had not mentioned this consideration when he was in Washington; if he had, there might have been a different story. This Soviet difficulty was not the concern of the United States government and it could happily flog Litvinov with his dilemma as he had our representatives on the other points.

> I told him that it was indeed curious that he was in the habit of saying to me that there were no difficulties in the matter of debts and claims except his relations with England and France; that there were no difficulties in the question of our consular districts except his relations with Japan and Germany; that there were no difficulties with regard to the use of our airplane[s] except his relations with Germany, Poland, and England. . . . I considered it deplorable that he should allow the relations between our two countries to be controlled by his relations with those countries which he considered to be his enemies.[81]

What the Soviet government was doing, Bullitt stated, was to say to the American government: "We shall not honor our agreement with the President. We shall make no payment either to the American corporations or individuals whose property we have seized. We shall make no payments on our indebtedness to the Government of the United States. . . . We shall, however, expect the Government and people of the United States to work with us loyally and intimately."[82]

The American government did understand the predicament of the Soviet government and saw that this may have been the crux of inability to reach a settlement, though it did not go as far as Litvinov when he stated that this was the "only obstacle"[83] to a settlement. American officials knew, for example, that the Soviet government was trying desperately to improve its credit position in Europe, that the situation was deteriorating rather than improving, and that the Soviet government had sometimes paid cash rather than accept the necessary credit terms. "It may, therefore, be assumed that, until this credit struggle has been decisively concluded, the Soviet Government might be averse to setting the precedent, so long resisted, of accepting controlled credits, such as those offered by the American Government."[84] And yet, one report from Moscow was that, "I have observed no indications that the Soviet Government has recently been under any pressure from third states to restrain it from concluding a settlement of debts and claims with the United States."[85]

Bullitt was willing to accept the Soviet assertion that the chief obstacle was in devising a method of distinguishing between the claims of the United States and those of other governments. "I venture to suggest that we should exercise whatever ingenuity we may possess in attempting to devise a basis of settlement which while acceptable to us could not be acceptable to France, Great Britain, and other claimants."[86] If the Soviets were honest in their assertion and would have signed a debt settlement if such a formula could have been found, this was the point of final breakdown. Repeatedly asked to suggest a solution, Troyanovsky said he had no proposals; faced with Bullitt's advice, just stated, the United States government found no answer, and negotiations collapsed. If the Soviets were only using a convenient afterthought to help protect their interests, no formula would have made any real difference, for they would have produced some other problem.

The way in which Litvinov used the other governments as argumentational crowbars gives credence to this latter theory. We have seen how he juggled the figures on interest rates. In March 1934 the Soviets were confidently talking about a 100,000,000 crown loan from Sweden; in April the Swedish Minister in Moscow said that it was "most unlikely" that his government would grant the loan; at the end of the month the Soviet government announced that it would not ratify the loan, presumably to save its prestige by not giving the Swedish legislature opportunity to reject it. The Soviet leaders talked about a new credit being arranged in Germany; Bullitt was told that "there will be no new loan agreement so long as the Soviet Government maintains its present hostility to the Hitler regime."[87] In August 1934, Soviet sources spread the story of a new $100,000,000 loan available in France. A secretary of the French Embassy said that "there is no project for a Soviet loan or a new commercial credit in France."[88] Again in November Moscow told of new commercial opportunities in France; "the French Embassy has no knowledge of any new financial proposal having been formulated."[89] The Soviet government, in other words, was willing to pressure the American government in an effort to get the best settlement it could, playing one government against another. Moscow may have used the same arguments with other governments.

Records of the debt negotiations demonstrate a greater lack of harmony among the Soviet negotiators than on any other issue. It was generally assumed by the outside world that the Soviet system was so monolithic that this could not be true, that only the democracies are handicapped by this fumbling technique, but such does not appear true here. Early in the negotiations, Bullitt cabled that "Troyanovsky has reported that he is in a helpless position being unable successfully to interpret the assurances which Litvinov gave in Washington or to contest the position taken by the Department."[90] A month later Litvinov told Bullitt that he had sent Troyanovsky a "severe reprimand" for not having dealt with the issue of the principal disagreement. Litvinov feared that "Troyanovsky's faulty knowledge of English rendered him incompetent,"[91] which was a peculiar thing to say in the midst of an important negotiation, but soon after this Hull wired Bullitt that one of Troyanovsky's reports was "most inaccurate."[92] It was not surprising, perhaps, that a Soviet official told Bullitt that Litvinov before his departure from Moscow "had given definite orders that the matter should be discussed not by Troyanovsky but by himself and Krestinsky."[93] Thus, the American Ambassador suggested to the Department that "Until I can report Krestinsky's views I believe that it would be inadvisable for the Department to negotiate with Troyanovsky who may or may not represent the point of view of his government."[94]

In July 1934, just before the negotiations started downhill, Litvinov reported a conversation between Troyanovsky and an official of the Department of State. Later that day Hull wired that "Contrary to Litvinov's statement to you, Troyanovsky has not made the inquiry alleged."[95] Two days later, Bullitt informed Litvinov "that Troyanovsky had not initiated any discussions at the Department. He replied that Troyanovsky had again misunderstood his telegraphic instructions and read a number of telegrams to prove this point."[96] Three weeks

later, Litvinov said that "he had again received an unintelligible telegram from Troyanovsky and had telegraphed . . . to obtain any proposals of the Department in written form so that he personally could
consider an actual text and not be dependent upon Troyanovsky's
interpretations which he feared might lead to further misunderstanding."[97] In Washington the Soviet Ambassador was having trouble, too.
"Mr. Troyanovsky commenced the conversation by saying that he had
had considerable difficulty in connection with the last exchange of
telegrams with Moscow since they were very much garbled."[98] The
fault was not confined to faulty communications. Wiley (the American
Chargé in Moscow) talked with Troyanovsky, back there for a period,
and reported that "from one or two facetious remarks it is evident that
his relations with Litvinov are not good."[99] Later Wiley reported that
"Troyanovsky's relations with Litvinov since his return have been
stormy,"[100] and that "it has been an open secret that Troyanovsky and
Litvinov have long been working at cross purposes."[101] A year later
Moore wrote Bullitt, "you and I understand that he has no influence
whatever."[102]

Much of this trouble may have been personal, a factor that must
plague all diplomatic establishments from time to time, yet it is
remarkable that Litvinov should have been so open about the matter
to the American Ambassador, and that, if the Russians did hope to
complete the negotiations successfully, nothing was done to replace
the diplomat.

But Litvinov's troubles were not monopolized by his relations with
Troyanovsky. Early in the negotiations Hull reported "Litvinov's
attitude wholly inconsistent with all that was understood when he was
here and from every point of view absurd."[103] In June 1934 Bullitt
talked with Litvinov.

> He began by refusing in the most categorical manner to alter his posi-
> tion on payment of indebtedness. I told him that I thought it was our
> duty to attempt to overcome the "misunderstanding" which had arisen
> with regard to his verbal understanding of the President. He replied
> "there is no misunderstanding" and asserted that the government of the
> United States was attempting to back out of the verbal agreement.[104]

It was at the end of this discussion that Litvinov said he and his government were ready to drop the matter of the debt permanently. A
month later, Bullitt had a "very long and intimate" conversation with
Voroshilov and "found out as I suspected that Litvinov had not given
Stalin and Voroshilov an altogether accurate version of our discussions
with regard to claims and indebtedness. . . . I feel sure that Voro-

shilov will use his influence with Stalin which is very great to soften Litvinov's obduracy."[105] Later, Radek told Bullitt that Voroshilov, "after a long conversation with me about 6 weeks ago had made a detailed report to Stalin on our position and had demanded that our proposals should be accepted."[106] Radek, who had read the dossier in Stalin's office, did not think that Litvinov had distorted the facts in his reports to Stalin.

Two weeks later, Hull told Troyanovsky that while he "did not want to go so far as to say that we felt that Mr. Litvinoff was trifling with the American government, he would say that it appeared to him that Mr. Litvinoff was indifferent with regard to the outcome of the negotiations."[107] Bullitt held a similar view. He wrote Moore, "I am convinced that the chief obstacle both to a successful conclusion of the negotiations with regard to debts and claims and to the establishment of really frank and friendly relations between our two governments is Litvinov himself."[108] A month later Bullitt reported that he had talked with Litvinov and found him "rather pulverized. . . . I suspect also that he had been thoroughly kicked around the Kremlin on the previous day. . . . Litvinov positively quivered when I brought Voroshilov's name into the conversation."[109] In November 1934 a high Soviet official privately visited the American Chargé in Moscow, predicting that a decision on the debt negotiations would be reached, with "the 'directive' given by the party leaders; not by the Foreign Office,"[110] which seemed to underscore either a lack of confidence in Litvinov or an unusual method of announcing foreign-policy decisions. Right after the breakdown of negotiations at the end of January 1935, Wiley reported from Moscow that he had

> discreetly reviewed and analyzed developments with Karakhan (who is an outstanding opponent of Litvinov). He declared that the way Litvinov had acted towards United States was "filled with dark spots." I suppose he will discuss matter with Kremlin. By another Soviet official, a reliable source, am informed that your press release came as complete surprise to Litvinov, that his position was not improved thereby.[111]

A few days later, Wiley added to this view:

> From various sources, I have been informed since the beginning of November that Mr. Litvinov was under fire; that his prestige was waning. This has been reported to me on many occasions by Soviet and foreign diplomatic contacts. From various reliable sources, I have now been told that the rupture of the negotiations in Washington has been grist to the mill of his opponents. Moreover, I have been given to understand that his veracity has been questioned in high Soviet quar-

ters which seem to doubt that, on his return from Washington, he reported accurately regarding his commitments to Mr. Roosevelt. I must add, however, that he gives no impression of being perturbed. . . . He has intimated to me, when insisting on his good faith, that his position was juridically impeccable.[112]

It appears, therefore, that Litvinov was having difficulty with a number of other Soviet officials, some of whom, unlike Troyanovsky, were his equals. It would also seem that the monolithicity of Soviet diplomacy was more apparent than real. On the other hand, much of this appearance may have been part of a game Litvinov was playing to prevent the United States government from getting the debt agreement he had promised in Washington. These "revelations" of personal clashes were almost too obvious to be impressive.

At the end of January 1935 the debt negotiations collapsed. The active diplomacy of fifteen months and the dreams of fifteen years were, at least for the moment, dead. It could not be foreseen then whether this was a tactical maneuver in the game, a dramatic move to produce new proposals, new hopes, and—perhaps—a settlement. Wiley reported from Moscow that Soviet officials considered the development to be of a "routine nature," believing that "American business interests will bring effective pressure on government to extend credits irrespective of results of our negotiations."[113] Litvinov was "demonstrably friendly" in social contacts, to convey the impression that cordial relations were unimpaired. He calmly stated that he thought it was a good thing for the negotiations to be "put on ice" for a time, that they might at some future time be resumed with greater hope for a successful conclusion. When asked what inspired his optimism, he replied that "political conditions would change and might greatly influence matters. I answered that the possibility of any such political change in the United States was indeed remote. He explained he had Europe in mind; not the United States. He did not clarify his cryptic allusion."[114] Other Soviet leaders, such as Radek and Umansky, were "definitely provocative . . . attempting to discredit rupture as childish and empty gesture . . . reflecting only petty irritation."[115]

The American Chargé in Moscow listed the factors that may have prevented a successful outcome to the negotiations:

An eastern or even Asiatic mentality in respect of financial and economic negotiations.

Policy of caution in respect of extensive foreign commitments, in the form of short or middle term credits, in excess of normal trade exchanges.

Disinclination to recognize even tacitly debts and obligations not directly incurred by the Soviet regime.

Fear of the possible resuscitation of dormant claims in third countries.

Resistance to any attempt at or implication of regimentation of foreign trade by other countries as a counterpoise to Soviet regimentation by means of the Soviet trade monopoly.[116]

He concluded that the first and last of these factors were of chief significance in determining Litvinov's remarks and attitude. As he said, "the Soviet Government has consistently refused to admit that what was sauce for the goose was admissible for the gander."

What developments occurred subsequently? Hull's decisive action on January 31, 1935, was no dramatic gesture for tactical advantage but the real end to the negotiations. As time passed, Soviet uneasiness was thought to be increasing. "This is probably attributable to growing realization of the fact that termination was not a mere tactical maneuver."[117] By the middle of May, Litvinov told Bullitt that "he was not averse to reopening the question," though he could "see no point in reopening it unless there was some possibility of agreement," and he thought "the difficulties insurmountable since the difference between the Governments was one of principle."[118] In both May and June, certain new variations were suggested by Troyanovsky and Moore, with no results.

In November 1936 Henderson, the Chargé in Moscow, summarizing the problems of the first three years of diplomatic relations between the two governments, believed that the ill-will created by the debt situation resulted from the fact that the American government "thus far has not taken an attitude sufficiently cooperative to satisfy the Kremlin with respect to the latter's policy of endeavoring to utilize Soviet relations with foreign countries for the purpose of obtaining merchandise and technical and financial assistance."[119] He did not think that the Soviet government would be willing to renounce its revolutionary policy of repudiating debts and nationalizing property or that there was much likelihood that the two governments could reach an agreement, especially since the Soviet economy had improved.

In 1937, Joseph Davies, the newly appointed Ambassador to Moscow, reported that Walter Duranty believed that, at that time, "the debt question was 'out,' "[120] because of Soviet relations with twenty-six other creditor governments. But in Moscow Rosengolts told Davies that he thought matters could be settled if practically approached, and he suggested negotiations by private parties, such as Rozov, the new head of Amtorg. The Commissar said that the British and French had been willing to extend credits to the Soviet government without any settlement of their debts, implying that there was still hope of persuading the United States to do the same. In October 1938 State Department officials were told that the Soviet government would welcome a reopening of the old debt negotiations but that it could not very well initiate the proposal. A Chinese financier, then in the United States, was suggested as a go-between, but Department officials refused to agree to such an intermediary.

This suggestion was doubly interesting because the Russians had taken the initiative. On June 5, 1938, when Ambassador Davies made his formal parting call on President Kalinin and Premier Molotov, Stalin came in and, after other discussion, said he wanted to talk about the Kerensky debt. He understood that a group of American bankers, having close contacts with President Roosevelt, were prepared to finance up to $200,000,000 of credits if the American government agreed and if a portion of the money were used to pay the Kerensky debt. Stalin said his government would be willing to pay $50,000,000 as extra interest on the credits over a period of twenty years. Davies stated that his instructions were "to take the position that we had done everything that we were honorably committed or required to do and that so far as we were concerned it was a closed book, unless and until the Soviet Union wished to reopen the matter and fulfill its honorable obligations." Stalin fell back on the argument of the Soviet debt to other governments, saying that "what he had in mind was a formula that would eliminate this difficulty. The Soviet Government could differentiate a debt . . . to the United States government from a debt claimed to be due to private citizens in the United States. Therefore the Soviet Government could settle the Kerenski debt without such incidental and attendant difficulty with France or England."[121] "Stalin stated that this payment would have to be in complete liquidation of all claims." The Ambassador said that it was "useless" even to submit the proposal to his government for the sum was less than that previously agreed to but perhaps the Kerensky debt could be taken care of and the other claims left for the future. Stalin at first demurred and then agreed. On June 9 Molotov handed a definite proposal to Davies, who wrote that "it was not either in terms of credit or amounts what I had understood the original proposal made by Mr. Stalin to be." To this, Molotov said that it was not a hard-and-fast proposition, that he would keep the situation from hardening, and that his government was "desirous of getting this debt matter cleared up because of their high regard for the United States,"[122] though the U.S.S.R. did not need the credits. Because the proposal had originated with Rozov, it would not be taken up by Troyanovsky in Washington, and Molotov preferred it not even be discussed with him. Back in the United States, Davies conferred with Rozov but the matter was postponed because of other negotiations then going forward. It was Davies' judgment that in June 1938 the Soviet government was "sincerely desirous of clearing up the misunderstanding and bad feeling which was engendered by the failure of the debt payment negotiations" and that "distinct advance was recorded in the fact that Messers. [*sic*] Stalin and Molotov frankly made this statement to me and said that they desired to meet the Government's obligations under the Litvinov agreement to the limit of the practicabilities."[123]

A year later, Secretary of the Treasury Morgenthau told the new Soviet Ambassador, Umansky, that "we were ready to take up the question of the Russian debt and I would like to have him inquire of his Government whether they would care to do likewise."[124] The Ambassador then left for his vacation, and there is no indication that he brought up the matter upon his return in November. There seemed little real disposition to believe that a discussion of the Stalin proposal would be useful. Governments had more important things to do at the end of 1939 than try to renew discussions of debts that were not likely to be paid.

And yet the question was not dead either. American citizens continued to write to the Department of State to inquire about the debt situation, and the Department continued to give reassuring but meaningless answers: "The Department is not in a position to indicate when it may become possible to obtain an agreement for the settlement of such claims, although it will not fail to take advantage of any favorable opportunity for concluding such an agreement which may arise."[125]

> Any American citizen who desires to file with the Department a claim against the Soviet Government based on the ownership of Russian bonds should submit a sworn statement showing when he became an American citizen, when his bonds were obtained, the kinds, amounts, and serial numbers of the bonds, the consideration paid therefor, and the name and nationality of the person from whom they were obtained. If the bonds were obtained after January 21, 1918 (the date of the Soviet repudiation), the claimant should also submit evidence in affidavit form showing the names and nationalities of prior holders of the bonds since that time.[126]

On August 4, 1939, Congress, by joint resolution, provided for a Commissioner of Claims of American nationals against the Soviet government, which led to another flurry of inquiries; the Department could only explain that no funds had been appropriated by Congress for carrying out the purpose of the resolution. (In 1955 the arrangement for the Commissioner of Claims was repealed.)

With the coming of the Second World War, the cycle of futility began again. Soon after the Soviet Union occupied the Western Ukraine and Western White Russia in September of 1939, it nationalized land, banks, and large industries there. Now new claims would arise. The Secretary of State ordered the Chargé in Moscow to "draft a reply . . . informing [the Commissariat] that you have been instructed by your Government to state that your Government looks to the Government of the U.S.S.R. for the compensation of any American nationals or firms who may have suffered losses as the result of nationalization of foreign property."[127]

Another aspect of the Kerensky debt resulted from action in the Second World War by which a group of White Russians were stranded in Western Europe. Countrymen in the United States hoped to bring some of them to this country but were confronted by problems of sponsorship and financial support. On March 5, 1941, Alexander Kerensky called at the Department of State to talk about this matter; he left with Warren, chief of the Visa Division, two undated memoranda. One reads:

> As you know, the Russian Provisional Government received in 1917 a large loan from the Government of the United States. The Provisional Government also had considerable sums of its own on deposit in this country. . . . This money remains to this date in a separate account of the United States Treasurt [sic]. . . .
>
> I believe it would be fair to appropiate [sic] a small fraction of this money, perhaps 50-75,000 dollars, for the relief of Russian emigres who have remained true to the principles of democracy.
>
> A. Kerensky[128]

After the German attack on the Soviet Union in 1941, the American Government decided that, despite these problems over earlier debts, American interests would best be served by making money and equipment available to the Soviet Union to fight against Hitler. A series of agreements were made, by which the Soviet Government came under the same Master Lend-Lease Agreement as other anti-Nazi governments. Announcement of these developments brought a wave of new protests to the State Department. A lawyer in Texas wrote to his Congressman who asked the Department to comment:

> A billion dollars of Lend-Lease Funds has been made available to the Soviet Government.

Is it not timely to consider the plight of American citizens who loaned Russia money in 1916 . . . ?

. . . . .

In view of the aid we have extended to save Russia Congress may decide that Russia should not be required to *pay* the $375,000,000 borrowed from our Government in 1916. However, in all fairness don't you think that the Soviet Government should recognize and *negotiate settlement* of its $90,000,000 indebtedness owed to *citizens* . . . and to the banks which advanced the credit?[129]

On November 27, 1941, Senator Robert A. Taft of Ohio took a similar view and then added:

I should be greatly obliged if you would let me know whether the State Department has called this matter to the attention of the Russian Government in connection with the new loan for $1 billion. . . . While it would not be advisable to embarrass the Russian Government by requiring payment at this time, it occurs to me that this is the time to press for a recognition of this debt, and some arrangement for its payment in the future.[130]

It is interesting, after all that had happened, that people would still expect a new pledge from the Soviet government to solve problems caused by its failure to honor old pledges. Hull's answers to such inquiries and protests were usually something like this:

The question as to the adjustment of obligations by the Soviet Government to nationals of the United States has been discussed at considerable length with that Government and will be further discussed as opportunity is afforded, but it has not been thought to be in the national interest to make the recognition of such obligations a condition precedent to the furnishing of such assistance as is now being given to the Soviet Government. That assistance is deemed to be in the interest of our own national defense.[131]

Thus, while the debt question kept simmering over the years until we were involved in the Second World War—Hull's answer to the Taft inquiry, just quoted, was dated the day after the Pearl Harbor attack—no more progress was made than during the main negotiations in 1934. Bullitt has written that he and others urged the President, in the summer of 1941, not to give financial aid to Stalin until the latter had given "formal, written, public pledges" on a number of matters. "But the President rejected the suggestion, on the ground that, although there was no doubt that Stalin would make such pledges, there was equally little doubt that Stalin would break the promises as soon as it might

suit him to break them. . . . The President concluded [that] pledges
from Stalin were not worth having."[132]

The obligations incurred by the Soviet Government under the Lend-
Lease arrangements (the total amount was more than ten billion dollars) led to the question of payment. This produced the same kinds
of stalemates that earlier administrations had encountered with the
Russians. The American government, playing the 1934 Soviet theme
in a different key, announced that it was "not prepared to make a
settlement with the Soviet Union that would be materially more favorable than the terms previously demanded from friends and allies of the
United States, such as Britain and France."[133] When Khrushchev
visited the United States in 1959 he complained about "discrimina-
tions" imposed on Soviet trade. He was informed that removal would
require congressional action and that a "fair agreement" on the Lend-
Lease indebtedness would create a much better atmosphere in the
country. Under Secretary of State C. Douglas Dillon told a press conference that the United States government even had some hopes that
Khrushchev might make some payment on the $180,000,000 borrowed
by the Kerensky government, though he cautioned against high hopes
that the Russians would pay Tsarist bonds. If the Russians settled the
Kerensky and Lend-Lease debts, said Dillon, the United States "probably would consider that the terms of the Johnson Act don't apply to
the Soviet Union."[134]

A new set of negotiations in January 1960 led nowhere. The Soviet
government took the position that a lend-lease settlement would have
to be accompanied by a trade agreement and extension of long-term
credits on terms acceptable to the Soviet Union. The Department of
State said: "In view of the absence of agreement between the two
governments concerning the terms of reference of these negotiations,
there would appear to be no common ground for their continuance at
this time";[135] they were suspended on January 27, 1960.

Thus, the question of debts was still alive after forty years. A small
payment had actually been made on the private claims, as we shall
see in Chapter VI. It was noted in Chapter I that at the time of recognition in 1933 the Swiss press was not impressed by the November 16
debt statement, suggesting that "this matter may probably be settled
by . . . never mentioning it again."[136] It might have been just as well
to have saved all the effort expended, since the results were so similar.

CONCLUSIONS

The question of debts and claims, as stated at the outset, loomed
very large in the thinking of many Americans. There was real hope

that the "agreement" Litvinov signed in Washington would produce some actual payment by the Soviet government. Disillusion, slow in coming, was all the more bitter when it arrived.

Nothing more needs to be said here about the discussions in Washington in November 1933 and the gentleman's agreement that resulted from them. That the American position was carelessly stated, to the subsequent discomfiture of the government, is all too apparent. Assumptions, impressions, and oral understandings were entirely inadequate as bases for this important aspect of a significant diplomatic endeavor. It was Litvinov, not the Americans, who pressed in February 1935 for publication of the November 15 memorandum. Just after the breakdown in January 1935, an editorial in *Za Industrializatsiyu* concluded, "It is obviously impossible to accuse the Soviet government of not having fulfilled any of its undertakings to the United States."[137] An undated, unsigned memorandum received by the Department of State in August 1938 stated the official Soviet position:

> The Soviet Government does not feel that failure . . . to arrive at a settlement has been due to a lack of cooperation on its part, but, as before, attributes the inconclusive outcome of the negotiations to differences in interpretation of the understanding reached between the President and Mr. Litvinov and considers the interpretation given on the American side a departure from this understanding. The absence of a settlement of this question does not in itself constitute, in the opinion of the Soviet Government, an obstacle to the development of close and friendly relations between the two countries.[138]

Whether the first part of this statement was, in fact, correct or not, the Soviet government was able to make its position sound reasonable and throw the blame on the American government. The purpose of American diplomacy is to prevent such results, whenever possible. The latter part of the statement, in a cynical fashion, is true. Moscow was realistic in claiming that it had established friendly relations with other governments to which it owed large sums of money, without making any arrangement at all for payment. And, in another sense, the Soviet government was doing exactly what these other governments were doing. Litvinov spoke truthfully when he exclaimed to Bullitt: "No nation today pays its debts. Great Britain has defaulted. Germany is defaulting. And no one will be able to make propaganda against the Soviet Union if we do not pay one dollar on a debt we did not contract."[139] It was the bitter truth.

The American position seems to have been based upon its legal rights and Soviet need for credit. Of the legal rightness of the American position there is no doubt, and there was no argument. The debtor was a revolutionary regime that did not consider itself bound by the principles of bourgeois law. In any case, legal right is often an inadequate justification; as Trotsky said, "We may regret it but life is not based on jurisprudence."[140] And yet the Soviet government did assume legal responsibility and has repeatedly admitted its liability. And Premier Khrushchev sounded like a capitalist conservative, just prior to his 1959 visit to the United States, when he said, "Without observance of the standards of international law and without the fulfillment of undertakings assumed in relations between states, there can be no trust, and, without trust, there can be no peaceful coexistence. . . . The Soviet Union has always fulfilled and will continue sacredly to fulfill its international undertakings."[141] This statement, however, did not produce any payments.

Apparently, also, the American government believed that the Soviet government needed the financial credits so badly that it would be forced to make a settlement. Admitting the domestic aspect of the problem—negotiation with Moscow was played against a political background of general debt negotiation—the American government must have thought it held all the trumps, to have initiated negotiations with Moscow simultaneously with the passage of the Johnson Act and the Export-Import Bank resolution. The Soviet government could not avoid the belief that it was being subjected to strong pressure. One Soviet official stated that these actions "gave them the impression . . . that this government was attempting to use pressure thereon and . . . in the seventeen years of their government they had never yet yielded when another nation attempted to apply force."[142] Since the American government had to push negotiations and press for a settlement, its antagonizing the Soviet government in this manner seems strange, indeed. The problem was not handled very adroitly; the American government did better with the other agreements made with Litvinov.

Yet the Soviet government may also have miscalculated. Over a period of years, it apparently believed that the pressure of American business groups would be so great that the United States government would have to capitulate, that Moscow could just lie low and wait. Since this tactic had worked with other countries, it is not surprising that it was applied to the United States. In such a case, the Soviet leaders may actually have supposed that the American leaders would have to accept a payment as low as $50,000,000, with no interest, and over twenty years, with the American government paying the bill by providing credit to Moscow. Nor were the Russians entirely wrong. Within six months of the end of the debt negotiations—on July 13, 1935—Washington and Moscow entered into a trade agreement by which Russia undertook to buy at least $30,000,000 worth of goods a year in the United States in return for which she received most-favored-nation treatment on tariff rates generally applied under the Trade Agreements Act of 1934. In the debt negotiations Washington preferred the role of "jilted suitor" to that of "partner to a shotgun wedding," but it did not want to be left out entirely.

Was there any real chance of settling the debt problem? Probably not. The two governments were too far apart on the basic principles, not just on the detailed adjustments, for us to expect that either would have made the concessions necessary for an agreement. It would be difficult to conclude from a study of these negotiations that the Russians were just stalling and never wanted a settlement. Studied against the background of the other differences between the two governments, Bullitt's suspicions of Soviet bad faith early in 1934, and the Soviet position on the 7th Comintern Congress just after the breakdown of the debt negotiations, there is no reason to believe that the Russians really wanted the agreement. They might have been forced into making such an agreement, under certain conditions, but those pressures did not arise in 1934, so that the Soviet leaders treated the United States as they had their other debtors. It was a peculiar application of most-favored-nation treatment. Secretary Hull seems to have been completely right when he said, halfway through the debt negotiations, "Personally I have little idea that the Soviet officials will come to any reasonable agreement. Litvinoff won his victory when he obtained recognition and regards everything else as of minor importance."[143]

Yet Litvinov may have been just as correct when he talked about political changes in the future. What the Soviet government may not have felt any need to agree to at one time, it may yet see is in its interest. Khrushchev's statements in 1959 show that the Soviet government has not forgotten the issue and is prepared to drag it out of the closet onto the stage whenever helpful to its cause. Unlikely though this seems at so late a date, if Moscow felt itself backed into a corner— by Chinese or other pressures—some payment might still be forthcoming.

CHAPTER VI

Soviet Claims and Assignments

CLAIMS

The financial problem was not confined to debts owed by the Soviet government to the American government and its nationals. There was, at least potentially, the chance of reciprocation, for the Soviet government had claims to money which, it asserted, was owed to it. Much of this claim arose out of the Allied intervention following the Bolshevist revolution; additional claims resulted from the period of uncertainty following the establishment of the Soviet regime. Since the American government had delayed recognition so long, the possible legal effect of recognition was particularly relevant.

The United States Supreme Court, in the case of *Oetjen* v. *Central Leather Co.*, had stated in 1918 the general rule for the American government: "When a government which originates in revolution or revolt is recognized by the political department of our government as the *de jure* government of the country in which it is established, such recognition is retroactive in effect and validates all actions and conduct of the government thus recognized from the commencement of its existence."[1] We have seen that Ambassador Boris Bakhmetyev, sent by the Provisional Government to the United States in 1917, continued to be the Russian representative in Washington until June 30, 1922, and was then replaced by Serge Ughet, the Financial Attaché, who was recognized as custodian of Russian government property in this country until November 1933. Under the rule of the Oetjen case, recognition of the Soviet government could have led to invalidation of the acts of Bakhmetyev and Ughet, with consequent liability resting on American citizens and corporations. Litvinov himself had underscored the significance of this problem in 1928 when, despite the lack of official relations between the two governments, he had sent a telegram to the State Department, protesting the decision of a United States District Court that ordered the Lehigh Valley Railway Co. to pay compensation to the owners of munitions destroyed in 1916 in the Black Tom explosion. "Compensation for the destroyed property," said Litvinov,

> has been paid to a certain Serge Ughet, who styles himself a representative of the said former Russian Governments. . . . Taking into consideration the fact that Ughet had no authority whatsoever from the present government of the state previously known as the Russian Empire, the Government of the Union of Soviet Socialist Republics protests against the payment to a private person of money belonging to the former Russian Treasury, the application of which to any account may be made only with the sanction of the sole lawful owner of such money, viz. the Union of Soviet Socialist Republics represented by its Government. The Government of the Union of Soviet Socialist Republics considers the delivery of the above sum to Ughet as an irregular act, and reserves to itself the full right of putting a claim for this sum upon the Government of the USA.[2]

Protection against such claim was necessary, and as the Department of State prepared the agreements it wished Litvinov to sign, this problem was not overlooked.

One of the agreements related to Allied intervention after the Bolshevik revolution. One area of American intervention had been Siberia, and Litvinov agreed to waive all claims arising out of this action:

> My Dear Mr. President: I have the honor to inform you that, following our conversations and following my examination of certain documents of the years 1918 to 1921 relating to the attitude of the American Government toward the expedition into Siberia, the operations there of foreign military forces and the inviolability of the territory of the Union of Soviet Socialist Republics, the Government of the Union of Soviet Socialist Republics agrees that it will waive any and all claims of whatsoever character arising out of activities of military forces of the United States in Siberia, or assistance to military forces in Siberia subsequent to January 1, 1918, and that such claims shall be regarded as finally settled and disposed of by this agreement.[3]

There are several points of interest in this statement. One is that the agreement applied to the Siberian expedition only; Litvinov did not include the Archangel and Murmansk expeditions, although the American negotiators must surely have tried to put all three in the same category. It might be said, next, that the Far Eastern situation in 1933 was responsible for Litvinov's willingness to waive claims arising from the Siberian expedition, although the records do not show that it was; he surely was conscious that his statement would convey such an impression. It was known that the American forces had restrained the Japanese during the Siberian episode; this may have influenced Litvinov. In any case, the first part of his statement seems to indicate that he had been impressed "following our conversations and following my examination of certain documents," as if he had not expected to waive any claims arising out of the action until he had been "convinced" while in Washington.

The middle part of the sentence is curious. There is the reference to the "attitude of the American Government toward . . . the inviolability of the territory of the Union of Soviet Socialist Republics." In the first place, the U.S.S.R. did not exist in the 1918-20 period. With the caution used in preparing the text of these agreements, it cannot be imagined that the American negotiators were so careless as to write "Union of Soviet Socialist Republics" when they should have written "Russian Socialist Federated Soviet Republic." Moreover, the reference to territorial inviolability seems out of place here, since it was a violation of this that the Soviet leaders had complained about for many years. This might be understandable if the American leaders had been able to impress Litvinov, by showing him that the United States government was helpful to the Soviet interests in 1918-20 and was still willing to demonstrate interest in Soviet sovereignty over the area at a time when it was repeatedly predicted that the Japanese were about to seize the Siberian coastal areas.

The Americans had no such leverage over claims arising out of the Archangel and Murmansk expeditions, and Litvinov was not pressed into a similar abandonment here. Soviet claims against the United States arising from the Siberian expedition were thus completely extinguished by the Litvinov agreement in 1933; claims based on the other two actions were left to be settled with the debt problem.

ASSIGNMENTS

Another important aspect of the matter of debts owed the Soviet government falls under the heading of assignments. Before this regime came to power, there was in the United States certain property belonging to the then-Russian government or to Russian nationals. The Soviet government now claimed this property, either as the successor to the Russian Provisional Government or as a result of the 1918 nationalization laws. If the Soviet government refused to accept full responsibility for money owed by its predecessor governments, this did not mean that it might not seek to collect money owed it as their successor. There was uncertainty about the scope of Soviet nationalization; for example, American banks refused to pay out money deposited by former Russian corporations and individuals, even when these included demands on the accounts over their own signatures, lest later the banks be held responsible for the funds by the Soviet government, as in the Cibrario case, cited below. The Soviet government had confiscated the property of its nationals in Russia; why could it not claim the funds of its nationals abroad?

In October 1933, when the recognition issue was coming to the fore, Frederic R. Coudert, member of a New York law firm, pointed out to the Department of State that the Soviet government had agreed in March 1921 to make no effort to obtain any property in Britain that had belonged to former Russian governments. Why should this principle not be applied in the United States as well?

> Would it not seem proper and necessary, that some arrangement be made, preparatory to the possible recognition of the Soviet Government, for these pending Russian suits? If, as we assume, the Soviet Government is not to be permitted to prosecute these claims, then an assignment thereof by the Soviet Government to the Government of the United States would appear requisite.[4]

Assistant Secretary Moore wrote a memorandum suggesting this as the best of several alternatives.

Such suggestions were obviously followed and, in one of the November 16, 1933, agreements, Litvinov agreed to waive all claim to this property, releasing and assigning it to the government of the United States:

> My Dear Mr. President: Following our conversations I have the honor to inform you that the Government of the Union of Soviet Socialist Republics agrees that, preparatory to a final settlement of the claims and counter claims between the Governments of the Union of Soviet Socialist Republics and of the United States of America and the claims of their nationals, the Government of the Union of Soviet Socialist Republics will not take any steps to enforce any decisions of courts or initiate any new litigations for the amounts admitted to be due or that may be found to be due it as the successor of prior Governments of Russia, or otherwise, from American nationals, including corporations, companies, partnerships, or associations, and also the claim against the United States of the Russian Volunteer Fleet, now in litigation in the United States Court of Claims, and will not object to such amounts being assigned and does hereby release and assign all such amounts to

the Government of the United States, the Government of the Union of Soviet Socialist Republics to be duly notified in each case of any amount realized by the Government of the United States from such release and assignment.

The Government of the Union of Soviet Socialist Republics further agrees, preparatory to the settlement referred to above, not to make any claim with respect to:

(a) judgments rendered or that may be rendered by American courts in so far as they relate to property, or rights, or interests therein; in which the Union of Soviet Socialist Republics or its nationals may have had or may claim to have an interest; or

(b) acts done or settlements made by or with the Government of the United States, or public officials in the United States, or its nationals, relating to property, credits, or obligations of any Government of Russia or nationals thereof.[5]

In simpler language, the Soviet government agreed not to take any action relative to this property but to release and assign it to the United States government. This was a full release by the Soviet government. The only obligation resting on the American government was to notify the Soviet government whenever any money was collected on the basis of the assignment. As Secretary of State Hull wrote to the Attorney General in 1934, "It was the purpose of the assignment in question to release and assign to the United States not only all amounts to which the Soviet government was entitled as the successor to former governments of Russia, but also all amounts to which the Soviet government considered it was entitled in my manner."[6]

One essential, obviously, was to list all Russian property in the United States, so that the American government would know what had been assigned to it. On August 25, 1933, Serge Ughet, the Financial Attaché and custodian of Russian property in the United States, had "assigned, transferred, set over and delivered unto the United States of America all property, of whatsoever nature and description . . . together with all claims and demands,"[7] with a list of such property attached. As matters turned out, this Ughet assignment was unnecessary, being covered up by the Litvinov assignment in November, but Ughet had succeeded in freeing himself (and the Provisional Government now dead for sixteen years) from further legal responsibility for the property. In October 1933 Ughet presented a list of the items in Table 4 as a basis for action by the Soviet government. This list was not identical to the earlier list.

TABLE 4[8]

RUSSIAN PROPERTY IN THE UNITED STATES

Real property	Russian Embassy, 16th Street, Washington	
Bank deposits	Guaranty Trust Co., balance of December 12, 1917	$4,976,722.78
	New York Trust Co., balance of August 11, 1926	46,584.18
	New York Trust Co., balance of November 11, 1927	11,680.00
	National City Bank, balance of September 30, 1933	151,784.01*
Claims	against Curtiss Aeroplane and Motor Corp.	$1,050,000.00
	against Canadian Pacific Railway Co.	384,118.07
	against National City Bank	140,000.00
	against U. S. Shipping Board	1,412,532.35
	against Guaranty Trust Co.	15,000.00

*Against this, there was an offset claim of $4,435,000.

Ughet admitted that there might be other items which had never come to his attention. In 1930, looking for a list of Russian property in the United States, he had written to the Department of State, "I recall quite distinctly the form of the list and that the total of the property, besides the government funds, enumerated in that list amounted to something like $15,000,000."[9] Neither the Department of State nor the Treasury could find such a list in 1933, and the items enumerated amount to only half of this figure. Thereafter, the Treasury circulated a questionnaire regarding Russian accounts in American banks. In January 1935, J. P. Morgan Co. listed several such accounts, none large, of which Ughet had no knowledge. He wrote, "The fact is that there are about $130,000 available to the United States, and that in itself is a pleasant surprise."[10]

A number of problems had to be surmounted, however, before these assignments could be collected. Most of the problems were legal and technical, though many of them contained at least an element of politics.

This was especially true of the Soviet government's confiscation of private property. When the American government, to buttress its position in court suits under the assignment, asked for an official statement from the Soviet government, the latter asserted "that the 1933 agreement has in view those rights of the government of the Union of Soviet Socialist Republics which are subject to realization on the territory of the United States and which have passed to the government of the Union of Soviet Socialist Republics by virtue of its succession to former governments of Russia or by virtue of its succession to private companies on the basis of legislation concerning nationalization."[11]

This idea did not, of course, commend itself to American public opinion. The New York State Court of Appeals, for example, ruled in January 1934 that, since the Soviet confiscation decree was "contrary to our public policy and shocking to our sense of justice and equity," the recognition of the Soviet government afforded "no controlling reason why it should be enforced in our courts."[12] "If our Government obtains title to these funds," wrote a lawyer who opposed the government's position on the assignments, "one link in the chain of title is a confiscatory decree of the Soviet Government so that our Government thereby becomes a receiver of confiscated funds. . . . But . . . our Government certainly should not receive from another government confiscated property which it would not be permitted to take under its own constitution."[13] The United States government, however, took the view that the nationalization was an internal affair, "a matter between the companies and the state that created them."

> In asking the courts to pass upon the legal effect of the assignment . . . this Government does not give approval to or admit the propriety of the Soviet nationalization decrees but seeks only to give effect to the assignment if, as a matter of law, the decrees had the effect of making the assets the property of the Soviet Government. . . . Such decision would not in our opinion affect the obligation of that Government to make compensation where rights of American nationals are involved.[14]

Another aspect of the nationalization controversy concerned the right of the Soviet government to assign title to the assets located in the United States. At the time of the nationalization decrees, there was no U.S.S.R. and the decrees were those of the R.S.F.S.R. Thus, in 1936, in the trial of the Moscow Fire Insurance Co., the attorney moved to dismiss the petition of the American government on the grounds that it had not proven any connection between the legal title of the R.S.F.S.R. and that of the U.S.S.R. The referee gave the government a period of time in which to present this proof, which set off a feverish search into Soviet law. The Department of State sent a call to the Embassy in Moscow for declarations or even a Soviet legal expert to testify at the trial. On September 22, 1936, the Embassy wired an interpretation from the Commissariat of Justice of the R.S.F.S.R. affirming that "the rightfulness of the transfer to the ownership of the Government of the U.S.A. by the Government of the U.S.S.R. of property situated abroad, nationalized according to the laws of the R.S.F.S.R., in particular the property of the insurance companies . . . is perfectly obvious."[15] The Embassy also enclosed an opinion by Professor Mark A. Plotkin, Vice-Director of the Legal Department of the People's Commissariat for Foreign Affairs, that "from the stand-point of Soviet law there is no doubt that the Government of the Union . . . had the right to assign to the Government of the U.S.A. the properties of the Moscow Insurance Co." stating that there were a number of precedents where the central government had dealt with objects nationalized by the government of the R.S.F.S.R. The Embassy expressed its disappointment, however, that Professor Plotkin was unwilling to go further and state formally that the foreign assets of the R.S.F.S.R. had become *ipso facto* the assets of the Union government, but the Soviet official maintained that he had gone as far as entitled under Soviet law, and that if he went any further "he would be venturing into ground which as yet had not been explored by the Soviet judicial legislative system."

Following this, the Embassy appealed to Litvinov himself, on January 7, 1937, and he agreeably stated, in a note of the same date, that "it was the purpose and intention of the Government of the Union of Soviet Socialist Republics to assign to the Government of the United States . . . all the amounts admitted to be due or that may be found due not only to the Union of Soviet Socialist Republics but also the constituent republics of the Union of Soviet Socialist Republics or their predecessors."[16] The issue was finally settled through an inter-pretation by the People's Commissariat of Justice of the R.S.F.S.R., which certified that "all nationalized funds and property of former private enterprises and companies, in particular by virtue of the decree of November 28, 1918 . . . the funds and property of the former insurance companies, constitute the property of the State . . . irrespective of whether it was situated within the territorial limits of the R.S.F.S.R. or abroad."[17]

Another question was of more general concern in the United States. By 1935 it had become apparent that, for the present at least, the negotiations over the debts had come to an impasse and that the creditors were not likely to be paid. The only assets being turned into cash were those involved in the assignments. These were being taken by the United States government and placed in a special fund in the Treasury. Congress had made no provision for their final disposition. If these funds were to be disposed of by Congressional decision, asked the President of the Foreign Bondholders Council, "I would like to ask you how this matter is likely to come before Congress for de-termination. . . . Just how should the Council proceed in order to have any claims of bondholders given consideration?" To this query, the Department's Legal Adviser replied:

Little thought has been given to the question as to whether the Department should make recommendations to the Congress with respect to the disposition to be made of funds which may be recovered under the assignment. . . . At the time the assignment was taken it was thought that there would be a general settlement of claims against Soviet Russia and that the amounts recovered under the assignment would be supplemented by payments by the Soviet Government.[18]

But that part of the plan had not materialized, and the United States government was, meanwhile, taking control of the only cash available or likely to be. Hence there were repeated protests to the Department of State against this practice. It was even suggested that the breakdown in debt negotiations required "as a necessary corollary the withdrawal of all litigation based on the Litvinoff assignment."[19] The Department rejected this view. Hull wrote the President that "the Department does not find any merit in the line of reasoning advanced in Mr. Polk's letter."[20] "The assignment made to the Government of the United States by the Soviet Government," wrote Assistant Secretary Moore, " . . . is not dependent upon the reaching of a final settlement of the question of debts and claims, and . . . this Department does not propose to direct the discontinuance of the litigation instituted in pursuance of that assignment."[21]

The counsel for one group proposed that the whole policy be changed. Under the current policy the funds obtained under the assignment would be distributed among the claimants against the Russian government. But, he said, the claims amount to seven or eight hundred million dollars, perhaps more with the interest, and there will be thousands of claimants, scattered all over the world. The distribution would involve an interminable and expensive proceeding so that no one would obtain more than a few cents on a dollar. Why then, he asked, did the American government not forego further litigation and let the funds revert to their original rightful owners? "All that is necessary . . . is a dismissal of the Government's case upon its merits. In that event the Insurance Department and the Banks where these funds are deposited will pay them to the owners without further delay."[22] The Secretary of State replied that "the assignment vested the ownership of the assets in question in the Government of the United States, which is one of the creditors of the Soviet Government and it would therefore seem that such assets could not be disposed of in the manner you propose without Congressional action."[23] The government was willing to forego any of this money for itself, agreeing to devote all amounts realized under the assignment to the benefit, in whole or in part, of American private claimants against Russia.[24]

The United States government believed, indeed, that it should press the assignment suits. "The Department of State considers that this government should make every effort possible to disclose assets which this government could claim under the assignment."[25] A conversation in 1939 between representatives of the Department of Justice and Assistant Secretary Moore and the Legal Adviser of the Department of State reaffirmed this view:

> It was the conclusion of those present . . . that the Executive branch of the Government is obligated to realize the assets which were assigned to the Government. . . .
>
> Mr. Moore pointed out that prior to the commencement of the suits based on the assignment, Mr. Frank L. Polk had personally suggested to the President that the Government should not treat the assignment as covering assets of private corporations nationalized by the Soviet Government and should not seek to recover such assets in the United States, but the President did not accept that view of the matter. . . . The question of the abandonment of the Government's claims to assets of these private corporations was brought to the Department's attention some months ago . . . and at that time the Department supported by the Department of Justice, took the position that it was obligated to take all appropriate steps to realize any assets which had accrued to this Government under the assignment and that the matter of determining whether the Government or creditors of the corporations were entitled to the assets was a matter for the courts to decide.[26]

During this discussion, there was consideration of the character of some of the claims. The representatives of the Department of Justice stated that they

> were not cognizant of one claim against these corporate assets which is held by a person who is an American citizen and who was an American citizen at the time the claim arose; that the interested parties are mostly aliens, or persons who have become naturalized citizens since their claim arose, "conservors" of the companies' assets, and attorneys.[27]

They were very skeptical "of the bona fides of many of the claims" and stated that the practical question is "whether the corporations' assets shall go to these people or to American claimants against the Soviet Government for the satisfaction, at least in part, of whose claims it has been the intention of the Government to make these funds available."

Insistence of the United States government on prosecuting cases under the assignment was, in part, the result of an important legal victory for the government. Prior to 1918 a Russian corporation, the Petrograd Metal Works, had deposited money with August Belmont in New York. The United States government sued Belmont's heirs for this money, on the ground that it had been confiscated under the Russian decree of June 28, 1918, and assigned to the United States in 1933. In 1936 the U.S. Circuit Court of Appeals, 2d Circuit, dismissed the complaint; the court recognized that the confiscation decree was effective, as applied to property physically located on Russian territory, but refused to permit its operation within the United States. The court said:

> Laws of foreign governments have extraterritorial effect only by comity and the public policy of the forum determines whether its courts will give effect to foreign legislation. It is very clear that it is contrary to the public policy of the state of New York to enforce confiscatory decrees with respect to property located here. Nor can the assignment . . . give the assignee any greater right than the assignor had.[28]

On appeal, however, the United States Supreme Court reversed this decision, and the Belmont case decision thus became the keystone of the American government's position on cases involving the assignment. The Supreme Court's decision read, in part:

> What another country has done in the way of taking over property of its nationals, and especially of its corporations, is not a matter for judicial consideration here. Such nationals must look to their own government for any redress to which they may be entitled. So far as the record shows, only the rights of the Russian corporation have been affected by what has been done; and it will be time enough to consider the rights of our nationals when, if ever, by proper judicial proceeding, it shall be made to appear that they are so affected as to entitle them to judicial relief. The substantive right to the money, as now disclosed, became vested in the Soviet Government, as the successor to the corporation; and this right that government has passed to the United States.[29]

This case, the first in which the Supreme Court had passed on the merits of the government's claims arising out of the assignment, became the precedent for the other cases then pending.

Yet there were those who considered this a Pyrrhic victory. "Does it not seem anomalous," wrote Professor Edwin Borchard to Assistant Secretary Moore,

> that after denouncing the Soviets for fifteen years for the confiscation of private property . . . we should now undertake to share in the plunder as assignees of the Soviets and have the Attorney General or Solicitor General of the United States appear in court to defend the validity of the confiscations and our own rights under them? For the few paltry million dollars of confiscated property that we would thus

acquire, we undermine a long-continued national tradition and make altogether paradoxical the United States refusal to recognize the Soviets because of their confiscatory policy. Moreover, it seems to me that we have weakened beyond expression the force of our claim that the confiscations of American property in Russia were illegal under international law; we thus seem effectively to have extinguished the several hundred millions of dollars of claims that we hold.[30]

Borchard did not say, as he might well have done, that one of the members of the court in the Belmont case had been Secretary of State in 1923 and had said that if the Soviet authorities were ready to restore the confiscated property of American citizens or make effective compensation, they could do so, as quoted in Chapter I.

Aside from the legal aspect, and the Department of State continued to maintain that its position was not one of upholding the confiscations, there was the practical side to which Borchard referred. The American government hoped to realize something like five million dollars from the assignment cases, and if, in so doing, it jeopardized hundreds of millions of dollars worth of claims, this was a self-defeating procedure. Looking back now, it is apparent that this was no real sacrifice, for there was no actual possibility of getting the Soviet government to pay its debts. Those who wondered whether the United States government would even obtain enough money from the assignment cases to pay the costs of prosecuting them were more realistic.

The Belmont case decision opened the way for the United States government to prosecute other cases. The files of the Department of State on these cases are voluminous, and the material is often very technical. There is no one place which lists all of the cases, or their status at a particular time, or the decision which was made. It has been found impossible to make a complete analysis of the matter, especially since the files are not generally open beyond 1941 and some of the cases were still pending at that time. The following discussion sets forth the general facts of some of these cases, as illustrations only, following which there will be an estimate of the money realized from these legal actions.

A list of cases was attempted in 1934, only a year after the assignment and long before the Belmont decision. A memorandum stated that the government had instituted litigation in the following seven cases, involving $6,639,910.62.[31]

> U.S. v. Guaranty Trust (U.S.)—$4,976,722.28; U.S. v. New York Trust Co. (Vladikavkas [sic] Railway)—$58,264.18; U.S. v. Morton Trust [sic] and Tractor Co.—$1,433.01; U.S. v. Bank of New York

and Trust Co. (Moscow Fire and Insurance Co.)—$1,080,399.54; U.S. v. President and Directors, Manhattan Co.—$245,307.60; Bettman v. The Northern Insurance Co. of Moscow—$126,000.00; (The U.S. attempting to intervene).

There were eight other cases, involving $4,050,118.07, where, it was said, the United States would probably institute suit as soon as additional information had been secured:

> Curtiss Airplane Co.—$1,050,000; Canadian Pacific Railway—$384,118.07; National City Bank (shoe contractors)—$140,000; Globe Indemnity Co.—$126,000; Baranowsky Co.—$1,000,000; Russian Reinsurance Co.—$100,000; 1st Russian Reinsurance Co.—$1,000,000; 2nd Russian Reinsurance Co.—$250,000.

The list of cases and the amounts involved do not always agree, from one time and place to another.

The Guaranty Trust Co. in New York had in its possession, belonging in whole or in part to the Soviet government, an amount of $6,540,-000; it had claims against the Soviet government of $7,540,000, though there was reason to believe that some of these were overlapping or even void. The Guaranty Trust Co. offered to compromise the matter by paying either the Soviet or the United States government one million dollars, but the United States wanted to get a final judicial decision on its rights, even at the risk of losing the $1,000,000. The Guaranty Trust Co. also had on deposit $1,740,000, plus approximately $400,000 of interest, in a special account in the name of the Russo-Asiatic Bank. The P. V. Baranowsky Co., Ltd., munitions manufacturers, had contracted to purchase powder in the above amount during the First World War, although the contract was cancelled in June 1916; the directors of the company, assembled in Paris after the Bolshevik revolution, started suit for the money. After November 1933, however, the United States government sued Guaranty Trust Co. for this deposit, under the Litvinov assignment. The case was still incomplete in 1944.

In the case of the New York Trust Co. and Vladikavkazky Railway Co., the United States claimed the deposit in the New York bank on the grounds either that the railway was nationalized and the money assigned to the United States or that the deposit never belonged to the railway but had been advanced to it by the Russian government.

At least nine Russian insurance companies were in business in the United States, prior to the Bolshevik revolution. In the 1920's, the state of New York began the liquidation of the five of these companies that operated there. It was estimated that after the settlement of all American claims against the American assets of these five companies, there would be a surplus of about $5,000,000. The Soviet government claimed this surplus by virtue of the nationalization decrees, but as early as 1926 the Department of State informed state officials—Ohio was also involved—that the United States government had an interest in any funds which might be claimed by the Soviet regime. Most of the balance was still on deposit in 1933 when the American government claimed it under the assignment.

The National City Bank held sizable deposits. In 1927 Russian representatives offered to pay the bank approximately $10,000,000 to take care of the whole matter; the bank offered to accept $24,000,000 but negotiations fell through. This was one of the very few Soviet offers of compensation. The Curtiss Airplane Co. claim involved a contract with the Imperial Russian government to deliver seaplanes, 90 per cent to be paid on shipment from New York and the remainder after acceptance by the Russian government. Since some of the planes were allegedly unsatisfactory, the payment was held up, and the United States government now claimed the 90 per cent which had been paid and the cost of transportation, which totalled approximately one million dollars. The Canadian Pacific Railway claim involved a contract entered into in New York in 1916 between the railway and the Russian Railway Mission. The Litvinov assignment would not seem to include this claim since no American national was involved.

There was also a claim on postal money orders which had been bought in the United States but never cashed in Russia. When this business was finally suspended in 1920, there remained a balance of slightly more than $1,500,000. Acting Secretary of State Phillips wrote to the Postmaster General in 1936, "it is the opinion of this Department that, subject to the right of the purchasers of the money orders to claim refunds upon the submission of proper proof of non-payment in Russia, the amount held by the Post Office Department should be considered as belonging to the United States under the assignments,"[32] and the money placed in the special account in the Treasury. This was done in 1955, being specifically mentioned in Public Law 285, to be discussed below.

The situation of the Russian Volunteer Fleet illustrates some of the complexities arising out of the conflicting claims. In 1879 the Imperial Russian government chartered the Volunteer Fleet, based on voluntary contributions of Russian citizens. Sometimes part of the Russian navy and sometimes not, it was reorganized in 1912, under the Ministry of Trade and Industry, and provided with government subsidy. In 1914 certain of its vessels were delivered to the Allies to strengthen their transport facilities. After the Bolshevik revolution, the control of the Russian Volunteer Fleet—at least for those vessels not in Russian ports—continued to be exercised by the Board of Directors, and for the vessels in American waters by Ambassador Bakhmetyev in Washington. On March 30, 1918, the U.S. Shipping Board hired five of these vessels and paid $1,830,417.55 to the Russian Embassy in Washington. When Ughet tried to get the remaining $23,643.75 still due on this contract, the Shipping Board asserted against this debt a credit of $31,278.22 against the Russian Volunteer Fleet. The United States claimed that the fleet was an instrumentality of the Provisional Government and that any money paid should go to Ughet, who would turn it into the United States Treasury as a set-off for obligations of the Russian government. On April 1, 1929, the United States Court of Claims dismissed the petition, on the ground that the Soviet government had not been recognized by the executive branch of the government of the United States, but the Supreme Court reversed this decision on February 24, 1931, and remanded the case to the Court of Claims. At this point, Ughet was sent to Europe by the Department of Justice to secure records for use in the trial. Though still recognized by the United States government as a Russian government employee, he was actually trying to get money for the American government. The case was still pending in the Court of Claims on November 16, 1933, when Litvinov specifically assigned the matter to the United States government. In February 1934 that government moved successfully to dismiss the petition. In 1937 bills were introduced into both houses of Congress to determine the amount of compensation and to pay the attorneys of the Russian Volunteer Fleet.[33] The bills were approved, whereupon a whole batch of new claims was presented.

The Cibrario case illustrates limitations upon the use of the Litvinov assignment. In 1918 the R.S.F.S.R. government opened an account in the National City Bank, on the basis of a contract with Jacques Roberto Cibrario, an Italian then in Moscow, who was to provide photographic equipment. He later obtained most of the money. In April 1937—after a whole series of problems and court trials—the Soviet government sued the National City Bank, to recover one million dollars, plus interest from July 24, 1918. The defendant pleaded, among other things, that the Cibrario matter was included under the Litvinov assignment, and the New York Supreme Court agreed with this contention. While the case was being appealed, the Soviet government asked the American government for a clarified interpretation of the Litvinov agreement. It was the Soviet government's view that

> the parties to the correspondence contemplated solely the inclusion of such fund to which title might come to the Union of Soviet Socialist Republics by succession from previous governments, or otherwise, namely, by the virtue of laws of nationalization of the Union of Soviet Socialist Republics. The *intent* excluded any sums or claims which arose de novo after November 7, 1917, and which have colloquially been termed as "fresh money" deposited by the Union of Soviet Socialist Republics or any of its constituent bodies.[34]

The American government was requested to agree with this interpretation. Immediately afterwards, members of the Department of State met with representatives of the Department of Justice, who stated that they were not inclined "to bring suit for the funds . . . on the ground that these funds were 'fresh money' and that it was not the intent of Mr. Litvinov's note to assign to the Government of the United States funds deposited in American banks by the Soviet Government."[35] The question then arose of the possibility of a new exchange of notes between the two governments which would clarify a number of points. There was general agreement that, in the absence of legal or political obstacles, such an exchange of notes would be helpful to both governments. "There is no doubt," wrote Henderson, "that the Soviet Government has treated American courts unfairly from an American point of view, and that it has been guilty of a number of sharp practices so far as American property rights are concerned. Nevertheless, the American Government should not resort to similar practices in matters affecting the Soviet Government."[36] This new exchange of notes took place on June 3, 1939. The case was finally settled out of court in July 1942 with an unstated amount of money paid to the Soviet representative.

The problem of the Litvinov assignments would appear to have absorbed a disproportionate amount of the time and attention of officials of the State, Justice, and Treasury departments. It is gratifying that some money was realized, but it was a small amount, hardly worth the effort. Over a period of nearly twenty years the United States government collected and deposited in the Treasury the sum of $9,114,444.66, derived from the Ughet and Litvinov assignments. This money came from these sources:[37]

TABLE 5

MONEY REALIZED FROM THE LITVINOV ASSIGNMENT

1935	J. P. Morgan and Co.	$167,857.84
1935	Belmont Estate	825.93
1937	Sargent and Williams (Kidder, Peabody Co.)	36,326.59
1938	Post Office Department (money orders)	1,500,000.00
1941	Globe Indemnity Co.	112,500.00
1941	All Russian Zemsky Union	87,500.00
1942	Northern Insurance Co.	118,767.49
1942	Belmont (Petrograd Metal Works)	25,225.68
1942	Johnson and Higgins	66,219.64
1942	Russian Reinsurance Co.	95,825.00
1942	Comptroller of the Currency	330.58
1943–45	First Russian Insurance Co.	1,275,782.26
1943	Moscow Industrial Bank	354.81
1946	New York Trust (Vladikavkazski Railway)	75,914.66
1946	Northern Insurance Co. of Moscow	195,823.12
1946	Manhattan Co. (2nd Russian Insurance Co.)	282.04
1947	Guaranty Trust Co. (Russo-Asiatic Bank and Baranowsky)	3,000,000.00
1948	Guaranty Trust Co. (Russo-Asiatic Bank)	364,939.69
1948	Samson Selig	1,250.00
1948	Guaranty Trust Co. (misc. accounts)	166,126.72
1950	Curtiss Aeroplane Co.	500,000.00
1952	National City Bank (misc. accounts)	1,023,711.95
1953	Bank of New York; Fifth Ave. Bank	298,700.66
		$9,114,444.66

This $9,114,444.66 was deposited in Special Deposit Account 3 in the Treasury to await a Congressional decision as to its eventual disposition. As some American citizens with claims against the Soviet government had predicted and feared, the amounts realized were a paltry percentage of those claims.

On August 9, 1955, the 84th Congress amended the 1949 International Claims Settlement Act by passing Public Law 285 (69 Stat. 562) which dealt with American claims against a number of European governments. Among other things, a Soviet Claims Fund was created, into which the Secretary of the Treasury covered "the funds collected by the United States pursuant to the Litvinov Assignment (including postal funds due prior to November 16, 1933)." Authority over these claims was granted to the Foreign Claims Settlement Commission, established in 1954, with arrangements for filing claims and granting awards.

In accordance with this law, the Commission received 4,130 claims totaling $3,583,259,924. The money derived from the Litvinov Assignment was to be used to pay private but not United States government claims. All validated claims of $1,000 or less were to be paid in full; on all other claims, there should be a first-round payment of $1,000, and then a prorated share of the balance.

The Commission made 1,900 awards, totaling $38,793,147. A few examples may be helpful. Susan Erskine Rogers had purchased a $1,000 bond issued by the Vladikavkazski Railway Co., later nationalized by the Soviet government. She sought $2,580, the face value of the bond plus interest. In 1957 the Commission validated this claim. Andrew H. Allen was awarded $4,000, plus interest until November 16, 1933, the day of the Litvinov Assignment, on the basis of confiscated Imperial Russian government bonds. Bert McCord had purchased $112,590 of Imperial Russian government bonds for $1,008.45; he was awarded his purchase price by the Commission. The Methodist Church was awarded $82,500 for land and buildings in Russia confiscated by the Soviet government in 1917. In 1958 the Allis Chalmers Manufacturing Company was awarded $62,162.25 (principal plus interest to November 16, 1933) for its confiscated bank deposits. The Singer Manufacturing Company claimed $100,096,398.41 as the owner of a company in Russia and its treasury notes and bank accounts. Some of this claim was denied, and the Commission ruled that the Singer Company had a credit claim of $25,787,207.86. Since, however, the Commission found that the total worth of the Russian subsidiary company was only $19,077,666.49, its award was for this amount.[38]

It should be remembered that these figures represent awards made by the Commission; the formula stated in the 1955 law was then applied to these awards. Approximately two-thirds of the $9,114,444.66 was left after the first-round payments; this permitted a payment of 9.717845 per cent of the award balances. The result was that individuals were paid less than $1,000,000 of the total, with the large industrial claims getting the balance, out of about $50,000,000 awarded to them.[39] It was not clear whether these payments represented a repayment of principal, interest, interest on interest, or a government gratuity, but at least the Litvinov Assignment money was exhausted, and the private claimants in the United States did receive something of what was owed them.[40]

IMPLEMENTATION

The matter of implementation does not bulk large when applied to the assignments. Litvinov made his promise to assign and, by his signature, this became an accomplished fact. From this point, the implementation was largely in the hands of the American government.

The most important consequence of the Litvinov Assignment, perhaps, was that it kept the Soviet government from entering American courts and muddying the legal waters. The claims and counterclaims were, in any case, so involved that any simplification was helpful. This also prevented the Soviet government from attempting to challenge or reverse any of the decisions made in this country before November 16, 1933, about the disposition of Russian money in the United States. From the legal standpoint, it was very important to keep the Soviet government out of these cases, so that the United States government could handle them.

As we have seen, there were many resultant legal problems and interpretations; on these the American government called upon the Soviet government for assistance. Over the years, the latter cooperated very well with the American requests for information and official statements of Soviet law to be used in the trials. The process of getting this information was often time-consuming and patience-wearing, but the records indicate that this was because of differences between the two legal systems rather than Soviet unwillingness to be helpful.

In May 1936, the Department of State raised with the Soviet Ambassador in Washington the question of bringing a Soviet expert to the United States to help straighten out some of the legal confusion in the Moscow Fire Insurance Co. case. The Ambassador promised to raise the question with his government; there was little action. In September the Secretary wired Henderson relative to getting "Zhukhovitsky or other Soviet legal expert in the United States to be suggested by Soviet Embassy."[41] A week later, Henderson informed the Department that Professor Mark A. Plotkin "does not believe any Soviet legal expert in the United States is sufficiently versed in Soviet constitutional law to testify on the point and is of the opinion that it is preferable to have no Soviet witness rather than one who might become entangled by Komar's shrewd cross examination. Zhukovitsky [sic] is a specialist in commercial law rather than in matters of the kind at issue."[42] It was then arranged for Plotkin himself to come to the United States, which he did late in the summer of 1936, and also in December 1938 for further testimony. When he was needed again in 1939, however, it was found that he was unavailable, having been purged.

Some of these trials dragged on, year after year. The Soviet government must on occasion have wondered why the United States government kept wanting more material, much of it of the same type. On one occasion, indeed, the Soviet Foreign Office complained that it had already provided the Guaranty Bank with 900 photostats in 1931-32. Only after the German attack on the Soviet Union in 1941, however, did the Soviet government fail to cooperate and then under the plea that the desired documents were in Leningrad, under siege, or had been scattered to various places in the country for safekeeping and could not be located. In one such situation, the Soviet official "wished it understood that the delays had resulted . . . not from any unwillingness on the part of the Soviet authorities to be of assistance in the matter."[43]

As we have seen, also, the two governments exchanged notes in June 1939 to provide a clearer understanding of the scope of the Litvinov Assignment, so as to exclude the Cibrario case.

The money derived from the assignment was not of great importance, and it is assumed that the Soviet government expected to get credit for all of this when the "final debt settlement" was made. The litigation was expensive; it has been estimated that more than $430,000 was spent on attorneys and other personnel involved in the cases, with another $100,000 spent for expert witnesses, printing, and so on.[44] These figures make no allowance for the time and effort of the staff of the United States government, regularly employed and devoting part- or even full-time attention to the cases over a period of eighteen years, but only for those specially employed from the outside for this work. The government did not receive any reimbursement out of the amounts derived from the cases, but turned the whole sum over to the private claimants, except for the 5 per cent administrative charge that the law had authorized the Foreign Claims Settlement Commission to deduct.

The problem of implementation of the agreement on assignments and claims, then, was not difficult. Relations between the two governments, regarding this problem, were cordial and cooperative, as was not normally true with the other Litvinov agreements. The Soviet government had little to do with the matter after November 16, 1933, and nothing directly to gain, so there was no reason for the kind of unpleasant haggling that characterized some of the other situations.

CHAPTER VII

Economic Espionage

The next part of the exchange differs from the others in several ways. Its exact nature and purpose are not even clear. It is evident that President Roosevelt raised the question of economic espionage in the Soviet Union. There was no exchange of views, no apparent request for a statement of policy, no promise, no agreement, only an explanation. This is the one part of the exchange, accordingly, that involves no specific commitment.

Had the American government not been concerned about it, the topic of economic espionage presumably would not have been raised, but Kelley had warned that this was one of the problems needing settlement prior to recognition: "the Soviet conception of espionage, especially economic espionage, is of such a broad nature that almost every foreigner in Russia commits acts which may readily be interpreted as violating the laws on this subject."[1] The American government, moreover, must have been apprehensive in view of the Metropolitan-Vickers trial, which occurred in Moscow during the first days of the Roosevelt Administration.

In the Moore Papers in the Hyde Park Library there is a draft proposal, marked "Judge Moore's draft," undated but presumably written sometime in November 1933, dealing with this subject. After two pages on noninterference in general comes the following:

The U.S.S.R. agrees that the following actions on the part of Americans in Russia shall not be interpreted as economic espionage:

The receipt of unsolicited information of any sort whatsoever from other parties;

The solicitation *by legal means* of information of any sort from government officials or employees connected with organizations which might reasonably be supposed to be charged with the distribution of such information.

The solicitation, collection, or transmission *by legal means* of general economic information, including information concerning economic trends and tendencies, internal and foreign economic or politico-eco-

199

nomic policies of the Soviet Government, measures of the Government in the domestic economic sphere or in foreign trade, the progress of politico-economic campaigns, difficulties encountered in various branches of national economy, and general conditions in these branches** but not including information concerning business and production secrets.**[2]

We can imagine that the President brought up the matter and Litvinov said that this was really no problem at all; he could explain it very briefly because economic espionage in the Soviet Union was not at all what it had been pictured to be. He would set the record straight, once and for all. In reply to a question of the President in regard to prosecutions for economic espionage, Mr. Litvinov gave the following explanation on November 16, 1933.

> The widespread opinion that the dissemination of economic information from the Union of Soviet Socialist Republics is allowed only in so far as this information has been published in newspapers or magazines, is erroneous. The right to obtain economic information is limited in the Union of Soviet Socialist Republics, as in other countries, only in the case of business and production secrets and in the case of the employment of forbidden methods (bribery, theft, fraud, etc.) to obtain such information. The category of business and production secrets naturally includes the official economic plans, in so far as they have not been made public, but not individual reports concerning the production conditions and the general conditions of individual enterprises.
>
> The Union of Soviet Socialist Republics has also no reason to complicate or hinder the critical examination of its economic organization. It naturally follows from this that everyone has the right to talk about economic matters or to receive information about such matters in the Union, in so far as the information for which he has asked or which has been imparted to him is not such as may not, on the basis of special regulations issued by responsible officials or by the appropriate state enterprises, be made known to outsiders. (This principle applies primarily to information concerning economic trends and tendencies.)[3]

The Nature of Economic Espionage

Litvinov began by stating that "the widespread opinion that the dissemination of economic information from the Union of Soviet Socialist Republics is allowed only in so far as this information has been published . . . is erroneous." This effort to assuage American suspicions was intended to be a statement of international policy, apparently, since it says "dissemination *from*" and not *within* the Soviet Union. After recognition, American representatives in the Soviet Union would be able to send economic information out of the country. And yet it says nothing positive as to what is permissible and legal. The remainder of the statement concerns securing information, not disseminating it. It had been widely stated that only information already published—since all newspapers and magazines in the Soviet Union are official, they contain only what the Soviet government censor allows—was suitable for general circulation. It had been assumed that if the Soviet government was willing to let its people know certain facts, it was safe for them to know these facts; if the government had not made such information available, it was not safe for the people to know or communicate it. Litvinov said that this statement was erroneous. This was precise; his explanation of the nature of the error was much less so.

He began by admitting limitations on the right to obtain economic information in his country. The right was limited there—as in other countries, he said—in the case of business and production secrets, and in cases involving such "forbidden methods" as bribery, theft, and fraud. He maintained that these were the "only" limitations on obtaining economic information. Although he did not attempt any definition of the terms "business and production secrets," he did admit that this category included the "official economic plans" that had not previously been made public but did not include "individual reports concerning the production conditions and the general conditions of individual enterprises." It seems to be a Soviet characteristic to appear to clarify something and leave it, intentionally or otherwise, almost completely muddied. The last part of the statement is vague, too. Everyone has the right to receive and talk about economic information, so long as this information has not been classified—by appropriate state agencies and on the basis of regulations issued by responsible officials—as being forbidden to be made known to outsiders. There is no attempt here to determine what matters might be forbidden to outsiders, which agencies are appropriate in this case, and what regulations might have been issued by those officials deemed responsible.

This explanation does not clarify much, and certainly does not show why the statement was erroneous. It should not have satisfied the American representatives participating in the 1933 negotiations; there is no evidence whether it did. But, then, there is no evidence that this statement proved satisfactory the first time it was used, for it was not prepared for the talks in Washington but only pulled out of Litvinov's pocket where it had been awaiting just such an occasion. In 1928 the Germans and Russians were trying to clear up some of the problems arising from the German-Soviet Commercial Treaty of October 1925. During the discussions, the German delegation asked to be enlightened on several questions relating to economic espionage.

The Soviet delegation, stating that this question "cannot be made the subject of negotiations at this conference"[4] but wanting to be helpful, said, only as an advisory opinion: "The widespread opinion that the dissemination of economic information . . ." and so on, using verbatim the explanation Litvinov offered in 1933.

A careful examination of this statement, in George F. Kennan's words,

> reveals that actually the possibility of obtaining economic information in Russia is, for outsiders, extremely limited. The official economic plans, unpublished information about which is included among the type of information which cannot be sought by outsiders, embrace nearly the whole of Russian economic life. Furthermore, experience has shown that it is often the most elementary and important economic facts which, on the basis of "special regulations issued by responsible officials or by appropriate state enterprises," cannot be made known to outsiders. . . . Limited acquaintance with the Soviet economic press is sufficient to show that certain of the most important and elementary statistics, such as the size of the grain crop, the issuance of currency, the production of gold, etc. are included in this category. Consequently, not only the asking for information on these subjects but also the mere acceptance of such information is classified as economic espionage. According to the "advisory opinion" of the Russian delegation, a foreigner who even happened to be told the size of the total grain crop in Russia could be convicted of economic espionage by a Russian court.[5]

This being true, it is easy to see how anyone in the Soviet Union who interested himself in the economic development of the country would become a prime suspect of this serious charge of economic espionage. An American official concluded that "in actual practice any foreigner attempting to obtain information in Soviet Russia is limited to official sources."[6]

Just what is "economic espionage"? It apparently includes most of the types of economic—business, industrial, agricultural—information which businessmen and diplomats are accustomed to collect in all free countries. In the United States the reports of the Treasury Department, the Federal Reserve system, the Departments of Commerce and Agriculture, the economic journals and the business pages of the daily newspapers are filled with information which, in the Soviet Union, would come within the list of carefully guarded state secrets, knowledge of which involves economic espionage. "We have no industrial secrets within the meaning of capitalist law," said Vyshinsky at the Metropolitan-Vickers trial in 1933, "but we have the concept of economic espionage."[7] Article 58 of the Special Section of the

Criminal Code defines espionage as "the transmission, theft, or gathering, for the purpose of transmission, of information which by its contents represents a particularly guarded state secret, to foreign states, counter revolutionary organizations, or private persons."[8] Economic and military espionage are about the same in the Soviet Union. "It would appear that the line drawn in Soviet Russia between ordinary economic information as understood in capitalist countries and information of a secret military nature is so faint that it can be considered as non-existing."[9]

It seems natural to an American that a businessman trying to establish business relations in the Soviet Union involving granting credits would want to know, in fairly detailed fashion, the current balance of payments abroad, or the amount of gold production or exportable stocks, since these facts involve the whole question of the Soviet government's ability to pay for foreign purchases. These are state secrets. Under such circumstances, it is easy to see the difficulties which the ordinary American business man might meet. We can understand why the American government was warned that in drawing up treaties "the question of the gathering of economic information should receive the most careful attention as to the possibility of including an article guaranteeing that ordinary economic information, as the term is used in all countries, be made available as soon as possible to the representatives of the governments concerned and to their nationals in the event that such information directly affects their business affairs."[10] Absence of adequate protection for foreigners in this matter was considered one of the chief deficiencies of the commercial treaties concluded by the Soviet government before 1933.

THE METROPOLITAN-VICKERS TRIAL

The American government was doubly apprehensive, surely, because of the Metropolitan-Vickers trial in Moscow in April 1933, involving "sabotage" and "wrecking" by twenty-five Russian officials and employees of Russian electric power stations, and six British engineers working in Russia for the Metropolitan-Vickers Co. The concern of the American government was twofold, based on the possibility of establishing relations with the Soviet government in the near future and also because of lack of agreement as to the reasons behind the trial. Some believed that the trial was a Soviet device for whipping up enthusiasm among Soviet workers, who were criticized in the Soviet press for not heeding Stalin's orders to "master the techniques of their jobs." Thus on the day after the arrests, *Pravda* published an editorial titled "No Quarter to the Enemies of the People!" It concluded: "Let us increase our class vigilance! Protect public (socialistic) property with greater vigilance, honorably, and conscientiously defend the interests of the Workers' and Peasants' State. *No mercy for the enemies of the people!*"[11] Others believed, instead, that the unbridled denunciation of Great Britain for its prompt and energetic intervention when the arrests were announced, showed that the British were a convenient whipping-boy, and William H. Stoneman of the *Chicago Daily News* reported that "the G.P.U. had had a dossier prepared on this case and that it was available for use at such time as the higher authorities . . . deemed it expedient."[12] In this version, the British action permitted the Soviet leaders to settle some old scores with the British. Another theory was that the trial was a smoke-screen to cover the failure of Soviet policies.[13] Or, on the other hand, this incident may have been used as an excuse for keeping Russian goods out of Britain, following the Ottawa agreements of the previous year, which was what happened when the British government embargoed certain types of Soviet goods as soon as the trial was concluded.

All of these possible explanations for the trial interested the American government which, if it established relations with the Soviet government, might find itself similarly involved at some future time. The *Times* of London saw this when it predicted that "the American government would bear this case in mind in considering the question whether or not to recognize the Soviets and to establish diplomatic relations with Russia."[14]

The Metropolitan-Vickers trial began on April 12 and lasted for six days. The general charge against the British engineers was that they caused intentional damage to equipment of electric power stations—which was a crime under Article 58-7 of the Criminal Code, the article on economic espionage—and other offenses such as giving and receiving bribes. Alan Monkhouse, one of the defendants, for example, was charged with "1. Espionage, including military espionage and 'obtaining secret information regarding new constructional works.' 2. Collecting information. (Mr. Monkhouse does not understand how this charge differs from the first.) 3. 'Diversional activity.' (*i.e.* disorganizing or wrecking work) . . . 4. Bribery."[15]

The trial opened up the question of the definition of "economic espionage." Strang (the British Chargé in Moscow) wired Sir John Simon in London that the "acts of economic espionage which Mr. Thornton has admitted amount to no more than collection of information for company on state of company's plant, general condition of the company, and prospects of future business. His admission of military espionage is founded on collection of three pieces of information which were common knowledge."[16] The American Minister in Riga emphasized this problem once more when, soon after the completion of the trial, he reported:

> The collection of what would in the ordinary way be called "business information," could easily be laid hold of and dignified for propaganda purposes into the sinister sounding "economic espionage." It is obvious that practically all commercial managers and agents abroad collect such public or factory or firm data, and by the way, it is the duty of all consular and diplomatic officers of all nationalities everywhere to gather and transmit such intelligence in some form or other to their respective governments. Information of the sort can easily be interpreted into some kind of connection or other with military manufacture particularly in view of the modern mechanization and chemicalization of present-day war.[17]

But repeated emphasis of this point did not produce much clarification of the meaning of "economic espionage," as the Soviets used it.

On March 14, 1933—nine days after discovery of a "plot" to sabotage Soviet agriculture and the same day that the arrest of the electrical engineers and specialists was announced—the Central Executive Committee issued a new order, having the force of law, "Regarding the Responsibility of Employees of Government Institutions and Enterprises for Acts of Sabotage," in which the C.E.C. "announced that the rights, granted to the United States Political Administration [the secret police] . . . to judge . . . cases dealing with diversions, incendiarism, explosions, damage of machinery in state enterprises and with other forms of sabotage . . . must be put into effect with exceptional severity in regard to employees of government institutions and enterprises detected in such crimes."[18] If the secret police were to use "exceptional severity" in such cases and if, following recognition, American workmen were to be employed in the Soviet Union, this order of March 1933 might well cause the same trouble as the British had experienced. Even in the Metropolitan-Vickers trial—which was not conducted by the secret police but, under pressure of the British government, in open, regular court under normal Soviet procedure— "absolutely no documentary evidence was introduced and . . . the only evidence was the verbal testimony of terrorized Russian employees of the company and the 'confessions' of the accused themselves."[19]

In view of this background, it is astonishing that the American government was willing to accept Litvinov's meaningless statement and hope to be better off than the British or Germans. The record does not show whether the American representatives tried to get an actual promise from Litvinov or, at least, a more specific statement. At any rate, the American government published this unsupported statement as a part of the record, according recognition without any further clarification. A precise statement would not necessarily have produced any better results, but it could have been defended with pride had the occasion demanded.

AMERICAN EXPERIENCE

The records of the Department of State during this period show that the government's concern with this problem was largely needless. At no time were there staged trials or even accusations of "economic espionage" against American citizens, although a number of Americans did work in the Soviet Union at one time or another. Some of these Americans had difficulties, as we saw in Chapter IV, but these were not problems of economic espionage.

The problems of this nature that did arise, strangely enough involved Russians, not Americans. It was they who were suspected of this type of impropriety, although the American government neither used the term nor made formal charges.

American engineers, for example, had difficulty in taking their drawings, blueprints, technical data, and documents out of the Soviet Union. Soviet customs officials maintained that such papers had to be examined, and that it would not be possible for the engineer to be present during the examination. Since several days or even weeks elapsed between the submission of these papers to the customs officials and their release for exportation, it was widely suspected that Soviet personnel used this opportunity to copy or photograph the documents and thus secure free information needed for the development of the Soviet economy.

Soviet practice was somewhat flexible. When Soviet officials insisted that a Mr. Riddell deliver his documents for examination, "documents, which contained matters of a highly confidential nature, remained in the possession of the customs authorities for several days, during which period all of them could have been copied or photographed."[20] When Mr. Nemidov, the representative of the Otis Elevator Co., told the Commissariat for Foreign Affairs in 1933 that "if the Soviet government persisted in its attitude . . . he would destroy all of his papers and his firm would not again permit plans or blueprints to enter the Soviet Union, the Commissariat, without any inspection, sealed in his presence his package of documents [and] . . . furnished him with certificates to be handed to the border authorities."[21] In March 1935 Mashinoimport (the Soviet machinery-importing agency) told Mr. Badger that his documents relating to construction of an oil refinery would have to be inspected, and refused to allow him to be present—"in the hour and a half examination most could have been photographed."

The American government was sufficiently concerned about this matter to protest, and on July 22, 1935, the Embassy in Moscow received a written reply from the People's Commissariat for Foreign Affairs declaring that "it is self-understood that the competent authorities intend in the future to permit foreign citizens to be present during the examination of documents which these persons take out."[22]

This assurance presumably solved the problem, but the Embassy reported that in February 1937 an American engineer had been required to turn over to the Soviet customs authorities

> all of his detailed drawings of an electric furnace which he had installed in Leningrad. . . . The customs authorities stated that it would be necessary to examine the documents carefully and forward them to the engineer in the United States at a later date by post. Although there is no definite evidence showing that the drawings were used or photostated, there appears to be little doubt . . . that the Soviet authorities actually made use of the documents to construct an electric furnace similar to the one purchased in the United States. . . . Apparently the practice of acquiring (requiring) foreign engineers to turn over their documents, drawings and data to the Soviet authorities for examination without the engineers being permitted to be present during the examination is still being carried out. . . . The promises given by the Soviet authorities [in July 1935] in this regard are no longer in force.[23]

The Embassy noted that the Soviet caution in 1937 was undoubtedly connected with the Great Purge of that period but added that this "does not change the fact that in their vigilance to run down spies the Soviet authorities also may find it convenient to use certain confidential information obtained during the examination of the documents which they could not otherwise obtain at any cost or could only obtain after the conclusion of a contract specifically providing that such information should be furnished."[24]

A month later, the problem arose again, this time involving three engineers of the Radio Corporation of America. On October 27, 1937, accordingly, the Secretary of State, stating that this action "constitutes a clear violation of the written assurances given to the Embassy by the People's Commissariat for Foreign Affairs on July 22, 1935," requested the Ambassador "to protest against the action taken by the authorities at Leningrad. In doing so, you may point out that if the assurances given by the Soviet Government . . . are again violated, this Government will have to consider whether measures should not be taken to bring the practices of the Soviet authorities in this respect to the attention of American business men prior to their departure for the Soviet Union."[25] The Embassy did not protest, however, since "the Radio Corporation desired that no protest be made, on the ground that any protest would only serve to alienate any future orders from the Soviet Government."[26]

Soviet officials used another variation of this technique with, apparently, the same motivation. Late in 1934 two American firms, E. B. Badger and Sons and Alco Products, submitted bids to Amtorg for the construction of a large oil-refining plant in the Soviet Union. Both companies were thereupon asked to send representatives to Moscow to negotiate with Mashinoimport. After three weeks of spirited competition and negotiation, each company was apparently told that it might have the contract if it would reduce its bid by 40 per cent. Both refused, complaining because "Amtorg, when inviting their respective firms to send representatives to Moscow, had not intimated that there was such a wide discrepancy between the amount of the bids and the prices which the Soviet government was willing to pay."[27] The most interesting part of the Badger representative's report to the American Embassy, however, was this:

> The type of questions put to Mr. Badger and himself . . . led him to believe that the Soviet Government was considering, in case it could not obtain the desired reduction in price, the possibility of using Soviet engineers to build the plant and of purchasing abroad only those machines which could not possibly be manufactured in the Soviet Union. . . . In his opinion, the Soviet engineers endeavored to obtain from the bidders a sufficient amount of technical information to enable themselves to prepare their own projects.[28]

This led the Embassy to "suggest that whenever possible American citizens who are planning to enter the Soviet Union for business or for other reasons be informed that they may not be able to take out of the country any documents which have not been previously turned over to the Soviet customs officials for inspection."[29] It also notified the Department that the members of other diplomatic missions in Moscow were accustomed to transmit in their diplomatic pouches documents used or prepared by their nationals in connection with business matters.

After the beginning of the Second World War, the Russians became more interested in American industry than ever before. Although their representatives had been permitted to visit plants in the United States which were producing goods for the Soviet Union, they now wanted access to whole plants. The problem came to the Department of State and the Acting Secretary was informed that

> the meeting was unanimously against . . . permitting Soviet engineers to enter the plants other than for normal inspection work in connection with goods which are destined for them. The list of the military secrets requested itself shows very efficient espionage. . . . The previous conduct of the Russian engineers in the plants made it plain that their real work was not limited to the nominal scope provided in the contract.[30]

It was the Russians and not the Americans, then, whose interest in production secrets led to difficulties between the two governments. A great bulk of economic information was publicly available in this country, and the Russians can be expected to have made careful extractions from this. During the Second World War, moreover, under the Lend-Lease program, they came into possession of many of the products of American industry. It is not apparent just how much of this kind of information came from the Soviet Union to the American government and industry. At any rate, Americans in the Soviet Union were not accused by the Soviet government of engaging in economic espionage. Even if they had been, this would not have been a violation of the Roosevelt-Litvinov agreements, for on this topic there was no agreement, only an implication.

CHAPTER VIII

"Normal" Diplomatic Relations

We have already seen that the Roosevelt-Litvinov agreements led to American recognition of the Soviet government, with the resulting establishment of diplomatic relations and exchange of ambassadors. President Roosevelt stated that his government "has decided to establish normal diplomatic relations. . . . I trust that the relations now established . . . may forever remain normal and friendly, and that our nations henceforth may cooperate for their mutual benefit and for the preservation of the peace of the world."[1] In reply, Litvinov said that his government was "glad to establish normal diplomatic relations" and that he shared "the hope that the relations now established may forever remain normal and friendly, and that our nations henceforth may cooperate for their mutual benefit and for the preservation of the peace of the world."[2] In his speech to the National Press Club on November 17, 1933, Litvinov emphasized this point: "Normal relations do indeed exist now among all nations of the world, but not in a few cases, mistrust and ill feeling, culminating sometimes in the most abnormal actions, are being nourished under the cover of normal relations. . . . It is in no such conventional or technical sense that we want normal relations with this country."[3] There seemed agreement, then, on the type of relations which, it was hoped, would result from this action.

While these terms were traditionally used on such occasions, it seems useful to see just what did result, what type of "normal diplomatic relations" did develop, and the degree to which there was cooperation for mutual benefit and the preservation of world peace. It was not to be expected in 1933 that diplomatic relations between these two governments would be the same as relations between most other governments, for the differences between the United States and the Soviet Union were not just the normal differences between governments. These two were antithetical to each other. How could they maintain "normal" relations? With their differences, could they be

210

really friendly? Was something more than the exchange of polite phrases possible or was this, too, a mirage to delude the weary observer?

THE HONEYMOON

Immediately after the exchange of notes on November 16, both governments undertook to turn the promise announced in the notes into fruition. Bullitt made a preliminary trip to Moscow within a few days after Litvinov left Washington, arriving on December 11 and remaining eleven days. He received a generous reception: an American flag was suspended over the entrance of the Hotel National when he arrived, his apartment had been "beautifully refurnished and was most comfortable"; the hotel was heated and the "food and service were good."[4] He was received "at once" by Litvinov and they had a brief, friendly conversation. The next day Bullitt had lunch *"en famille* with Litvinov,"* who was "delighted" with the remarks Bullitt proposed to make when presenting his credentials. "As a special politeness, contrary to diplomatic precedent," Litvinov gave Bullitt a copy of the reply which President Kalinin would make.

On December 13 the American Ambassador presented his credentials. After the formalities, Kalinin took him aside, saying that "he felt as if he were welcoming someone he had known for a long time." Everyone in Russia "considered the President completely out of the class of the leaders of capitalist states." "Kalinin said that he hoped that I would travel in every part of the Union of Soviet Socialist Republics. . . . He told me that I could go any place I might wish in the entire Union by plane. . . . There would be no restrictions whatever on my movements." The press comments were "undeservedly complimentary."[5]

On the 15th Bullitt talked with Rosengolts (the Foreign Trade Commissar) and Molotov. That evening Litvinov gave a formal dinner "in my honor" and the next night "I was Litvinov's guest at the ballet." On the 20th "I dined with Voroshilov at his apartment in the Kremlin." Litvinov "remarked to me that the persons present constituted the 'inside directorate.' . . . After dinner I had a long talk with Stalin." "Before I left Stalin said to me, 'I want you to understand that if you want to see me at any time, day or night, you have only to let me know and I will see you at once.' . . . After I had said good-bye to Voroshilov and the others, Stalin went to the door . . . with me and said, 'Is there anything at all in the Soviet Union that you want?' " Following numerous other conversations, "Litvinov gave a tremendous reception for me" on the 21st.

And so Bullitt returned to Washington, flushed with the welcome he had received and the many kindnesses the Soviet officials had showered on him. There could hardly be doubt that the Roosevelt Administration had made the appropriate decision in recognizing the Soviet government, or that friendly relations between these governments might well be the deciding factor in the preservation of world peace. After a stay in Washington, Bullitt returned to Moscow to begin officially his work as Ambassador. But, as we saw in Chapter V, when he visited Litvinov on March 15 to begin the negotiations on the Soviet debts, "Litvinov expressed objection to almost every sentence of the draft."[6] From here on, the warm welcome was rapidly replaced with the cool air of a late Moscow winter. Less than two weeks later, Bullitt reported "several instances in which the Soviet Government does not seem disposed to carry out understandings between it and the Government of the United States."[7] The first was the debt talks; "an even more extraordinary 'misunderstanding' has arisen with regard to the property which was promised to us for the construction of our new Embassy"; a third resulted from the "unwillingness of the Soviet Government to carry out the verbal promise which was made to me . . . that the State Bank would supply us with paper roubles. . . . These three extraordinary incidents indicate clearly that oral promises of members of the Soviet Government are not to be taken seriously." Bullitt was still cheerful, however, having the impression "that the 'misunderstandings' have been produced not so much by bad faith as by inefficiency. The members of the Soviet Government seem disposed to make promises without taking into consideration all the factors involved."[8] But he had already discovered a fundamental truth in dealing with the Soviet government and he issued a clear warning for the future: "In every case understandings with the Soviet Government or representatives thereof should be made in writing or should be confirmed at a later date by a written document."

In the first week of April 1934 Bullitt had "a completely unsatisfactory discussion" on the debt situation with Litvinov, who maintained that "he had said his last word and made his maximum offer . . . so far as he was concerned the matter was closed."[9] Never again would the relations between the American and Soviet governments be completely warm and friendly. It had been a very brief honeymoon; now the parties were at odds over a number of issues, with the friction never being completely removed.

It is easy to say, looking back, that there was no chance for truly friendly relations, but the leaders of the 1930's did not know this. They tried sincerely, even desperately on occasion, to solve the problems and get relations back on the basis of December 1933. But a series of problems arose and continued to exist over the years, preventing this, until by the end of the decade it had become clear that "normal" relations between them were always clouded by doubt and suspicion, even hostility, and that this was the best that could really be expected.

FRICTION AND HEAT

Let us turn to a discussion of some of these problems which meant—as in the case of the other Roosevelt-Litvinov agreements—such a difference between hope and realization. All governments have problems with other governments; there would be no need for diplomats if this were not so. It is assumed that most governments are sincere in their efforts to solve their problems and reduce the friction, so that friendly relations can be achieved. The real tragedy of American-Soviet relations in the 1930's came when it became apparent that, at least for the foreseeable future, there was no such possibility in the case of these governments. Examination of a few of these problems will show why this awareness developed as it did.

One problem involved housing facilities. An American overseas Mission would normally buy, rent, or lease buildings it required and control and maintain them as it desired. This was not possible in Moscow where the Soviet government owned and controlled all real property. One reason for Bullitt's trip to Moscow in December 1933 was to arrange for offices and housing, which would be needed by the American Mission in the Soviet capital. The Soviet government offered several places to Bullitt, who selected two—Spaso House, as the Ambassador's residence, and Mokhovaya Building, an office building overlooking Red Square, to be used for both offices and residences. While neither was completely adapted to the new uses, both offered good possibilities. "Because the Russians hope that our leasing of the two Moscow properties is merely to provide temporary quarters while a permanent establishment is being built," wrote Bullitt, "they have leased us buildings which they would not rent to any other government and at more reasonable rents than other governments have obtained for inferior properties."[10] Quarters would be cramped until these buildings could be prepared for American occupancy: "Until May 1 it will be necessary for us to house nearly all the staff and offices in a hotel. . . . I shall be glad to confine my own quarters to two bedrooms and to take into the house some of the secretaries, assistants or code clerks. After May 1 it will probably prove best to have all the offices, except my own personal office, located in the office-residence-building."[11]

It then became apparent that the Americans had a great deal to learn about Soviet operations. Because it was necessary to deal with Burobin (Central Bureau for Services to Foreigners), negotiation of leases took months of painstaking effort and building repairs took additional months. No space was available except as Burobin provided it, and Moscow was crowded, with every square foot in demand. As early as May 1934 the prospective Embassy staff had outgrown the space provided by Burobin: "You will note that I have made no provision for Hodgson and a visa control office in the consulate. This decision is due solely to lack of office space and living quarters. . . . Unless we can obtain additional quarters in Moscow it will be necessary, therefore, either to leave the visa-control office in Riga or establish it in Leningrad."[12] On another occasion the Ambassador wired: "Our need for stenographers is so urgent that if the Department has no funds available I should be glad to consider paying the travel expenses to Moscow of one or more men from my personal funds."[13] But there was no housing available even if personnel and funds had been. The fact is that never since early 1934 has enough office and living space been made available to the American government by Burobin, with resultant difficulties in operating the Embassy and consequent friction between the two governments.

Since this situation was thought temporary in 1934, it could be endured. In December 1933 Bullitt had found a choice location for a new Embassy building, to be constructed as a sign of the permanence of our diplomatic relations and an impressive symbol of the American government. Thus, when Stalin asked Bullitt on December 20, "Is there anything at all in the Soviet Union that you want?" Bullitt was ready:

> I told him that I should be glad to know that the property on the bluff overlooking the Moscow River might be given to the American Government as a site for an Embassy. Stalin replied, "You shall have it." The next day Litvinov told me that Stalin had given orders to the Moscow Soviet that the property in the park should be ours if we wished to have it.[14]

This must have seemed too good to be true. Indeed it was, for on March 28, 1934, Bullitt reported difficulties. He had carefully described the property and had secured two letters from the Soviet Ambassador in Washington so as to be sure of the ground before approaching Congress for an appropriation. But on March 25 a Foreign Office official in Moscow told him that the Soviet Ambassador must have deciphered the telegram incorrectly, that the Moscow Soviet would not give up the land as described. Bullitt replied that the matter was settled; that I had received a promise from Stalin and assurance from Litvinov that Stalin had given orders in accordance with his promise; that the agreement had been confirmed in writing by Troyanovsky; and that I could not agree to any alteration whatsoever in this agreement. . . . It was not wise for the Soviet Union to create the belief in the United States that a promise of Stalin, backed by an assurance of Litvinov, plus a written confirmation by the Soviet Ambassador in Washington, was worthless.[15]

At this point Bullitt emphasized the necessity of committing all agreements with the Soviet government to writing.

With such an introduction to the problem of constructing an Embassy building, the American government moved cautiously. The more the matter was studied, the more difficult the problem seemed. An American architect was hired in 1934; after an on-site inspection, he listed a number of problems:

The building methods in use are strangely primitive. . . . There is little or no machinery, no mechanical short-cuts, and no sense or ordered economy.

. . . In Moscow it takes from three to five years to construct a building of average size. . . .

We must send over an experienced organization . . . for all the sub-trades, with at least six mechanics in each of the ten important trades. . . . It will be necessary to house our own organization. . . .

Their standard brick is heavy, large, full of fissures and difficult to handle, and at least 60% are broken in shipment. . . .

There is no seasoned lumber in Russia, no good mill work, no decent window glass, no rolled steel of standard sizes, no good metal work of any kind. Their so-called galvanized steel corrodes the day after it is installed.[16]

The chief difficulties, however, revolved around the Embassy's inability to obtain written assurances from the Soviet government. The American government was never able to get a statement that the property would be exempt from taxes under the customary rule of international law, or that the lease could be renewed. The American government was never able to obtain written assurances from the Soviet government as to the cost of brick, cement, or sand; the wages to be paid to Soviet workmen; transportation costs within the Soviet Union; and exemption from customs duty of materials imported from abroad. Negotiations became stymied on the conversion rate to be used; there were as many rates as commodities, varying from 29–1 for gravel to 2½–1 for cement. "There are no itemized costs available . . . so that an accurate agreed conversion on the entire construction

. . . is practically impossible."[17] Bullitt was promised specific figures by one Soviet agency in September 1934; in November he was referred to another agency. In January 1935 the Embassy was instructed "to present personally to Litvinov a formal note. . . . The Soviet Government should give us the written assurance within a fortnight if work is to be begun in the Spring."[18] Five weeks later the Embassy reported that "despite repeated efforts to obtain a reply . . . no reply has been forthcoming from the Foreign Office. The Foreign Office stated today . . . that it was impossible to give any definite indications when it would be."[19] When the reply came in early March, it was not satisfactory to the American government.

Early in January 1935 Secretary Hull suggested that "if you derive from Litvinov the impression that the Soviet Government is attempting to make the construction of the Embassy impossible you might intimate that such action would be peculiarly inappropriate at the present moment,"[20] which was the first indication that the whole effort might be futile. The discussion had now dragged over a year with no prospect that the problems could be solved, and in the summer of 1935 the American government decided to abandon the project. The Soviet government later made inquiries, but the American government, still unable to obtain satisfactory assurances on the questions discussed, refused to proceed with the construction program, telling the Soviet government that we no longer wished it to reserve the site for our needs.

This left the American government with the buildings already under lease, plus some additional space that Burobin made available under considerable pressure. The same types of problems continued. The question of renewing the lease for Spaso House, for example, was discussed with the chief of Burobin on October 10, 1936. A reply was promised to the Americans for October 13, then for the 15th, 17th, 21st, 24th, and then "in a few days." A draft lease was not submitted until November 24.

There were difficulties in obtaining estimates from Burobin for painting, redecorating, and repair work. Estimates were often so excessive as to make the work impossible.[21] If the work was ordered, the chances were about even that it would not be completed.[22] No Soviet contracting organization could deal with foreign missions in Moscow, but in 1937 Demaree Bess (the *Christian Science Monitor* correspondent in Moscow) told the Embassy that he knew some workmen who were willing to do repair work. It was suggested that one of the men come to the Embassy where such work was often needed. Several days later the man appeared, bearing a card of introduction from Demaree Bess. The man had been stopped outside the Embassy by the secret police guard, taken first to headquarters, then to Lubyanka prison where he was stripped, his clothes searched, the linings ripped out, and his collar taken apart. After several days, during which his neighbors were questioned, he was released and showed up again at the Embassy, still willing to work. In July 1939 Burobin tried to have the Embassy perform building repairs, although the lease specifically provided that this was Burobin's responsibility. The housing situation did not produce "normal," "friendly" relations between the two governments but a series of annoyances that made matters difficult for both of them.

A second problem concerned the papers required of American diplomats. It is necessary for diplomats as well as private citizens to carry passports and to obtain visas when entering a country, though normally this latter action is done quickly and automatically in the case of diplomats. At times the Soviet practice followed the accepted rule. "Up to a few months ago it was possible for me to send diplomatic passports up to the Soviet Embassy with a note requesting a visa and have the visa accorded while the messenger waited."[23] But there were enough exceptions to make Soviet action in any individual case uncertain. Visas were never refused to diplomatic officials,[24] but they suffered varying delays. When Ambassador Davies' passport was sent to the Soviet Embassy, it took a week to obtain the visa.

Soviet officials in Washington denied that visa applications by bearers of diplomatic passports had to be referred to Moscow but the delays seemed to indicate that this was not true. Thus, one American Military Attaché in Riga was held up for months waiting for action on his visa application, and he finally gave up his trip to Leningrad. And Page, when being transferred from Riga to Moscow, had to wait more than ten days. Pressly waited almost a month in December 1937 when being transferred to Moscow, and Lieutenant Seidel, a language officer in Riga, waited from February to June for a visa "notwithstanding repeated representations on the part of the American Embassy in Moscow."[25] Occasionally, when delays of this type occurred, the travel orders of the diplomat required him to proceed, and thus personnel destined for Moscow arrived in Berlin without a Soviet visa, having been told that it would be ready for them there, only to find that the Soviet Embassy in Berlin had to obtain authorization from Moscow before the visa could be issued, necessitating further delay. In a similar situation, the Freers were kept waiting in Stockholm for ten weeks. When they obtained their visas, they proceeded to Leningrad only to find that all trains had been commandeered by the Soviet government to transport delegates to the meeting of the Supreme Soviet in Moscow. "Other Missions with more interchange of tourists and travelers put the squeeze play on the Soviets, when it comes to visas, but we have very few going and coming—only United Nations Russian personnel, who are special cases."[26]

One American official said, "I had thought that some of the delay might be attributed to the inexperience of new minor officials at the Soviet Embassy in Washington but I believe now it is part of the general policy."[27] In 1938, when the number of these visa cases had become a matter of concern to the American government, the Soviet Embassy in Washington denied that there was any such policy or even practice. "No difficulties in granting visas to American diplomatic officers are known to the Soviet Government or to its Embassy or Consulates in the United States, nor were any specific cases ever brought to their attention."[28] In calling this statement "surprising," American officials pointed to several of the cases cited above. Later, however, the American Ambassador in Moscow was assured that instructions had been issued to speed up issuance of visas to Americans. "While I am not too optimistic about a permanent continuation of this improvement, I have hopes that the improvement will not bog down too soon."[29] Later, Ambassador Kirk noted that his application for a visa to visit Germany, from Moscow, had taken ten days though, confronted by this, Vyshinsky "apologized, saying there must have been a mistake, as his office had strict orders to honor immediately any application from the American Ambassador."[30]

It should be stated, in all fairness, that the problem of visas for diplomats involved a minor rather than major problem between the two governments. In fact, it may be wondered why the Soviet government even bothered to annoy the American officials with a problem of this kind.

Far more serious was the Soviet policy restricting foreign diplomats from traveling freely in the Soviet Union. One important function of diplomats is to ascertain and report on conditions and attitudes in the host country, so that the home government can better shape policy toward it. Freedom to travel is considered mutually beneficial to both governments. This has not been the Soviet view.

We have already seen that, when Bullitt presented his credentials in December 1933, Kalinin said "that he hoped that I would travel in every part of the Union of Soviet Socialist Republics, and I told him that I should be delighted to do so. . . . He told me that I could go any place I might wish in the entire Union . . . that there would be no restrictions whatever on my movements."[31] During the early period of diplomatic relations between the United States and the Soviet Union, there was relative freedom of movement for diplomats within the Soviet Union. There were numerous administrative problems. Trains, hotels, and restaurants, all of which were operated by the Soviet government, required reservations. Getting reservations was often tantamount to obtaining the permission of the Soviet government to travel, but this did not prove too onerous. One Soviet Ambassador in Washington pointed proudly to the fact that Ambassador Davies, Mr. Kennan, Mr. Durbrow, and Lieutenant Colonel Faymonville had been aided by the Soviet government in traveling through industrial and agricultural areas of the Soviet Union as far as the Far Eastern Region.

Soon, however, the freedom was restricted. In September 1935 the Soviet government adopted a policy that "persons not permanently residing within the border zone and in prohibited areas along the border shall not be allowed to enter them without permission from organs of the People's Commissariat for Internal Affairs of the U.S.S.R."[32] In May 1941 the American Embassy in Moscow was notified by the Soviet Foreign Office that

> from this date a procedure has been established by the Government of the Union of Soviet Socialist Republics in accordance with which the travel, in the territory of the Union of Soviet Socialist Republics, of diplomatic and consular representatives of foreign states in the Union of Soviet Socialist Republics, as well as of employees of foreign embassies, missions, and consulates, may take place only on condition that a preliminary notification be filed by these persons with the appropriate authorities of the People's Commissariat for Foreign Affairs, the People's Commissariat for Defense and the People's Commissariat for the Naval Fleet, concerning projected trips, in which connection the route, the stopping places, and the duration of the trip shall be indicated for the purpose of registering these trips with the above mentioned authorities.[33]

"Simultaneously," the Soviet note declared, "the points and districts of the Union of Soviet Socialist Republics enumerated in the list attached herewith are declared forbidden areas." A list of fifty Soviet cities and regions followed, ending with "in addition to this, all points located in the frontier zone." As the Embassy saw, "the list of forbidden points and districts is virtually all-inclusive." A few days later, it notified the Department that "It appears most unlikely that official authorization will be granted to visit any of the forbidden areas excepting in rare cases."[34]

A week later the Department of State expressed the hope that "members of the Embassy will continue to travel as much as possible, such travel being of course in strict conformity with the new regulations."[35] Asking the Embassy to list all known refusals and cases of discrimination, the Department stated that it was considering controlling travel of Soviet diplomats in the United States but added that "we do not wish to do so until we have had an opportunity to learn of the effect of the Soviet restrictions upon the travel of our personnel and whether the Soviet authorities are resorting to discrimination."

The effect of the Soviet decree began to be felt almost at once. By May 22 diplomatic representatives of two countries were refused authorization to visit Odessa and Leningrad. On May 31 Ambassador Steinhardt cited several instances of refusal and discrimination, and hoped that the Department would take "immediate retaliatory action of a nature sufficiently severe to induce the Soviet authorities to change their present policy."[36] On June 5 he reported that the Soviet authorities had granted permission to Mr. and Mrs. Erskine Caldwell (then of *Life* magazine) "to visit Kiev, Odessa, Sochi, Yalta, Batum, Tiblisi, and Baku if they so desire as well as Rostov. All of these are in areas which diplomats are forbidden to enter."[37] Later that day, Steinhardt talked to Lozovsky of the Soviet Foreign Office about "the refusal of permission to members of the Embassy staff to visit places such as Leningrad while such permission was granted to American writers whom the Soviet authorities hoped would write well of the Soviets." Lozovsky said that there was no discrimination, "as the rule applied to all of the members of the Diplomatic Corps but seemed surprised to learn that permission had been refused to members of the American Embassy staff to visit Leningrad."[38]

On June 6 the Embassy decided to test the Soviet decree, delivering to the Foreign Office notification of the intention of two members of the staff "to visit on June 8 a museum at Yasnaya Polyana which is about 100 miles from Moscow, not in a forbidden zone and a place frequently visited by tourists."[39] On the following day, the Foreign Office telephoned the Embassy to say that

> as the proposed visit had "not yet been registered" it would not be possible . . . to make the visit. In reply the Commissariat was informed that its note of May 16 merely required the Embassy to notify the Commissariat of intended visits . . . and that as such notice had been given the Embassy did not understand upon what basis the Commissariat now undertook to state that this trip could not be made.
>
> The Commissariat was, therefore, requested to reply in writing. The Commissariat replied that the trip had "not been registered" and that no written reply would be made.[40]

Steinhardt understood that permission to make a similar local trip to a nonforbidden zone had also been refused the Hungarian Minister and the Italian Military Attaché but that no objection had been raised when an attaché of the German Embassy proposed to go to Vladimir; he had gone and returned.

Authorities in Washington were now apparently satisfied with the evidence and on June 7, 1941, Secretary Hull notified Ambassador Umansky that, in view of the Soviet restrictions placed upon American diplomatic and consular representatives and employees in the Soviet Union, the United States Government, "on the basis of reciprocity," requested employees of the Soviet Embassy and Consulates in the United States not to travel outside "the immediate vicinity" of the District of Columbia, "without formally notifying the Department of State . . . and . . . obtaining the permission of the Department . . . to engage in such travel."[41] The information required for such travel duplicated Moscow's requirements. It was orally explained that "immediate vicinity" meant, "for the time being, within 100 miles of Washington not including the city of Baltimore; and within 50 miles of the city in which Soviet consuls maintained residence," New York, Los Angeles, and San Francisco.

Events prevented this problem from becoming a major diplomatic obstacle to "friendly relations." Two weeks after the State Department action, Germany attacked the Soviet Union. Suddenly it was more to the interest of the United States to help the Soviet Union defeat Hitler than for Washington and Moscow to argue about diplomatic travel. A week after the attack, the Department notified the Embassy in Moscow that, believing that the new situation obviated the application of reciprocity of travel restrictions, "we are prepared either to annul or relax the restrictions."[42] Ambassador Steinhardt said he would "appreciate authorization to offer to make these gestures in return for such concessions as I may deem appropriate,"[43] and on the same day he was authorized to do so. On July 3 he made eight suggestions to Lozovsky; two days later Lozovsky agreed to some of the suggestions but "was not yet prepared to give me a reply as to the mutual removal of travel restrictions."[44] On July 15 the Department said that it was trying to "eliminate as rapidly as possible various points of friction" between the two governments and that it had "informed the Soviet Ambassador that restrictions on travel in the United States of Soviet diplomatic and consular officers and employees have been lifted."[45]

"It is assumed," said the Acting Secretary of State, "that, in view of our attitude . . . the Soviet Government will show a disposition to relax its restrictions upon the Embassy staff which are interfering with their freedom of movement and handicapping their work."[46] But this was too optimistic. On July 16, Steinhardt stated that, after almost two weeks, he had "received no reply to my inquiry as to whether the Soviet authorities are agreeable to the mutual removal of travel restrictions";[47] diplomatic records do not indicate that the Soviet government ever agreed to do this. Steinhardt also said that Umansky's statement of July 10 that the American military attachés in Moscow "were being granted full facilities to proceed to the front is not in accordance with the facts"; it was thought that the Soviet Ambassador was engaged in wishful thinking. If the American government wanted to remove points of friction and travel restrictions, there was no indication that the Soviet government was similarly inclined.

Soviet restrictions on diplomatic travel were not just a wartime measure. Moscow has continued this policy, though we need not go into details here. In June 1953 Moscow announced that large areas of the Soviet Union were still closed to foreign travel. In March 1956 travel to the Caucasus was banned during the de-Stalinization disturbances; in April 1957 Western diplomats were refused permission to travel in Central Asia, the Caucasus, and the Crimea, and permits for travel to Kiev and Yasnaya Polyana were denied. The Department of State protested on May 13, 1957: "On more than 36 occasions since July 1, 1956, Embassy officers have been prevented from visiting areas of the U.S.S.R. open to travel by foreigners, according to the Ministry's notes."[48] The American government retaliated with a reciprocal arrangement in which certain American areas were matched with certain Soviet areas, and certain American cities with their counterparts in the Soviet Union. When Premier Khrushchev attended meetings of the United Nations General Assembly in September 1960, the American government requested that "arrangements be made for Mr. Khrushchev to reside in the closest convenient proximity to the headquarters of the United Nations and that his movements—other than those connected with arrival and departure—be limited to those required by his official mission, not beyond Manhattan Island."[49] In 1962 the American government announced that it was lifting restrictions on travel in the United States for Soviet tourists but continuing the twenty-five-mile ban for Soviet diplomats. Again and again—most recently in November 1963—the American government has proposed discussions on removal of travel bans in both countries. No Soviet action has been forthcoming; often the Soviet government has not even acknowledged proposals.

It was not just that the Soviet government forbade diplomatic travel to certain areas. For a number of years the American Ambassador was accompanied wherever he went by a secret-police guard—"to protect him," though it was not clear just what this meant—so that the Soviet authorities always knew where he was. This was a special guard for him[50]—and the British and German Ambassadors—in addition to the normal surveillance of all Embassy personnel carried on by the secret police. The ostensible purpose of this guarding was not to prevent Embassy employees from travelling, though it sometimes had this effect.

The result of these restrictions on travel by foreign diplomats in the Soviet Union was a whole series of annoyances—both personal and organizational—which created and fostered friction between the two governments, and kept their relations from being "normal" and "friendly," as was the professed goal.

Another indication that relations between the two governments were not carried on under the rules of normal diplomatic usage was the controversy over the value of Soviet currency. The Soviet government—almost alone of the major powers—did not list its currency, and does not today, on the world money markets, so that there was no internationally accepted value to the ruble. The value depended upon actions of the Soviet government and bore no necessary relation to the purchasing power of the ruble.

During Bullitt's visit to Moscow in December 1933, Litvinov told him that "the Soviet Government had no objection to our charging consular fees in the Soviet Union either in dollars or in paper roubles at a paper rouble rate to be fixed by ourselves in accordance with the rates outside the Soviet Union."[51] He was also assured that the State Bank would supply the American Embassy with the paper rubles needed for the current expenses of the staff "at a fair rate of exchange." At this time the official rate for the ruble was two to the dollar; on the black market it varied from twenty-five to fifty to the dollar. George Kennan wrote: "If local currency had been purchased at the official rate the cost of operating the mission and the cost of living for members of the staff would have been prohibitive."[52] Because of the understanding between Bullitt and Soviet leaders, the Department of State issued a strict order against buying rubles on the black market.

> You should have instructions issued at once to your entire staff to the effect that Soviet currency . . . must be obtained only from the Embassy . . . and that no individual may effect any transaction in foreign exchange except through the channel established by you. . . . The Department will regard any violation of the provisions of this instruction as a serious offense to be punished by severe disciplinary action involving in flagrant cases separation from the Government service. It is requested that you obtain from each officer and employee a signed statement . . . to the effect that the Department's requirements in these matters have been made known to them and their families.[53]

When Bullitt and the staff arrived in Moscow, however, the "understanding" proved not to be in effect. It was explained that the Commissariat of Finance could not fix a rate for the American Embassy without doing the same for all foreign missions. Litvinov said he had told the State Bank to give the Embassy as many rubles as it needed; the State Bank refused to do so. At this time Bullitt sent his report to the Department suggesting "several instances"—including this one—in which the Soviet government did not seem disposed to carry out its understandings with the American government. Finally, after more negotiations, Bullitt said to Litvinov, "It seems to me that we have embarrassed you greatly by our attempt to play fair and to live in accordance with your laws and the extraordinary monetary regime you have established." "That is quite true," said Litvinov, "and if the worst comes to the worst you know that we shall have no possible objection to your obtaining paper roubles in any way that you see fit."[54] Divilkovsky told Bullitt: "You must have the paper roubles. We shall, of course, not inquire in any way where you obtain them." When Bullitt told Litvinov that he "objected strongly to being put in the position of having a written law waived thus by him orally, Litvinov said he could do nothing more about the matter."[55]

When the American and Soviet governments could not agree on a practical basis, the American Embassy—and every other Mission in Moscow—was forced to obtain its supplies of local currency outside the country, at rates of exchange that fluctuated greatly, and bring the money in by diplomatic courier. By 1937, with the Soviet government apparently controlling the supply of rubles outside the country, the price in Paris, Stockholm, or Warsaw had gone up so much that they cost practically the same as in Moscow.

One specific consequence of the artificially established exchange rate and the power of the Soviet government to revalue its currency at any time came in January 1936 just after the ruble had been "stabilized."

> I told Mr. Skvirsky that we had been paying to Intourist a rental of $80 a month for a garage, and that Intourist had informed the Embassy . . . that commencing January 1st the rental would be 1730 rubles. . . . This represented an increase from $80 to approximately $346 . . . or over 300 per cent.[56]

Again and again, the Embassy staff in Moscow was victimized by extortion of this type.

What did the Soviet government say to this? How did it justify its policy? Ignoring the human and economic aspects of the situation, it said only that the policy was nondiscriminatory:

> The Soviet Government has established its exchange rates in accordance with its fixed financial policy. . . . There is of course no discrimination whatsoever in the treatment of the American Embassy . . . in regard to questions of currency, as compared to other foreign missions accredited to the Government of the Union.[57]

There was no disputing these statements, which were completely factual, even if inadequate and perhaps irrelevant. The fact than an agreement, made freely by the Soviet government in December 1933, had been broken was not even mentioned.

A final abnormal situation developed when the Soviet government insisted on inspecting goods being imported or exported by members of the Embassy staff in Moscow, and levying charges on these goods. It has been international practice that diplomats are not subject to taxation, including customs duties, and that no inspection is made of their personal effects. The Soviet government, however, did not follow this rule.

By 1937 the problem had become prominent in relations between the two governments and it became more acute during the next few years. The Soviet government differentiated between diplomatic and consular officers. The former presented no great problem at first, receiving their merchandise with no import duties levied on them. Consular officers were not so favored, and the problem would have been worse had the United States government been able to establish consular offices in the Soviet Union as it had planned. Bertel Kuniholm of the State Department wrote: "Since the problem of attending to the simple business of living requires so much more time and effort in the Soviet Union than elsewhere, it is incumbent that freedom from unnecessary discomfort and irritation on the part of an arrogant and belligerent Soviet bureaucracy in some measure be assured our consular representatives."[58]

The problem was more complicated in taking goods out of the Soviet Union. Starting in 1936 when Bullitt left Moscow, the Soviet customs authorities inspected minutely even the Ambassadors' furniture, furnishings, and effects; this had previously been done only for subordinate personnel. The Soviet excuse was that it was necessary to levy export duty on articles purchased on the Soviet Union. Certain books were subject to duty; special representatives examined every art object, charging duty according to their appraisals. The officer had to prove that every article had been brought into the Soviet Union or risk an export tax of 100 per cent or even more. This meant that upon arrival the officer must

> open all of his packing cases in the presence of customs officers and have everything listed and checked. . . . This means that every book, every phonograph record, every piece of jewelry, etc. must be listed, so that subsequently everything can be identified. This necessitates a tremendous amount of work, in fact, several days of typing, etc., making out duplicate lists in several copies, by the officer himself.[59]

In 1937 new regulations altered Soviet practice in two ways. Effects other than personal luggage of Chiefs of Mission and Counselors would now be inspected at home and those of all others at the customs house, whereas previously all diplomatic officers could have the inspection at home. Chiefs of Mission, who previously were not charged appraisal fees, were now to be charged 3 per cent of the determined export value of all dutiable effects. "General indignation" stirred the Diplomatic Corps in Moscow into a movement to formulate an official protest. The Department of State, agreeing with the views of the diplomats, was unable to see

> how a system of inspection . . . which can only involve expense and delay to the officers . . . which cannot but result in great inconvenience and irritation, and which does not evidence proper regard for the dignity of the diplomatic office, will serve the interests of the Soviet Government or any agency thereof.
>
> The Department is not aware of any principle of international law that would justify the levying on effects acquired by a chief of mission and taken by him out of the country of any tax, regardless of what the tax may be called.[60]

In January 1938 the Embassy in Moscow sent a list of the fees and duties charged by the Soviet government, including 550 rubles for Wiley, 2,000 for Shantz, and 1,013 rubles for appraisal fee and 28,310 duty for Ambassador Davies.[61] (At the time the official exchange rate was five rubles to the dollar.)

The Soviet government did not consider this a serious problem. When the Soviet Ambassador called at the Department of State in April 1938, he admitted that there had been difficulties, but "it seemed to him that they were all very small questions."[62] American officials pointed out that Moscow might consider these matters trivial but, from their view, "it was their cumulative effect which was creating an exceedingly difficult atmosphere and which could not be belittled." The Americans called attention to one member of the staff who had recently spent thirty-three days doing nothing else than getting his effects out of the Soviet Union and a Secretary of Embassy who was told to export some forty-one volumes of his private library within a month or have them confiscated. Even though Dr. Rumreich had documents to prove that some of his effects had been imported into the Soviet Union, he was charged "a small export duty."

The Soviet Ambassador in Washington once protested when a Soviet official, Zaikin, only a Vice Consul, was required to open "all his trunks and bags" on arrival at New York. The Soviet Ambassador stated that he was astonished at this action on the part of the United States customs officials. . . . He was certain that American consular officials entering the Soviet Union were granted the usual customs courtesies."[63]

Soviet regulations on customs formalities and their administration annoyed the American government. Not "normal" in diplomatic usage, the regulations were not conducive to "friendly relations" as conceived in the 1933 negotiations.

This cataloguing of the ways in which the two governments found it difficult to get along well together could go on almost endlessly. Some of these ways were official: the arrest of four Soviet citizens employed by the American Embassy, Soviet cancellation of subscriptions to newspapers and magazines that the Embassy depended on for information, or the failure of the Soviet government to reply to 323 diplomatic notes in 1938 and 300 in 1940. Some were more personal: Burobin's failure to maintain a constant supply of hot water or make repairs in the buildings occupied by the staff, lack of adequate dentists and physicians to care for the physical needs of the staff, failure of the electricity just when the evening news was being broadcast, or a sudden refusal to allow Embassy cars to turn at corners where turns had always been made. Some were obviously intentional and picayune, such as the insistence of the Soviet customs officials on one occasion that several dozen fresh eggs being brought into the Soviet Union be broken open, on the plea that it was necessary to see whether or not they were diseased. It was no wonder that the American government declared Moscow a "hardship post," and worried that the staff members might not be able to stand up under the constant mental strain produced by Soviet irritations.

CONCLUSIONS

Some of these departures from normal diplomatic practice resulted from the fact that the Soviet regime was revolutionary and unorthodox; it sought to be different from its bourgeois enemies. Other problems arose from differences in political, economic, and social theory in the two systems. Others seemed to come from an almost childish Soviet delight in antagonizing and frustrating its enemies who, relying on the traditional rules of international law and diplomatic usage, found themselves unable to cope with this strange new system. With their basic differences, the two governments, even with the best of goodwill, would have found it difficult to be on truly friendly terms. Perhaps only a major shift in policy by one or the other would have made this possible. One official noted that the American representation in Moscow was "in a position particularly to feel the shock of the contact" between the two systems, and that many of the irritations could be traced "for the most part to the fact that representatives of foreign governments, regardless of what might be their personal feelings towards the Soviet regime, or the extent to which they may be in the good favor of the Soviet government, are nevertheless products of what is deemed to be a hostile system and therefore automatically subjected to suspicion and restriction."[64] Bullitt reported that Litvinov "expressed with his customary cynicism the view that there was no such thing as friendship or 'really friendly' relations between nations."[65] This may have been cynicism, since he appeared to hope for them in his letter to President Roosevelt on November 16, 1933. But it also held a considerable degree of realism, for Litvinov understood that Soviet leaders had no real interest in being friendly with those they sought to destroy; nothing more than a semblance of friendship was possible, at best. Only two years earlier, Litvinov had told a League of Nations group, "I have no intention of creating the impression that there is any harmony of interests between the capitalist system and the Soviet system. . . . These two systems are fighting each other and they will continue to do so; this fact is inherent in their simultaneous existence."[66]

At the end of the debt negotiations in January 1935, Hull instructed the Embassy in Moscow to convey to the Soviet government "the fact that the Government of the United States has desired and does desire the most friendly cooperation with the Soviet Union but that Litvinov has shown so little disposition to permit the development of friendly relations . . . that the Government of the United States is convinced that no real friendship can be developed so long as he adheres to his present attitude."[67] It is not clear whether Hull realized the impossibility of Litvinov's changing his basic attitude and still retaining his post in the Soviet system, or whether Litvinov, with a belief based upon the "scientific truth" of the Communist ideology, considered that the whole world was in process of changing to his views.

Bullitt, who had swallowed his initial enthusiasm and hope through

the painful process of firsthand contact with the Soviet grindstone, had
learned this:

> We should not cherish for a moment the illusion that it is possible to
> establish really friendly relations with the Soviet Government or with
> any communist party or communist individual. . . . The keynote of our
> immediate relations with the Soviet Union should be patience. . . . We
> should neither expect too much nor despair of getting anything at all.
> . . . We should remain unimpressed in the face of expansive professions
> of friendliness and unperturbed in the face of slights and underhand
> opposition.[68]

In any case, relations with the Soviet government were frequently
characterized by friction rather than friendliness. Some of this is attributable to personalities. Chapter V shows that both Soviet and
American leaders mistrusted the first Soviet Ambassador, Troyanovsky.
Konstantin Umansky, who replaced him in 1939, was little better.

> Oumansky was one of the most difficult foreign diplomats with whom
> we ever had to deal. He was insulting in his manner and speech, and
> had an infallible faculty for antagonizing those of us with whom he
> came in contact. Overbearing, he made demands for concessions as if
> they were a natural right, and protested our acts as if they were heinous
> offenses. In my opinion he did much harm to Russian-American
> relations.[69]

Elsewhere Hull wrote: "Oumansky, a walking insult when at his
worst"; "Oumansky said rather sarcastically—sarcasm poured from the
Ambassador like wheat from a thresher"; and "Oumansky, who thought
that firmness meant rudeness, was difficult to deal with at best."[70]

But it was not just the personalities of the diplomats sent to Washington. One of the most frustrating experiences of American-Soviet
relations came in 1939/40 when Ward (the American consul in Moscow) went to Lwow, at the suggestion and invitation of the Soviet
government, to take charge of Ambassador Biddle's possessions left
behind in the evacuation of Poland in 1939. Between October 23, 1939,
and April 18, 1940, there were fifty-one American messages dealing
with the problem, at the end of which time matters stood exactly as
they had before the Embassy directed the first message to the Soviet
Foreign Office. "Should the Soviet Ambassador here ever find occasion
to complain against any lack of cooperation on our part," wrote
Edward Page of the State Department, "I suggest that this file be
handed to him for perusal."[71]

At about the same time, Under Secretary of State Welles prepared a memorandum titled "Certain Matters Affecting Soviet-American Relations":

> The difficulties and irritating experience which our representatives continue to encounter in the Soviet Union strongly operate to injure the relations between the two countries. It is firmly believed that it will be almost impossible to have what might be truly called cordial relations so long as the Soviet authorities continue to employ methods which seriously hamper the proper functioning of the Embassy and alienate the American personnel.
>
> . . . It cannot be too strongly emphasized that the above-mentioned irritations and annoying incidents, which show no signs of decreasing, not only prevent our Embassy from functioning in a normal manner but also make it appear that the attitude of officials responsible for them is not friendly to the United States.[72]

Admiral William Standley, who may well have been appointed Ambassador to Moscow because he represented the "hard" rather than "diplomatic" type of governmental relations, wrote that, "since my arrival here the Embassy . . . had been continually subjected to delays, interference and indifference on the part of subordinate Soviet officials and that it appeared to me that almost a studied effort was being made to thwart its cooperative spirit which Stalin had agreed in my first interview should exist."[73] On April 6, 1945, Ambassador Averell Harriman cabled from Moscow: "I cannot list the almost daily affronts and total disregard which the Soviets evince in matters of interest to us."[74] On another occasion, Secretary of State George Marshall told Stalin, after reciting a long list of communications not answered by the Russians, that "such conduct was not merely discourteous but that it amounted to an attitude of contemptuousness, and if their design was to earn our ill will they were going about it most successfully."[75]

It was not just frustration and bad manners, however, that annoyed the Americans. Downright deceitfulness characterized some Soviet action. In 1948, Secretary of Defense James Forrestal wrote, with reference to the Berlin blockade, then in its seventy-fourth day:

> The sheer duplicity of the Soviets during these negotiations is beyond the experience of the experts in the State Department, with the result that any future promise made by the Soviets is to be evaluated with great caution. It appears that they do not mind lying or even our knowing that they lie, as long as it is for the benefit of the state.
>
> . . . The directive issued [from Moscow] to the four governors [military governors in Berlin] has been completely disregarded by Sokolovsky. . . . He has disavowed practically all of the four-power conference proposals agreed to by Stalin and Molotov.[76]

Matters were worse than usual during two periods of our diplomatic relations: the Great Purge period, 1936-38, and the Cold War period, especially 1947-52. At these times the Soviet government made obvious attempts to isolate its people from contacts with foreigners, including diplomats, and to keep relations to the barest minimum. Particularly during the days of the Great Purge, when most of the Soviet Foreign Office and Foreign Service officials were replaced, aloofness and timidity were best for those who were left to talk with Americans, until one State Department official made clear to the Soviet Ambassador in Washington "that if our officers in Moscow were to receive no more cooperation from the Soviet authorities than they were receiving at this time, and were to be expected to continue under the difficulties they were encountering . . . we would not be justified in continuing to maintain the present staff of officers in Moscow."[77]

But when Ambassador Laurence Steinhardt talked to Umansky, then in Moscow, the latter

> made it quite clear that he and the Soviet authorities take the position that we should continue as in the past to immediately extend every possible courtesy and facility while expecting nothing in return under pain of being accused of retaliation, the consequences of which, he tells me, will be the irritation of the Soviet authorities and a complaint by him to Mr. Hull in person. . . . Unless we take a firm position . . . we must expect a steady encroachment resulting in increased demands upon us and further curtailment of the meager courtesies now accorded us.[78]

It was easy for President Roosevelt to say, "I think we should match every Soviet annoyance by a similar annoyance here against them,"[79] but retaliation by the American government was not a simple matter.

> The situation in many countries—and particularly in the United States —is such that it is an easy matter for Moscow to circumvent the governments of these countries and to deal directly with private individuals, firms, and organizations. It has its trade delegations, its local communist parties, its foreign newspaper correspondents, and its various disguised agents, to help it in these efforts. Thus the Soviet leaders have been able to proceed to curb the scope of activity of the Moscow diplomatic corps, confident that no retaliatory measures which might follow could effectively disturb their own business with the outside world.[80]

It was this, as much as anything else, that kept the American government from seriously considering breaking off the diplomatic relations established with Moscow in 1933.

There seemed no real chance of ever establishing the kind of cordial relations that were normal in dealing with most other governments. What looked like an opportunity for cooperation and peaceful endeavor in 1933 was only a will-o'-the-wisp, but no government could know this before pursuing these ends. Perhaps, after all, Secretary Hull understood the situation very well. On the eve of Hitler's invasion of the Soviet Union, he wrote that our policy toward the Soviet Union embraced these points:

> Make no approaches to Russia.
>
> Treat any approaches toward us with reserve until the Russians satisfied us they were not maneuvering merely to obtain unilateral concessions for themselves.
>
> Reject any Soviet suggestions that we make concessions for the sake of improving American-Soviet relations, and require a strict *quid pro quo*.
>
> Make no sacrifices of principle in order to better relations.
>
> Let Russia understand that we considered an improvement in relations to be just as important, if not more so, to Russia than to the United States.
>
> Make the principle of reciprocity the basis of our day-to-day relations.
>
> In general our policy toward Russia was one of firmness but friendliness.[81]

This was a far cry from the goal set by President Roosevelt (as quoted at the beginning of this chapter, p. 210).

CHAPTER IX

Evaluation

BROKEN PROMISES AND HOPES

It is clear that the Soviet government did not implement the Roosevelt-Litvinov agreements as expected at the time of signature. Whether American expectations were justifiable, they were not realized, and this has clouded American-Soviet relations ever since. More recent Soviet violations of agreements have somewhat obscured those discussed in the previous chapters, but they are only a continuation of the patterns of the first few years of our diplomatic relations. The violations were most obvious in the cases of the agreements on interference in internal affairs, legal rights of nationals in the Soviet Union, and payment of the Soviet debts, though the last was really a violation of an assumption rather than a formal agreement. Nowhere else was the Soviet government openly defiant of the agreements but in the case of the 7th Congress of the Communist International, and this became the symbol around which American disillusionment with its Soviet policy was centered. The many instances of Soviet failure to accord American nationals in the Soviet Union their rights aroused less official anger in Washington than Soviet violations of the other two agreements mentioned. Seldom was a diplomatic document so bluntly phrased as Secretary Hull's telegram of August 30, 1935, in which he wrote, with reference to the 7th World Congress: "In its reply of August 27, 1935, . . . the Soviet Government almost in so many words repudiated the pledge which it gave at the time of recognition that 'it will be the fixed policy of the Government of the Union of Soviet Socialist Republics not to permit . . . and to prevent' the very activities against which this Government had complained and protested."[1] Writing several years after this event, Hull was still gravely concerned about it. "We were now back almost to where we had started. We had official relations with Moscow, but they rested on no bedrock of friendship and cooperation."[2] And Assistant Secretary of State Berle

233

wrote a memorandum for Hull in 1940, preparatory to a visit by Umansky, suggesting that:

> It might be pointed out that we are sick and tired of the pretense that the Russian government has nothing to do with propaganda activities here . . . of the whole farce of Russia's insisting that she be treated in all respects as a friendly nation while she left-handedly carries on a campaign plainly hostile to the system of this country. . . .
>
> Until there is, in good faith, an actual carrying out of the terms of the Roosevelt-Litvinov agreement, we have, specifically:
>
> (1) No interest whatever in assisting the Soviet government with our ships and resources;
>
> (2) No reason to permit a Soviet engineer or any other kind of Soviet visitor, to visit our plants;
>
> (3) In requisitioning machine tools or forbidding exports of materials, no particular reason to give special consideration to Soviet needs; and
>
> (4) Every reason to take obvious measures for internal and external defense, exactly as the Soviet Government has done, including defence [sic] against Soviet intrigues.[3]

When Hull wrote about our inability to settle the debt problem, he denoted the Soviet action as "unfortunate,"[4] indicating how much less serious this violation appeared. After all, the Soviet government was only one more in a procession of European governments defaulting on First World War debts to the United States.

Some of the other agreements made in November 1933 were of relatively little importance. The Soviet government generally honored the agreement on freedom of worship for Americans in the Soviet Union, though its antireligious policy remained a target of active opposition. Little was ever heard of the statement on economic espionage, and that on Soviet claims and assignments was of little importance except insofar as it kept our courts free from countersuits. The few million dollars raised from the assignment cases did little to make Americans feel more kindly toward the Soviet government.

All in all, it was not a happy story from the American point of view. The Soviet government received no credit for having faithfully lived up to the agreements on numerous occasions, when there were so many other instances where it failed to do so.

The American government was doubly sensitive about these violations because of the feeling, which grew as years went by and violations continued, that it had probably been outsmarted in the November 1933 negotiations. There was general agreement that the Soviet leaders had had only one real interest: recognition. If they could obtain this uncon-

ditionally, as with other governments, so much the better. If they had
to pay a price, they would, keeping it as low as possible. When the
Americans insisted on attaching conditions to recognition, the Russians
agreed but managed subsequently to see that they did not have to give
up very much for what they wanted. The Soviet leaders, then,
achieved their goal; the American leaders, hopeful at first, later saw
that they had not obtained theirs, and were properly annoyed at this
turn of events. As soon as the Russians attained recognition, they lost
interest in the promises made by Litvinov; when the Americans realized that they were not getting what they had hoped, they had only
the promises to fall back on. As early as April 1934 Moore concluded,
"It is now quite apparent that Litvinov when he was here was not
serious about any phase of the negotiations except recognition, and
that he is now indifferent to all the assurances he gave in respect to
other phases."[5] Secretary of State Dulles later emphasized that "it is
never prudent to trade performance on our part against promises on
the part of the Soviet Communists."[6] Both sides left the negotiation
table confident; the satisfaction of the Russians lasted longer than that
of the Americans. Indeed, given the warnings and experiences of other
governments, it was a bitter brew the Americans had to swallow, and
probably no satisfying explanation will ever be made as to why the
American government was not more cautious when it knew so much
about Soviet performance.

In retrospect it is not clear why the Americans should have refused
recognition until they had achieved their goal, just because they held
the initial whip-hand. It was possible to continue to withhold recognition, and some have argued that this would have been preferable. It
might have been possible to get a definite Soviet promise to pay the
debts, or even some actual transfer of money, before recognition, but
it was not possible to put the Soviet government on probation, to make
Moscow suspend operations of the Comintern for five or ten years, or
to hold out until the first hundred American nationals had received
protection of their legal rights in the Soviet Union. Recognition involved a single act, all in one day; implementation was a continuing
development, over the years. The two things were not of the same
nature.

On the other hand, Moscow, too, may have been disappointed by
the developments. Soviet leaders must have considered recognition a
tremendous psychological boost for their system. Yet they may have
been dismayed later to discover that the Americans actually expected
the promises to be fulfilled and were willing to jeopardize friendly
relations in the event of failure. After all, no other government had

seriously tried to hold Moscow to its word. There had been words of anguished frustration but, once uttered, they were soon forgotten and not made the basis for foreign policy. Moscow seemed to have great difficulty in correctly assessing American public opinion. Litvinov once complained to an American, "Yes, we are always expecting more than we should from America."[7] The Soviets may well have discovered that some strain of puritanism led the American government to expect even diplomats to fulfill their promises.

And the Americans did expect this. "It has been—and continues to be—the natural expectation of this Government that the Soviet Government would adhere strictly to all those engagements,"[8] wrote a State Department official several years after Litvinov had made the agreements. It was not just something they wanted; they really expected the promises to be fulfilled and were willing to protest non-fulfillment and even extort a price from the Russians because of it. In the long run, the Soviet leaders, who may have thought initially that they had obtained recognition without having to pay a price, may have discovered that it was they—not the Americans—who were receiving public scorn.

Out of the Soviet failure to fulfill Litvinov's promises came a widespread belief that "you can't trust promises made by the Russians." This was not just within the walls of chanceries; it was trumpeted to the skies, around the world, until the Soviet reputation for duplicity was unequalled in modern diplomacy. When the Soviet government failed to fulfill its agreement in the case of the 7th World Congress, one newspaper said that this action "must remind all those who still believe in the sincerity of the Soviets' intentions and activities of the pronouncement of Lenin: 'Sign with one hand—and cross out and tear up agreements with the other.' "[9] After half a dozen years of Soviet violations, one official wrote that "it becomes apparent that no action or policy should be based upon the word of the Kremlin however solemnly pledged."[10]

It is interesting, in view of American opinion of these Soviet violations, to read Harry Hopkins' report of his conference with Stalin on July 30, 1941, in which the head of the Soviet government spoke

> of the necessity of there being a minimum moral standard between all nations and without such a minimum moral standard nations could not co-exist. He stated that the present leaders of Germany knew no such minimum moral standard and that, therefore, they represented an anti-social force in the present world. The Germans were a people, he said, who without a second's thought would sign a treaty today, break it tomorrow and sign a second one the following day. Nations must fulfill their treaty obligations, he said, or international society could not exist.[11]

Present leaders of the American and Soviet governments could condemn Stalin for the same sin, though on different grounds.

The Department of State later brought the record up to date, declaring that "the instability of peace the world over is due, in large measure, to deliberate Soviet policy and actions and to the wholesale Soviet violation of basic agreements. . . . Before the court of world opinion, it stands indicted for disregarding its international treaties and agreements, openly flouting protocols and promises, and encouraging violations of basic human rights by other treaty signatories."[12] In 1953 a House committee devoted 138 pages to violations by the Soviet government and its satellites. Two years later a Senate committee "studied nearly a thousand treaties and agreements . . . which the Soviets have entered into not only with the United States, but with countries all over the world. . . . Its government has broken its word to virtually every country to which it ever gave a signed promise."[13]

Shortly after he became President, Truman was visited by Molotov, who was on his way to the San Francisco Conference. The President was angry at Soviet failure to fulfill the Yalta agreements. Finally Molotov said, "I have never been talked to like that in my life." "I told him, 'Carry out your agreements and you won't get talked to like that.'"[14] And Secretary of State Dulles later labeled this officially as a matter of Soviet policy: "They are a nation—perhaps the first nation—which has turned treaty-breaking into a regularly accepted means of gaining their ends in the world."[15] This was twenty-five years after the first Soviet violation of the Roosevelt-Litvinov agreements.

BREAK DIPLOMATIC RELATIONS?

It was natural that steps would be taken to combat this situation. "I think that the Soviet Ambassador should be called in," wrote Assistant Secretary Moore, "and made to understand that the conduct of his government is so intolerable as to lead to the belief that there is hardly any value in maintaining an American Embassy in Moscow."[16] At least, Moore concluded, "it does not seem to me that there should be any haste . . . in appointing a successor" to Ambassador Davies.

But the loudest protests against Soviet violations came from Congress. As early as January 1935 Senator Key Pittman (Chairman of the Senate Foreign Relations Committee) sent Secretary Hull a copy of Senate Concurrent Resolution 7 which stated that "it is the sense of the Senate and House of Representatives of the United States that the diplomatic recognition by the Government of the United States of America of the Union of Soviet Socialist Republics should be withdrawn."[17] In his reply of February 9, Hull pointed out that this could not be done, that only a breach of diplomatic relations was possible. The greatest flurry of congressional opposition came at the time of the Soviet attack on Finland. Representative Bolles of Wisconsin introduced a resolution to prevent the use of any government appropriation for maintenance of our Embassy in Moscow. Had the resolution passed, it would have effectively severed our relations with the Soviet Union. In February 1940 Representative McCormack of Massachusetts offered an amendment to an appropriations bill to strike out the amount allocated for the salary of the American Ambassador in Moscow. Although this amendment was approved by the House (88–86) on a standing vote, it was defeated on a teller vote.

On January 19, 1940, Pittman sent Hull a copy of a resolution submitted the previous day by Senator Arthur Vandenberg of Michigan:

> Resolved, That the President is requested to report to the Senate, if not incompatible with the public interest, whether the Union of Soviet Socialist Republics has fulfilled the obligations of the Litvinoff agreements of November 16, 1933 upon which our diplomatic relations with the Union of Soviet Socialist Republics were then and are now made wholly contingent.

In reply, Hull stated that "although the agreements . . . were concluded simultaneously with the establishment of diplomatic relations . . . the maintenance of diplomatic relations has not been made 'wholly contingent' . . . on the fulfillment by the Soviet Government of the obligations set forth in these agreements."[18] He also spoke of representations made to the Soviet government when violations occurred.

On March 16, 1940, Pittman wrote Hull again, enclosing a resolution introduced the previous day, which, after calling attention to the Russo-Finnish war and the Soviet government's failure "to abide by the Litvinoff agreements of 1933," "Resolved, That it is the sense of the Senate that the President of the United States should recall the United States Ambassador to the Union of Soviet Socialist Republics, and suspend further diplomatic relations with that country." In his reply of March 25, Hull suggested:

> This Department obviously will encounter difficulties in meeting its responsibilities connected with the conduct of American foreign relations, including the protection of American citizens and interests abroad, if this Government adopts the policy of withdrawing its diplomatic representatives . . . whenever this Government disapproves of the manner in which the government of that country treats a third country. . . .

Similarly, it would not be to the best interests of this Government, in my opinion, for it to follow the policy of suspending diplomatic relations with other governments merely because it feels that they have broken obligations to it.[19]

Others were tempted, in view of the Soviet provocation, to reply by ending the diplomatic relations which appeared to be so futile. This would have ended the treatment suffered by our diplomats in Moscow, but the Department refused to admit that it would be helpful to our national interests. As Hull wrote Pittman, "Whenever this Government has cause to believe that another government has failed to live up to agreements with it, it is accustomed to make use of the very channels which exist by virtue of diplomatic relations, in order to bring this failure to the attention of the other government."[20] To end these relations would be self-defeating; it would remove the means of correcting the grievances.

And, in any case, we had a great deal to lose by breaking diplomatic relations with the Soviet government, perhaps more than our opponents. Moscow had numerous sources of information in the United States: the American press, TASS, Amtorg, the well-disciplined members of the American Communist Party, the Red International of Labor Unions, and all the "front organizations" listed in Chapter II, in addition to its diplomatic and consular representatives. On the other hand, the American government was almost solely dependent upon its official representatives in Moscow for information about the Soviet Union. There were a few American correspondents there and some temporary visitors, but the government had no press association comparable to TASS, no trading organization, no Soviet sections of American political parties, and no front organizations. A breach of diplomatic relations would end the official information-gathering and -reporting activities in both countries; it would leave the Soviet government with all of its other sources in the United States, while the American government would have essentially nothing in the Soviet Union on which to depend. In this light, recognition was more useful to the United States than to the Soviet Union, and so was continuance of diplomatic relations. Moscow may have achieved the initial psychological gain at the time of recognition; we profited, year in and year out, in a practical fashion. Moscow had paid little or no price for its victory, while we had to pay the price of daily anger and frustration. The Department of State concluded that our results were worth this price; by defeating all the resolutions mentioned above, Congress agreed.

WHAT HAVE WE LEARNED?

American-Soviet relations in the first years after the Roosevelt-Litvinov agreements were the first official relations between the two governments. It is appropriate to inquire what we learned—or should have learned—during the first years of official relations. If we did not achieve in practice the fulfillment of all of our 1933 hopes, perhaps the lessons learned were valuable as a basis for future action.

It is much easier to assess the short-run than the long-run results; the former were more tangible and specific whereas the long-run are more general and philosophical, with no documentary evidence yet available. There is every reason to believe that the American government learned a great deal during this period about Soviet diplomacy, both its personnel and techniques. Before the debt negotiations had collapsed at the end of the first year of diplomatic relations, some analysis of Soviet diplomats had been made (as shown in Chapter V). The Great Purge led to wholesale replacement of officials, both in the Foreign Office in Moscow and in the Foreign Service abroad, but the young men of the 1930's are the senior officials with which the American government has had to deal in more recent years. If any allowance is made for personality in the Soviet system, we should be better able to do business with these men on the basis of thirty years of experience.

Those in charge of American relations with the Soviet Union should also have learned a great deal about the methods of Soviet diplomacy. It should have been apparent fairly early, for example, that one of Moscow's techniques was a constant switching from one matter to another, with the use of "double talk" or "aesopian language" to becloud the central issue and keep the opponent from concentrating upon it to Soviet disadvantage. It should also have been recognized that it was a standard Soviet technique to start off by arousing the most roseate hopes, only to dash them afterwards with cold opposition. The differences in the reception of Bullitt in December 1933 and March 1934 (discussed in Chapter VIII) illustrate this technique. Inability of low- and middle-rank Soviet officials to take any initiative or to have any flexibility of negotiation was another technique obvious in the 1930's. A corollary to this was that the Americans understood the necessity of talking to high-level Soviet officials—the higher the better—whenever they wanted action or decision.

American officials should have learned—but it is not clear that they did—how readily the Soviet government made promises and how worthless these promises were. The differences between the agreements of November 16, 1933, and their later realization—or lack of it—illustrates this. Secretary Dulles emphasized this in a press conference on November 29, 1955: "I have frequently said . . . that I thought it would always be reckless for the United States substantially to alter its position in reliance merely of promises made by the Soviet Union as to what they might do in the future."[21] This has apparently been one of the more difficult lessons to learn. Knowing well of Soviet perfidy, we have still found it hard to keep our desire to get along with others from riding roughshod over what we rationally know needs to be done.

Associated with this, and also not completely learned yet, is the idea that in dealing with the Soviet government it is necessary to obtain a *sine qua non* for every concession made to them. This would seem natural for a people of "Yankee horse traders" or "hard-headed businessmen." Yet, time and again, we have discovered that failure to be sufficiently specific in writing an agreement, or desire for haste in achieving a desired result, has doomed us to later disillusionment. This lesson should have been learned from our experiences with the Roosevelt-Litvinov agreements, but it plagues us even now, thirty years later. It is a standard Soviet technique, for example, to offer an "agreement in principle." Bullitt recognized this in 1936: "We should, I think, take a vow right now *never to accept anything in principle,* but only to discuss concrete detailed proposals."[22] In 1945 General John Deane, on the basis of his wartime negotiations with the Russians, wrote, "It has been my experience that an 'agreement in principle' means exactly nothing to the Russians. They are, therefore, generous in making such agreements."[23] In summarizing a three hundred-page analysis of Soviet negotiating techniques, Professor Philip Mosely has said that

> one of the main pitfalls in wartime Anglo-American negotiations with the Soviet Union was the tendency to rely upon reaching an "agreement in principle" without spelling out in sufficient detail all the steps in its execution. After long and strenuous debates, studded with charges, accusations and suspicions, it was undoubtedly a great relief to reach a somewhat generally worded agreement and to go home. Prodded by manifold public and party duties, anxious to prove to themselves and to their people that current agreements and postwar cooperation with the Soviet Government were genuinely possible, facing "deadlines" with respect to the expectations of legislatures and of public opinion, the western leaders often approached these negotiations under serious disadvantages.[24]

This truth should have been learned in the 1930's, so that there would be no necessity for postwar recriminations over wartime negotiations, but it was not.

It may also be true, as stated earlier, that no agreement, however carefully worked out, can guarantee the desired results when one of the parties is unwilling to fulfill the agreement. In such a case, a carefully conducted negotiation is still preferable, if only for the sake of defending the record when it is attacked later. One such lesson was apparently learned: "in every case understandings with the Soviet government or representatives thereof should be made in writing or should be confirmed at a later date by a written document."[25]

One bitter lesson learned from these experiences by some, though far from all, of the American people was that their national interest was not the sole factor to be considered. It was easy, when we had little responsibility in international affairs, to believe that "others" made the mistakes and "we" could have done better. Somewhere along the road from isolation to international leadership we had to discover that our domestic leaders did not possess the whole truth, that it was impossible for us—just because we were Americans—to outmaneuver all other peoples of the world, and that no government could have its own way all the time. Secretary of State Byrnes said at the Paris Conference in October 1946, "two states can quickly reach an understanding if one is willing to yield on all demands. The United States is unwilling to do that. It is equally unwilling to ask it of another state."[26] Much of this education resulted from our relations with the Soviet Union after 1933. Chagrin, embarrassment, and frustration are frequent concomitants of learning, whether it involves an individual or a people. Yet there are still many Americans who do not realize this, who blame only a single man or a political party for the fact that we did not accomplish all that we set out to do. Had other individuals been in office at the time, some things would have been done differently, but there is no evidence that the achievements would have been more notable.

There is one important lesson, apparently, that we have not learned, and that is how best to deal with the Soviet government. There were those, some of them in high places, who were dissatisfied with the basic philosophy of our approach to the Soviet government; they would have preferred a stronger, firmer policy toward Moscow. On one occasion, Sumner Welles said that our policy should have been firmer and that he had expressed that view to President Roosevelt "who concurred, but said that he had no success with Hull, who, as he phrased it, wanted to rely on the linger-and-wait policy of a domestic politician, with the result that instead of shaping events he had permitted events to shape him."[27] It is difficult to convince some people that a president whose claim to greatness rests on his ability to get things done as he wanted them could transfer blame to his Secretary of State on so important a matter. Secretary Stimson is quoted as believing "that the Americans tended to give way too easily on these smaller questions, leaving the Russians with the impression that they had only to be disagreeable to get what they wanted."[28] But apparently he, too, had misjudged them, for it has been said that in the two years after the Second World War "the behavior of the Russians . . . filled him with astonishment and regret."[29]

It might be expected that those who had to meet the unpleasantnesses of Soviet officials day after day would have believed in a firmer policy. In 1940 Umansky proposed a series of talks with Department of State officials, to clear the air of the friction that characterized our relations. Although no great good was expected out of these conversations between Umansky and Welles, it was thought that some benefit might result. One official thought this an error:

> Soviet authorities have been more recalcitrant, uncooperative, and stubborn than usual during the past three or four weeks. This is easy to explain. As long as the attitude in Washington was unfriendly, we were getting results here. . . . The moment these people here get it into their heads that we are "appeasing them, making up to them, or need them," they immediately stop being cooperative. . . . I assume that the "higher ups" . . . are still fooling themselves into believing that the Soviet government responds to kindness or evidence of good will. My experience has been that they respond only to force and if force cannot be applied, then to straight oriental bartering or trading methods.[30]

And the diplomats in Moscow, who really bore the brunt of relations between the two governments, had it the worst of all, and should, perhaps, have argued most insistently for a firmer policy. One did, writing:

> My observation of the psychology of the individuals who are conducting Soviet foreign policy has long since convinced me that they do not and cannot be induced to respond to the customary amenities, that it is not possible to create "international good will" with them, that they will always sacrifice the future in favor of an immediate gain, and they are not affected by ethical or moral considerations, nor guided by the relationships which are customary between individuals of culture and breeding. Their psychology recognizes only firmness, power and force. . . . They must be dealt with on this basis and on this basis alone. . . . It has been my own experience that on every occasion that either the Department or the Embassy has made concessions to the Soviet Government or approached it in a spirit of friendly cooperation or good will, these gestures have been received by the Soviet authorities with marked suspicion and a disposition to regard them as evidence of weak-

ness, whereas on each occasion that our attitude has stiffened the Soviet authorities have regarded our demeanor as evidence of self-confidence and strength and have promptly reacted by a more conciliatory attitude which has noticeably increased our prestige. Nor have I found any evidence of resentment or bitterness at the reciprocal application of unpleasant measures.[31]

The Ambassador's views were obviously not accepted by his government. A week later, when the Soviet Union was attacked by Hitler, the American government hastened to withdraw its travel restrictions on Soviet diplomatic personnel in the United States, unfreeze blocked Soviet funds in American banks, and end by making "concessions" of ten billion dollars' worth of Lend-Lease materials for which almost no reciprocity was asked and no thanks or repayment received by the United States. The point here is not whether the words of the ambassador or the subsequent acts of his government were correct or in error, for the words were written in a situation that the events of the next few days changed almost entirely. The point is that the American government was not able to agree on how its own interests, vis-à-vis the Soviet Union, could best be advanced. Almost a decade had elapsed since inauguration of diplomatic relations. There had been a thousand occasions on which to assess Soviet leaders and policies, yet we did not know in June 1941 how to deal with them. Hull, writing after he left office, admitted that

> it might be said that the President and I were taken in by Russia's promises and written pledges, that we should have realized it was impossible to do business with Soviet Russia . . . and consequently that we should have adopted the policy of the mailed fist toward Russia right from the beginning.
> But as we went back over our relations with Moscow I felt, and President Roosevelt did too, that there was ample reason for the policy of friendship that we adopted.[32]

Hull would be expected to justify the policy of the Department of State during his administration, but outsiders could not decide whether Atherton and Steinhardt or Roosevelt and Hull had the better answer on how to deal with the Soviet government.

It should also be said that in the autumn of 1962, faced with Soviet missiles and troops in Cuba, the American government still did not know how to deal with Soviet leaders. If the newspaper reports are to be believed (since diplomatic documents are not yet available for this period) the group around the President was divided into "hawks" and "doves," arguing whether or not a strong, firm, blunt policy would be best.

We have not been so uncertain in our dealings with other governments. Perhaps it is some sense of morality, or legality, or tradition on our part. Perhaps it is the genius of the Soviet government somehow to be able to delude us, in which case this is a major diplomatic victory for that government. In 1946 George Kennan wrote a memorandum about the Soviets:

> We have here a political force committed fanatically to the belief that with the United States there can be no permanent modus vivendi, that it is desirable and necessary that the internal harmony of our society be disrupted, our traditional way of life be destroyed, and international authority of our state be broken, if Soviet power is to be secure. . . . The problem of how to cope with this force is undoubtedly the greatest task our diplomacy has ever faced and probably the greatest it will ever have to face.[33]

American diplomacy has not yet solved that problem.

If it still confronts us, we need not conclude that our relations with Moscow have been fruitless. Writing in 1938, Ambassador Davies asserted that, despite the irritations, "the Mission of the government of the United States here has received more consideration and favor from this government during the past year than has any other foreign state."[34] When Secretary Dulles was asked for an evaluation, on the twentieth anniversary of the recognition of the Soviet government, he said that he believed that "on balance over the twenty-year period the United States has gained more than it has lost through recognition. The gain was particularly notable during the period of the Second World War."[35]

It is true, indeed, that establishment of diplomatic relations between the two governments was the most important single factor on which the Second World War anti-Hitler coalition rested. No price was too great to have the Soviet Union involved in this conflict on the same side as the United States, rather than on the sidelines waiting to pick up the pieces, as many experts expected and feared.

It was suggested earlier that President Roosevelt was chiefly concerned with the domestic situation in the United States and the effect of Soviet recognition on American opinion. Kennan has asserted, in fact, that the President exchanged these promises with Litvinov "only" because of their psychological impact on the American people and was not worried about their later effectiveness. If so, the exchanges were basically successful. This dramatic step captured attention; American insistence on obtaining promises from the Russians reassured the people; there was a chance for more export trade; war did not break out in the Far East. The step was a "typical Roosevelt coup." And no

one, outside a small group of experts, followed the diplomatic laby-
rinth of the decade closely enough to see what progress was actually
made. There was frustration and anger on occasion but this was
largely momentary. The 1930's were filled with too many events and
too much drama for the general public to focus long on any single
aspect. From this angle, November 1933 marked a notable step forward. It might even be said that anything gained later through Soviet
fulfillment of the Litvinov promises was actually a bonus, welcome
but unexpected.

If we did not achieve all that we wished from the Roosevelt-
Litvinov agreements, we can have considerable satisfaction. We did
not receive payment on the debts, but the money would have produced no great effect on the national budgets of the postdepression
years. We did not stop the operations of the Comintern in the United
States, though the danger of communism to our system was not much
greater because of Soviet failure to implement this agreement. In turn,
the menace of international communism was brought home—to us and
to many other peoples—far more clearly because of Soviet violation of
its promise on this matter. On this the Soviet government was its own
worst enemy and we, the beneficiary. In protecting the rights of some
of our nationals in the Soviet Union, we did better than any other
government. There was, without much question, temporary improvement in the international situation, especially in the Far East, just
after recognition. If there was no long-term improvement, it was
because the American and Soviet governments could not agree. The
result was beneficial to us in several ways, as we learned more about
the real nature of the Soviet system. No other government was more
successful in dealing with Moscow than we and that, considering our
inexperience, was no mean accomplishment. We kept our self-respect,
also no small matter in a democracy. It would seem evident, also, that
much of the basis of our current leadership of the free world was laid
during the decade after 1933. Our policies and our diplomatic methods
commended themselves to other governments when they were forced
later to choose sides in a polarized world. This list of benefits, if not
what we hoped it would be, may be as much as we had a right to
expect.

Appendix

Identification of Officials

The following list is included to aid the reader in identifying American and Soviet officials important in the text, giving the positions that involved them in American-Soviet relations. The spellings are those used in *Foreign Relations of the United States*.

Atherton, Ray: Counselor of the American Embassy in London

Bakhmetyev, Boris A.: Ambassador of the Provisional Government of Russia to the United States, 1917-22

Bakhmetyev, Georgi: Ambassador of the Imperial Russian Government to the United States, 1911-17

Bogdanov, Peter A.: Chairman of the Board of Directors, Amtorg Trading Corporation, New York, 1928-34

Bohlen, Charles E.: Vice Consul, Consul, Third Secretary of the American Embassy in Moscow, 1934-35, 1937-40; Division of Eastern European Affairs, Department of State, 1935-37; Ambassador of the United States to the Soviet Union, 1953-57

Bullitt, William C.: Special Assistant to the Secretary of State, 1933; Ambassador to the Soviet Union, 1933-36

Byrnes, James F.: Secretary of State, 1945-47

Carr, Wilbur J.: Assistant Secretary of State, 1924-39

Castle, William R.: Assistant Secretary of State, 1927-33

Chicherin, Georgi V.: People's Commissar for Foreign Affairs, 1918-30

Colby, Bainbridge: Secretary of State, 1920-21

Cole, Felix: Counselor of Legation—Riga, Kovno, and Tallinn, 1930——

Coleman, Frederick W. B.: Minister of the United States to Estonia, Latvia, and Lithuania, 1922-31

Davies, Joseph E.: Ambassador of the United States to the Soviet Union, 1938-39

Davis, Norman H.: Chairman, American delegation to the General Disarmament Conference, Geneva

Dillon, C. Douglas: Under Secretary of State for Economic Affairs, 1958-59, Under Secretary of State, 1959-60, Secretary of the Treasury, 1961——

Dimitrov, Georgy: Elected Secretary General of the Executive Committee of the Communist International by the 7th World Congress, 1935

Divilkovsky, Ivan A.: Secretary General of the Collegium, People's Commissariat for Foreign Affairs

247

Dulles, John Foster: Secretary of State, 1953-59

Dunn, James C.: Special Assistant to the Secretary of State, 1934; Chief, Western European Division, Department of State, 1935; Adviser on Political Relations, Department of State

Faymonville, Philip R., Major (later Lieutenant Colonel): American Military Attaché in the Soviet Union, 1934-39

Forrestal, James: Secretary of Defense, 1947-49

Francis, David R.: Ambassador of the United States to the Imperial Russian Government and the Provisional Government, 1916-18

Grew, Joseph C.: Ambassador of the United States to Japan, 1931-41

Gromyko, Andrei A.: Chief, Division of American Countries, People's Commissariat for Foreign Affairs, 1939; Counselor, Soviet Embassy in Washington, 1939-43; Ambassador to the United States, 1943-46; Deputy Minister of Foreign Affairs, First Deputy Minister, Minister, 1946, 1949, 1957——

Hackworth, Green H.: Legal Adviser, Department of State, 1931-46

Harriman, W. Averell: Chairman, Special Mission to the Soviet Union, 1941; Ambassador to the Soviet Union, 1943-46

Henderson, Loy W.: Second Secretary of the American Embassy in the Soviet Union, 1934-36; First Secretary, 1936-38; Assistant Chief, Division of European Affairs, Department of State, 1938-42; Counselor of Embassy and Chargé d'Affaires in Moscow and Kuibyshev, 1942

Hughes, Charles E.: Secretary of State, 1921-25

Hull, Cordell: Secretary of State, 1933-44

Kalinin, Mikhail I.: Chairman, Presidium of the Supreme Soviet (titular head of the Soviet government)

Karakhan, Lev M.: Assistant People's Commissar for Foreign Affairs, 1931-34

Kelley, Robert F.: Chief, Division of Eastern European Affairs, Department of State, 1926-37

Kennan, George F.: Third Secretary of Embassy, Moscow, 1934-35; Second Secretary, 1935-37; Division of European Affairs, Department of State, 1937-38; Minister-Counselor, Moscow, 1945; Ambassador to the Soviet Union, 1952

Kerensky, Alexander F.: Prime Minister, Provisional Government of Russia, 1917

Khrushchev, Nikita S.: Member, Presidium of the Central Committee (CPSU), 1939-64; 1st Secretary, Central Committee, 1953-64; Chairman, Council of Ministers, 1958-64

Kirk, Alexander C.: Consul General and Counselor, American Embassy in the Soviet Union, 1938-39

Kohler, Foy D.: Ambassador of the United States to the Soviet Union, 1962——

Krassin, Leonid B.: People's Commissar for Foreign Trade

Krestinsky, Nikolay N.: Assistant People's Commissar for Foreign Affairs

Kuniholm, Bertel E.: Third Secretary of Embassy, Moscow, 1934-35;

Second Secretary, 1936; Division of Eastern European Affairs, Department of State, 1936-37

Kuusinen, Otto: Leading Comintern official

Lansing, Robert: Secretary of State, 1915-20

Lenin, Vladimir I.: Leader of the Bolshevik revolution; President, Council of People's Commissars until 1924

Litvinov, Maxim M.: People's Commissar for Foreign Affairs, 1930-39

Lozovsky, Solomon A.: Secretary General, Red International of Trade Unions; Executive Committee of the Communist International; Assistant People's Commissar for Foreign Affairs, 1939

Manuilsky, Dmitry Z.: Presidium, Executive Committee of the Communist International

Marshall, George C.: Secretary of State, 1947-49

Messersmith, George S.: Assistant Secretary of State, 1937-40

Moffat, J. Pierrepont: Chief, Division of European Affairs, Department of State, 1932-34, 1937-40

Molotov, Vyacheslav M.: Chairman, Council of People's Commissars, 1930-41; People's Commissar for Foreign Affairs, 1939-49

Moore, R. Walton: Assistant Secretary of State, 1933-37; Counselor, Department of State, 1937-41

Morgenthau, Henry, Jr.: Under Secretary, Acting Secretary, Secretary of the Treasury, 1933-45

Packer, Earl L.: Assistant Chief, Division of Eastern European Affairs, Department of State, 1928-36

Page, Edward, Jr.: Third Secretary, American Embassy in the Soviet Union, 1935, 1937-38; Division of European Affairs, Department of State, 1938-42

Phillips, William: Under Secretary of State, 1933-35

Plotkin, Mark A.: Assistant Chief, Legal Division of the People's Commissariat for Foreign Affairs, 1935-38

Potemkin, Vladimir P.: Assistant People's Commissar for Foreign Affairs, 1937-40

Radek, Karl B.: Soviet publicist and editor

Roosevelt, Franklin D.: President of the United States, 1933-45

Rosengolts, Arkady P.: People's Commissar for Foreign Trade

Rozov, David A.: Chairman, Board of Directors, Amtorg Trading Corporation, New York City; Assistant People's Commissar for Foreign Trade, 1938

Rubinin, Evgeny V.: Director, 3rd Western Political Division, People's Commissariat for Foreign Affairs

Rumreich, Dr. Adolph S.: Public Health Surgeon, attached to the American Embassy in the Soviet Union

Rusk, Dean: Assistant Chief, Division of International Security Affairs, Department of State, 1946; Director, Office of United Nations Affairs, 1947-49; Assistant Secretary of State, 1949; Deputy Under Secretary of

State, 1949-50; Assistant Secretary of State, 1950-51; Secretary of State, 1961——

Rykov, Alexey I.: Chairman, Council of People's Commissars until 1930

Sayre, Francis B.: Assistant Secretary of State, 1933-39

Skinner, Robert P.: Minister to Estonia, Latvia, and Lithuania, 1931-33

Skvirsky, Boris E.: Soviet trade representative in the United States prior to recognition; Counselor, Soviet Embassy in the United States, 1934-36

Stalin, Iosif V.: Secretary General, Central Committee (CPSU/B); Premier, 1941-53

Standley, William H.: Ambassador of the United States to the Soviet Union, 1942-43

Steinhardt, Laurence A.: Ambassador of the United States to the Soviet Union, 1939-42

Stimson, Henry L.: Secretary of State, 1929-33

Stomonyakov, Boris S.: Assistant People's Commissar for Foreign Affairs

Trotsky, Lev D.: Communist leader and associate of Lenin, from the Bolshevik revolution until 1924; in exile thereafter

Troyanovsky, Alexander A.: Soviet Ambassador to the United States, 1934-39

Ughet, Serge: Financial Attaché of the Russian Provisional Government in the United States from 1917, becoming custodian of Russian property, 1922-33

Umansky, Konstantin A.: Chief, Press Section of the People's Commissariat for Foreign Affairs, 1931-36; Counselor, Soviet Embassy in the United States, 1936-39; Soviet Ambassador to the United States, 1939-41

Vinogradov, Sergey I.: Assistant Chief, Third Western Political Division, People's Commissariat for Foreign Affairs; in charge of the American desk, 1937-39

Voroshilov, Kliment E.: Marshal; People's Commissar for Defense

Vyshinsky, Andrey Y.: Assistant People's Commissar for Foreign Affairs, 1939-49

Ward, Angus I.: Consul, Second Secretary, Chief—Consular Section of the American Embassy in the Soviet Union, 1934-40; Consul, Vladivostok, 1940-41

Weinberg, Khaim S.: Assistant Chief (Chief, after 1937), 3rd Western Political Division, People's Commissariat for Foreign Affairs, 1935-38

Welles, Sumner: Assistant Secretary of State, 1933-37; Under Secretary of State, 1937-43

Wiley, John C.: Counselor, American Embassy in the Soviet Union, 1934-35

Yaroslavsky, Emelyan: Chairman, Central Council of the Union of Militant Atheists of the Soviet Union

Zinovyev, Grigory E.: prime organizer of the Communist International; President, Executive Committee of the Communist International

Notes to Chapters

Since much of the research for this book was done in the Department of State Files in the National Archives, many notes refer to materials there. For documents in these files, the initials DSF are used, followed by the file and document numbers. Thus DSF 711.61/71 means that the cited document, 71, is to be found in the National Archives in Department of State File 711.61. Some of these documents have been printed, at least in part, in the series, *Foreign Relations of the United States*. Since for most students these volumes are more easily accessible than the documents themselves, I have cited *Foreign Relations* wherever possible, using the initials *FR*, followed by the year, volume, and page. For the volume in the *Foreign Relations* series entitled *The Soviet Union, 1933-1939*, the initials *FRSU* are used. Since *Foreign Relations* includes file numbers, they are not repeated here. When materials in the Franklin D. Roosevelt Library at Hyde Park, New York, are cited, the initials RL are used. Where no city of origin is included for telegrams and dispatches to the Department of State from abroad, the reader may assume that they involve the United States Embassy in Moscow. When such a message originated elsewhere, that fact is noted.

Chapter I. RECOGNITION OF THE SOVIET GOVERNMENT

1. There was apparently a mixup of names and the "wrong man" was dismissed. (Letter, Secretary Hull to Attorney General Cummings, November 21, 1935, DSF 311.6154 Guaranty Trust Co. [U.S.]/15.) There is some variance in the spelling of Russian names. Except in direct quotations, the spelling used in the *Foreign Relations* volumes has been used here.

2. When Litvinov came to the United States in 1933 to arrange for recognition, he brought his commission dated June 21, 1918, signed by Lenin and Chicherin, as evidence of his long wait for personal acceptance by the American government. (*New York Times*, Nov. 5, 1933, p. 18.)

3. Tel., Secretary Lansing to Ambassador Davis (London), Jan. 8, 1920, *FR* 1920, III, 445.

4. Letter, Secretary Colby to Italian Ambassador Avezzana, Aug. 10, 1920, *FR* 1920, III, 466.

5. *Ibid.*, 467-68.

6. Tel., Secretary Hughes to American Consul in Reval, Dec. 18, 1923, *FR* 1923, II, 788.

7. Most of these favored recognition of the Soviet Government—S.J. Res. 145 and 177, 67th Cong., and the following Senate Resolutions: 293, 67th Cong.; 50, 68th Cong.; 74, 69th Cong.; 44, 70th Cong.; 12, 71st Cong.; 73, 72d Cong.; and 15, 73d Cong. Two other Senate resolutions—263, 72d Cong., and 21, 73d Cong. —authorized committee investigations of conditions in Soviet Russia with respect to recognition.

8. A comparable situation had arisen in January 1933 when Ambassador Grew in Tokyo had refused to sign an Address to the Emperor prepared by the interim

Dean of the Diplomatic Corps, Soviet Ambassador Troyanovsky. When he checked with Washington, however, he was informed that it was permissible for him to sign the address and to call on and receive Troyanovsky, so long as he made it clear that he was not entering into relations with him as a representative of the Soviet government. (Joseph Grew, *Ten Years in Japan* [N.Y., Simon and Schuster, 1944], pp. 58-59.)

9. Just a few days before the 1932 elections, a letter was addressed to Roosevelt by Prince Paul Chavchavadze (Executive Secretary of the United Russian National Organizations in America) in which he said that it was with profound satisfaction that "we learned that, if elected President of the United States, you would have no intention of granting diplomatic recognition to the Soviet government." (Roosevelt Papers, President's Secretary's File, Box 14, RL.)

10. Memorandum by Kelley, Nov. 3, 1933, p. 20, DSF 861.44 Litvinov/15.

11. Six months later, however, Litvinov was talking to Bullitt about placing a "considerable" amount of orders in the United States, a very different tune. Desp. from Bullitt, Jan. 4, 1934 (On Board Steamship "Washington"), FR 1933, II, 840.

12. Desp. from Grew (Tokyo), March 6, 1933, DSF 861.01/1859.

13. Desp. from Brodie (Helsinki), March 7, 1933, DSF 761.94/596.

14. Desp. from Grew (Tokyo), March 9, 1933, DSF 761.94/595.

15. Desp. from Marriner (Paris), March 16, 1933, DSF 761.94/599.

16. Desp. from Grew (Tokyo), Aug. 14, 1933, DSF 861.01/1949.

17. Hull to Roosevelt, Sept. 21, 1933, FR 1933, II, 790.

18. Memorandum by Hornbeck, Oct. 11, 1933, DSF 761.94/638. This view was reiterated from the Soviet side after recognition when Bullitt reported from Moscow that "everyone in Moscow believes that time is running in favor of the Soviet Union and that within a year and a half the Soviet Union will be impregnable. . . . Litvinov, Voroshilov and many other Soviet leaders have expressed the opinion to me that the largest single deterrent to an attack by Japan this spring was recognition of the Soviet Government by the U.S. . . . They are aware that if the honeymoon of December and January . . . should not culminate in a rapid divorce an attack by Japan would become more likely. For this reason, but for no other, I am inclined to believe that they will not allow their relations with the U.S. to become as unpleasant as their relations with Great Britain." (Desp. from Bullitt, April 1934, DSF 761.94/734.) Bullitt reported that a Japanese attack was regarded as certain by all members of the Soviet government and Communist Party, and that Stalin had introduced General Egorov, his Chief of Staff, as "the man who will lead our Army victoriously against Japan when Japan attacks." (Desp. from Bullitt [On Board Steamship "Washington,"], Jan. 4, 1934, FR 1933, II, 837.)

19. An analogous situation developed in 1963/64. With the general easing of Cold War tensions, interest in the trade possibilities between the United States and the Soviet Union quickened. It was accelerated by the rapidly expanding trade of certain American allies—especially Britain, France, and Japan—with the Soviet Union. Some American businessmen favored relaxation of restrictions on nonstrategic trade. Since the Russians are getting what they want elsewhere, they asked, why should we have to hold off, why should we not have a share of the orders now going to others? Secretary of Commerce Luther Hodges suggested that this debate was not something initiated by our government but rather "a natural outgrowth of the changing political climate in the world," and Secretary of State

Rusk cautioned against optimistic hopes of any significant increase in trade: "There are some serious problems. There is not a strong economic base for large expansions of trade between our two countries. There is not a great deal . . . in the Soviet Union that we would wish to buy." (*New York Times*, March 12, 1964.) But the pressure was there, and soon the United States government was talking with the Russians about the purchase of $250,000,000 worth of American wheat, with the negotiations dragging on and on, plagued by the same kinds of problems that had characterized earlier American-Soviet talks. It was not clear either that the Russians really wanted the wheat badly or that the American businessmen and farm leaders were looking beyond immediate possibilities for profit.

20. Memorandum by Kelley, Nov. 3, 1933, pp. 20-21, quoting *International Press Correspondence*, Jan. 12, 1933, vol. 13, no. 2, pp. 40-41, DSF 861.44 Litvinov/15.

21. Letter, Hull to Frank C. Walker, Oct. 29, 1933, Moore Papers, Box 18, RL.

22. Desp. from Skinner (Riga), Feb. 24, 1933, DSF 861.01/1849.

23. Desp. from Cole (Riga), July 26, 1933, DSF 661.1115/551. The bank credit amounted to approximately $50,000,000 and was arranged by the German government.

24. Desp. from Carlson (Tallinn), Jan. 14, 1933, DSF 861.5017 Living Conditions/581. Attached to the file copy of this despatch is a note by Kelley: "Mr. Rogers: Worth noting—Mr. Seljamaa is one of the best informed diplomats in Russia. RFK."

25. Letter, Castle to Fred L. Eberhardt, March 3, 1933, *FRSU*, 5.

26. William C. Bullitt, "How We Won the War and Lost the Peace," *Life*, vol. 25 (August 30, 1948), p. 84.

27. Henry Morgenthau, Jr., "The Morgenthau Diaries. Part III—How F. D. R. Fought the Axis," *Colliers* (October 11, 1947), p. 21.

28. Moore Papers, Box 18, RL.

29. Roosevelt Papers, Official File 220-A, Box 4, RL.

30. Cordell Hull, *The Memoirs of Cordell Hull* (New York, Macmillan, 1948, 2 vols.), p. 293.

31. *Ibid.*, p. 297.

32. Morgenthau, "Diaries," p. 21.

33. Letter, Roosevelt to Kalinin, October 10, 1933, *FRSU*, 17-18. Kelley later told Robert Browder that the text was "worded and reworded with the object of insuring the appointment of Litvinov," on the theory that the choice of the Soviet negotiator would probably determine the success or failure of the negotiations. Kelley also stated that an unoffical copy of Roosevelt's letter was sent to Moscow, through Skvirsky, for tentative approval, before the letter was officially dispatched. (Robert Browder, *The Origins of Soviet-American Diplomacy* [Princeton, Princeton University Press, 1953], pp. 116-17.) The file copy in Washington bears the notation: "Correct. Boris E. Skvirsky."

34. Letter, Kalinin to Roosevelt, Oct. 17, 1933, *FRSU*, 18.

35. Desp. from Skinner (Riga), Feb. 24, 1933, DSF 861.01/1849.

36. Tel., Secretary Hull to Legation in Riga, April 15, 1933, DSF 361.4121/2.

37. Letter, Moore to Kelley, Oct. 24, 1933, Moore Papers, Box 18, RL.

38. Memorandum, Moore to Hull, October 24, 1933, Moore Papers, Box 18, RL. Attached to the file copy of this memorandum is a note: "October 27, 1933. Mr. Moore: I inquired of the Secretary's office regarding the attached and they

say your memorandum is on his desk now and that they think he is going to take it up at the Cabinet Meeting this afternoon. A"

39. Memorandum by Hackworth, Oct. 28, 1933, Moore Papers, Box 18, RL.

40. Memorandum, Moore to Hull, Nov. 4, 1933, Moore Papers, Box 18, RL.

41. Memorandum by Moore, undated, Moore Papers, Box 18, RL.

42. Memorandum by Moore, Oct. 4, 1933, *FRSU*, 16.

43. Lassa F. L. Oppenheim, *International Law* (London, Longmans Green, 1920/21), I, 136.

44. Personal letter, Brown to Hull, Oct. 27, 1933, DSF 711.61/345.

45. Memorandum by Moore, Nov. 10, 1933, Moore Papers, Box 18, RL.

46. Memorandum "by Judge Moore," Oct. 4, 1933, DSF 711.61/289⅓.

47. Hull, *Memoirs*, p. 206.

48. Memorandum by Bullitt, Oct. 4, 1933, *FRSU*, 16-17.

49. Radio address by Moore, Nov. 22, 1933, DSF 800.51 W89 U.S.S.R./85½.

50. Hull, *Memoirs*, p. 299.

51. "Bullitt began walking me to work in the mornings in order to pump me about the latest developments. At first this annoyed the President, on the ground that Bullitt was going over Hull's head. . . . But, as affairs developed, he entrusted the negotiations more and more to Bullitt." (Morgenthau, "Diaries," p. 21.)

52. Secretary of State, Press Conference, Oct. 21, 1933, Moore Papers, Box 18, RL.

53. Secretary of State, Press Conference, Oct. 28, 1933, Moore Papers, Box 18, RL.

54. Memorandum by Hull, undated, Roosevelt Papers, President's Secretary's File, Box 23, RL.

55. Hull, *Memoirs*, p. 300.

56. *New York Times*, Oct. 29, 1933, I, 3.

57. *New York Times*, Nov. 8, 1933, p. 24.

58. *Ibid.*

59. *New York Times*, Nov. 5, 1933, p. 18.

60. Hull, *Memoirs*, p. 300.

61. In the Library at Hyde Park is a Memorandum for the Secretary of State, dated March 3, 1934: "Mr. Kannee forwards envelope of miscellaneous papers and clippings re Litvinoff conferences and states that these were left on the mantle in Mr. McIntyre's room during the conferences. Mr. Kannee states that he put them in Mr. McIntyre's desk and called them to the attention of Mr. Bullitt who said, "leave them there, they are not important." (Roosevelt Papers, Official File, Box 799, RL.)

62. Memorandum by Moore, Nov. 9, 1933, Moore Papers, Box 18, RL.

63. *Ibid.*

64. *Ibid.*

65. Litvinov refused to sign the agreements on the Communist Party and religious freedom "so persistently that he was handed a schedule of steamship sailings and told to sign or go home." (Bullitt, "How We Won the War . . . ," p. 84.) The *New York Times* reported, in a despatch written on November 10, that "expectation in some quarters of a possible agreement on recognition prior to tonight had caused the development yesterday and today of various rumors of hitches in the Soviet-American conferences." (*New York Times*, Nov. 11, 1933, p. 1.) At the same time, Duranty stated that "in some quarters it had been expected that a

decision might be reached this afternoon." (*Ibid.*, p. 9.) On the following day, Duranty gave as the reason for the prolongation of the negotiations the American government's decision to require "substantial assurances on major differences prior to recognition," and said that "it is understood that the course of events has surprised M. Litvinoff." (*New York Times*, Nov. 12, 1933, p. 1.)

66. It is not entirely clear just when this occurred. Browder states (p. 132) that on the afternoon of November 9 "Litvinov was scheduled to see the President but the appointment was canceled," so that the President could meet with the negotiators from the Department of State. Moore's memorandum, referring to the negotiations with Litvinov on Wednesday, November 9, says that on that afternoon the negotiators handed Litvinov the proposed agreement on religious questions. (Memorandum by Moore, Nov. 9, 1933, Moore Papers, Box 18, RL.) Apparently, then, there were two conferences on the afternoon of November 9, one between Litvinov and the State Department team and the other involving the State Department and the President. It is clear that Litvinov and Roosevelt met on the 10th; since there is no reference to any meeting that morning, the meeting on the afternoon of the 10th was apparently the first "working meeting" between Roosevelt and Litvinov.

67. The most thorough account of these meetings will be found in Browder (pp. 130-41) on the basis of interviews with Phillips, Bullitt, and Kelley.

68. Memorandum by Bullitt, Nov. 15, 1933, *FRSU*, 26.

69. Letter, Roosevelt to Litvinov, Nov. 16, 1933, *FRSU*, 27.

70. Tel., Acting Secretary Phillips to Hull, Nov. 22, 1933, *FRSU*, 41.

71. Circular Telegram to all Diplomatic Missions Abroad, Nov. 17, 1933, *FRSU*, 39.

72. Radio address by Moore, Nov. 22, 1933, *FRSU*, 42.

73. Hull, *Memoirs*, p. 292.

74. The D.A.R. chapters in Leonia, New Jersey, and Manville, Rhode Island, passed identical resolutions opposing the appointment of Bullitt as Ambassador, charging, among other things, that he had married "Louise Bryant Reed, wife of the late John Reed, a communist who lies buried in the walls of the Kremlin and was given highest military honors by the Soviet Government for his work in directing communist propaganda." (DSF 123 Bullitt, William C./12 and -/33.)

75. *New York Times*, Nov. 12, 1933, p. 3.

76. *New York Times*, Nov. 14, p. 10, and Nov. 18, p. 2.

77. Radio address by Moore, Nov. 22, 1933, DSF 711.61/406.

78. *Ibid.*

79. Letter, Senator J. Hamilton Lewis to Hull, Dec. 4, 1933, enclosing letter from President W. D. Scott, DSF 711.61/438. A paper in the Roosevelt Library identifies this scholar as Professor Paul Haensel, for many years a financial adviser to the Soviet government.

80. Editorial, *Osservatore Romano*, Nov. 11, 1933, quoted in Desp. from Long (Rome), Nov. 15, 1933, DSF 711.61/401.

81. Editorial, London *Times*, Nov. 20, 1933, attached to Desp. from Cox (London), Nov. 21, 1933, DSF 711.61/460.

82. Editorial, *Nationalzeitung* (Basle), Nov. 1933, quoted in Desp. from Greene (Berne), Nov. 23, 1933, DSF 711.61/414.

83. Desp. from Greene (Berne), Nov. 23, 1933, DSF 711.61/414.

84. Editorial, *Izvestia*, Nov. 20, 1933, *FRSU*, 44-46.

Chapter II.   NONINTERFERENCE IN INTERNAL AFFAIRS

1. *Congressional Record,* 73d Cong., 1st sess., vol. 77, part 2, p. 1543, April 12, 1933.

2. Desp. from Skinner (Riga), Feb. 24, 1933, DSF 861.01/1849.

3. Memorandum by Kelley, Oct. 20, 1933, p. 89, DSF 811.00B/1608.

4. *Ibid.,* pp. 89-93.

5. *Ibid.,* pp. 182-83.

6. *Ibid.,* p. 135.

7. *Ibid.,* p. 98.

8. Hull, *Memoirs,* p. 299.

9. *Ibid.,* pp. 300-01.

10. Letter, Litvinov to Roosevelt, Nov. 16, 1933, *FRSU,* 28-29.

11. Hull, *Memoirs,* p. 299.

12. Morgenthau, "Diaries," p. 21.

13. Editorial, London *Times,* Nov. 20, 1933, attached to Desp. from Cox (London), Nov. 21, 1933, DSF 711.60/460.

14. Memorandum by Kelley, Nov. 3, 1933, p. 102, DSF 861.44 Litvinov/15.

15. *Ibid.,* p. 146.

16. Joseph J. Thorning, S.J. "What Russian Recognition Means," *America,* L, no. 9 (Dec. 2, 1933), 201; copy in Moore Papers, Box 18, RL.

17. *Washington Post,* Nov. 18, 1933, p. 4. The quotation in the *New York Times* is slightly different. In this, Litvinov was quoted as saying: "The Communist party of America is not concerned with the Communist party of Russia and the Communist party of Russia is not concerned with the Communist party of America." (*New York Times,* Nov. 18, 1933, p. 1.) In turn, the version made available to the Russian people was very different, viewing the agreement as most ordinary: "there was the inevitable question of propaganda. In another letter I assured the President that the relations of the Soviet Government and the governments of other countries were based on the principle of mutual non-interference in internal affairs. I stated the mutual obligations undertaken by the Soviet Government and other governments with which normal relations were established. These obligations were extended to the United States." (Quoted in Browder, p. 149.)

18. *New York Times,* Nov. 22, 1933, p. 8.

19. Memorandum by Kelley, Oct. 20, 1933, p. 26, quoting *International Press Correspondence,* vol. 7, no. 59, Oct. 20, 1927, DSF 811.00B/1608.

20. *Ibid.,* p. 19, quoting *Collection of Laws and Orders,* 1917, no. 8, Article 112.

21. *Ibid.,* quoting *Works* of L. Trotsky, III, Part 2, 1925, 141-42.

22. *Ibid.,* quoting Stenographic Report, 2d Congress, Communist International, p. 126.

23. Memorandum by Kelley, Nov. 3, 1933, quoting Litvinov's note to the British government, Sept. 27, 1921, DSF 861.44 Litvinov/15.

24. *Ibid.,* p. 21, quoting *Izvestia,* no. 272, Nov. 28, 1924.

25. *Idem.,* quoting *Pravda,* no. 274, Dec. 2, 1924.

26. *Ibid.,* pp. 101-102, quoting *Izvestia,* July 31, 1928.

27. *Ibid.,* p. 132. In this memorandum Kelley wrote a twenty-two-page account of the British experience with the Soviet government's "non-interference" pledges, apparently in the belief that this was of very great relevance to the needs of the United States government.

28. *Ibid.*, p. 2.

29. *Ibid.*, pp. 214-15. A later compilation showed the following Soviet Commissars and Ambassadors who appeared to be delegates to various Comintern Congresses. Those marked with an asterisk were definitely identified as such: Antonov-Ovseenko*, Minister to Poland, Congress 4; Chicherin*, Commissar, 1; Karakhan*, Ambassador to Turkey, 2; Khinchuck*, Ambassador to Germany, 4, 5; Kobetski, Minister to Greece, 3; Kollontai*, Minister to Sweden and Mexico, 2, 3; Krassin*, Ambassador to Great Britain, 5; Krestinski, Assistant Commissar and Ambassador to Germany, 2; Litvinov*, Commissar, 2; Lunacharski*, Minister to Spain, 2, 3, 4, 5, 6; Minkin, Minister to Uruguay, 4; Pastukhov, Minister to Persia, 5; Rakovski*, Ambassador to France, 2; Raskolnikov*, Minister to Bulgaria, 5, 6; Sokolnikov*, Ambassador to Great Britain, 2, 4, 5; Ustinov, Minister to Estonia, 2; and Vorovski*, Ambassador to Italy, 1.

30. Memorandum by Kelley, Oct. 20, 1933, p. 21, quoting *Izvestia*, no. 252, Nov. 7, 1927, DSF 811.00B/1608.

31. *Ibid.*, p. 22, quoting Jablonski from *International Press Correspondence*, vol. 9, no. 13, March 1, 1929.

32. Desp. from Cole (Riga), May 26, 1933, pp. 126-27, quoting from *Voprosy Leninizm*, Moscow, 1931, p. 541, DSF 800.00B Communist International/135.

33. New York *Daily Worker*, Feb. 21, 1929, p. 3.

34. *Organized Communism in the United States*, House of Representatives, Committee on Un-American Activities, 85th Cong., 2d sess., Aug. 19, 1953, p. 91.

35. Desp. from London, Jan. 8, 1931, DSF 811.00B/1212.

36. Desp. from Brodie (Helsingfors), April 23, 1931, DSF 811.00B/1222.

37. Memorandum by Packer, Sept. 15, 1931, DSF 811.00B/1262.

38. Desp. from Coleman (Riga), Sept. 18, 1931, DSF 811.00B/1264.

39. Memorandum by Kelley, Oct. 20 1933, p. 47, DSF 811.00B/1608.

40. Desp. from Skinner (Riga), April 12, 1933, quoting Stenographic Report, 11th Plenary Session, ECCI, p. 69, DSF 800.00B Communist International/134.

41. Desp. from Skinner (Riga), March 27, 1933, annex 1, enclosing Proclamation of ECCI, March 5, 1933, and "Up the Struggle Against Fascism," *Pravda*, no. 64, March 6, 1933, DSF 800.00B Communist International/132.

42. Tel. from Cole (Riga), Nov. 8, 1933, DSF 811.00B Party, Workers (Communist)/49.

43. Desp. from Cole (Riga), May 26, 1933, quoting *Pravda*, no. 251, Sept. 11, 1931, p. 3, DSF 800.00B Communist International/135.

44. Desp. from Coleman (Riga), Nov. 25, 1929, quoting *Pravda*, Nov. 15, 1929, DSF 811.00B Party Workers (Communist)/12.

45. Memorandum by Kelley, Oct. 20, 1933, p. 68, quoting letter from Political Secretariat of ECCI to Central Committee (CPUSA) from *The Communist*, May 1931, DSF 811.00B/1608.

46. Desp. from Cole (Riga), May 26, 1933, pp. 12-13, DSF 800.00B Communist International/135.

47. *Ibid.*, pp. 69-70, quoting *Pravda*, no. 282, Oct. 11, 1932.

48. *Ibid.*, p. 70, quoting *International Press Correspondence*, 1932, no. 49, p. 1064.

49. Desp. from Coleman (Riga), March 5, 1931, quoting Litvinov's speech to Council of People's Commissars, Feb. 18 1931, DSF 811.00B/1211. The Hawley-Smoot tariff law, June 18, 1930, barred goods produced by "forced labor," with Russia as the intended target.

50. Desp. from Skinner (Riga), April 12, 1933, pp. 55-56, 800.00B Communist International/134.

51. *Ibid.,* p. 64.

52. Desp. from Cole (Riga), July 6, 1932, DSF 811.00B/1338.

53. Desp. from Skinner (Riga), April 12, 1933, p. 141, quoting *International Press Correspondence,* no. 54, Oct. 22, 1931, DSF 800.00B Communist International/134.

54. *Ibid.,* p. 144.

55. *Ibid.,* pp. 64-65.

56. *Ibid.,* pp. 148-49.

57. Desp. from Lane (Riga), Sept. 2, 1936, DSF 800.00B Communist International/196.

58. *Ibid.,* p. 5.

59. Diplomatic Serial, Acting Secretary Castle to Diplomatic and Consular Officers, July 18, 1931, *FR* 1931, II, 983.

60. Memorandum by Kelley, Oct. 20, 1933 p. 3, DSF 811.00B/1608.

61. Desp. from Skinner (Riga), April 12, 1933, Annex I, p. 6, quoting from *Program,* p. 27, DSF 800.00B Communist International/134.

62. Thorning, "Russian Recognition," p. 200, Moore Papers, Box 18, RL.

63. Benjamin Gitlow, *The Whole of Their Lives* (N.Y., Scribners, 1948), pp. 264-65.

64. New York *Daily Worker,* Nov. 21, 1933, p. 6.

65. Desp. from Cole (Riga), March 1, 1934, DSF 811.00B Party, Workers (Communist)/56.

66. Memorandum, Moore to Bullitt, May 23, 1934, Moore Papers, Box 3, RL.

67. Memorandum by Moore, June 5 1934, Moore Papers, Box 3, RL.

68. Letter, Moore to Bullitt, June 26, 1934, Moore Papers, Box 3, RL.

69. Tel., Secretary Hull to Embassy in Moscow, Aug. 14, 1934, *FRSU,* 132.

70. Desp. from Gwynn (Riga), Dec. 6, 1934, DSF 811.00B/1581.

71. Desp. from Ward, Feb. 5, 1935, DSF 811.00B/1587.

72. Memorandum by Kelley, Nov. 3, 1933, pp. 24-25, quoting *International Press Correspondence,* vol. 9, no. 71, Dec. 27, 1929, DSF 861.44 Litvinov/15.

73. Memorandum by Packer of conversation with Troyanovsky, Oct. 9, 1935, DSF 811.00B/1683. Again in 1944 the Soviet Government complained that cases of war materials, arriving in the Soviet Union, contained "packages of anti-Soviet newspapers," and the American government investigated the responsibility for this, while disclaiming any responsibility. (Tel., Secretary Hull to Embassy in Moscow, April 21, 1944, DSF 711.61/995.)

74. Tel. from Bullitt, Sept. 26, 1934, DSF 861.00 Congress, Communist International VII/2.

75. Tel. from Bullitt, June 22, 1935, *FRSU,* 219-20.

76. Tel. from Bullitt, July 2, 1935, *FRSU,* 220.

77. Tel., Hull to Embassy in Moscow, July 3, 1935, *FRSU,* 221.

78. Tel. from Bullitt, July 8, 1935, *FRSU,* 222.

79. Tel. from Bullitt, July 13, 1935, *FRSU,* 223.

80. Tel. from Bullitt, Aug. 6, 1935, *FRSU,* 237.

81. Memorandum by Kelley, Aug. 20, 1935, enclosure no. 4, pp. 1 and 5, DSF 861.00 Congress, Communist International VII/114.

82. Tel. 363 from Bullitt, Aug. 21, 1935, *FRSU,* 244.

83. Tel. 367 from Bullitt, Aug. 21, 1935, *FRSU,* 247.

84. The American Naval and Air Attachés had been withdrawn from Moscow in February 1935 (Tel., Secretary Hull to Embassy in Moscow, Feb. 6, 1935, *FRSU*, 177) as a protest to the breakdown of the debt negotiations. This action did not affect continuance of Soviet service attachés in Washington.

85. Tel. 366 from Bullitt, Aug. 21, 1935, DSF 861.00 Congress, Communist International VII/59. A similar version will be found in *FRSU*, p. 246.

86. Tel. from Bullitt, Aug. 25, 1935, *FRSU*, 250.

87. Department of State *Press Releases*, vol. 40, Aug. 25, 1935, *FRSU*, 251.

88. Tel. from Bullitt, Aug. 27, 1935, *FRSU*, 252-53.

89. Tel., Secretary Hull to Embassy in Moscow, Aug. 28, 1935, *FRSU*, 254.

90. Tel. from Bullitt, Aug. 29, 1935, DSF 711.61/542.

91. Tel., Secretary Hull to Embassy in Moscow, Aug. 30, 1935, DSF 711.61/542b.

92. "Your views were of course carefully weighed," Moore wrote to Bullitt, "and the conclusion finally reached by the President that it is best to do nothing further at this moment than for the Secretary to issue the statement you have already seen. He was not swayed by the opinion of any individual but acted very independently, and of course with the desire to save you from any personal embarrassment. My own belief is that there is such a seething now with respect to the political situation, and the new developments in the Ethiopian matter . . . that very little further attention is likely to be given our relations with the Soviet, unless that Government should make a nasty statement in reply to ours or do something definitely showing its purpose to carry on the world revolution movement." (Letter, Moore to Bullitt, Sept. 3, 1935, Moore Papers, Box 3, RL.)

93. Statement by the Secretary of State, issued Aug. 31, 1935, Department of State *Press Releases* vol. 40, *FRSU*, 258-59. The Secretary's language was much milder later; in his *Memoirs* (p. 1251) he said only that the Soviet Government had "evaded" its promise.

94. Desp. from Bullitt, Aug. 31, 1935, pp. 24-25, DSF 861.00 Congress, Communist International VII/116.

95. Tel. from Bullitt, Aug. 29, 1935, DSF 711.61/542. Speaking in another context, Hull declared in 1940 that "there is no existing secret pact, agreement, or understanding of any kind whatsoever between the United States of America or (and?) the Union of Soviet Socialist Republics." (Letter, Hull to Sol Bloom [Chairman, House Committee on Foreign Affairs], July 13, 1940, DSF 711.61/744).

96. Tel. from Bullitt, Nov. 9, 1935, *FRSU*, 264-65.

97. Memorandum of Conversation, Packer and Walter Duranty, Dec. 10. 1938, in Desp. 106 from Riga, DSF 861.00 Congress, Communist International VII/668.

98. Desp. from Nielsen (Warsaw), Sept. 3, 1935, DSF 861.00 Congress, Communist International VII/119. This paragraph was pencil-noted by two different readers in the Department of State.

99. Memorandum by Packer, Nov. 27, 1935, DSF 811.00B Party, Workers (Communist)/71.

100. Later an Embassy official said that it had been informed that this society is "subordinated in all major questions of policy to the press department of the Central Committee of the All-Union Communist Party." (Desp. from Henderson, Jan. 29, 1936, DSF 800.00B Communist International/179.)

101. Tel. from Bullitt, Oct. 7, 1935, DSF 711.61/563.

102. Tel. from Bullitt, Oct. 25, 1935, DSF 711.61/568.

103. Memorandum by Packer, Aug. 20, 1936, DSF 800.00B Communist International/190.

104. *Ibid.*

105. Tel., Secretary Hull to Embassy in Moscow, Aug. 27, 1936, DSF 800.00B Communist International/188B. The second sentence in the telegram is hand-inserted, in the file copy, and initialed E.L.P[acker].

106. Tel. from Lane (Riga), Aug. 28, 1936, DSF 800.00B Communist International/188½.

107. Tel. from Henderson, Sept. 9, 1936, DSF 800.00B Communist International/193.

108. Tel. from Lane (Riga), Sept. 22, 1936, DSF 800.00B Communist International/198.

109. Tel. from Lane (Riga), Oct. 16, 1936, DSF 800.00B Communist International/204.

110. Desp. from Lane (Riga), Sept. 23, 1936, DSF 800.00B Communist International/201.

111. Tel. from Packer (Riga), Jan. 13, 1937, DSF 800.00B Communist International/212.

112. *Organized Communism in the United States,* pp. 99-107.

113. Tel. from Steinhardt, Jan. 6, 1941, *FR* 1941, I, 597.

114. Memorandum, Feb. 10, 1941, DSF 811.00B/1871½.

115. New York *Daily Worker,* May 24, 1945, p. 9.

116. *Ibid.,* p. 1.

117. In 1936 Ambassador Bullitt, then stationed in Paris, reported that the Soviet leaders had asked the attitude of the French government about a possible transfer of the Communist International headquarters to Paris, but that the attitude was negative. (Tel. from Bullitt [Paris], Nov. 26, 1936, DSF 800.00B Communist International/209.)

118. *New York Times,* Nov. 23, 1951, p. 1.

119. *American Foreign Policy, 1950-1955,* Department of State Publication 6446, General Foreign Policy Series 117, 1957, 2 vols., II, 1954-55.

120. Editorial, Syracuse *Herald-Journal,* Oct. 17, 1952.

Chapter III.   FREEDOM OF WORSHIP

1. Desp. from Coleman (Riga), Jan. 7, 1931, DSF 861.404/330.

2. Desp. from Coleman (Riga), May 21, 1930, quoting *Izvestia,* no. 58, Feb. 28, 1930, DSF 861.404/320.

3. Letter, Cotton to Wilbur, March 3, 1930, DSF 861.404/294. Following recognition of the Soviet government, this question was brought to the attention of the Department of State. In 1934, for example, the Department was asked about the possibility of the Lutheran church exploring with the Soviet Embassy in Washington the question of sending a representative to the Soviet Union to assist members of the church there. (Memorandum of Conversation, Packer and Mssrs. Morehead and Long, April 6, 1934, DSF 861.404/380.) The President of Goshen College wanted to know how to send a commission to the Soviet Union to investigate conditions of life and worship among Mennonites there. (Memorandum of Conversation, Packer and Dr. H. S. Bender, Aug. 18, 1936, DSF 861.404/402.) In both cases, the Department refused to become involved in any way, suggesting

that it was "highly inadvisable for any foreigner to interfere in internal affairs in that country." This view did not, however, prevent the United States Senate from passing a resolution in February 1953 suggesting that the "vicious and inhuman campaigns conducted by the Soviet Government and its puppet governments," "such as the persecution of Greek Orthodox congregations, the imprisonment of Roman Catholic prelates, the harassment of Protestant denominations, the supression of Moslem communities . . . and most recently the increasing persecution of the people of the Jewish faith, deserve the strongest condemnation." (Sen. Res. no. 84, 83d Cong., 1st sess., Feb. 27, 1953, in *American Foreign Policy, 1950-55*, II, 1961.)

4. On January 3, 1963, a group of thirty-two Soviet citizens besieged the American Embassy in Moscow, claiming to be Evangelical Christians who had come 2,100 miles from Siberia; the group pushed past the Soviet police guards at the Embassy and sought to be sent out of the U.S.S.R. to a place where they could practice their religious beliefs. Embassy officials reluctantly called the Soviet Foreign Office, and the weeping peasants were taken away by bus. "It is deeply distressing to us," said a Department of State official, "that there should be, in any country, restrictions on the free exercise of religion. . . . Nevertheless, this unhappy situation concerns Soviet citizens on their own territory. . . . [The American Embassy] is in no position to intervene in . . . complaints of Soviet citizens against conditions in their country." (*Washington Post*, Jan. 4, 1963.)

5. Eleanor Roosevelt, *This I Remember* (New York, Harper, 1949), p. 134.

6. Memorandum by Moore, Nov. 9, 1933, Moore Papers, Box 18, RL.

7. Hull, *Memoirs*, p. 301.

8. Memorandum by Moore, Nov. 9, 1933, Moore Papers, Box 18, RL.

9. For the letters exchanged by Roosevelt and Litvinov, see *FRSU*, pp. 29-33.

10. Letter, Moore to Roosevelt, Nov. 11, 1933, Moore Papers, Box 18, RL.

11. In 1936 the Department was notified that "in the past it has been the practice to discriminate against members of [Soviet] religious congregations by administrative measures in cases where the use of violence was considered inadvisable. Thus many of them have been refused permission to live in a city in which the religious denomination to which they belong have a congregation. Others have not been permitted to obtain employment, others have been ejected from their living quarters on the ground that the space was needed by persons performing more useful work, and so forth." (Desp. from Henderson, Sept. 28, 1936, DSF 861.404/403.)

12. Desp. from Coleman (Riga), May 21, 1930, quoting Moscow *Bezbozhnik*, no. 13, March 5, 1930, DSF 861.404/320. Later the Department received the text of a new law, eighteen pages long: "Resolution for Procedure in Carrying into Effect the Decree 'Concerning the Separation of the Church from the State and of the School from the Church.'" (Desp. from Cole [Riga], May 4, 1934, DSF 861.404/385.)

13. Memorandum by Kelley, Nov. 3, 1933, p. 152, DSF 361.4121/20.

14. Thorning, "Russian Recognition," p. 200; copy in Moore Papers, Box 18, RL.

15. Letter, Parker to Roosevelt, Nov. 13, 1933, DSF 861.404/366.

16. Letter, Leiper to Hull, Jan. 28, 1935, DSF 861.404/388.

17. Desp. from Wiley, March 13, 1935, DSF 861.404/392.

18. Desp. from Wiley, March 5, 1935, enclosing Letter, Wade to Bullitt, Feb. 7, 1935, DSF 861.404/391.

19. Desp. from Wiley, March 5, 1935, DSF 861.404/391.

20. It should not be thought that there has been no Protestant ministration to Americans in Moscow since 1933. During the early years of the American Embassy, some help came from the Lutherans, who were under the semiprotection of the German Embassy which made numerous representations on their behalf. On November 14, 1936, the Department was notified of the arrest of Pastor Streck, the only Lutheran Evangelical Pastor remaining in Moscow, and the one who ministered to the members of the Evangelical faith at the American Embassy. The previous May he had baptized the child of one American Vice Consul and was, on the day arrested, to have performed a marriage ceremony for another Vice Consul. Since Pastor Streck was a Soviet citizen, the United States government could not intervene directly in the case, though Bullitt suggested that the Secretary of State call in the Soviet Ambassador in Washington to ask him if this meant that the Soviet Government was beginning a campaign against those who minister to the members of the American Embassy in Moscow. (Tel. from Bullitt [Paris], Nov. 14, 1936, DSF 861.404/408.) More recently, the Protestants in the American Embassy staff have been ministered to by the British chaplain, who lives in Helsinki and comes to Moscow for a week every two months or by the Bishop of Fulham who comes two or three times a year. Both of these clergymen deal only with foreigners, and the Soviet government has raised no known objection to their work in Moscow. None of this comes under the Roosevelt-Litvinov agreement since they are not American nationals. At other times, lay readers have conducted Protestant services in Moscow.

21. In 1936 Bishop Neveu returned to France for medical attention, on the strength of a Soviet government promise that he would be given a re-entry permit. After he had left, however, the Soviet leaders refused to grant him the entrance visa, although diplomatic representations were made by the French government on his behalf. Early in 1939, for example, Premier Daladier told Ambassador Bullitt that he "would this evening give orders . . . that until Mons. Neveu had received a visa to return to the Soviet Union, no Soviet subject, whether a government official or not, should receive a visa to France." "I reminded Daladier," said Bullitt, "that the French Ambassador in Moscow last spring had been informed that the Soviet Government might give Mons. Neveu a visa but that he would be arrested and would disappear the moment he stepped over the frontier. Daladier said that in that case he would order the immediate arrest of the Soviet Ambassador and all his staff. I have discussed this matter with Mons. Neveu recently and he desires to take the risks. I am informed also that the Church desires him to take the risks." (Tel. from Bullitt [Paris], Feb. 14, 1939, DSF 851.5122 American Church/53.) Actually, Neveu never did return to the Soviet Union, his entrance visa being granted by the Soviet government the day after he died in Paris in 1946.

22. Since the only place where any sizable groups of Americans resided was Moscow itself, the application of the agreement has been confined to that area.

23. Tel. from Bullitt (Paris), Aug. 24, 1938, DSF 861.111/793.

24. Tel., Secretary Hull to Bullitt, Aug. 26, 1938, DSF 861.111/793.

25. Tel. from Harriman, Feb. 14, 1944, DSF 861.404/559.

26. Tel. from Hamilton, May 26, 1944, DSF 861.404/572.

27. Tel. from Kennan, Nov. 20, 1944, DSF 861.404/11-2044.

28. Georges Bissonnette, *Moscow Was My Parish* (New York, McGraw-Hill, 1956), p. 270.

29. *New York Times*, March 8, 1955.

30. *Ibid.*

31. Quoted in U.S. note to the Soviet Government, June 27, 1955, *American Foreign Policy, 1950-1955,* II, 2000.

32. Statement by the Department of State, March 2, 1955, *American Foreign Policy, 1950-1955,* pp. 1999-2000.

33. U.S. note to the Soviet Government, June 27, 1955, *American Foreign Policy, 1950-1955,* p. 2001.

34. *Ibid.*

35. *Ibid.,* p. 2002.

36. Department of State *Press Release* 636, Jan. 4, 1955. See also Department of State *Bulletin,* vol. 33, no. 855, Jan. 14, 1955, 785.

37. U.S. note to the Soviet Government, June 27, 1955. *American Foreign Policy, 1950-1955,* pp. 2003-2004. This problem was complicated by the fact that most of the Russian Orthodox group in the United States had split off from the Moscow church after 1917, contending that the Moscow Patriarchate had fallen under the domination of the Soviet regime. This claim was prominently re-iterated during the Second World War when leaders of that church in the Soviet Union took a most cooperative role in the Soviet war effort. There had been constant friction between the two groups in the United States over control, finances, and functions. It was unlikely that Moscow, in wanting Archbishop Boris to reside in the United States, was ignorant of this situation and of the political possibilities resulting therefrom. "In all of the Patriarchate's foreign contacts the Soviet state must have had a conscious interest, since without its consent no Soviet citizen can travel abroad." (Anderson, Paul B., "The Orthodox Church in Soviet Russia," *Foreign Affairs* vol. 39, no. 2 [January 1961], p. 308.)

38. Soviet note, November 10, 1955, *Department of State Bulletin,* vol. 34, no. 862, Jan. 2, 1956, p. 21.

39. Statement by the Department of State, November 15, 1955, *American Foreign Policy, 1950-1955,* pp. 2003-2004.

40. *Department of State Bulletin,* vol. 34, no. 862, Jan. 2, 1956, p. 20.

41. Tel. from Kennan, Nov. 20, 1944, DSF 861.404/11-2044.

42. Bissonnette, *Moscow Was My Parish,* p. 7.

43. *Ibid.,* p. 48.

44. Memorandum by Henderson, Jan. 20, 1939, attached to Tel. from Kirk, Jan. 17, 1939, DSF 861.404/429.

45. Tel., Secretary Hull to Embassy in Moscow, Jan. 20, 1939, DSF 861.404/429. The French Embassy in Moscow, which offered official protection to the church of St. Louis des Français and the apartment where Fr. Braun resided, also opposed his taking even a temporary assignment at the Polish church, be-cause of "possible detriment to the interests of the French church." (Desp. from Kirk, Jan. 18, 1939, DSF 861.404/430.)

46. Letter, Welles to Taylor, Nov. 19, 1941, DSF 861.404/450.

47. Desp. from Henderson, Sept. 18, 1936, enclosure 2, DSF 861.404/404. The *New York Times* reported on March 12, 1964, that Israeli diplomats in Moscow had been accused of using a Moscow synagogue to distribute Zionist propaganda. An article in *Trud,* the trade union newspaper in Moscow, said that Abraham Agmor, Counselor of the Israeli Embassy, was a purveyor of "na-tionalist literature that is alien to the minds and hearts of the Soviet populace."

48. On this episode, see Walter B. Smith, *My Three Years in Moscow* (Phil-adelphia, Lippincott, 1950), pp. 287-89.

49. Bissonnette, on his last day in Moscow, told his congregation: "My dear brethren, . . . I ask you to go to the father in the church of St. Louis des Français. If you cannot confess in Russian or Polish just tell the father you want absolution and you will receive it." (*New York Times,* March 4, 1955.)

50. Another incident, having nothing to do with the Litvinov agreement but illustrating the complications resulting from the Soviet government's antireligious policy, occurred in 1960 when President Gronchi of Italy visited the Soviet Union. The Soviet government agreed to arrange his schedule so that he could attend Mass on Sunday in Leningrad. Since all Catholic churches there had been closed long ago, it was necessary for the Soviet government to reopen one of them for the service, and then "permit" Fr. Dion in Moscow to travel to Leningrad to celebrate the Mass. (Syracuse *Herald-Journal,* Jan. 2, 1960.)

51. Tel. from Steinhardt, Feb. 17, 1941, *FR* 1941, I, 996.

52. Tel. from Steinhardt, Feb. 28, 1941, *FR* 1941, I, 997.

53. Tel. from Steinhardt, March 19, 1941, *FR* 1941, I, 998.

54. Tel. from Steinhardt, March 15, 1941, DSF 861.404/439.

55. William H. Standley and Arthur A. Ageton, *Admiral Ambassador to Russia* (Chicago, Regnery, 1955), p. 159. The draft prepared by the Legal Adviser in the Department of State in 1933 proposed that American clergymen in the Soviet Union "shall not be placed in a position less advantageous with respect to the rental of living quarters and the purchase of food and other necessities of life than that of the most favored of citizens of the United States of America possessing no ecclesiastical status" but this had been eliminated by Litvinov.

56. Tel. from Steinhardt, Feb. 17, 1941, DSF 861.404/437.

57. Bissonnette, *Moscow Was My Parish,* pp. 171-72.

58. "Few people realize that a minister of cult (clergyman, priest, rabbi, mulla, etc.) is called upon by law to pay an income tax rate of 40% of his actual revenue or the revenue the government income tax inspector merely thinks or arbitrarily stipulates he must be getting." (Letter, Fr. Braun to Myron C. Taylor, Oct. 5, 1941, DSF 861.404/459.)

59. In 1936 Representative John McCormack informed the Secretary of State that there were 896 Roman Catholic priests in the Soviet Union in 1917 but only 30 at liberty in 1936. Some had died of natural causes, but most had been sent to prison camps or had disappeared, and their fate was unknown though suspected. The American Embassy in Moscow informed the Department, at about the same time, that before the Revolution there were 500 churches in Moscow but only 20 were left then, and that there had been 192 Lutheran churches in the territory now included in the Soviet Union but that there were only 12 left, one in Moscow and none from there east to the Pacific. In 1941 Fr. Braun wrote that "every single Catholic member of clergy in the U.S.S.R. has been arrested, imprisoned or exiled!!! The very last priests . . . were arrested in 1939. All the parishes (Catholic) in the Soviet Union were disorganized and effectively closed by 1939 with the exception of one church in Leningrad and one in Moscow. . . . The Evangelical clergy (Lutheran) fared no better here in the capital or especially in the Odessa region or the Volga provinces where their numerous churches have all to the last been closed." (Personal letter, Myron C. Taylor to Secretary Hull, Nov. 5, 1941, enclosing photostated letter, Fr. Braun to Taylor, Oct. 5, 1941, DSF 861.404/459.)

Chapter IV. LEGAL PROTECTION FOR AMERICAN NATIONALS

1. Memorandum 5 by Kelley, Nov. 20, 1933, p. 1, DSF 361.11/4089½.

2. Memorandum, *Foreigners in Russia*, p. 3, enclosure with Desp. from Cole (Riga), Nov. 3, 1933, DSF 361.4121/20.

3. Quoted in *ibid.*, p. 137.

4. *Ibid.*, p. 158.

5. Memorandum by Kelley, Nov. 20, 1933, pp. 10-11, DSF 361.11/4089½.

6. Memorandum, *Foreigners in Russia*, p. 156, enclosure with Desp. from Cole (Riga), Nov. 3, 1933, DSF 361.4121/20.

7. Memorandum by Kelley, Nov. 20, 1933, p. 14, DSF 361.11/4089½.

8. The Library at Hyde Park contains an undated paper, with the heading, "The Legal Adviser," dealing with "Tentative Projects to be Entered into with Soviet Representatives at the time of Recognition." Among the rights listed here is this: "The Consul shall have the right to interview the prisoner at any time and in private, if desired." The last words are crossed out in pencil. (Moore Papers, Box 18, RL; for the full text of this Roosevelt-Litvinov exchange, see *FRSU*, 33-34.)

9. This statement is based upon a reading of the document. A curious contradiction arose in 1938 when M. N. Gorin, a Soviet citizen, was arrested in Los Angeles. Ambassador Umansky called Henderson (Assistant Chief, Division of European Affairs, Department of State) to request that Mikail I. Ivanoushkin (Soviet Vice-Consul in New York) be permitted to talk with Gorin. "I asked Mr. Oumansky if his request . . . was based on the exchange of notes which took place on November 16, 1933. . . . Mr. Oumansky apparently hesitated before replying to my question and I therefore pointed out that 'it might be difficult for the State Department to endeavor to arrange for such an interview except on the basis of those notes. Mr. Oumansky thereupon answered my question in the affirmative, stating that his request was based upon the agreement entered into between the United States and the Soviet Government by virtue of the exchange of notes.'" (Memorandum by Henderson, Dec. 14, 1938, DSF 311.6121 Gorin, M.N./15.) Later in the same memorandum, Henderson is even more specific. In a conversation with an official of the Department of Justice, "I said that in view of the existence of an agreement between the United States and the Soviet Government according to which Soviet consular officers would be permitted without delay to visit Soviet nationals in prison. . . ." Nothing in that agreement gives Soviet consuls any such right and no other agreement than that of November 16 is known. The explanation would seem to be that Henderson, momentarily forgetting that this agreement—unlike some of the others of the same date—was not reciprocal, operated upon a faulty premise. At any rate, this incident gave the United States government an opportunity to demonstrate to the Soviet government, by example, how we would like to be treated when one of our nationals was arrested in the Soviet Union.

10. Green H. Hackworth, *Digest of International Law* (Washington, Government Printing Office, 1942), III, 1-2.

11. Enclosure with Desp. from Messersmith (Berlin), April 28, 1931, DSF 861.012/31.

12. Instruction, Secretary Stimson to Consul General (Berlin), April 12, 1932, *FR 1932*, II, 523, 525. It was recognized that the Soviet government had a peculiar interest in some of these people. Earlier, Chicherin had written: should

a foreigner "himself declare that he ceases to be a citizen of that state? That would mean that he would be deprived of the right to return to the country from which he came," to which Kennan commented, "This rather uncommunistic sentimentality about the poor workers does not conceal very well what was in the back of Chicherin's mind, namely, the fear that carefully trained foreign agitators might not be allowed back into their respective countries. And it is perfectly evident that the Soviets are never going to encourage their American sympathizers to get formally 'naturalized' in Soviet Russia." Both the Chicherin article and Kennan's memorandum, "On the Status of American Communists Residing in the U.S.S.R. and Exercising Political Rights and Privileges Therein," are enclosed with the despatch from Berlin, cited in n. 11, above.

13. Unnumbered instruction, Secretary Hull to Embassy in Moscow, May 20, 1935, DSF 861.111/661.

14. Memorandum by Kelley, Nov. 3, 1933, pp. 203-204, quoting Desp. from Oslo, Nov. 22, 1926, DSF 861.44 Litvinov/15.

15. In January 1941 Under Secretary Welles and Ambassador Umansky were discussing the case of Roszkowski who, it was said, "had been seized by the Soviet authorities subsequent to the invasion of Poland. The Ambassador stated that . . . he was certain that Mr. Welles would not use such an expression as 'invasion of Poland.' Mr. Welles asked the Ambassador what words should be used. . . . The Ambassador said that he would suggest words somewhat as follows: 'Subsequent to the adherence of Western Ukraine and Western White Russia to the Soviet Union.' Mr. Welles said that perhaps Mr. Oumansky might also object to his use of the word 'seized'; perhaps he would prefer him to say that Mr. Roszkowski had 'been adhered to by the Soviet authorities.' " (Memorandum of Conversation of Jan. 8, 1941, p. 18, Welles-Oumansky Conversations and Related Memoranda, June 1940-April 1941.)

16. Tel., Secretary Hull to Embassy in Moscow, Dec. 28, 1940, DSF 361.1121 Roszkowski/2.

17. Memorandum by Henderson, Dec. 16, 1940, *FR* 1940, III, 427.

18. Tel. from Steinhardt, Dec. 30, 1940, DSF 361.1121 Roszkowski/3.

19. *Ibid.*

20. Memorandum of Conversation, Welles and Umansky, Jan. 21, 1941. DSF 311.6121 Gorin, M. N./37.

21. Tel. from Steinhardt, Dec. 16, 1940, *FR* 1941, I, 927.

22. Letter, Barr to Embassy in Moscow, quoted in Desp. from Bullitt, Jan. 4, 1935, DSF 361.1115 Barr, Edward/6.

23. Desp. from Henderson, Feb. 7, 1938, DSF 361.1115 Barr, Edward/13.

24. Desp. from Ward, Dec. 21, 1938, DSF 361.1121/8.

25. This area contained a number of foreign-born, chiefly Finns and Norwegians, who had been recruited in groups in the United States and Canada by the Karelian Technical Aid, an organization believed to be working through Amtorg.

26. Memorandum by Henderson, Nov. 30, 1938, DSF 361.1121 Nausiainen, Elmer J./16.

27. Desp. from Davies, May 11, 1938, *FRSU*, 719.

28. Memorandum by Kennan, June 1, 1938, DSF 361.1121 Sviridoff, George/21.

29. Desp. from Ward, Aug. 26, 1935; quotation is from note on file cover of this document, DSF 861.111/671.

30. Instruction, Secretary Stimson to Consul General (Berlin), April 12, 1932, *FR* 1932, II, 524.

31. Tel. from Hanson, April 23, 1934, DSF 861.111 American Passport/69.

32. Tel., Secretary Hull to Embassy in Moscow, Dec. 14, 1940, *FR* 1941, I, 926-27.

33. Desp. from Ward, Dec. 21, 1938, DSF 361.1121/8.

34. Desp. from Kirk, Aug. 17, 1938, *FRSU*, 723.

35. Desp. from Schantz, Aug. 10, 1934, DSF 861.111 American Passport/72.

36. "Kalinin was the individual charged with the granting of exit visas to Soviet citizens based on renunciation of Soviet citizenship." (*FR* 1941, I, 946.)

37. Desp. from Schantz, Aug. 10, 1934, DSF 861.111 American Passport/72.

38. Memorandum by Phillips of Conversation with Litvinov, Nov. 20, 1933, DSF 701.6111/742.

39. *New York Times*, Nov. 17, 1963.

40. Letter, Kelley to Mrs. Lasek, Oct. 31, 1932, 361.1121 Holub, Kasian/6.

41. Tel., Acting Secretary to Embassy in Moscow, April 23, 1934, DSF 800.51 W89 U.S.S.R./39A.

42. Memorandum, Moore to Sayre, July 19, 1934, DSF 800.51 W89 U.S.S.R./39A.

43. Tel. from Bullitt, April 28, 1934, DSF 125.813/14.

44. Note, V. H. James to "Mr. Stevens," July 12, 1947, DSF 125.631/17.

45. *Department of State Bulletin*, vol. 16, no. 417, June 29, 1947, p. 1307.

46. The United States was not alone in this treatment by the Soviet government. In 1938 American representatives in Moscow wrote about the "peremptory and arbitrary demands of the Soviet Government" in closing the consulates of fourteen foreign governments. (Desp. from Henderson, Feb. 18, 1938, DSF 761.00/293. See also Desp. from Davies, April 1, 1938, DSF 861.00/11778.)

47. Tel. from Bullitt, April 28, 1934, DSF 125.813/14.

48. Memorandum by Green, Dec. 26, 1939, DSF 700.00116 M.E./14.

49. Tel., Secretary Hull to Embassy in Moscow, Dec. 28, 1939, DSF 361.11 Employees/360.

50. Tel. 1156 from Steinhardt, Dec. 29, 1939, DSF 361.11 Employees/361.

51. Tel. 1157 from Steinhardt, Dec. 29, 1939, DSF 700.00116 M.E./24.

52. Tel. from Steinhardt, Jan. 23, 1941, DSF 861.5151/185.

53. Memorandum by Henderson, undated but "around July 27-August 1, 1940," DSF 711.61/777.

54. Tel. from Thurston, Aug. 2, 1940, DSF 138 U.S.S.R./602.

55. "The Soviet authorities with rare exceptions do not permit persons who have finally received permits to depart from the recently occupied territories to return even though they may only have travelled to Moscow." (Tel. from Steinhardt, Oct. 31, 1940, DSF 811.111 Refugees/636.) This meant that anyone who was permitted to come to Moscow took the risk that, denied an American visa, he would be exiled to Central Asia or some other remote region which the Soviet government wished to populate.

56. Tel. from Thurston, Aug. 12, 1940, DSF 861.111/835.

57. Tel. from Steinhardt, Oct. 10, 1940, DSF 861.56/192.

58. Memorandum of Conversation by the Under Secretary of State, Jan. 15, 1941, DSF 711.61/801.

59. *Ibid.*

60. Desp. from Kirk, Aug. 31, 1938, DSF 361.1121 Nausiainen, Elmer J./2.

61. *Ibid.*

62. Desp. from Messersmith (Berlin), April 15, 1931, DSF 861.111 American Passport/45.

63. Letter, Harry Alpert to Department of State, Nov. 8, 1937; Desp. from Ward, Feb. 25, 1938; and Desp. from Ward, April 16, 1938; DSF 361.1115 Alpert, Bessie/1, -/4, and -/6.

64. Letter, James Henderson to the Secretary of State, Aug. 20, 1936; Desp. from Ward, Nov. 27, 1936; and Letter, Department to James Henderson, Dec. 21, 1937; DSF 361.1115 Brady, William H./1, and -/7 and -/8.

65. Desp. from Schantz, Sept. 7, 1934, DSF 361.1115 Cronk, Harry C/6.

66. Desp. from Ward, June 1, 1938, DSF 361.1115 Comisaroff, Nicholas.

67. Desp. from Henderson, Aug. 26, 1937, and Desp. from Davies, May 11, 1938, *FRSU,* 491-92, 719-20.

68. Desp. from Ward, Jan. 9, 1936, DSF 361.1121 Wuori, Bruno H./1.

69. Memorandum by Kennan, Nov. 21, 1937, DSF 361.1121 Hrinkevich, Frank/4.

70. Tel. from Kirk, Nov. 14, 1938, *FRSU,* 723.

71. Memorandum by the Secretary of State of Conversation with Ambassador of the Soviet Union, Dec. 11, 1937, *FRSU,* 499.

72. Tel., Secretary Hull to Embassy in Moscow, Jan. 5, 1938, *FRSU,* 709.

73. Tel. from Henderson, Jan. 17, 1938, *FRSU,* 710-11.

74. One case of detention, however, involved an American diplomat, who was supposed to be immune from this kind of treatment if anyone was. Arthur R. Ringwalt, en route to Peiping through the Soviet Union, was stopped at Negoreloe, a border point, and detained overnight. When the Ringwalts arrived at the Soviet border, their possessions were, contrary to international usage, minutely examined by the customs officials and certain papers were retained. They were then forbidden to proceed because their visas were not in order. A request to telephone the Embassy in Moscow was refused. The border official also refused to allow Ringwalt to send a note to Moscow with a Japanese courier who was proceeding on the train, although the latter was permitted to accept a calling card, for delivery to the American Embassy. When the Embassy learned of Ringwalt's detention, it tried to telephone him but was informed that he "was out for a walk," though he had been told he could not leave the station. A telegram was delivered later, just as the Ringwalts were permitted to proceed. The Soviet Foreign Office, in reply to an American protest, contended that "the reason for the failure of the Embassy to reach Mr. Ringwalt by telephone . . . [was] that 'it would have taken too much time to have him come from his hotel to the telephone apparatus located at the local post office,'" though the fact was that the hotel was the second floor of the building in which the post office was the first floor. (Desp. from Kirk, Dec. 5, 1938, DSF 861.111/799.) Two months later, Frank A. Schuler, Jr., Third Secretary at American Embassy in Tokyo, also had trouble at Negoreloe. (DSF 861.111/807.) It is evident that the Soviet policy was not confined to "marginal" or lawbreaking American citizens.

75. Enclosure to Desp., Secretary Hull to Embassy in Moscow, Oct. 30, 1934, DSF 361.4121/20.

76. This would seem to be consistent with Article 3 of the Soviet Citizenship Law of 1921 which stated that "every person residing in the territory of the U.S.S.R. is considered a citizen of the U.S.S.R. if his citizenship of a foreign state is not approved." (Desp. from Ward, July 29, 1938, DSF 361.1115 Kujala,

Arthur J./5.) The burden of proof, thus, is on the citizen rather than the government, which makes it important for all those claiming American citizenship to keep their American passports or other evidence of citizenship in order to be able to "prove" their citizenship, when challenged.

77. Memorandum, *Foreigners in Russia,* Desp. from Cole (Riga), Nov. 3, 1933, enclosure: *Weekly of Soviet Justice,* nos. 36-37, 1928, pp. 1008-1009, DSF 361.4121/20.

78. Desp. from Ward, Nov. 9, 1938, DSF 361.1121 Argilander, Verner A./1.

79. Desp. from Ward, May 11, 1938, *FRSU,* 719-20.

80. Memorandum by Moore, Moore Papers, Box 18, RL.

81. Tel. from Steinhardt, Aug. 15, 1941, *FR* 1941, I, 993.

82. Tel. from Thurston, Dec. 11, 1941, DSF 360M.1121 Devenis, Michael.

83. Tel. from Davies, Oct. 21, 1937, *FRSU,* 493.

84. Tel., Secretary Hull to Embassy in Moscow, Oct. 23, 1937, *FRSU,* 493-94.

85. Tel. from Davies, Oct. 29, 1937, *FRSU,* 494.

86. Tel. from Davies, Nov. 11, 1937, *FRSU,* 495.

87. Memorandum by Kennan, Nov. 24, 1937, DSF 361.1121 Hrinkevich, Frank/10.

88. Enclosure with Desp. from Ward, Nov. 29, 1937, DSF 361.1121 Hrinkevich, Frank/12. Enclosed is a memorandum of the interview between Hrinkevich and Page and Durbrow, on Nov. 14, 1937. The quotations here are taken from pp. 6-7 of the record of the interview.

89. *Ibid.,* p. 8 of the interview.

90. Memorandum by Kennan, Nov. 24, 1937, DSF 361.1121 Hrinkevich, Frank/10. Page of the Embassy staff noted that "it would not appear however that, with the exception of the first two months of solitary confinement, Hrinkevich was treated badly in jail. This undoubtedly was due to the interest in him manifested by the Embassy." (Memorandum by Page, DSF 361.1121 Hrinkevich, Frank/56.) After his deportation from the Soviet Union, however, Hrinkevich was asked to execute an affidavit regarding the conditions of his imprisonment. In this statement, his period of solitary confinement totalled eight months— "For a year I was never taken outside, except when taken to the different authorities, never spoke to anybody." (*Ibid.*) In October 1938 he was conducted across the Soviet border and in 1939 he and his family were reunited in the United States, a particularly happy circumstance since it was his refusal to abandon his family in the Soviet Union which apparently led to all of his trouble.

91. Tel. from Henderson, Feb. 10, 1938, DSF 361.1115 Robinson, Donald L./117.

92. This case was exceptional in that the prisoner was allowed to be interviewed by foreign representatives before the conclusion of the investigation by Soviet authorities, on the understanding that this action did not constitute a precedent.

93. Desp. from Henderson, Feb. 15, 1938, DSF 361.1115 Robinson, Donald L./136.

94. Desp. from Kirk, March 8, 1939, DSF 361.1115 Kujala, Arthur J./15.

95. *Ibid.*

96. Desp. from Kirk, April 18, 1939, *FRSU,* 907.

97. Tel. from Grummon, June 7, 1939, DSF 361.1115 Kujala, Arthur J./19. Attached is a memorandum written by Page, dated June 13, which states that

"it is not believed that the F.O. official would have made the statement regarding the probability of the case being reviewed unless he had been informed that the G.P.U. seriously intended to release and deport Kujala. Consequently, although the Soviet Government has again flagrantly broken its pledge . . . it is possible that any strong protest at this time, which would be entirely justified, might prejudice the case. It is therefore suggested that no formal protest . . . be made at the present time; that such action be deferred for a month or six weeks in order to give the Soviet authorities sufficient time to review the case."

98. Tel. from Grummon, June 27, 1939, DSF 361.1115 Kujala, Arthur J./21.

99. Tel. from Steinhardt, Aug. 18, 1939, DSF 361.1115 Kujala, Arthur J./25.

100. Tel. from Standley, Sept. 15, 1942, *FR 1942*, III, 767.

101. See *FR 1942*, III, 550, 563.

102. Tel., Secretary Hull to Embassy in Moscow, Dec. 13, 1939, *FRSU*, 914.

103. Enclosure with Desp. from Steinhardt, Dec. 27, 1939, Enclosure 1, *FRSU*, 916.

104. Enclosure with Desp. from Steinhardt, Dec. 27, 1939, Enclosure 2, *FRSU*, 917.

105. *Ibid.*, 918.

106. Desp. from Steinhardt, Feb. 21, 1940, DSF 361.1115 Kujala, Arthur J./46.

107. Quoted in *ibid*.

108. *Ibid*.

109. Memorandum by Page, April 8, 1940, DSF 361.1115 Kujala, Arthur J./48. In 1933, at the time of Metropolitan-Vickers case, the British representatives in Moscow quoted a Soviet Foreign Office official as saying that "from moment that preliminary investigation is complete visitors are no longer bound by condition not to speak to accused on substance of the case." (Unnumbered Desp. from Atherton [London], April 7, 1933, DSF 361.4121/7.) This view was confirmed in a telegram sent to the Department from Moscow in January 1938, saying that "statements made by members of other diplomatic missions tend to show that for some time at least the Soviet authorities have been refusing to permit representatives of foreign governments to visit their nationals in Soviet prisons until after investigations have been completed. Although thousands of foreigners have been arrested during the last year, in apparently only a few instances have visits of diplomatic or consular officers been allowed. It seems that even these visits have been permitted only after sentence has been passed or decision to deport has been reached." (Tel. from Henderson, Jan. 26, 1938, *FRSU*, 716.)

110. *Ibid*.

111. Tel., Secretary Hull to Embassy in Moscow, April 19, 1940, DSF 361.1115 Kujala, Arthur J./47.

112. On the Powers trial, see *Department of State Bulletin*, vol. 43, no. 1104, Aug. 22, 1960, p. 276; no. 1105, Aug. 29, 1960, p. 350; and no. 1106, Sept. 5, 1960, p. 361.

113. *New York Times*, Nov. 17, 1963.

114. *New York Times*, Nov. 16, 1963.

115. Memorandum by Henderson, April 14, 1939, DSF 800.00B Rubens, Adolph A./43.

116. The Embassy's request for a copy of the court record in the Hovi trial, for example, was denied by the People's Commissariat for Foreign Affairs on the grounds that Soviet regulations allowed copies to be issued only to persons

participating in the case. (Desp. from Bohlen, July 15, 1938, DSF 361.1121 Hovi, Albert/3.)

117. Quoted in Letter, Pierrepont Moffat to Walter S. Throop, January 22, 1938, DSF 361.1115 Robinson, Donald L./82.

118. Desp. from Ward, March 15, 1938, DSF 361.1121 Hovi, Albert/1.

119. Desp. from Skinner (Riga), April 7, 1933, enclosure 5, *Izvestia*, no. 80, March 24, 1933, p. 1. DSF 361.4121/5. Foreign lawyers, however, might be present at the trial and Rubinin thought it might be possible for them to confer with the defending counsel.

120. Desp. from Ward, March 15, 1938, DSF 361.1121 Hovi, Albert/1.

121. Desp. from Ward, April 29, 1936, DSF 361.1121 Wuori, Bruno H./2.

122. Memorandum by Henderson, Jan. 4, 1938. (This date should be 1939, not 1938 as in the Archives.) DSF 800.00B Rubens, Adolph A./37. Elsewhere, Henderson noted that "in Soviet jails at the present time there are thousands of foreigners who have been detained for months and even years without trial." (Memorandum by Henderson, April 14, 1939, DSF 800.00B Rubens, Adolph A./43.) Litvinov complained at one stage about American ingratitude: "The Soviet Union has done and was disposed to do more for the United States than for any other country . . . [yet] more adverse publicity and acclaim had been given to the detention of one American citizen who was obviously tainted with crime, than had been given to hundreds of Germans and prisoners of other nationalities who had been detained and who, after months of imprisonment, still had not been interviewed by the diplomatic representatives of their country." (Desp. from Davies, March 4, 1938, DSF 124.61/123.)

123. Tel. from Grummon, June 9, 1939, DSF 800.00B Rubens, Adolph A./48.

124. Memorandum, *Foreigners in Russia*, Nov. 3, 1933, p. 97, DSF 361.4121/20.

125. Memorandum by Henderson, Dec. 17, 194, FR 1940, III, 432.

126. Tel. from Steinhardt, Sept. 20, 1939, DSF 361.11 Employees/357.

127. Tel. from Steinhardt, Feb. 1, 1940, *FR* 1940, III, 252.

128. Tel. from Steinhardt, Nov. 19, 1940, *FR* 1940, III, 406.

129. *Department of State Bulletin*, vol. 17, no. 441, Dec. 14, 1947, p. 1195.

130. *Department of State Bulletin*, vol. 22, no. 559, March 20, 1950, p. 433.

131. *Ibid.*, p. 435.

132. Memorandum, Jan. 18, 1939, DSF 360d.1121 Hovi, Albert/9.

133. Tel. from Steinhardt, March 17, 1941, *FR* 1941, I, 941.

134. Tel. from Steinhardt, Nov. 5, 1940, *FR* 1940, III, 234-35.

135. Memorandum, Welles to Roosevelt, Nov. 22, 1940, *FR* 1940, III, 236.

136. Tel. from Steinhardt, Jan. 9, 1941, *FR* 1941, I, 598.

137. Tel. from Steinhardt, May 30, 1941, *FR* 1941, I, 618-19.

138. Circular Telegram, Secretary Hull to Embassy in Moscow, June 5, 1941, *FR* 1941, I, 619.

139. William H. Stoneman of the Chicago *Daily News* is quoted as saying that he "felt that the vigorous action of the British had been a great surprise to the Polit Bureau and that the consequences of their action in holding the trial were far from what they had expected. . . . The Soviet authorities had unquestionably underestimated the length to which the British Government would go in exercising their traditional policy of protecting their nationals abroad and that the embargo placed upon Russian goods by England was an unexpected

blow." (Desp. from Crocker [Stockholm], May 8, 1933, enclosing a memorandum of conversation with Stoneman, DSF 361.4121/17.) This estimate was concurred in by the American Legation in Riga: "The energetic action of intervention on behalf of its nationals undertaken by the British Government would appear to have had considerable effect . . . the extent of the (Soviet) retreat under British pressure is not to be overlooked. . . . 5 out of 6 Englishmen were released on bail. The case was transferred from the secret OGPU to a public tribunal. The accused were to have such a defense as intimidated Russian lawyers could give. British observers and legal advisors were to be permitted. Out of 6 accused Britishers the verdict releases 4 and only 2 are given very light sentences." (Desp. from Skinner [Riga], April 21, 1933, DSF 361.4121/10.)

140. Memorandum by Bartley Gordon, *FR* 1942, III, 768-70.

141. Desp. from Steinhardt, Aug. 21, 1939, DSF 361.1115 Kujala, Arthur J./36.

142. "You will recall the recent despatch of our Embassy in Moscow . . . containing the statement that more than 20,000 Greek citizens have been arrested." (Memorandum by Henderson, Nov. 30, 1938, DSF 361.1121 Nausiainen, Elmer J./6.)

143. *Ibid.*

Chapter V. SOVIET DEBTS

1. Quoted in Memorandum, May 26, 1933, p. 23, DSF 861.51/2601.

2. Tel. from Francis (Petrograd), Jan. 26, 1918, DSF 861.00/1029.

3. Memorandum by Kelley, July 27, 1933, *FRSU*, 7.

4. Memorandum, May 26, 1933, pp. 71-72, DSF 861.51/2601.

5. Memorandum by Kelley, July 27, 1933, *FRSU*, 10-11.

6. Memorandum 3 by Kelley, Oct. 20, 1933, pp. 6-7, DSF 461.11/198½. In several cases there were offsets which, if allowed, would alter the final amount of the claim.

7. Quoted in Memorandum 3 by Kelley, Oct. 20, 1933, pp. 9-10. DSF 461.11/198½.

8. Quoted in Desp. from Coleman (Riga), Dec. 31, 1924, p. 145, DSF 861.51/2601.

9. Quoted in Memorandum, May 26, 1933, pp. 146-47, DSF 861.51/2601. The text of the agreement is in Louis Fischer, *The Soviets in World Affairs* (London, Jonathan Cape, 1930), II, opposite p. 767.

10. Memorandum 1 by Kelley, Oct. 20, 1933, p. 20, DSF 800.51 W89 U.S.S.R./13¾.

11. *Ibid.*, p. 19.

12. *Ibid.*, pp. 20-21.

13. Quoted in Memorandum 2 by Kelley, Oct. 20, 1933, pages IV-1, DSF 861.51/2622½.

14. Memorandum 8 by Kelley, Nov. 3, 1933, p. 33, quoting *Pravda*, no. 107, April 17, 1932, DSF 861.44 Litvinov/15.

15. Quoted in Memorandum 3 by Kelley, Oct. 20, 1933, pp. 13-14, DSF 461.11/198½.

16. Quoted in Memorandum, May 26, 1933, p. 114, DSF 861.51/2601.

17. Quoted in Memorandum 2 by Kelley, Oct. 20, 1933, pp. IV-11, DSF 861.51/2622½.

18. Tel., Secretary Lansing to Embassy at Vologda, April 5, 1918, DSF 861.00/ 1416.

19. Tel. from Haynes (Helsingfors), to Commission to Negotiate Peace (Paris), March 11, 1919, enclosing message from Bullitt, DSF Paris Peace Conference 184.02202/4.

20. Tel. from Bullitt (Helsingfors) to Commission to Negotiate Peace (Paris), March 16, 1919, pp. 8-9, DSF Paris Peace Conference 184.02202/5.

21. Memorandum by Bullitt for the President and Commissioners Plenipotentiary to Negotiate Peace, Undated, March 25 (?), 1919 (*sic*, in original), DSF Paris Peace Conference 184.02202/11.

22. Tel. from Copenhagen, Nov. 2, 1920, reporting statement by Mr. Vanderlip to American Legation (Copenhagen), Aug. 30, 1920, DSF 861.44 Litvinov/15, p. 143.

23. Quoted in Memorandum 2 by Kelley, p. V-2, DSF 861.51/2622½.

24. Quoted in Memorandum 8 by Kelley, Nov. 3, 1933, p. 30, DSF 861.44 Litvinov/15.

25. *Ibid.*, p. 28.

26. Quoting Jan Rudzutak, Commissar of Railways, in Memorandum 2 by Kelley, p. V-3, DSF 861.51/2622½.

27. Memorandum 2A by Kelley, Oct. 25, 1933, *FRSU*, 23-24.

28. Memorandum by Bullitt, Nov. 15, 1933, *FRSU*, 25.

29. Memorandum by Roosevelt and Litvinov, Nov. 15, 1933, *FRSU*, 26-27.

30. Joint Statement by Roosevelt and Litvinov, Nov. 16, 1933, *FRSU*, 37.

31. Memorandum, May 26, 1933, pp. 137-38, DSF 861.51/2601.

32. Tel., Acting Secretary to Hull, Nov. 22, 1933, *FRSU*, 41.

33. Memorandum, December 7, 1933, Moore Papers, Box 18, RL.

34. Department of State *Press Release*, May 5, 1934, DSF 800.51 W89 U.S.S.R./47.

35. Opinion of the Attorney General, quoted in *ibid.*, p. 10.

36. Tel. from Bullitt, June 16, 1934, DSF 800.51 W89 U.S.S.R./72.

37. Tel., Secretary Hull to Embassy in Moscow, April 5, 1934, DSF 800.51 W89 U.S.S.R./27.

38. Memorandum by Moore, April 28, 1934, Roosevelt Papers, President's Secretary's File, Box 14, RL.

39. Tel. from Bullitt, April 8, 1934, *FRSU*, 80. The copy of this telegram in the Roosevelt Library contains marginal marks in red pencil around this sentence.

40. Tel. from Bullitt, June 9, 1934, *FRSU*, 104-105.

41. Tel. from Bullitt, Sept. 7, 1934, DSF 800.51 W89 U.S.S.R./77.

42. About this time Bullitt wrote a "personal and confidential letter" to Moore, saying, "I think we shall find the Russians stiff-necked so long as they feel their international position is secure. . . . At the moment, they believe that Litvinov will be able to put through either the Eastern Locarno agreement or an alliance with France and Czechoslovakia and that their rear will be completely protected in case of an attack by Japan. Moreover, they feel certain that Japan does not intend to attack them this autumn or next spring, and they believe that the strength of the Soviet Army in the Far East will be so great by next summer that Japan will not dare attack." (Letter, Bullitt to Moore, Sept. 8, 1934, Moore Papers, Box 3, RL.)

43. Tel., Secretary Hull to Embassy in Moscow, Oct. 1, 1934, *FRSU*, 153.

44. Memorandum by Bullitt (then in Washington), Jan. 30, 1935, *FRSU*, 168-69.

45. Memorandum by Kelley, Jan. 31, 1935, *FRSU*, 170-71.

46. Tel., Secretary Hull to Embassy in Moscow, Jan. 31, 1935, *FRSU*, 171. It might be useful, while mentioning this reduction in the Embassy staff, to recall a memorandum written later by Kennan on the same subject: "It scarcely seems that there is anything to be gained by cutting the staff of the mission. . . . Any further curtailment on our own part would be merely to cripple the mission in carrying out work which is useful to our Government. . . . This would hardly be effective in influencing the Soviet Government, since it is precisely what that Government wants us to do. . . . Their ideal of a foreign mission in that city would be an important chief of mission with practically no staff—a person whose presence would contribute to the prestige of their Government but who, deprived of adequate assistance, would be unable to furnish his own Government with any great amount of information concerning developments in Russia." (Memorandum by Kennan, March 24, 1938, DSF 124.61/130.)

47. A letter from Albert F. Coyle, Chairman of the American Committee of Creditors of the Soviet Union, dated May 5, 1934, expressed the hope that the lump sum settlement would not be less than $300,000,000. (DSF 800.51 W89 U.S.S.R./21A.)

48. Memorandum by Moore of interview between Roosevelt and Troyanovsky, April 30, 1934, *FRSU*, 86.

49. Tel. from Bullitt, May 21, 1934, *FRSU*, 99.

50. Letter, Moore to Sayre, July 19, 1934, *FRSU*, 120.

51. Tel. from Bullitt, March 15, 1934, *FRSU*, 66-67.

52. Tel., Secretary Hull to Embassy in Moscow, March 17, 1934, *FRSU*, 67.

53. Tel. from Bullitt, March 18, 1934, *FRSU*, 68.

54. Tel. from Bullitt, March 21, 1934, *FRSU*, 69.

55. Tel. from Bullitt, April 2, 1934, *FRSU*, 75.

56. Tel. from Bullitt, April 5, 1934, DSF 800.51 W89 U.S.S.R./27.

57. Tel., Secretary Hull to Embassy in Moscow, May 18, 1934, *FRSU*, 98-99.

58. Memorandum by Kelley, Aug. 3, 1934, *FRSU*, 127.

59. Memorandum by Kelley, Aug. 10, 1934, *FRSU*, 129-30.

60. Memorandum by Kelley, Aug. 24, 1934, *FRSU*, 135-36. "The legal principle in which the Soviet leaders were interested came from Roman law: *do ut des.* (We pay if you give.)" Quoted in Memorandum of May 26, 1933, p. 78, DSF 861.51/2601.

61. Memorandum by Kelley, Sept. 5, 1934, *FRSU*, 141.

62. Tel., Acting Secretary of State to Embassy in Moscow, Sept. 7, 1934, *FRSU*, 162.

63. Tel. from Bullitt, Oct. 10, 1934, *FRSU*, 158-59.

64. Memorandum by Kelley, Jan. 31, 1935, *FRSU*, 171.

65. Tel. from Bullitt, July 17, 1934, *FRSU*, 118.

66. *Ibid.*

67. Memorandum by Roosevelt and Litvinov, Nov. 15, 1933, *FRSU*, 27.

68. Memorandum by Moore, April 28, 1934, Roosevelt Papers, Personal Secretary's File, Box 14, RL. This paper is also attached to DSF 800.51 W89 U.S.S.R./85½.

69. Tel. from Wiley, Oct. 20, 1934, *FRSU*, 160.

70. Quoted in Tel. from Wiley, Feb. 27, 1935, *FRSU*, 185.

71. Tel. from Bullitt, July 17, 1934, *FRSU*, 118.
72. Tel. from Bullitt, March 15, 1934, *FRSU*, 66.
73. Tel. from Bullitt, April 18, 1934, *FRSU*, 85.
74. Tel. from Bullitt, July 17, 1934, *FRSU*, 118.
75. Memorandum by Kelley, Aug. 24, 1934, *FRSU*, 136.
76. Tel. from Bullitt, Oct. 20, 1934, *FRSU*, 160.
77. Tel. from Bullitt, Oct. 10, 1934, *FRSU*, 158.
78. Tel. from Bullitt, May 9, 1934, *FRSU*, 92.
79. Tel. from Wiley, Feb. 14, 1935, reporting conversation of Captain Nimmer (U.S. Naval Attaché) and Voroshilov, *FRSU*, 183.
80. Tel. from Bullitt, July 9, 1934, *FRSU*, 115.
81. Tel. from Bullitt, Oct. 10, 1934, *FRSU*, 159.
82. Tel. from Bullitt, June 16, 1934, *FRSU*, 109.
83. Tel. from Bullitt, Oct. 5, 1934, *FRSU*, 155.
84. Desp. from Wiley, Feb. 6, 1935, *FRSU*, 180.
85. *Ibid.*, p. 179.
86. Tel. from Bullitt, Sept. 13, 1934, *FRSU*, 145.
87. Tel. from Bullitt, April 17, 1934, *FRSU*, 84.
88. Tel. from Bullitt, Aug. 3, 1934, *FRSU*, 126.
89. Tel. from Wiley, Nov. 10, 1934, *FRSU*, 162.
90. Tel. from Bullitt, April 13, 1934, *FRSU*, 84.
91. Tel. from Bullitt, May 9, 1934, *FRSU*, 91.
92. Tel., Secretary Hull to Embassy in Moscow, May 11, 1934, *FRSU*, 93.
93. Tel. from Bullitt, May 21, 1934, *FRSU*, 100.
94. Tel. from Bullitt, June 8, 1934, *FRSU*, 103.
95. Tel., Secretary Hull to Embassy in Moscow, July 7, 1934, *FRSU*, 114.
96. Tel. from Bullitt, July 9, 1934, *FRSU*, 115.
97. Tel. from Bullitt, July 30, 1934, *FRSU*, 124.
98. Memorandum by Kelley, Aug. 10, 1934, *FRSU*, 129.
99. Tel. from Wiley, Oct. 20, 1934, *FRSU*, 160.
100. Tel. from Wiley, Nov. 10, 1934, *FRSU*, 162.
101. Tel. from Wiley, Nov. 18, 1934, *FRSU*, 163.
102. Letter, Moore to Bullitt, Oct. 1, 1935, Moore Papers, Box 3, RL.
103. Tel., Secretary Hull to Embassy in Moscow, May 23, 1934, *FRSU*, 101.
104. Tel. from Bullitt, June 16, 1934, *FRSU*, 108-109. Just previous to this, Bullitt had written to Moore, with reference to the verbal agreement: "Unless we can get Litvinov to negotiate on the basis of our understanding of that agreement, it is, in my opinion, useless to discuss either the amount to be paid by the Soviet Government or interest rates." (Letter, Bullitt to Moore, May 4, 1934, Moore Papers, Box 3, RL.)
105. Tel. from Bullitt, July 27, 1934, *FRSU*, 127.
106. Tel. from Bullitt, Sept. 15, 1934, *FRSU*, 147.
107. Memorandum by Kelley, Aug. 10, 1934, *FRSU*, 130.
108. Personal and confidential letter, Bullitt to Moore, Sept. 8, 1934, Moore Papers, Box 3, RL.
109. Personal and confidential letter, Bullitt to Moore, Oct. 6, 1934, Moore Papers, Box 3, RL.
110. Tel. from Wiley, Nov. 13, 1934, DSF 800.51 W89 U.S.S.R./149.
111. Tel. from Wiley, Feb. 3, 1935, *FRSU*, 175.
112. Desp. from Wiley, Feb. 6, 1935, *FRSU*, 179-80.

113. Tel. from Wiley, Feb. 3, 1935, *FRSU*, 175.
114. Tel. from Wiley, Feb. 5, 1933, *FRSU*, 177.
115. Tel. from Wiley, Feb. 9, 1935, *FRSU*, 181.
116. Desp. from Wiley, Feb. 6, 1935, *FRSU*, 178-79.
117. Tel. from Wiley, March 6, 1935, *FRSU*, 185.
118. Tel. from Bullitt, May 16, 1935, *FRSU*, 188.
119. Desp. from Henderson, Nov. 16, 1936, *FRSU*, 314.
120. Desp. from Davies, Jan. 19, 1937, *FRSU*, 359.
121. Desp. from Davies, June 9, 1938, Enclosure 1, *FRSU*, 576.
122. *Ibid.*, Enclosure 2, *FRSU*, 579.
123. Unnumbered despatch from Davies (Brussels), Jan. 17, 1939, DSF 800.51 W89 U.S.S.R./247. See also *FRSU*, 597.
124. Quoted in Letter, Department of the Treasury to Department of State, June 30, 1938, DSF 800.51 W89 U.S.S.R./248.
125. Letter, Secretary Hull to Hatton W. Sumners (Chairman, House Judiciary Committee), Nov. 5, 1941, DSF 861.51/2900.
126. Letter, Hackworth to Percy Wien, Aug. 18, 1939, DSF 800.51 W89 U.S.S.R./244.
127. Tel., Secretary Hull to Embassy in Moscow, May 16, 1940, *FR* 1940, III, 201-202.
128. Memorandum by Henderson, March 5, 1941, DSF 811.111 Refugees/1109.
129. Letter, John D. McCall to Congressman M. H. West, Nov. 14, 1941, DSF 861.51/2908.
130. Letter, Senator Taft to Secretary Hull, Nov. 27, 1941, DSF 861.51/2910.
131. Letter, Secretary Hull to Senator Prentiss M. Brown, Sept. 29, 1941, DSF 861.51/2881.
132. Bullitt, "How We Won the War . . . ," pp. 91-92.
133. *New York Times,* Jan. 9, 1960.
134. *Wall Street Journal,* Oct. 1, 1959.
135. Department of State *Press Release* 42, Jan. 27, 1960.
136. Desp. from Greene (Berne), Nov. 23, 1933, DSF 711.61/414.
137. Tel. from Wiley, Feb. 4, 1935, enclosure, DSF 800.51 W89 U.S.S.R./173.
138. Memorandum of Oral Conversation, received in Department of State, Aug. 31, 1938, p. 7, DSF 124.61/134.
139. Tel. from Bullitt, June 16, 1934, *FRSU*, 109.
140. Memorandum, May 26, 1933, quoting *Izvestia*, Sept. 30, 1923. DSF 861.51/2601.
141. *New York Times,* Sept. 13, 1959.
142. Memorandum by Keith Merrill of conversation with Rubinin. April 25, 1934, DSF 861.51/264½.
143. Tel., Secretary Hull to Embassy in Moscow, Sept. 15, 1934, *FRSU*, 146.

Chapter VI. SOVIET CLAIMS AND ASSIGNMENTS

1. 246 U.S. 302-303.
2. Memorandum by Kelley, Nov. 3, 1933, pp. 207-208, quoting the Litvinov telegram of Feb. 6, 1928, DSF 861.44 Litvinov/15. The fact that Ughet had

deposited most of the million dollars derived from this case in the United States Treasury does not alter the legal aspect of the problem.

3. Letter, Litvinov to Roosevelt, Nov. 16, 1933, *FRSU*, 36.

4. Letter, Coudert to Kelley, Oct. 19, 1935, DSF 311.6154 Bankers Trust/48.

5. Letter, Litvinov to Roosevelt, Nov. 16, 1933, *FRSU*, 35-36.

6. Letter, Secretary Hull to Attorney General Cummings, Sept. 21, 1934, DSF 411.61 Assignments/6.

7. Letter, Ughet to Department of State, Aug. 25, 1933, DSF 411.61 Assignments/2a.

8. Letter, Ughet to Department of State, Oct. 26, 1933, DSF 411.61 Assignments/1¼.

9. Letter, Ughet to Kelley, May 16, 1930, DSF 311.6153/4.

10. Letter, Ughet to Department of the Treasury, Jan. 18, 1935, DSF 411.61 Assignments/37½.

11. Note, signed by Troyanovsky, July 21, 1936, 411.61 Assignments/97.

12. *Vladikavkazsky Railway Co. v. N.Y. Trust Co.*, 263 N.Y. 360 and 189 N.E. 456. DSF 411.61 Assignments/8.

13. Memorandum for the Secretary of State by Smith W. Brookhart, Counsel, Oct. 18, 1938, DSF 311.6153 Russian Reinsurance Co./85.

14. Letter, Moore to Joseph A. Conroy, Oct. 19, 1936, 411.61 Assignments/125.

15. Tel. from Henderson, Sept. 22, 1936, DSF 411.61 Assignments/110.

16. Tel. from Henderson, Jan. 9, 1937, DSF 411.61 Assignments/145.

17. Tel. from Henderson, Dec. 3, 1937, DSF 411.61 Assignments/170.

18. Letter, Hackworth to Francis White, June 3, 1941, in reply to inquiry of May 22, 1941, DSF 861.5 Bondholders/12.

19. Letter, Frank Polk to Department of State, March 11, 1935, DSF 311.6154 Guaranty Trust Co. (Baranowsky)/57.

20. Secretary Hull to Roosevelt, Nov. 16, 1935, DSF 311.6154 Guaranty Trust Co. (Baranowsky)/68.

21. Letter, Moore to F. H. Koschwitz, Feb. 16, 1935, DSF 411.61 Assignments/35.

22. Memorandum for the Secretary of State, prepared by Smith W. Brookhart, Counsel, Oct. 18, 1938, p. 7, DSF 311.6153 Russian Reinsurance Co./85.

23. Letter, Secretary Hull to Brookhart, Nov. 3, 1938, DSF 311.6153 Russian Reinsurance Co./85.

24. The *Pink* case was later cited by the supporters of the Bricker Amendment as an instance where the United States government had pushed aside state rights and deprived citizens of their rights and property. Louis H. Pink, formerly Superintendent of Insurance for the State of New York, thereupon wrote a letter to the editor of the *New York Times* (published Feb. 13, 1954) refuting Bricker's charge, pointing out that no citizens lost rights or property under the Litvinov Assignment.

25. Letter, Department of State to Secretary of the Treasury, June 18, 1934, DSF 411.61 Assignments/4a.

26. Memorandum by Yingling, Dec. 21, 1939, DSF 411.61 Assignments/271. It has been suggested that the original intention may have been to apply the assignment only to money deposited to the credit of the Russian governments and then, when the debt negotiations collapsed, an imaginative mind saw the possibility of including corporate assets as well. The records indicate that this was not true. In March 1934 when the debt negotiations were just getting under

way, Kelley was already talking about the corporate assets of the Baranowsky Company. (Memorandum, Kelley to Hackworth, March 19, 1934, DSF 311.6154 Guaranty Trust Co. [Baranowsky]/20½.) Assistant Secretary Moore agreed that "there would be no objection to claiming property and assets in the United States of Russian corporations." (Note, Hackworth to Kelley, April 2, 1934, *ibid.*/23½. A marginal note on this document states, "Mr. Sweeney of the Department of Justice informed April 12, 1934. RFK"). If this suggestion coincided with the original intention, the phrasing of the assignment agreement turned out to be most convenient for the American government.

27. Memorandum by Yingling, Dec. 21, 1939, DSF 411.61 Assignments/271.

28. Letter, U.S. Attorney Lamar Hardy to Kelley, Aug. 12, 1936, enclosing opinion of the court, DSF 411.61 Assignments/101½.

29. 301 U.S. 332.

30. Letter, Borchard to Moore, May 13, 1937, DSF 411.61 Assignments/155.

31. Memorandum for the Assistant Attorney General, Oct. 1, 1934, DSF 411.61 Assignments/19½.

32. Letter, Phillips to Postmaster General, June 23, 1936, DSF 411.61 Assignments/76½.

33. In 1942 the United States Court of Claims approved payment of $125,000 legal fees and $13,800 reimbursement to Charles Recht et al.; $10,000 and $3,800 to Coudert Brothers; and $8,000 fees to Victor Gartz. Other petitions were denied. (Letter, Department of Justice to Secretary of State, March 3, 1942, DSF 411.61 R92/178.)

34. Note, Umansky to Moore, Dec. 8, 1938, enclosing previous Soviet statement of interpretation, DSF 311.6154 R92/45.

35. Memorandum by Henderson, Dec. 9, 1938, DSF 311.6154 R92/48.

36. Letter, Henderson to Ralph Hill, Jan. 27, 1939, DSF 311.6154 R92/54.

37. These figures were provided by C. T. Brannan, Bureau of Accounts, Department of the Treasury, during an interview and are based on deposits actually made into the Treasury. But, on March 11, 1954, a subcommittee of the House Committee on Foreign Affairs was told that the amount was $9,114,444.36. (Hearings, 83d Cong., 2d sess., p. 31.) Both of these amounts, in turn, are at variance with those contained in a report prepared for the Department of Justice by Paul Sweeney and Herman Marcuse who represented the government in a number of the Litvinov Assignment cases. Their report shows that $7,142,-235.05 was collected as a result of litigation, $1,500,000 from the Post Office Department, and $330.58 from the Comptroller of the Currency, for a total of $8,642,565.63. Further, both the Department of Justice and the Archives records show the collection of $1,433.01 in 1934 from the Morton Truck and Tractor Co., although the Treasury Department's figures list no such deposit. Interviews with Brannan, Marcuse, and Sweeney failed to explain these differences. The actual deposits total $9,114,444.66.

38. Foreign Claims Settlement Commission of the United States, *10th Semi-annual Report* to the Congress for the period ending June 30, 1959, Part V, pp. 180-82, 203-204, 209, and 263-73.

39. The figures in this paragraph were taken from the *New York Times* of Sept. 8, 1957; May 18, 1959; Aug. 23, 1959; and Nov. 29, 1959.

40. One unexpected result of the government's "beneficence" was that each bond sharing in the award had to be stamped for verification; this act was later viewed as an "alteration" of the bond, making it "unfungible" or unexchange-

able. This affected the subsequent value of the bond but, since there has been no further action on the matter and no more money available, this point is academic.

41. Tel., Secretary Hull to Embassy in Moscow, Sept. 16, 1936, DSF 411.61 Assignments/106a.

42. Tel. from Henderson, Sept. 22, 1936, DSF 411.61 Assignments/110.

43. Tel. from Dickerson (Kuibyshev), Nov. 24, 1942, 411.61 Assignments/92.

44. Interview with Paul Sweeney, Department of Justice, April 16, 1963.

Chapter VII.   ECONOMIC ESPIONAGE

1. Memorandum by Kelley, July 27, 1933, DSF 711.61/287¾.

2. Draft agreement, Moore Papers, Box 18, RL. In the draft the last sentence was crossed out between the double asterisks, so that the sentence ended with "branches." In both of the last two paragraphs, the phrases "by legal means," indicated by single asterisks, were crossed out, and inserted in pencil was the phrase "in good faith and . . ." followed by three undecipherable words which look like "without harmful—or wrongful—intent."

3. Statement by Litvinov, Nov. 16, 1933, *FRSU*, 34-35.

4. Memorandum by Kelley, Oct. 20, 1933, pp. 7-8, DSF 361.11/4089½.

5. Desp. from Skinner (Riga), April 5, 1933, enclosing this memorandum by Kennan at pp. 48-49, DSF 661.0031/30.

6. Memorandum, *Foreigners in Russia*, Nov. 3, 1933, pp. 80-81, DSF 361.4121/20.

7. *Ibid.*, pp. 78-79.

8. *Ibid.*, p. 75.

9. *Ibid.*, pp. 78-79.

10. *Ibid.*, pp. 80-81.

11. Desp. from Skinner (Riga), April 7, 1933, enclosure 3, *Pravda*, no. 73, March 15, 1933, p. 1, DSF 361.4121/5.

12. Desp. from Crocker (Stockholm), May 8, 1933, enclosing memorandum of conversation with William H. Stoneman, DSF 361.4121/17.

13. Desp. from Skinner (Riga), April 7, 1933, p. 18, DSF 361.4121/5. In this despatch, another supposition was voiced (p. 22): "to furnish the Russian public with a plausible excuse for reduced machinery imports due in reality . . . to Russia's inability to assume even long-term credit obligations abroad,—perhaps even to an anticipation that it will be unable to meet obligations already incurred as a result of failing export trade."

14. Quoted in Desp. from Skinner (Riga), April 7, 1933, DSF 361.4121/5.

15. Unnumbered despatch from Atherton (London), April 7, 1933, enclosing Cmd. 4290—Regarding the Arrest of Employees of the Metropolitan Vickers Co. at Moscow, quoting p. 15, DSF 361.4121/7.

16. *Ibid.*, p. 17.

17. Desp. from Skinner (Riga), April 21, 1933, pp. 6-7, DSF 361.4121/10.

18. Desp. from Skinner (Riga), April 7, 1933, quoting from enclosure 2: *Pravda*, no. 73, March 15, 1933, p. 1, DSF 361.4121/5.

19. Desp. from Crocker (Stockholm), May 8, 1933, DSF 361.4121/17.

20. Desp. from Wiley, March 29, 1935, DSF 861.111/654.

21. *Ibid.*

22. Tel. from Bullitt, July 24, 1935, DSF 861.602/267.

23. Desp. from Henderson, Sept. 29, 1937, DSF 361.11 Employees/349.

24. *Ibid.*

25. Instruction, Secretary Hull to Embassy in Moscow, Oct. 27, 1937, DSF 361.11 Employees/349.

26. Memorandum by Kennan and Page, July 19, 1938, *FRSU*, 660.

27. Desp. from Wiley, March 26, 1935, DSF 861.111/656.

28. *Ibid.*

29. *Ibid.*

30. Memorandum by Acting Secretary Berle, July 30, 1941, DSF 811.22761/59.

Chapter VIII. "NORMAL" DIPLOMATIC RELATIONS

1. Letter, Roosevelt to Litvinov, Nov. 16, 1933, *FRSU*, 27.

2. Letter, Litvinov to Roosevelt, Nov. 16, 1933, *FRSU*, 28.

3. *Washington Post*, Nov. 18, 1933, p. 4.

4. Desp. from Bullitt (On Board Steamship "Washington"), Jan. 4, 1934, *FRSU*, 55.

5. *Ibid.*, pp. 56-62.

6. Tel. from Bullitt, March 15, 1934, *FRSU*, 66.

7. Desp. from Bullitt, March 28, 1934, *FRSU*, 71.

8. *Ibid.*, p. 74.

9. Tel. from Bullitt, April 8, 1934, *FRSU*, 79-80.

10. Memorandum by Bullitt: "Budget Argument for Moscow," February 10, 1934, DSF 124.611/113. The Germans were scattered in five different parts of Moscow, while the British had paid £. 20,000 to buy off and evict families, put £. 5,000 in permanent improvements into their Embassy, and had to pay £. 5,000 a year as rent.

11. Desp. from Bullitt (On Board Steamship "Washington"), Jan. 4, 1934, DSF 123 Bullitt/32.

12. Tel. from Bullitt, May 24, 1934, DSF 125.6316/77.

13. Tel. from Bullitt, April 28, 1934, DSF 125.813/14.

14. Desp. from Bullitt (On Board Steamship "Washington"), Jan. 4, 1934, *FRSU*, 60.

15. Desp. from Bullitt, March 28, 1934, *FRSU*, 73.

16. Letter to Secretary Hull from H. T. Lindeberg, June 13, 1934. DSF 124.611/167. In 1935 Bullitt noted that Mokhovaya Building, completed only a year before, already required two months of repair work. (Tel. from Bullitt, June 3, 1935, DSF 124.611/266.)

17. Tel. from Cudahy (Warsaw), Jan. 8, 1933 (*sic*, but date should be 1934), DSF 124.611/62.

18. Tel., Secretary Hull to Embassy in Moscow, Jan. 8, 1935, *FRSU*, 270.

19. Tel. from Wiley, Feb. 15, 1935, DSF 124.611/231.

20. Tel., Secretary Hull to Embassy in Moscow, Jan. 8, 1935, *FRSU*, 270.

21. In 1950 the Swedish Embassy in Moscow needed some minor repairs. The Swedish estimate was $500; the Burobin bid was $4,000. When the Soviet government refused entrance visas to Swedish workmen, the Burobin bid was accepted. (*New York Times*, Sept. 21, 1950.)

22. On Burobin's cleaning of the radiators in Spaso House, see Lydia Kirk, *Postmarked Moscow* (New York, Scribners, 1952), pp. 200, 206.

23. Note, Ruth Shipley to Pierrepont Moffat, August 19, 1937, DSF 861.111/719.

24. There was a refusal in 1934, a special type of case involving Captain William A. Worton, U.S.M.C., an Attaché for Language Study at Peiping, who wanted to travel by sea to Vladivostok, then by rail to Kharbarovsk and return to Peiping through northern Manchuria. Bitner, the Soviet Counselor of Embassy in Peiping, refused to issue the visa, pointing out to Captain Worton "that obviously his mission was one of observation and not purely pleasure." Captain Worton made no attempt to conceal the fact "that his journey was semi-official." (Desp. from Johnson [Peiping], Aug. 29, 1934, DSF 861.111/639.)

25. Memorandum by Kennan, July 19, 1938, *FRSU*, 659.

26. Lydia Kirk, *Postmarked Moscow*, p. 150.

27. Note, Ruth Shipley to Pierrepont Moffat, Aug. 19, 1937, DSF 861.111/719.

28. Memorandum of Oral Conversation, undated but received in the Department from the Soviet Embassy on April 28, 1938, DSF 124.61/134.

29. Desp. from Steinhardt, Aug. 16, 1939, DSF 861.111/814.

30. Lydia Kirk, *Postmarked Moscow*, p. 198.

31. Desp. from Bullitt (On Board Steamship "Washington"), Jan. 4, 1934, *FRSU*, 56.

32. Desp. from Cole (Riga), Nov. 2, 1935, enclosure: Resolution of Sept. 5, 1935, DSF 861.111/677.

33. Tel. from Steinhardt, May 17, 1941, *FR* 1941, I, 881-82.

34. Tel. from Steinhardt, May 22, 1941, *FR* 1941, I, 883.

35. Tel., Secretary Hull to Embassy in Moscow, May 28, 1941, *FR* 1941, I, 883.

36. Tel. from Steinhardt, May 31, 1941, DSF 124.61/173.

37. Tel. from Steinhardt, June 5, 1941, DSF 124.61/175.

38. Tel. from Steinhardt, June 6, 1941, *FR* 1941, I, 751.

39. Tel. from Steinhardt, June 9, 1941, DSF 124.61/177.

40. *Ibid.*

41. Secretary Hull to Embassy in Moscow, June 7, 1941, *FR* 1941, I, 884.

42. Tel., Acting Secretary of State to Embassy in Moscow, June 28, 1941, *FR* 1941, I, 889.

43. Tel. from Steinhardt, July 1, 1941, *FR* 1941, I, 889.

44. Tel. from Steinhardt, July 5, 1941, *FR* 1941, I, 890.

45. Tel., Acting Secretary of State to Embassy in Moscow, July 15, 1941, *FR* 1941, I, 900.

46. *Ibid.*

47. Tel. from Steinhardt, July 16, 1941, DSF 361.1121/21.

48. *American Foreign Policy. Current Documents,* 1957, Department of State Publication 7101, 1961, p. 743.

49. *New York Times,* Sept. 11, 1960.

50. "At least 30 or 40 people are employed for the open observation and protection of the Ambassador's movements." (Memorandum by Kennan, Nov. 24, 1937, DSF 124.61/119.)

51. Desp. from Bullitt, March 28, 1934, *FRSU*, 74.

52. Memorandum by Kennan, Nov. 24, 1937, DSF 124.61/119.

53. Instruction, Secretary Hull to Embassy in Moscow, Feb. 14, 1934, DSF 124.613/494B.

54. Desp. from Bullitt, March 28, 1934, DSF 124.613/527.

55. Desp. from Bullitt, March 28, 1934, and Desp. from Bullitt, April 2, 1934, DSF 124.613/527 and -/528.

56. Memorandum by Kelley, Jan. 9, 1936, *FRSU*, 281.

57. Memorandum of Oral Conversation, undated but received in the Department from the Soviet Embassy, April 28, 1938, DSF 124.61/134.

58. Memorandum by Kuniholm, May 26, 1937, *FRSU*, 443.

59. *Ibid.*, pp. 444-45.

60. Memorandum by Kuniholm, May 26, 1937, DSF 661.11241/13.

61. Tel. from Henderson, Jan. 21, 1938, *FRSU*, 630.

62. Memorandum by Moffat, April 16, 1938, *FRSU*, 646.

63. Memorandum by Henderson, Dec. 7, 1939, *FRSU*, 862.

64. Desp. from Henderson, Nov. 16, 1936, *FRSU*, 317.

65. Tel. from Bullitt, Nov. 9, 1935, *FRSU*, 265.

66. Memorandum by Kelley, Nov. 3, 1933, p. 8, quoting Litvinov's speech of May 18, 1931, before the League of Nations Commission of Enquiry for European Union, DSF 861.44 Litvinov/15.

67. Tel., Secretary Hull to Embassy in Moscow, Jan. 31, 1935, *FRSU*, 171.

68. Desp. from Bullitt, April 20, 1936, DSF 861.01/2120.

69. Hull, *Memoirs*, p. 743.

70. *Ibid.*, pp. 807, 809, 971.

71. Memorandum by Page, May 17, 1940, DSF 123 Biddle, Anthony J.D./216.

72. Welles-Oumansky Conversations and Related Memoranda, pp. 17-18.

73. Tel. from Standley, July 5, 1942, *FR* 1942, III, 606.

74. Walter Millis, ed. *The Forrestal Diaries* (New York, Viking, 1951), p. 40.

75. *Ibid.*, pp. 266-67.

76. *Ibid.*, p. 482.

77. Memorandum by Dunn, Jan. 13, 1938, *FRSU*, 628.

78. Tel. from Steinhardt, Aug. 31, 1939, *FRSU*, 850-51.

79. Roosevelt Papers, President's Secretary's File, Box 14, RL.

80. Memorandum by Kennan, Nov. 24, 1937, *FRSU*, 446-47.

81. Hull, *Memoirs*, pp. 972-73.

Chapter IX.   EVALUATION

1. Statement by the Secretary of State, Aug. 31, 1935, *FRSU*, 258.

2. Hull, *Memoirs*, p. 306.

3. Memorandum by Berle, May 29, 1940, DSF 711.61/732½.

4. Hull, *Memoirs*, p. 304.

5. Personal letter, Moore to Bullitt, April 10, 1934, Moore Papers, Box 3, RL.

6. Department of State *Press Release* 622, Nov. 17, 1953.

7. Samuel N. Harper, *The Russia I Believe In* (Chicago, University of Chicago Press, 1945) p. 249.

8. Letter, Pierrepont Moffat to C. P. Oakes, Feb. 12, 1938, DSF 711.61/636.

9. Desp. from Nielsen (Warsaw), Sept. 3, 1935, quoting *Kurjer Warszawski*, no. 235, August 28, 1935, DSF 861.00 Congress, Communist International VII/119.

10. Memorandum by Page, Oct. 3, 1940, *FR* 1940, III, 229-30.

11. Report by Harry Hopkins of conference with Stalin, July 30, 1941, *FR* 1941, I, 803.

12. Department of State Memorandum, June 1950 in *American Foreign Policy, 1950-1955,* p. 1937.

13. *Soviet Political Treaties and Violations,* Staff study for the Committee on the Judiciary, 84th Cong., 1st sess., Doc. 85, 1955, p. iii.

14. Harry S Truman, *Memoirs* (Garden City, Doubleday, 1955), I, 82.

15. Department of State *Press Release* 650, Dec. 3, 1957, p. 5.

16. Letter, Moore to Messersmith, Nov. 2, 1937, DSF 124.61/119.

17. Letter, Senator Pittman to Secretary Hull, Jan. 21, 1935, DSF 711.61/517.

18. Letter, Pittman to Hull, Jan. 19, 1940, enclosing S. Res. 219, 76th Cong., 3d sess., Jan. 18, 1940; reply, Hull to Pittman, Jan. 30, 1940; DSF 711.61/704.

19. Letter, Pittman to Hull, March 16, 1940, enclosing S. Res. 246, 76th Cong., 3d sess., March 15, 1940; reply, Hull to Pittman, March 25, 1940; DSF 711.61/718.

20. Letter, Hull to Pittman, Jan. 30, 1940, DSF 711.61/704.

21. Department of State *Press Release* 671, Nov. 29, 1955, pp. 4-5.

22. Personal and confidential letter, Bullitt (in Paris) to Moore, Nov. 29, 1936, Moore Papers, Box 3, RL.

23. Millis, *Forrestal Diaries,* pp. 27-28.

24. Mosely, Philip, "Some Soviet Techniques of Negotiation," in Raymond Dennett and Joseph E. Johnson, eds. *Negotiating with the Russians* (Boston, World Peace Foundation, 1951) p. 289.

25. Desp. from Bullitt, March 28, 1934, *FRSU,* 74.

26. *A Decade of American Foreign Policy, Basic Documents, 1941-49,* prepared at the request of the Senate Committee on Foreign Relations by the Staff of the Committee and the Department of State, 81st Cong., 1st sess., Doc. 123, 1950, p. 89.

27. Millis, *Forrestal Diaries,* pp. 172-73.

28. Henry L. Stimson and McGeorge Bundy, *On Active Service in Peace and War* (New York, Harper, 1947/48), p. 608.

29. *Ibid.,* p. 646.

30. Memorandum by Atherton, Nov. 26, 1940, *FR* 1940, III, 408.

31. Tel. from Steinhardt, June 17, 1941, *FR* 1941, I, 765.

32. Hull, *Memoirs,* p. 1467.

33. Millis, *Forrestal Diaries,* pp. 138-39.

34. Desp. from Davies, April 1, 1938, DSF 711.61/650.

35. Department of State *Press Release* 622, Nov. 17, 1953.

Note on Sources

The present book does not depend on the same type of sources as most other books. With the avowed purpose of presenting the information available to the Department of State, the author necessarily relied almost exclusively on official sources.

The bulk of the research was done in the Security Search Room of the National Archives, where the Department of State records were made available. The records are arranged by file number, based on a master classification system; within each file, the documents are arranged by date. Thus the first number is that of the file and the second is that by which documents in that file are classified: 124.61/1508 means that the file number is 124.61 and that the document is 1508 in that file. The system used in the National Archives is that used for footnotes in the present work that cite the documents.

The files most helpful in research on this topic, with a general title of the materials, are as follows: 124.61 and 124.611, the Embassy in Moscow; 311.6153 and 311.6154, assignments and claims; 361.11, 361.1115, and 361.1121, protection and welfare of American nationals; 411.61 and 461.11, assignments; 711.61, relations between the U.S. and the USSR; 800.51, financial affairs; 800.51 W89 U.S.S.R., Communism in the Soviet Union; 800.00B Communist International, that organization; 811.00B, Communism in the U.S.; 861.00 Congress, Communist International VII, that meeting; 861.111, residence and travel in the USSR; 861.404, religion; 861.44, special persons, especially 861.44 Litvinov; and 861.51, financial affairs and bonds. Many of these files have subsidiary numbers.

The researcher was free to use Department of State documents in the "open period," which goes up through 1941. Some scattered items from the next two years were also made available, on special request, where they did not involve security matters, but there was no access to the complete record after 1941, a fact the reader must keep in mind. Fortunately, of course, the main patterns of American-Soviet relations were established in the years 1933-41, so that availability of records in this period makes it possible to study the subject quite thoroughly from the American point of view.

The Archives also contain a folder from Research Group 59 (Office of Eastern European Affairs, USSR Section, 1917-40) entitled "Welles-Oumansky Conversations and Related Memoranda, June 1940-April 1941" which, though duplicated in part by other documents, contains some useful materials of the talks between the Under Secretary of State and the Soviet Ambassador in Washington.

The other main source of documentary materials was the Franklin D. Roosevelt Library at Hyde Park, New York. Two sets of papers were most valuable on the present topic: Group 13, the Papers of President Roosevelt; and Group 55, the Papers of R. Walton Moore. Among the Moore papers were: Box 3, seven folders on William C. Bullitt; Box 8, folders on Hull and the Johnson Bill; Box 17, folders on President Roosevelt; and Box 18, four folders on Russia. Among the Roosevelt papers, the following were used: (1) *President's Secretary's File*, Box 14, Russia; Boxes 20, 21, and 22, State Department; Box 23, Hull; Box 24, Moore; and the folder on Russia from the *Safe File*. (2) The *Official File*, 220, four boxes on Russia; 20, the State Department; 799, Bullitt; 263, two boxes on Communism; and 1913, Joseph E. Davies. (3) The *President's Personal Files*, 1124, Bullitt, and 2605, Moore.

Although the documents as such are not available for the period after 1941, some are obtainable from a series of Department of State Publications. In July 1957 the Department published *American Foreign Policy, 1950-1955*, two volumes listed as Publication 6446, General Foreign Policy Series 117; since then the series has been entitled *Current Documents*, with each volume covering a single year. These volumes contain a selection of documents which can be released within the prescribed twenty-year publication limit, and certain excerpts were useful for the present work. The *Department of State Bulletin* relates to recent events but was generally less helpful for this type of research than other publications. The Office of News in the Department of State contains files of the departmental *Press Releases* and the *Verbatim Reports* of the Secretary of State's Press Conferences.

Certain publications of the Committee on Un-American Activities of the House of Representatives contain information on Communist activities, especially *The Strategy and Tactics of World Communism*, (80th Cong., 2d sess., House Document 619, 1948) and *Organized Communism in the U.S.* (85th Cong., 2d sess., August 1953.)

Among the nonofficial sources, special mention needs to be given to Robert T. Browder's *The Origins of Soviet-American Diplomacy* (Princeton University Press, 1953) because this treatment dovetails with the period covered here, as explained in the Foreword. Other important secondary sources used are mainly those written by or about the people involved in American-Soviet relations since 1933, including the Reverend Georges Bissonnette's *Moscow Was My Parish* (N.Y., McGraw-Hill, 1956), Ambassador William C. Bullitt's "How We Won the War and Lost the Peace," (*Life*, vol. 25, August 30, 1948, pp. 83-97), Ambassador Joseph F. Davies' *Mission to Moscow* (N.Y., Simon and Schuster, 1941), Ambassador David R. Francis' *Russia from the American Embassy* (N.Y., Scribners, 1921), Benjamin Gitlow's *The Whole of Their Lives* (N.Y., Scribners, 1948), Ambassador Joseph C. Grew's *Ten Years in Japan* (N.Y., Simon and Schuster, 1944), Secretary Cordell Hull's *The Memoirs of Cordell Hull* (N.Y., Macmillan, 1948, 2 vols.), Lydia Kirk's *Postmarked Moscow* (N.Y., Scribners, 1952, Walter

Millis' editing of *The Forrestal Diaries* (N.Y., Viking, 1951), Secretary Henry Morgenthau, Jr.'s "The Morgenthau Diaries, Part III—How F.D.R. Fought the Axis" (*Colliers*, October 11, 1947, pp. 20-21, 72-79), Ambassador Walter B. Smith's *My Three Years in Moscow* (Philadelphia, Lippincott, 1950), Ambassador William H. Standley and Arthur A. Ageton's *Admiral Ambassador to Russia* (Chicago, Regnery, 1955), Secretary Henry L. Stimson and McGeorge Bundy's *On Active Service in Peace and War* (New York, Harper, 1947-48), and Harry S Truman's Memoirs (Garden City, Doubleday, 1955-56, 2 vols.). Of a different nature is *Negotiating with the Russians*, edited by Raymond Dennett and Joseph E. Johnson (Boston, World Peace Foundation, 1951).

Index

Adams, John Quincy, 2
Alexander I, 2
Allis-Chalmers Manufacturing Co., 196
All-Russian Zemsky Union, 195
All-Union Communist Party: *see* Communist Party, Soviet Union
Alpert, Harry, 110
America, 31, 32
American Communist Party: *see* Communist Party, United States
American Embassy in Moscow:
  construction, new building, 214-16
  currency problem, 223-25
  customs duties and inspection, 225-27
  housing facilities, 213
  political asylum, 261
  travel in Soviet Union, 218-23
American Federation of Labor, 10, 42, 43
American nationals, 66, 91-93, 102, 125
American-Russian Chamber of Commerce, 5
Amtorg: *see* Soviet Union, Government of
Anti-Comintern Pact, 6
Anti-Subversive Activities Act, 57
Archangel, 2, 14, 16, 24, 180, 181
Arola, John, 96-97, 112
Assignments: 192, 234, 277
  amounts obtained, 194-95
  clarification notes (1939), 194
  payments made, 196
  Soviet Claims Fund, 195
Assumptionist Order, 70, 72, 76
Atherton, Ray, 244
Austria, 28
Azerbaijan Petroleum Trust, 43

Bakhmetyev, Boris A., 2, 156, 179, 193
Bakhmetyev, Georgi, 2
Baranowsky, P. V., Company, 191, 195, 278
Barghoorn, Frederick, 103, 128, 136
Barr, Edward, 96, 97, 136

Belgium, 141
Belmont, August, 188
Belmont case decision, 189-90
Belmont estate, 195
Berle, Adolf A., 233
Berlin, 217, 230
Bess, Demaree, 216
Bezbozhnik, 66
Biddle, Anthony D., 229
Bissonnette, Fr. Georges, 71, 73-76, 78, 85, 264
Bittelman, Alexander, 36
Black Tom explosion, 180
Bogdanov, Peter A., 4, 5, 7
Bohlen, Charles E., 73, 85
Bolshevik, 42
Borah, William E., 27
Borchard, Edwin, 189-90
Boris, Archbishop, 73-77, 79, 263
Borodin, Mikhail M., 44
Boston, 21
Brady, William H., 110
Brannan, C. T., 278
Brassard, Fr. John A., 71, 73, 82
Braun, Fr. Leopold, 70-72, 77, 79-81, 83-85, 263, 264
Browder, Earl, 35, 43, 46, 47, 54-58
Browder, Robert, vi, 253, 255
Brown, Philip M., 15
Buchanan, Sir George, 68
Bukharin, Nikolay I., 34
Bulgaria, 28
Bullitt, William C.: 166, 167, 178
  as Ambassador, 21, 211-13, 218-19, 225, 240
  currency, 223, 224
  debt problem, 145, 147, 149, 150, 152, 153, 155-64, 168, 174, 273, 275
  diplomatic relations, 212, 228, 241
  legal rights, 99, 104, 105
  new Embassy building, 214, 215
  noninterference, 44-48, 50, 53
  recognition, 10, 16, 17, 20, 252, 254

religious rights, 63, 71, 262
    trade, 252
Burobin: *see* Soviet Union, Government
    of
Byrnes, James, 242

Cahiers du Communisme, 58
Caldwell, Erskine, 220
Canadian Pacific Railway Co., 184, 191,
    192
Carr, Wilbur J., 103
Castle, William R., 5, 9, 40
Catherine the Great, 1
Chavchavadze, Prince Paul, 252
Chicago, 21, 103
Chicherin, Georgi V., 2, 3, 33, 34, 144,
    145, 147, 251, 257, 265
China, 28
Cibrario case, 182, 193-94
Claims of American nationals: 16
    Siberian expedition, 180, 181
Colby, Bainbridge, 3
Cole, Felix, 9, 25, 55
Coleman, Frederick, 62
Comintern: *see* Communist International
Comisaroff, Nicholas, 111
Communist International: 16, 24, 25,
    30-34, 38, 40-42, 45, 48, 51, 52,
    54-56, 235, 246, 260
    and American Communist Party, 37,
    57
    and RILU, 39
    and Soviet government, 31, 33, 34,
    41, 44, 45, 47, 49, 51, 52
    dissolved, 57
    ECCI, 33, 35, 36, 37, 39, 40, 43,
    44, 47, 55
    representatives, 35
    6th World Congress, 33-35, 41
    7th World Congress, 42, 44-49, 53,
    56, 58, 178, 233, 236
Communist International, 36-37, 43,
    54-56
Communist Party, U.S.S.R. (CPSU):
    31, 32, 34, 42, 259
    Central Committee, 34, 205
    front organizations, 38-40, 239
    19th Party Congress, 59

Communist Party, United States: 10,
    27, 32, 37, 39, 41-43, 45, 46,
    52, 54, 55, 58, 60, 239, 254, 256
    and Communist International, 35, 37,
    57
    Farmer-Labor Party, 46, 54
Conferences, International
    Geneva Disarmament (1932), 4
    Genoa (1922), 145
    Pan American, Montevideo (1933),
    17
    Paris Foreign Ministers (1946), 242
    Paris Peace (1919), 145
    Prinkipo (1919), 144, 145
    San Francisco (1945), 237
    World Economic, London (1933),
    5, 11
Consular convention, 90, 91, 103-04
Consular districts, 105
Consulates, 267
Consuls, 48, 50, 51, 225
Coolidge, Calvin, 3
Cotton, Joseph P., 62
Coudert, Frederic R., 182
Credits to Soviet Union, 9, 10, 21
Creighton, Albert M., 5
Cronk, Harry, 110-11
Cuba, 244
Curtiss Airplane and Motor Co., 184,
    191, 192, 195
Czechoslovakia, 28, 273

Daily Worker (N.Y.), 37, 41, 42, 55,
    58
Daladier, Edouard, 262
Dana, Francis, 1
Daughters of the American Revolu-
    tion, 255
Davies, Joseph E., 170, 171, 173, 219,
    226, 245
Davis, Norman H., 5
Day, Donald, 54-56
Deane, John, 241
Debts, Soviet: 13, 21, 212, 233, 246,
    259
    collapse of negotiations, 155
    credit, 160
    gentlemen's agreement, 150, 160,
    162, 176

interest payments, 161-63
loan, 157, 159-61
nationalization, 173
relation to other governments, 163-66
repudiation by Soviet government, 140
Roosevelt-Litvinov memorandum, 151
Denmark, 28
Department of State: 87, 171, 172
assignments, 182, 184, 185, 187, 188, 190, 192, 194, 197
currency, 223
customs restrictions, 226
debt problem, 142, 152, 154, 155, 158, 174
diplomatic relations, 239, 243
Division of Eastern European Affairs, 17, 27, 148
economic espionage, 206, 209
Legal Adviser, 42, 186, 188, 264-65
legal rights, 101, 106, 132
noninterference, 42, 54, 57, 59
recognition, 10, 12, 17, 19-21
religious rights, 73, 74, 76, 79, 260
Soviet violations, 237
travel in Soviet Union, 219-22
Devenis, Michael, 99-100, 119, 136
Dillon, C. Douglas, 175
Dimitrov, Georgy, 46, 48, 54
Dion, Fr. Louis F., 71, 75-77, 82, 264
Diplomatic relations with Soviet Union: 245
"agreement in principle," 241
currency problem, 223-25
customs restrictions, 225-27
miscellaneous restrictions, 227
restrictions on travel in United States, 220-22
severance of, 47, 237-39
Soviet techniques, 240
travel in Soviet Union, 218-23
visas, 217
Divilkovsky, Ivan, 17, 224
Dominican Republic, 14
Drypool, Sol, 100, 106, 109
Duclos, Jacques, 58
Dulles, John Foster, 235, 237, 240, 245
Duranty, Walter, 18, 22, 52, 161, 170, 254
Durbrow, Elbridge, 120, 219, 269

Economic espionage: 24, 234
German-Soviet Treaty, 201
Litvinov statement, 200
state secrets, 202-203
Egorov, Alexander I., 252
Equitable Life Assurance Society, 143
Espionage, 134, 135
Estonia, 28, 56
Expatriation, 93, 99

Far Eastern situation, 6, 180, 245, 246
Faymonville, Philip R., 219
Finland, 238
First Russian Reinsurance Co., 191, 195
Fischer, Louis, 44
Fish, Hamilton, Jr., 10
Foreign Bondholders Council, 186
Foreign Claims Settlement Commission, 198
Forrestal, James, 230
Foster, William Z., 35, 46, 47, 58
France, 17, 28, 41, 44, 141, 148, 162-66, 175, 252, 273
Francis, David R., 2, 140, 147

Georgia, 28
Germany, 4, 17, 28, 33, 41, 92, 135, 141, 145, 162-65, 176, 218, 221
Gitlow, Benjamin, 36, 41
Globe Indemnity Co., 191, 195
Gorin, M. N., 123, 265
GPU: *see* Police
Great Britain, 15, 17, 28, 33, 41, 49, 141, 146, 148, 162-65, 175, 176, 252
Green, William, 10
Grew, Joseph C., 6, 251
Guaranty Trust Co., 143, 184, 190, 191, 195, 198

Habicht, Hermann R., 134
Hackworth, Green H., 14, 93, 153
Haensel, Paul, 255
Haiti, 14
Harriman, W. Averell, 230
Hatalowich, Ivan, 113
Hawley-Smoot tariff law, 257

Helsinki, 36, 134, 262
Henderson, W. Loy: 170, 271
  assignment, 194
  legal rights, 97, 98, 116, 118, 129, 139, 265
  noninterference, 55
  religious rights, 79
Hitler, Adolph, 4, 6, 173, 221, 232, 244
Hodges, Luther, 252
Holland, 36
Hopkins, Harry, 236
Hornbeck, Stanley K., 7
Hovi, Albert, 129, 130, 134, 270
Hrinkevich, Frank, 114, 120, 121, 269
Hughes, Charles Evans, 3, 5
Hull, Cordell: 166, 167, 231
  assignment, 183, 187
  debt problem, 154, 155, 157, 164, 170, 174, 178, 234
  diplomatic relations, 228, 232, 238, 239, 242, 244
  legal rights, 124
  new Embassy building, 216
  noninterference, 29, 30, 42, 48, 50-51, 55, 233, 259
  press conferences, 17
  recognition, 7, 10, 11, 17, 18, 22
  religious rights, 63, 68
  trade, 8
  travel in Soviet Union, 221
  Umansky, 229

Imperial Russian government, 140, 149, 192, 196
International Claims Settlement Act (1949), 195
International General Electric Co., 143, 144
International Harvester Co., 143
International Organization to Help Revolution in Foreign Countries (MOPR), 24
International Press Correspondence, 36, 40
International Red Aid (MOPR), 38
International Workers Relief (Mezhrabpom), 24
Intervention, allied, 3

Intourist: *see* Soviet Union, Government of
Italy, 17, 41, 49, 92, 135
Ivanoushkin, Mikail, 265
Izvestia, 25, 34, 130

Japan, 4, 21, 28, 164, 252, 273
Johnson Act, 148, 153-54, 160, 175, 177

Kalinin, Mikhail I., 4, 11, 12, 102, 171, 211, 218, 267
Karakhan, Lev M., 168, 257
Kelley, Robert F.:
  assignment, 278
  currency, 224
  debt problem, 148, 153
  legal rights, 87, 88, 104
  memoranda, 13, 148
  noninterference, 27-29, 31, 34, 41, 52, 53, 256
  recognition, 12, 17, 20, 253
  religious rights, 66, 67
Kennan, George F., 98, 114, 202, 219, 223, 245, 266, 274
Kennedy, John F., 82, 128
Kerensky, Alexander, 173
Kerensky government, 16, 149, 156, 175
Kerensky loan, 148, 171, 173
Khrushchev, Nikita S., 128, 175, 177, 178, 222
Kiev, 78
Kohler, Foy D., 128
Kolchak regime, 148, 149
Kovno, 56, 62, 119
Krassin, Leonid B., 146, 147, 257
Krassnoff, Peter, 100
Krestinsky, Nikolay N., 48, 49, 51, 52, 166
Kujala, Arthur, 114-15, 123-25, 127, 130, 131, 137, 138, 270
Kuusinen, Otto W., 39

Laberge, Fr. George A., 71, 72, 78, 81, 86
Lancaster, W. W., 4, 5
Lansing, Robert, 3, 147

Latvia, 28, 49, 117

Legal rights, protection of: 12, 233, 246
  access to Embassy, 103, 106-10
  investigation by Embassy, 110-11
  right to fair trial, 103, 129-31
  right to notification of arrest, 90,
    103, 111-19
  right to visit and interview, 91, 92,
    103, 119-28

Lehigh Valley Railway Co., 180

Leiper, Henry Smith, 68

Lend-Lease, 173, 175, 209, 244

Lenin, Vladimir I., 33, 145, 147, 236,
  251

Leningrad, 103-05, 111, 207, 214, 217,
  220, 264

Lewis, J. Hamilton, 23

Lithuania, 100, 135

Litvinov, Maxim M.: 166, 167, 169,
  257
  assignment agreement, 182, 186, 187,
    193, 194
  claims, Soviet, 179-81
  currency, 223-24
  debt problem, 144, 147, 149, 150,
    152-64, 167, 170, 176, 212, 275
  diplomatic relations, 210, 211, 215,
    228
  economic espionage, 200, 205
  negotiations in Washington, 18-20
  pledge on legal rights, 90, 94, 103,
    111, 116, 120, 123, 271
  pledge on legal rights reinterpreted
    by Molotov, 126-27
  pledge on noninterference, 29, 31-34,
    42, 44, 45, 47, 52, 256
  pledge on religious rights, 63-67, 71,
    73, 74, 81, 86, 264
  prestige, 167-69
  recognition, 2, 5, 7, 11-13, 17, 19,
    21, 22, 251, 254, 255
  trade, 5, 252
  violations of pledges, 42, 43, 45, 47,
    48, 49, 51, 54, 72, 74, 114, 124,
    135-36, 137-39, 233-34, 236, 238

Lloyd George, David, 145, 146

Lovestone, Jay, 36

Lozovsky, S. Abramovich, 35, 39, 47,
  119, 133, 220, 221

Lubyanka Prison, 128, 217

Lutheran Church, 262, 264

Lwow, 133, 229

McCormack, John, 238, 264

Manchuria, 4, 6

Marcuse, Herman, 278

Marshall, George C., 230

Martens, Ludwig C. A. K., 2

Matsuoka, Yosuke, 6

Metropolitan-Vickers case, 90, 130, 199,
  202-06, 270

Mexico, 14, 15

Mokhovaya Building, 213, 280

Molotov, Vyacheslav M.: 45, 82, 124,
  171, 211, 230, 237
  reinterprets Litvinov pledge on legal
    rights, 126-27
  U.S. government rejects interpreta-
    tion, 127

Monkhouse, Alan, 204

Mooney, Tom, 46

Moore, R. Walton:
  assignment, 182, 187-89, 278
  debt problem, 148, 153, 154, 159,
    160, 167, 170
  diplomatic relations, 237
  economic espionage, 199
  legal rights, 19, 104, 119
  Litvinov pledges, 235
  noninterference, 30, 42, 259
  recognition, 13-17, 19-23, 235, 253,
    255
  religious rights, 63, 65, 67

Morgan, J. P., Co., 184, 195

Morgenthau, Henry, Jr., 10, 11, 17,
  30, 150, 162, 172

Morton Truck and Tractor Co., 190, 278

Moscow *Daily News*, 5

Moscow Fire Insurance Co., 185, 186,
  191, 197

Moscow Industrial Bank, 195

Mosely, Philip, 241

Most-favored-nation, principle of, 88,
  91-92, 178

Muenzenberg, Willi, 39

Murmansk, 16, 24, 180, 181

Mutual Security Act (1951), 58, 59

MVD: *see* Police

National City Bank, 4, 142, 184, 192, 193, 195
National Council of Churches, 70
Nationality, dual: 93, 94, 96, 97, 110, 112, 113, 120
    Litvinov on, 94
National Press Club, 32, 210
Nationalzeitung (Basle), 24
Negoreloe, 268
Neveu, Bishop Pie, 70, 81, 262
New York City, 48, 103, 227
New York Life Insurance Co., 143
New York Times, 5, 59, 99, 128, 254, 256, 263, 277
New York Trust Co., 184, 190, 191
Nicholas II, 2
Noninterference: 41, 53, 233
    by United States government, 59
    Litvinov statement, 29-30
Nordeen, Hjalmar S., 101, 112
Northern Insurance Co. of Moscow, 191, 195
Norway, 28, 92, 94
Nousiainen, Elmer J., 97, 109

Odessa, 104, 220, 264
Oetjen v. *Central Leather Co.,* 179
Oggins, Isaiah, 124
Osservatore Romano, 24
Otis Elevator Co., 206
Oumansky: *see* Umansky

Page, Edward, Jr., 269
Paris, 28, 146, 224, 260
Parker, Rev. George L., 68
Peiping, 281
People's Commissariat for Foreign Affairs: 90, 168, 216, 240
    assignment, 186, 198
    economic espionage, 206, 207
    legal rights, 97, 100, 101, 107, 108, 110, 112-15, 117, 119, 121, 123, 124, 126, 128, 136-38, 268, 270
    noninterference, 33, 37, 50, 52
    relation to People's Commissariat for Internal Affairs, 117-19
    religious rights, 83
    travel in Soviet Union, 220

People's Commissariat for Internal Affairs, 83, 108, 118, 124, 131, 219
Persia, 28
Petrograd, 2
Petrograd Metal Works, 188, 195
Petrozavodsk, 97, 130
Petty, Robert, 136-37
Pfister, Johannes, 117
Phillips, William, 13, 17, 20, 153, 192
Pittman, Key, 237-38
Plotkin, Mark A., 185-86, 197
Poland, 28, 33, 95, 108, 132, 164, 266
Police:
    GPU, 37, 134, 135, 204, 270, 272
    MVD, 73
Polish Catholic Church, 79, 263
Polk, Frank L., 187
Potemkin, Vladimir P., 123
Powers, Francis Gary, 127-28, 130
Pravda, 36, 56, 146, 203
Prinkipo: *see* Conferences
Profintern, 35, 48; *see also* Red International of Labor Unions
Propaganda, Soviet: 16, 18, 20, 27, 31, 32, 41
    anti-Soviet, in United States, 50
    Litvinov statement on, 29, 30
    Soviet promises to other governments, 28
Provisional Government of Russia, 2, 12, 140, 149, 173, 179, 181, 183, 193
Pyk, Irene T., 113

Radek, Karl B., 33, 168, 169
Radio Corporation of America, 207-08
Rakovsky, Khristian G., 29
Recognition of Soviet government: 178, 234, 235, 251
    by other governments, 13
    conditions to, 14-16, 19
    Japanese threat, 6, 7
    notification of, 21
    reactions to, 22-25
    Roosevelt letter on, 20-21
    Soviet desire for, 4, 5, 15, 16, 18
    trade, 7
    unconditional, 17, 18

U.S. policy on, 2-4
U.S. press survey on, 10
Red International of Labor Unions (RILU): 38-40, 42, 43, 237
and Communist International, 39
and Trade Union Unity League, 39
Reed, John, 255
Reentry permits, 23, 72
Refugees, 59, 135
Religion:
agreement on religious rights, 63-65, 234
American Jews in Soviet Union, 68
American Protestants in Soviet Union, 68-70
American Roman Catholics in Soviet Union, 70-86
rights for Americans in Soviet Union, 10, 16, 18, 20, 23, 78
Soviet government policy on, 61, 80, 260-61
Richard, Fr. Joseph, 71, 82
Riga, 8, 12, 27, 36, 42, 54, 55, 81, 87, 88, 100, 106, 205, 214, 217, 272
Ringwalt, Arthur R., 268
Roberts, Rev. Donald V., 70
Robins, Raymond, 143
Roman Catholic Church, 73, 80, 264
Roosevelt, Franklin D.:
assignment, 188
debt problem, 150, 156, 160-62, 174
diplomatic relations, 210, 231, 232, 242, 244
economic espionage, 200
legal rights, 91, 129
letter to Kalinin, 11
noninterference, 30, 32, 42, 44, 48, 50, 52, 55
recognition, 4, 10, 11, 17-22, 24, 245, 252, 254
religious rights, 63, 64, 71, 73, 81
Rosengolts, Arkady P., 163, 170, 211
Roszkowski, Mieczyslaw, 95-96, 113, 266
Rozov, David A., 170, 172
Rubens, Mrs. Adolph, 115-16, 122, 126, 129, 130-31
Rubinin, Evgeny, V., 154, 271
Rusk, Dean, 104, 253
Russia, 135, 146

Russian Orthodox Church, 76, 79, 263
Russian Reinsurance Co., 191, 195
R.S.F.S.R., 181, 186; *see also* Soviet Union, Government of
Russian Volunteer Fleet, 182, 192-93
Rykov, Alexey I., 33, 62

S. S. Berengaria, 17
St. Louis des Français, 81, 82, 263, 264
St. Petersburg, 68
San Francisco, 48
Sayre, Francis B., 104
Schweiger, John, 101-102
Scott, Walter Dill, 23, 255
Seattle, 21
Second Russian Reinsurance Co., 191, 195
Seljamaa, Julius, 9, 253
Siberian expedition, 24, 180, 181
Singer Manufacturing Co., 143, 196
Skinner, Robert P., 8, 12
Skvirsky, Boris, 4, 21, 224, 253
Sokolnikov, Grigory Y., 31
Sokolovsky, Vasily, 230
Soviet Union, Government of:
Agitation and Propaganda School, 36
Amtorg, 4, 10, 24, 36, 37, 47, 110, 144, 158, 159, 171, 208, 239, 266
Burobin, 82, 85, 214, 216, 217, 227, 280, 281
Burovitz, 136
Civil Code, 88
Code of Criminal Procedure, 117, 129
Communist International, 31, 33, 34, 41, 44, 45, 47, 49, 51, 52
Council for Religious Affairs, 81, 82
Council of People's Commissars, 158
Executive discretion, 89
Intourist, 47, 224
Mashinoimport, 206, 208
Nationalization of property, 141, 181, 185, 186
People's Commissariat of Justice, 117, 185, 186
R.S.F.S.R., 186
Society of Militant Atheists, 66, 80
Soviet Information Bureau (Washington), 4, 21
State Bank, 212, 223, 224

State secrets, 202-03
TASS, 239
Technical Aid Society, 94
See also People's Commissariat for
    Foreign Affairs; People's Commis-
    sariat for Internal Affairs
Spaso House, 82, 213, 216, 281
Speier, Edward H., 136
Stalin, Iosif V., 7, 27, 34, 45, 46, 54,
    59, 146, 167-68, 171, 172, 174-
    75, 211, 214, 215, 230, 236,
    252
Stalingrad, 111
Standley, William H., 85, 230
Steinhardt, Laurence A.:
    diplomatic relations, 231, 244
    legal rights, 96, 107, 113, 119, 124-26,
        132, 133, 135, 137
    noninterference, 57, 82
    religious rights, 85
    travel, 220-21
Stimson, Henry L., 93, 243
Stockholm, 217, 224
Stomonyakov, Boris S., 120
Stoneman, William H., 204, 271
Strang, Sir William, 204
Sviridoff, George, 98, 112, 118
Sweden, 33, 92, 165, 280
Sweeney, Paul, 278
Switzerland, 33

Taft, Robert A., 174
Taylor, Myron C., 80
Third International: see Communist
    International
Thorning, Joseph F., 31
Times (London), 24, 31, 204
Tokyo, 6, 251
Trade, 5-9, 24, 252-53
Travel:
    in Soviet Union, 218-23
    in United States, 220-22, 244
Treaties and agreements:
    Anglo-Soviet Trade Agreement
        (1921), 146
    Brest-Litovsk (1918), 145
    General (1924), 146
    German-Soviet (1925), 65, 67, 90,
        92, 111, 120, 126, 201

German-Soviet Agreement (1928),
    92, 125
Rapallo (1922), 145, 163
U.S.-Soviet Trade Agreement (1935),
    177-78
Trotsky, Lev D., 33, 34, 177
Troyanovsky, Alexander A.:
    as Ambassador, 21, 162, 166, 167,
        170, 229, 252
    debt problem, 153-59, 165, 172
    diplomatic relations, 215
    noninterference, 32, 42, 43
Truman, Harry S, 237
Turkey, 28, 92

Ughet, Serge, 2, 21, 156, 179, 180,
    183, 184, 193, 276
Umansky, Konstantine A.: 17, 51, 265
    debt problem, 169, 172
    diplomatic relations, 231, 243
    evaluation as Ambassador, 229
    legal rights, 95, 108, 266
    travel in Soviet Union, 221, 222
    violations of Litvinov pledge, 234
United Nations, 58, 218, 222
United States, Government of:
    Commissioner of Claims, 172-73
    Congress, 4, 14, 237-38
    Department of Justice, 188, 193, 194,
        265, 278
    Export-Import Bank, 154, 155, 158,
        159;
        resolution on credit, 154, 158, 177
    Federal Trade Commission, 153
    Foreign Claims Settlement Commis-
        sion, 195-96
    Post Office Department, 192, 195
    Public Law #285, 195
    Reconstruction Finance Corporation,
        5
    Shipping Board, 193
    Treasury Department, 153, 184, 195,
        277
    Treaty-making power, 14
    See also Department of State

Vacuum Oil Co., 143
Vandenberg, Arthur H., 238

Vinogradov, Sergey I., 123
Visas:
American, 48, 50, 76, 267
diplomatic, 217, 218
Soviet, entrance, 23, 65, 71, 75-77, 94, 262, 280, 281
Soviet, exit, 72, 94, 131-37
Vladikavkasky Railway, 190, 191, 195, 196
Vladivostok, 14, 16, 105, 281
Vologda, 2
Voorhis Act: *see* Anti-Subversive Activities Act
Voroshilov, Kliment E., 45, 155, 167-68, 211, 252
Vorovsky, Vatzlav, 144
Vyshinsky, Andrey Y., 72, 202, 218

Wade, Bp. Raymond J., 69
Walker, Frank C., 8
Walsh, Fr. Edmund A., 10, 23
Ward, Angus I., 122, 229
Warsaw *Courier*, 53

Weinberg, Khaim S., 116, 118
Weinstone, William, 43
Welles, Sumner, 80, 95, 109, 132, 229, 242, 243, 266
Wilbur, Ray Lyman, 62
Wiley, John C., 153, 167-69
Wilson, Woodrow, 144
Woll, Matthew, 42, 43
Workers International Relief (Mezhrabpom), 38-40
Worship: *see* Religion
Worton, William A., 281
Wuori, Bruno H., 113, 130

Yalta, 237
Yaroslavsky, Emelyan, 66, 80
Yasnaya Polyana, 220, 222

Zagorsk, 78
Zaikin, Dmitry I., 227
Zinovyev, Grigory E., 33
Zorin, Valerian, 128

A NOTE ABOUT THE AUTHOR

DONALD G. BISHOP has spent two decades studying and teaching comparative government, British government, Soviet government, and administration of American foreign relations. He is Professor of Political Science and Chairman of the International Relations Committee of the Maxwell Graduate School of Citizenship and Public Affairs at Syracuse University. A native of Altoona, Pennsylvania, Professor Bishop grew up in Akron, Ohio, earning his A.B. at the University of Akron, his A.M. at Princeton, and his Ph.D. at Ohio State. He has also studied at the London School of Economics, Oxford University, and the Royal Institute of International Affairs, as well as the Universities of Amsterdam and Neuchatel. The author of *The Administration of British Foreign Relations* (1961) and *The Future of the New French Political System* (1959), Professor Bishop is coauthor with Marguerite J. Fisher of *Municipal and Other Local Governments* (1950) and editor of *Soviet Foreign Relations: A Book of Documents and Readings* (1952).